MOUNTAINS
AND A MUSTARD SEED
A FAMILY'S JOURNEY OF HOPE

Nicole Allen

ISBN 978-1-64300-481-5 (Paperback)
ISBN 978-1-64300-221-7 (Hardcover)
ISBN 978-1-64300-222-4 (Digital)

Covenant Books, Inc.
11661 Hwy 707
Murrells Inlet, SC 29576
www.covenantbooks.com

Dedicated in loving memory to two beautiful souls who touched my life deeply. I am so grateful that God allowed our paths to cross in this world. Until we meet again in the next.

Mary B. Hubbard
and
Iole Biamonte (Orsini)

Truly I tell you, if you have faith as small as a mustard seed, you can say to this mountain, "Move from here to there," and it will move. Nothing will be impossible for you.

—Matthew 17:20

"God has created me to do Him some definite service. He has committed some work to me which He has not committed to another. I have my mission. I may never know it in this life, but I shall be told it in the next. I am a link in a chain, a bond of connection between persons. He has not created me for naught. I shall do good; I shall do His work. I shall be an angel of peace, a preacher of truth in my own place, while not intending it if I do but keep His commandments. Therefore, I will trust Him, whatever I am, I can never be thrown away. If I am in sickness, my sickness may serve Him, in perplexity, my perplexity may serve Him. If I am in sorrow, my sorrow may serve Him. He does nothing in vain. He knows what He is about. He may take away my friends. He may throw me among strangers. He may make me feel desolate, make my spirits sink, hide my future from me. Still, He knows what He is about."

—Blessed John Henry Newman

CONTENTS

PREFACE

$\mathcal{M}$y husband Joe and I have been married for twenty-three years and have twelve children. Let me begin by answering all the questions that you are undoubtedly asking yourself right off the bat. All twelve kids are ours, we are not a blended family, and I gave birth to each of them. One at a time. We have six girls and six boys—Angela, Joseph, Patrick, Christina, Grace, Clare, Callum, Sarah, Katie, Ryan, Michael, and Noah. In that order. Yes, we know what causes it; and yes, we are Catholic. We have always trusted God to determine the size of our family, so there could be more. Finally, yes, we definitely have our hands full.

You may be wondering how a mom of twelve has time to write a book. To be perfectly honest, I really didn't have the time. It took several years, from the time the seed was planted, and God had everything to do with me completing it. I was prompted to write our story by friends, family, and even perfect strangers. More convincingly, the nudges from the Holy Spirit were what moved me forward. There were dozens of excuses not to write it, but every single time I talked myself out of it, those familiar words would be spoken again, always by someone new. "Wow, you have such an incredible story, you really should write a book." Or during Mass or meditation, I clearly heard the promptings internally, *Write the book.*

I've never been one to share personal information with total strangers, I'm half Irish, and Irish folks are private. Growing up, I was guarded, and taught never to air dirty laundry. I learned to be proud. As an adult, I felt compelled to keep up my persona of having the perfect life as wife and mother, living the American Dream, never exposing anything even remotely negative. Any worries, fears, anxieties, or struggles that we dealt with as a family were kept hidden away, like skeletons in a closet.

We truly were living the American Dream, by society's standards, but our family was far from perfect. Life for us was easy and comfortable for most of our marriage. Along with each of Joe's many career changes and promotions, life got easier and even more comfortable. We continued to move forward, on a steady climb on the roller coaster of life. There were a few minor dips in the ride but nothing that we didn't quickly recover from. We never had any major struggles, and we were thrilled about the ride, very much enjoying the climb. The first eighteen years of our marriage could easily be summarized by a quote from the movie *God's Not Dead*: "Sometimes the devil allows people to live a life free of trouble, because he doesn't want them turning to God."

I don't know if the devil has that much power, but I never felt like we had troubles that were too big for Joe and I to handle on our own. I didn't really feel like I needed to turn to God for anything. Life was great.

We had reached a point where we were ready to begin a steady coast in our virtually worry-free life. We had come to a sweet spot of sorts. Our kids were happy and healthy, we were living in an awesome house, Joe's career was promising, and we were financially comfortable. As any thrilling roller-coaster ride will do, the bottom dropped without a hint of warning. That was the point where I was jerked into the realization of how vulnerable I was, and where my search for God began. What I quickly discovered was that he had always been there, I just hadn't been paying Him much, if any, attention.

As I began to reflect on my life, the big moments and milestones that I had taken for granted. I was able to see the exact points where God had been there, guiding the way, and I was amazed. I began to see clearly, in real time, how He was with me daily in all the moments, the big ones and the seemingly insignificant ones, equally. He proved to be there through the people He put into my path, the places He led our family, and the way things just always seemed to work out in precise detail, and perfect timing. God instances, not coincidences.

This is my conversion story. I know I am not unique in the response to my conversion. When you have experienced something so profound, you are compelled to share it with others, to be a living witness and to inspire hope. You just can't keep it to yourself. People relate to real-life experiences better than theories. They are inspired when you let down your guard and shed the pretenses.

People are starving for hope today. I have come to learn this by simply talking to people. I talk to everyone, and I smile pretty much all the time, without even realizing it. People have told me this, so I suppose it's true. I am generally a friendly person, and people tend to talk to me, no matter where I go. When our roller coaster began its violent descent, I talked to people about what was going on. I told my friends from church, teachers, and parents at the kids' school, ladies from my knitting group, the greeters and cashiers at Walmart, and folks in the doctor's office. I didn't just walk up to them and assault them with tales of my woes, I simply inserted whatever seemed appropriate, into the conversation.

What I discovered was that I wasn't alone, and many times they too had stories that they shared with me. It seemed as though these spontaneous sharing episodes inspired hope in people. Friends and complete strangers thanked me, oftentimes because their situations didn't seem so bad after hearing about ours. I felt like a walking *Guidepost* magazine. Soon, I began to see how sharing bits of my life, about how God was providing for our family, was spreading rays of hope. I started actively looking for opportunities to share more. I think that God must have been enjoying it because it seemed that the more I shared our story, the wilder and crazier our life became. The roller coaster continued to gain speed, but as it did, He sent lifelines, which gave me more reason to hope and have faith. I continued to smile through it all.

Friends and strangers alike were astonished, and often asked how I could be so joyful and positive, when things seemed to be going so wrong on so many levels. The events that took place in our life—and when I say *events*, I mean multiple stresses, fears, heartaches, betrayals, and dramas—looked like a train wreck from the outside. Ridiculous as it sounds, I was able to feel incredible hope and joy through it all. Certainly there were times I felt desperate, angry, and frustrated; but when I remembered to turn to God, I was able to find the peace and strength I needed. No matter what else happened in my life, after that conversion, I knew that God would be with me. Hence, this book. I have to confess, putting my whole self out there was a huge decision, and I was absolutely terrified to write it.

The purpose for telling my story—the good, the bad, and the ugly—is quite simply to give hope. I guarantee that every single person who reads it will relate to some, or multiple, parts of it or will know someone who can. We all have struggles. If you are alive, you have struggled. I'm sure that you have probably heard it said that God doesn't give you more than you can handle. When the bottom fell out, and the struggles compounded in every way imaginable, I wasn't so sure that I believed it. I am here to tell you that it is the absolute truth. I believe that if you ask God for help, He will give you the strength that you need to get through anything. If you pay attention, you too will see His hand as your life unfolds, in real time, and He very often sends aid through human angels. No matter how dark, hopeless, and painful your situation may be, He is there, waiting for you to seek Him.

ACKNOWLEDGMENTS

*T*his book would never have been possible without the love, support, and encouragement of several people. First and foremost, I want to thank my husband, Joe—my rock and the love of my life. There is no one I would rather travel this journey with. Thank you for being a strong leader, for always taking good care of us, and for being an outstanding role model.

Our children—Angela, Joseph, Patrick, Christina, Grace, Clare, Callum, Sarah, Katie, Ryan, Michael, and Noah. Without you, there would be no story. I thank God for each and every one of you every day. I love you all beyond words.

Cathy and Al Morin, and Bob and Nanette Mazzuca, for encouraging me to write those epistles, the springboard for this work.

Judy Wilmurt, for being the first to read my manuscript, and for sharing my excitement along the road to publication.

Fr. Lawrence D'Anjou, for validating my story and encouraging me to persevere in getting it out.

My sister Bridget Ouellet, for the marathon chats, for being my sounding board, and my cheerleader. For knowing when to be patient and when to nudge me out of my comfort zone.

My brother-in-law, David Allen, for the pep talks and big pushes.

Bob "the Bus Driver" Javens and Troy Scotchburn, for taking the time to read, review, and make notations of my typos as I worked through revisions.

This work has been a labor of love, discerned through much prayer. I give thanks to God for the gifts he has blessed me with and the courage to share them. I am especially grateful that he placed each of you in my life.

ONE

A Prayerful Giant

I am incredibly grateful for my Catholic roots. Joe and I recently had the privilege of hearing Matthew Kelly, a famous motivational speaker and author, speak at our parish. One of the things he spoke about that I could really identify with was about great families. He's done a lot of research and has talked to a lot of people. What he has discovered is that all the greatest and happiest families that he has met have one thing in common, a prayerful giant. It might be a grandmother, grandfather, aunt, uncle, mother, or father; but somewhere down the line, there is a prayerful giant. Matthew Kelly defines a prayerful giant like this:

> A prayerful giant is someone who covers their family with prayer, anchoring the family in God's grace. They pray constantly for their families, surrounding them with God's protection.

I hope that you can trace back to the prayerful giant in your family. If you can't, or if they are so distant that you don't have a clear memory of one, you may want to consider becoming the prayerful giant for your family. My maternal grandmother, Mary B. Hubbard (Hegarty), was our family's prayerful giant. She came to Canada from Donegal, Ireland, with her father, when she was just seventeen years old. She married my grandfather, Simeon Stanley Hubbard, when

15

she was nineteen years old. They met when she began working on his family's farm in Forest, Ontario, cooking for the farmers during the thrashing. My grandfather was seventeen years older than her, and together they had sixteen children, eleven girls and five boys. She was widowed in her early forties, long before I was born, and even several months before the birth of my mother, the youngest of the sixteen.

I grew up in Niagara Falls, Ontario, and Gramma Hubbard spent a lot of time at our house in my formative years. Her visits would sometimes last for several months at a time. She was unequivocally the most influential model of faith in my life, and probably the closest person I knew to be a living saint. She was humble, wise, and kind. She could be stern if she saw any of us kids behaving badly, but I never once saw her lose her temper. She was generous with what precious little she had, and she owned practically nothing. She didn't have any investments, and I don't think she ever even had a bank account. She never owned a house or a car, and she never held a driver's license. Even her wardrobe was modest and sensible, consisting of only a few summer and winter dresses, a couple pairs of shoes, and some winter boots. Her most treasured possessions were her prayer books, chaplets, and rosaries and some rescued statues of her favorite saints, which she kept in her room at my aunt Annie's house.

Gramma Hubbard was in constant prayer, and I am fairly certain that she had a direct line to God because she always seemed to get answers. People often asked her to pray for them. They asked for prayers for their children and grandchildren, for friends who were ill, a job for a husband, for someone with an addiction, and for a return to the faith of a loved one. I know that she prayed for an end to abortion, the poor, vocations, and the holy souls in purgatory, those in her own family, and those who had no one to pray for them, and she encouraged us to do the same. With each new day, I have no doubt that she had something new to pray for, in addition to her usual prayers. I am certain that she prayed for lots of things that I will never know about, but what I do know is that she prayed constantly.

Gramma Hubbard was already in her seventies when I was a child of six or seven. I observed her at that age praying quietly with her prayer books, the familiar blue pieta book and her other devotionals, sitting in the chair in the corner of the living room or next to the kitchen window. She always had a rosary in her hand or in her pocket, and she attended daily Mass as often as she was able. My aunts Mary and Jane would often come by to pick her up to take her to church, other times she took the city bus that stopped in front of our house. If my mother had errands to run or shopping to do, Gramma would come along, but preferred to sit in the car saying her prayers while the rest of us went into the stores. At home, she would excuse herself each afternoon to "do her homework." Homework was when she would go off to her room to pray.

It was not only these obvious times, when I saw her praying with her books, that left a lasting memory. It was the times that I heard her, when she didn't know I was listening, that are stamped onto my heart. Her soft murmuring from behind the bathroom door as she got ready for Mass, when she was in her bedroom, or while she was washing her stockings and underthings by hand in the big laundry tub in our basement. Just about any time she was alone, I heard her. Her quiet prayers, petitions, and daily chats with her Lord. I heard her tell Jesus how much she loved Him and asking Him to help her. It was a clear sign and confirmation of what I already knew in my heart, Gramma Hubbard was the real deal. She loved God, and her faith was solid as a rock. I found great comfort and safety in her presence.

She was humble and quiet, never showy or preachy. She always sat in the back pew, her veiled head bowed in prayer. I can clearly picture her on her knees in St. Anne's Church, in downtown Niagara Falls, with brilliant sunlight pouring through the stained glass windows, rocking back and forth ever so slowly in deep meditation. I wonder now if maybe that rock that I sometimes find myself doing with a baby in my arms at church might be that same rock. She'd had sixteen babies of her own, and I'm certain that she brought them each to Mass with her. Perhaps that rock had stayed with her into her old age.

Always a lady, Gramma Hubbard was modest in her dress. She never wore slacks, always a dress or a skirt, and I only ever saw her legs below the knee. She wore panty hose, the "L'eggs in the egg" kind, and she always saved the egg for us. We couldn't wait for it to be our turn to get the egg. We'd put treasures and things inside and decorated them with stickers and markers. It was a real treat. I wish they still made those L'eggs in the egg. I know my kids would love getting the egg. Gramma Hubbard never wasted anything. I watched her carefully fold up brown paper bags and foil wrap to be saved and used again, all well before the recycling era ever evolved. Everything about her was practical. She never wore makeup, other than Labello lip balm and Chantilly sachet fragrance. She didn't take tub baths but once a month. She didn't want to waste all that water. She washed every morning in the little powder room in our basement, not even using the bigger, brighter bathroom upstairs.

She used Final Net spray on her silver hair, and combed it out each morning. She always looked and smelled like she'd just stepped out of a salon. She washed her hair with a yellow bar of Sunlight soap about once a month, on what I what I like to recall as her beauty days, one of my favorite things to watch. She'd come out from her tub bath wearing her dusty-rose bathrobe, zipped up to the neck, and down to the floor, and settled herself at the kitchen table where my mother would set her hair in gray prickly rollers and pink plastic picks. She would insist that my mother use Dippity-Do gel so that it would hold up all month. She wore a kerchief for the rest of the day, checking her curls every few hours to see if they were dry, and would tease them out when they were done. That's about as fancy as she got, and she was the most beautiful woman of grace that I have ever known, through and through.

Never one to indulge, Gramma's diet was simple. Every day without fail, she ate an egg, boiled or poached, with a slice of toast, a boiled potato, and a banana. She ate fish every Friday and Wednesday. Fish cakes were a staple in our house, and on occasion, fillet of sole was a treat for her. She ate canned tuna and salmon and loved rye bread with caraway seeds. She also loved raisin bread and buttermilk. Now and then she would eat Arrowroot biscuits, and she often ate soda crackers to settle her stomach. She kept white powdery peppermints or humbugs in her pocket. I remember her drinking Red Rose tea before she gave it up for Lent one year, substituting it for boiled water. She never drank tea again once Lent was over. She also gave up bacon another year, and after Lent was over, she never ate it again. Being a bacon lover myself, I was amazed at her self-control. I had tried to give things up for Lent, year after year, failing after only a few days. I couldn't imagine ever trying to give up bacon. She never made a show of her sacrifices, she would just politely and quietly decline if someone offered it to her without giving a reason. I came right out and asked her about it. I knew she loved bacon and Lent was over, so I couldn't understand why she would want to keep up the sacrifice when she didn't have to. She explained to me that she decided to continue not eating it as a way of continuing her fast. She said that sometimes prayer and fasting was needed to answer some prayers than just prayer alone. I never asked her what it was that she was praying for, guessing that it must have been something pretty important for such drastic measures. I am certain that she made countless sacrifices that I will never know about.

Gramma Hubbard had a great devotion to the Blessed Virgin Mary. She prayed the rosary daily, and when she was visiting us, we said it with her together as a family, on our knees. She wore a large Miraculous Medal and a brown scapular at all times, with great faith. I know this because she needed to have a chest X-ray for a suspected bronchitis or pneumonia. When she returned from the appointment, she was visibly distressed that she had to be stripped down to a hospital gown with only her medal and scapular. The X-ray technician had instructed her to remove them, but she refused. I remember being in awe of her courage. I definitely would have been afraid to go against the rules, but more than that, I would have been embarrassed about someone seeing that I wore medals or scapulars. She was not ashamed of her faith or the sacramentals.

She prayed novenas regularly, asking the holy saints to intercede for her for some petition, help with decisions she had to make, or for someone who had asked for her prayers. One of her favorite saints was St. Anthony, who she taught us to pray to for help with finding lost things. She always promised him money for the poor, St. Anthony's Bread money, as she called it, in thanksgiving for answered prayer. She prayed to St. Thérèse the Little Flower, who sent roses from heaven, and she almost always received a rose in response to her prayer. When I was old enough to walk to the local florist by myself, and had some babysitting money, I brought her roses. I knew she was always praying to St. Thérèse, though I never knew exactly what it was she was praying for. She received roses a lot, so she sometimes would ask St. Thérèse to send her a specific colored rose as a sign. She was not superstitious, she truly believed with a childlike trust. Of course she never told anyone what color she was waiting for, but she always got an answer. She also had a great affection for St. Francis of Assisi. I came to realize that it was this special saint and his virtues that she modeled her life after with her simplicity, humility, and prayer life.

Gramma Hubbard became a Secular Franciscan—a Third Order Franciscan, as she called it, after she was widowed. She didn't talk about it much at all. I may have heard her mention it once or twice, but regretfully, I never asked her about her vocation. When we went to her visitation at the funeral home after she died, I was startled to see her dressed in a brown Franciscan habit. It was then that I recalled what she had mentioned years earlier about becoming a Third Order Franciscan. She looked like the saint that I believed her to be. Her very life, as I recall her memory, was the essence of what true Christianity should be. It was what I aspire to be in my life, though I have a very long way to go. While I witnessed her in her seventies and eighties in my youth, teenaged years, and young adulthood, I did not know all the details of her life. I knew only what she shared with me and what I observed myself, without ever pressing her with questions. I never wanted to invade her privacy.

At the stage of life that I am in, now in my forties, I know that her life could not have been easy. There are so many things I would love to ask her if she were here, about her life and her faith. I have wished, over the years, that she could be among my own family, holding and rocking my babies, and sitting in my living room saying her prayers. I believe that Gramma Hubbard must have experienced life in a more exaggerated way than people do today. Poverty, hardship, struggles, anticipation, fear, excitement, joy, peace, loss, and heartache. Leaving her family behind in Ireland, coming to a new country with her father, working excessively hard, marrying young, and raising a huge family. Having just enough to get by, losing her husband in her early forties with several young children still to raise on her own, and others at various stages of their lives with struggles of their own. She never spoke in detail of those things to me, but my guess is that she must have felt every emotion in its rawest form.

I truly believe that it is not the experiences that we have in life—the good, the bad, and the ugly—but how we respond to them that define who we become. I did not know her while she journeyed through all the experiences that made up the better part of her life, but I believe that Gramma Hubbard responded in faith, prayerful trust, and love to everything that God handed her. I miss her, and I think of her every single day. I wish that I could thank her for her example in my life. She taught me the importance of scattering seeds, which I pray I do effectively. I know I did not fully realize how extraordinarily special Gramma Hubbard was when she was with me. It wasn't until she was advanced in age, shortly after I got engaged, when I witnessed an act of love and kindness that I felt the depth of her heart. I had no idea that she would, more than two decades later, continue to be a living part of my life, even from the other side. I never imagined that I would feel her presence with me as I experienced hardships and struggles, but I did. I felt her with me every day, sensing that she had experienced many of the very same trials a lifetime earlier in her own life. Our connection is multifaceted. Not only was Mary B. Hubbard my grandmother, she was also my godmother and confirmation sponsor. Our bond was forged by the Holy Spirit.

TWO

The Early Years

Niagara Falls, Ontario

I'm a cradle Catholic. I went to a French Catholic elementary school, École St. Antoine, from junior kindergarten to grade six, Our Lady of Mount Carmel for grades seven and eight, and then attended two public high schools, Westlane and Stamford. Despite having strong Catholic roots and examples in my life, I didn't feel particularly religious growing up. Our family went to Mass every Sunday, I received all my sacraments and was fairly well catechized, but I definitely didn't have what I would call a relationship with God. My prayer life consisted of a lot of gimme prayers. God was who I went calling on when I needed something—help with a test, to spare me some punishment, or to attain whatever random items that I wanted. I would sometimes make promises, bribing Him only *if* I got the answer that I desired. I wasn't good at keeping my promises, and I can't say for sure that I even remembered to thank Him properly for the prayers that I felt He answered.

My childhood and teenaged years were ordinary. I was a good student, had nice friends, and there were no earth-shattering events that occurred that brought me to my knees. Life for me was fine. I came from a working class family, the oldest of eleven children, I was mature beyond my years, and had a lot of responsibilities. I learned from a very young age how to cook, clean, and change diapers. My mother worked for a few years when I was very young, before becoming a stay-at-home mom when I was four or five.

I knew early on that I wanted to be a stay-at-home mom, just like my mother. She was a fine example of how to keep it all together. She kept a clean and organized house, cooked dinner every night, and kept us kids neat, clean, and well-disciplined. She loved to entertain, and went all out with cooking and baking. She decorated and set a beautiful table, always making sure that things were perfect. She made a good impression, and appearances were very important to her.

My parents were very particular about how I spent my leisure time. I was a Brownie; took guitar, singing, and swimming lessons, gymnastics; sang in the church choir; volunteered at Dorchester Manor, the local nursing home; and babysat most of the neighborhood kids. During my teen years, I was introduced to the pro-life movement, and participated in prayer vigils, Life Chain, and volunteered with Right to Life, Birth Right, and Campaign Life. We made regular trips to Toronto to pray, picket, and sidewalk counsel outside of Henry Morgentaler's abortion clinic. I helped with Christmas baskets, church fund-raisers, and anything else that my mother was involved in. She dabbled in a lot of different things and often took on the lead roles, so I got a taste at an early age of being involved in the community.

When I was in middle and high school, a lot of kids my age were allowed to go to concerts and parties. I wasn't. I was allowed to go to approved movies, the mall, or out to dinner with my friends. I had classmates who were allowed to wear makeup and date. I had to wait till I was sixteen for both. I knew kids who experimented with drugs and alcohol and smoked cigarettes. I was way too afraid to try drugs, but I did try smoking. My dad was a smoker till I was in high school, and I used to walk to the Avondale store to buy him his cigarettes. That was way before there were any regulations on selling tobacco to minors. The only rule that they eventually introduced at the store was that you needed to bring in a signed note from an adult. All the clerks at the store knew my family, and that my dad occasionally sent me to buy his cigarettes. Most of the time, when I handed the clerk the note from my dad for a pack of Player's Light king-size cigarettes, they would return the note to me with the change. One time, I decided to keep the note so that I could use it again later. I had been intrigued by the "cool" kids who hid around the back of the middle school at lunch, smoking in their little circle. When my mother went out of town for a few days to visit her family in Sarnia, I decided that it was the perfect opportunity to experiment.

I took the recycled note that I had saved to the store, along with my babysitting money, and had no trouble at all buying a pack of cigarettes. I walked to Fern Park, at the end of our street, and was relieved to find it empty of kids and parents. I huddled down in the big wooden fort and lit a cigarette. I honestly had no clue what to do with it and am quite sure I didn't inhale. I just basically sucked in mouthfuls of smoke and blew them out till the cigarette was gone. I lit a second one. Same thing. I felt incredibly annoyed that I had wasted my hard-earned money on something that was obviously so dumb. I had no idea what the fascination was. I threw the rest of the pack into the trash can and walked home, never to touch cigarettes again.

As a senior in high school, I was not what you would call popular. I was not into sports or music, and although I got decent grades, I wasn't particularly studious. My favorite subjects were fine arts, creative writing, and home economics. High school for me was something I needed to get through, not something that I enjoyed. I wasn't one of the cool kids that enjoyed liquid lunches on Fridays at the Bon Villa, the local bar across the street from the high school. I eavesdropped on the stories during my English class, which was right after lunch. I wasn't interested in drinking, but at the time, I thought it would have been nice to be one of the "in" crowd. They seemed to be having a lot more fun than I was. None of my friends were partiers, but we decided that before we graduated, we would try it.

Drinking age in Ontario was nineteen, and we were all underage, but that was part of the thrill. It was a well-known fact that they didn't check for ID at the Bonnie. Before the last school dance of the year, we planned to join the club. There were five of us altogether, including my best friend since junior kindergarten, Michelle Casimir.

24

We decided that we would all go to the Bonnie for a beer before the dance, just so that we could say that we did. Being responsible kids, not wanting to drink and drive, we walked to the bar. Giggling and giddy, we gathered our wits and tried to compose ourselves next to an overgrown hedge at the edge of the parking lot. As soon as we got up our nerve and began to make our way toward the steps, I saw my uncle Roy stumble out the door. Frozen in my tracks, I gasped and told everyone to run. Thinking back on it now, I am pretty sure that my uncle hadn't been in any condition to even recognize me, but at the time, it had scared me enough to bolt.

Our plan to have a beer hadn't been completely spoiled. We decided to walk to the VIP Korean Restaurant down the street instead. After being seated by the waitress, all five of us ordered the same thing, an egg roll and a Labbatt Blue. The waitress looked at us like we were crazy, but she brought us our order without asking for ID. The Korean families that had been eating their dinners when we walked in stared at us the entire time we were there. The beer tasted gross. I didn't enjoy it in the least, but I drank it anyway. I still can't drink beer, I never acquired a taste for it. I kept the bottle cap as a souvenir, and my mother found it in the pocket of my jacket when she washed it. She questioned me about it and was quite shocked when I admitted to her that I had indeed had a beer. It was so out of character for me. She yelled at me, but I don't remember being punished for it. I hadn't done anything to really disappoint my parents up until that time that I can recall, and it would be a few years before I would disappoint them again.

THREE

One Snowy Night

Niagara Falls, Ontario, 1989

I need to begin this chapter with a disclaimer. It's about how Joe and I met. It has been written—and is intended—to be read from the mind-set that I was in at the time, and not from the place of faith and understanding that I reached later on. We did a lot of things wrong. If we could have a do-over, we both agree that we would have done things differently. We also agree, however, that because of God's infinite and unfathomable mercy, we have been redeemed. God has the power to turn the bad things in our lives and use them for good, and He has definitely done so in our lives.

And so I begin. Joe and I met at the Ramada Coral Inn hotel in Niagara Falls, Ontario, where I was working as a front desk clerk. He was the president and CEO of Allen and Associates, a consulting company that he owned, and he stayed at the hotel regularly as a corporate guest. He worked as a human resources consultant for Ford Glass. Coincidentally or not, he had a contract with the plant in Niagara Falls where my dad worked. Joe travelled to multiple Ford Glass plants throughout the Unites States and Mexico, and came to the Niagara Falls plant about twice a month. Although we had no romantic attraction whatsoever in the beginning, or for several months after our introduction, I still remember the day that we met.

I was a new employee at the hotel, which was owned and operated by the Orsini family. It was the summer of 1989, and I had finished high school, with no desire of going to college. I was ready to join the workforce, earn a paycheck, and move out on my own. I wanted to find Mr. Right, get married, and start a family. That had been my plan from a very young age. My mother saw an ad in the newspaper that the Ramada Coral Inn was hiring. They were looking for front desk clerks, and she insisted that I apply for the job. I chuckle a little bit to myself every time I recall this story because I am pretty sure that she wished more than once that she never saw that job advertised. I know she definitely regretted insisting that I apply for it.

Those were the days way before Internet job searches, when you got dressed up, went to the place of business, and asked to fill out an application that was printed on real paper. When you spoke to a manager who sized you up and decided whether to interview you or waved you off with the promise of a phone call. I got an immediate interview and was hired on the spot. Robert Orsini, the younger son of one of the owners, was the one who hired me. He was only a few years older than me, had been raised in the business, and was already managing the hotel.

Two brothers, Joe and Gus Orsini, had married two sisters, Mary and Anna. They had immigrated to Canada from Italy and bought the Coral Inn, which evolved into the Ramada Coral Inn, and the Ramada Suites and Conference Center. They were a wonderful, well-respected, hardworking family; and they ran a very successful business. I loved working for them and learned the job quickly.

I enjoyed dressing up in my navy-blue skirt and blazer, white blouse, and coral chiffon scarf. With my makeup and hair done, and high heels on, I felt sophisticated. The front desk area and office overlooked the indoor/outdoor swimming pools and restaurant. The atmosphere was fun and friendly, with a wide range of guests, from vacationing families to foreign tour groups, seniors, sports teams, and couples on their honeymoons. Everyone always seemed to be in a good mood. Now and then there were cranky, hard-to-please guests, but I didn't mind the challenge, and did my best to make them smile.

The businessmen and businesswomen who had contracts with local companies and stayed frequently got special rates.

The night I met Joe, I was working with Iole, Joe Orsini's daughter. It was late summer, and I had only been working at the hotel for about a month or so. I loved working with Iole, who was always sweet and very patient. As we began our shift, and checked the availability of rooms, and the reservations that had yet to arrive, Iole remarked that Mr. Allen had a reservation. She asked me if I had met him yet. I told her that I didn't think so, and if I had, I couldn't recall. She laughed and said, "Oh, if you met Mr. Allen, you'd remember. He's one of my favorite corporate guests."

Later that evening, he arrived at the desk to check in. I noticed that he was a very tall, more than six feet, and in good shape. He was a young-looking brown-skinned man. What I remember the most about that first meeting was his personality. He was exuberant and had a confident, self-assured presence about him. Now remember, I mentioned that there was no romantic attraction initially, but I certainly appreciated his full-of-life personality. He was smiling when he walked up to the desk, putting both hands down on it. He greeted Iole and me. He playfully pointed to her, saying, "I remember your name. Wait a minute. Hang on. It's like a song."

Then he started to chant, "Yolee! Yolee! Yolee!"

We both stood there giggling at his silliness. Iole made the introductions and showed me his reservation, pointing out his special corporate rate, and I checked him in. From that point on, he became my favorite corporate guest too. He always seemed to be in a good mood, was friendly, and full of personality. It was eight months before the sparks began to fly.

Fast-forward to early March 1990, a couple of days before my twentieth birthday. March weather in Niagara Falls is always unpredictable. The sun had been shining brilliantly when I arrived for my three-to-eleven shift. There was no hint of the blizzard that had been forecasted. After clocking in and getting updated by my coworker from the previous shift, I checked the available rooms and glanced over the reservations. A weekday in March was never busy at the hotel, and with the impending storm, it was virtually deserted.

Several reservations had cancelled. Snowflakes had begun to fall. The big fluffy ones that make it impossible to see your hand in front of your face, and they were accumulating rapidly.

As I looked over the few guests who had yet to check in, my heart skipped a beat when I saw his name. Joseph Allen. I was startled by the sudden rush of excitement and butterflies at the mere sight of his name. I found myself anxious for his arrival. During his last hotel stay, he had come up to the front desk to say hello before heading into the restaurant. It wasn't unusual for him to do so, but that evening, his hand had brushed past—no, it had lingered over—mine, just a little longer than a friendly pat, sending electricity up my arm and through my whole body. I don't recall thinking about him between his previous stay and that snowy evening, but seeing his name on the reservation definitely made my head swim and my heart flutter. I spent my whole shift waiting for his arrival.

The snow continued to fall, fluffy steady puffs, with not even the slightest breeze. It came straight down and piled up quickly. Evening fell, and the sky grew darker, looking like a perfect Christmas night, calm and peaceful. Everyone that had been due to check in had either arrived or cancelled their reservations. Everyone except for Mr. Allen. The roads were deserted. People were hunkered down, waiting out the storm. I waited anxiously, half expecting that he would call to cancel, but hoping that he wouldn't. At ten o'clock, Derek, the night-shift desk clerk who was scheduled to relieve me, called to say he would be two hours late. Gus Orsini offered to come in so that I could go home, but I told him that I didn't mind waiting. It didn't make sense for him to come out in the storm. I called my parents to let them know I would be late.

It was a strange feeling, being alone in the hotel. All was quiet in what was usually a hub of activity. The restaurant and pool had been closed for hours, and the guests all seemed to be in for the night. The only sounds I heard were the humming of the ice maker and pop machines, and the scraping of the snowplows and salt trucks. As isolated as I was, I wasn't afraid. I found the solitude wonderfully peaceful. Mr. Allen still hadn't checked in. I hoped that the extra two hours would give me the chance to see him.

Shortly after midnight, Derek called to let me know that he was on his way. I had parked my car in the first parking space, next to the entrance. I had watched it slowly get buried in snow all evening, from the front lobby window. I drove a 1987 Honda Civic, so it didn't take much for it to get covered. I decided to go out to clear off the heavy layer of snow while I waited for Derek. The snow hadn't let up for hours. The air was still and fresh, and not at all cold. The sky was clear, but black as pitch, and with the streetlights illuminated, the crisp contrast of the white flakes was breathtaking. For a moment, I stood gazing up to the heavens, taking in the beauty.

As I waded my way back to the entrance, stomping the snow from my boots, I noticed that Derek had arrived. I told him that he would no doubt have a very quiet night. I let him know that there was only one reservation yet to arrive, Mr. Allen. We both agreed that the odds were he'd been delayed due to the weather, and that he most likely wouldn't arrive at all. It was really coming down out there. Derek said that the plows and salt trucks were out in full force, but it didn't look like it would be stopping any time soon. I said goodnight and walked out toward my still-running car in the parking lot.

Noticing the headlights turning onto the street that ran down the side of the hotel, I hesitated. There were no other cars on the road, so the lights seemed out of place. Something made me wait to see where the car was going. As it pulled into the virtually empty parking lot, I stood next to my open door, sensing that it was him, but needing to see with my own eyes. The car door opened, and his tall frame unfolded, pulling out a single bag. It was Mr. Allen. When he looked up and saw me standing there, he flashed a familiar smile and said, "Hey."

I smiled back and casually approached him to say hello. Before I could even utter the word, I was scooped up into the biggest, warmest bear hug of my life. With my head spinning, buried in his chest, I couldn't process exactly what it was that I felt. It had all happened so quickly. I enjoyed the warm moment caught up in his arms. Before he let me go completely, he kissed me. Right on the lips. I wasn't completely certain if his affections were a manifestation of his sheer relief, having just survived a crazy Canadian winter storm, navigating through whiteout conditions, multiple flight cancellations and delays, or if he was genuinely happy to see me. I wondered if he had been having the same fluttery feeling as I had all evening. Once we backed out of our embrace, we nervously stammered about the weather, his nightmare flight, and the wild road conditions. I don't remember walking back to my car, or even the drive home, but I do remember not sleeping much. A warm glow enveloped me, and I couldn't stop smiling. I was anxious for my next shift at work so I could find out if what I had experienced was more than just a friendly greeting.

When I saw Mr. Allen the next afternoon, all signs seemed to indicate that the feelings were mutual. Words were not spoken, but they were conveyed by eye contact and body language. Each of us searching the other, looking for the connection, and the way he squeezed my hand when he greeted me, and how he lingered, just a little longer, at the front desk when he came and went. It was the week of my birthday, and I must have mentioned it, because when he returned from his evening jog, he handed me a portable CD player and a Linda Rondstadt and Aaron Neville CD. Their song, "Don't Know Much (but I Know I Love You)," had played over the lobby radio when he stopped by the desk. It was a song that I liked, and when he sang along to it, I realized we shared the same taste in music. After sensing that we were both feeling the same way about each other, the butterflies and heart flutters became uncontainable. Throughout the day I replayed the hug and kiss in the parking lot, and I played what I claimed to be our song, over, and over, and over.

I had casually mentioned the name *Joe Allen* to my parents when we had first been introduced because of his connection with the Ford Glass plant where my dad worked. My dad said that he had seen him around. The new feelings that had suddenly emerged had changed my entire demeanor, and it was obvious to my parents that something was up. When I started mentioning Joe Allen's name again, it didn't take long for them to figure it out. I knew in my head that the conditions for a relationship were not ideal; however, my heart spoke much louder. Joe was fourteen and a half years my senior. A yet-to-be twice-divorced father of one, and a non-Catholic African American. I was a twenty-year-old cradle Catholic, never-married white female, with no kids. I was fully aware that this was not the dream my parents had for their firstborn.

FOUR

Joe versus the Volcano

Niagara Falls, Ontario, 1990

I don't think that my parents wanted to believe that I could be in love with Joe. I gushed about how nice he was, so friendly with a vibrant personality and great sense of humor. They had several questions, and although I knew they wouldn't be happy to hear the answers, I was completely honest with them. My mother was visibly distraught while my dad remained silent. She was clearly upset by the fact that Joe was still legally married to his second wife. I explained to her that their marriage was over. The fact that he also had a son complicated matters. On top of everything was the significant age difference and, although they didn't say so at first, that he was black. I told them that none of the things that they considered to be obstacles mattered to me. The whole thing had come way out of left field for them, so I know they had to be in shock. As a mother, I know I would be, but as a twenty-year-old, my heart was bursting with all the crazy emotions of new love. I told my parents that Joe and I had made a date to see a movie that night. My mother objected. I was an adult with my own car, so I made the decision to go despite her protests. We went to see *Joe versus the Volcano*. Little did we know it then, Joe would come face-to-face with a real live volcano. My mother.

My relationship with my mother had worked well up until I fell in love with Joe. She had always been the dominant parent in our

33

household. I knew what was expected of me, and I rarely ventured out of that realm. I had always been the good girl, respectful, responsible, and mature beyond my years. From a young age, I learned not to go against the grain. It was through my observations of situations with many different people throughout my life—relatives, friends, and acquaintances—that I learned that there were conditions to my mother's affections. She had a strong personality and a low tolerance for those who disagreed with her opinions. She surrounded herself with like-minded people but seemed to have no trouble ending friendships when differences surfaced. People came and went, relationships were built quickly and ended abruptly. Although I never knew all the details, I felt sad many times over the loss of friendships. As the loyal daughter, I learned to follow my mother's lead, associating with who was in and avoiding who was out. I never betrayed her trust, even when my heart felt the injustice.

When I made it clear to my mother that I planned to continue seeing Joe, she tried everything in her power, including calling his soon-to-be ex-wife, in an attempt to dig up dirt. She tried to plant seeds of doubt in my mind, informing me that Joe had been married not once but twice, something that he had already told me. Joe had shared everything about his past with me in great detail, and none of the so-called secrets that my mother thought she would shock me with were of any surprise at all. She tried to convince me that because Joe was a frequent traveler, he undoubtedly had a girl in every port. She told me that I shouldn't think I was anyone special. None of her attempts to break us up worked. In fact, they brought us closer together. For my entire life, I had been the obedient child. Now that I was an adult, my mother frantically tried to maintain her control.

I was well aware of the fact that I was going against the rules of the Catholic Church, but at the time, it wasn't that important to me. A tiny voice inside my head whispered warnings that I was entering into dangerous territory. I brushed them aside with the hope that everything could be repaired with an annulment. I had no tangible knowledge of the annulment process. It was a term that I had heard tossed around, but nothing I had any experience with. My uneducated understanding was that it was a Catholic divorce. I had no idea what the process involved, how long it could take, or even if Joe could get not only one, but two of them. I never seriously considered the very real possibility that I might fall into a state of mortal sin. None of those things were at the top of my list of worries. All I knew and cared about was that Joe and I were in love and we wanted to get married. I believed that everything would come out in the wash.

My mother all but went out of her head with sadness, disappointment, anger, fear, and frustration. She had been accustomed to having all the control, and she fought to maintain her power. It was a losing battle. The two of us were in a constant state of debate over the situation, and the tension was ever present. I am certain that she prayed for our relationship to fizzle out on its own, but the more she badgered me about it, the more I sought refuge in Joe. Several weeks went by with my mother and I adamantly opposed to each other. I refused to stop seeing Joe, and after some ugly words, she told me to get out of the house. I don't think she actually expected me to leave. As far as she was concerned, I had no place to go. She was right, I really didn't have a place to go. My good friends were all away at university, and Joe was traveling on business. My mother knew that Joe wouldn't be able to easily rush to my aid. I had my own car though, so I drove to a phone booth and called him collect. I told him that my mother had just kicked me out. He was well aware of how my mother felt about him, and although he didn't like that our relationship was causing tension between my mother and me, we both viewed it as her problem, not ours.

Joe told me to go to the Western Union Station and wait for a money order. He said he would make a hotel reservation for me. He wired three thousand dollars to me, and I checked into the Viscount Hotel. I stayed there until he arrived the next day. I still have no idea why I called my mother, but I did. It must have been to let her know that I was okay, so she wouldn't worry. She was surprisingly calm over the phone and told me that she wanted to meet with the two of us to discuss the situation. Joe and I were cautiously encouraged. At least she was willing to talk. She told us what time we should meet her at the Campaign Life office in downtown Niagara Falls.

When we arrived at the office, she was already there, waiting in a very businesslike sort of way. Not surprisingly, she was alone. My father was not the confrontational type. My mother explained that my father was much too angry to come to the meeting. That was something that I found odd, because he had remained virtually silent on the topic, leaving all the talking to my mother. My father was not one to show emotion. I don't doubt that he was probably hurt and disappointed, but he definitely didn't seem angry. My mother sat across from the two of us at a long boardroom table and told us what we both already knew. She didn't approve of our relationship, and speaking for my father, neither did he. The reasons she gave us was that Joe's divorce was not yet final. She said that until such time as his marriages were annulled, she would not approve of us dating. She reminded us of the fact that I was a Catholic, and was going against church teaching. She also questioned Joe's motives. He informed her that if I had been just a fling for him, he certainly wouldn't have agreed to her interrogation. He told her that he loved me and intended to marry me. He was not holding me hostage and wasn't in any rush to get married. We could wait for an annulment, but it was unreasonable to not be allowed to see each other in the meantime.

The meeting ended with no resolution. We refused to put our relationship on hold, and my mother refused to support it. Joe and I left together, and I promised her that I would return home that night. Joe and I discussed the meeting over dinner at the Casa D'Oro, a great Italian landmark restaurant in downtown Niagara Falls. We were unwavering in our resolve to be together, and we wouldn't let anyone stand in our way.

My dad has always been a man of few words. My mother did most of the talking and made the decisions about pretty much everything. My father remained silent, to me at least, on the subject of my relationship with Joe. My mother would have had me believe that he was in grave distress over it all. I don't claim to know what their private conversations were like. All I knew was what I witnessed myself. What she said he said, I took with a grain of salt. The words my father finally did speak to me shocked me like none other, because they were not consistent with the way I had been raised.

Joe was out of town again, traveling on business. I had just returned from work. My mother had been growing increasingly distressed by the fact that Joe and I were showing no signs of breaking up, and it seemed to me that it was consuming her entire life to the point of panic. The timing, for what I would describe as an intervention, had no doubt been planned for when Joe would be, once again, not readily accessible. It was just me and my parents. My dad was sitting at the kitchen table. There was no leading up to his statement.

"You don't mix colors."

I don't for one second believe that my father is, or ever has been, a racist. I don't know if he ever believed the words that came out of his mouth, or if it was a desperate attempt, prompted by my mother, to convince me that our relationship wouldn't work. I never asked him if he believed it, I just stood there staring at him in disbelief. It was the only exchange he ever offered on the subject.

After my father's statement, my mother gave me an ultimatum. I would have no contact with Joe, no communication whatsoever until such time as he was not only divorced, but that both his marriages were annulled by the Catholic Church. Only then would she allow and support our relationship. If I refused to end the relationship, I would have to move out. I would need to pay my portion of my car insurance in full. I had been paying it in three installments up till that point, but she insisted that I had to pay it in one lump sum for the year, $1,500. She also said that I would need to take my father's name off as cosigner on my car loan. The choice was mine to make. My decision was an easy one. It took me a couple of weeks to make all the arrangements, but I didn't have to think twice about it.

I talked to my *mémère*, my dad's mom, who lived only a few blocks away. I told her about the whole situation. She said she had an extra bedroom and was willing to let me move in. I told her that I would pay rent. She didn't want to take any money, but I insisted. I paid her a hundred dollars a month for a bedroom. When I told my father about my plan, he agreed that it was a good idea. He said I was old enough to move out and thought it would be good for my grandmother too. He helped me move my stuff into my *mé*mère's house. She was happy to have me living with her, and I am pretty sure that my dad was relieved that some of the tension had been eliminated from his house.

I very much enjoyed my newfound freedom. I was anything but a wild child, but I enjoyed the peace and calm of being away from my mother. I had been given a promotion at work, from front desk clerk to accounts payable and receivable. I still helped out on the front desk when it got busy, but I worked exclusively at the new Ramada Suites and Conference Center, from nine to five. I had not divulged my relationship with Joe to my employers or coworkers, and Joe began staying at a different hotel whenever he came to town on business. When his contract with Ford Glass ended, he rented an apartment in St. Catharines with the intention of moving into it after we got married. He told me that I could move into the apartment right away if I wanted to. It was paid for and sat empty for the most part. When Joe was in town, I did spend time there and, on occasion, even spent the night. I had my own key and enjoyed the solitude after work when Joe was away. I loved the little apartment, but I didn't move in.

We made plans for our future. Instead of staying at his brother's house in Memphis where he had been living, he spent his time in St. Catharines, at the apartment, in between his business trips. When I decided that it was time to inform my boss, Robert, about our relationship, we met for coffee. I told him everything. Including the fact that my parents did not approve and had essentially disowned me. Robert was surprised to hear that Joe and I had been dating. He knew Joe fairly well, being that he had been a frequent guest for several years. Robert told me what a great guy he thought Joe was, and made no judgments about us dating. He offered his support and encouragement and said he hoped that my parents would come around. All my closest friends knew about our relationship, and I told the rest of my coworkers after my meeting with Robert. I told them we were planning to get married. There were some raised eyebrows, and I did hear a few rumors circulating around, though no one said anything to my face. Nothing bothered us. We were in love, and that was all we cared about.

FIVE

My Mémère

Niagara Falls, Ontario, 1990–1991

I missed my brothers and sisters. I had never been away from my family for any real length of time. Moving out of a busy house full of younger brothers and sisters, into my *mé*mère's much quieter place, was kind of a culture shock. Any attempts I made to visit my siblings were met with a cold shoulder. In fact, I was shunned. I quickly realized that one of the consequences of my decision to move out and continue my relationship with Joe was that I wouldn't be welcome at home at all. Not to live there, nor to visit. I wasn't allowed to see my siblings. This hurt me, but not enough to make me change my mind. I stayed away.

I began to reconnect with relatives who I had lost contact with over the years, mostly my father's siblings. Even though we all lived in the same city, in close proximity, we rarely saw them. It hadn't always been that way. I have very distinct memories of visiting my *mé*mère fairly regularly as a child, always around the holidays and often on weekends. Her house was always filled with music and laughter, and there was always something cooking. My aunts babysat us often, and I have fond memories of the fun times, when as a young girl, my sister Bridget and I had sleepovers at my aunt Kathy's tiny upstairs apartment. She took the two of us all over town to all the tourist attractions, mini putt, french fries at Jake's fry wagon, and ice cream under the Rainbow Bridge. We cooked dinner together in her Pepto Bismol–pink kitchen and stayed up late watching movies with a giant bowl of buttered popcorn. I helped my *mé*mère at the law offices where she had a cleaning job. Sometimes on Saturdays, I rode the city bus downtown, and she paid me twenty dollars for helping her dust, vacuum, and wash coffee pots and mugs in the office kitchenette.

My most favorite childhood memories are the ones spent with my relatives on both my parents' sides of the family. I am not exactly sure when it happened, but at some point, the visits grew less frequent and further apart. It was understood by all of us that my mother didn't think that my dad's family quite measured up. Living at my *mé*mère's house allowed me to visit and get to know my aunts and uncles on an adult level. They accepted Joe and I and showed us unconditional love. They were genuinely happy that I had sought them out after several years of separation.

My father's family had not lived without hardship. My dad was the second oldest of a large family. Born in Tracadie, New Brunswick, he had come to Niagara Falls as a teenager to work with his uncle Marcel, who owned a moving business. My dad sent money home to his family in New Brunswick until they joined him in Niagara Falls. My *pé*père, Stanley, whom I have very few memories of, was also my godfather. He had initially moved to Niagara Falls with his family, but eventually returned to New Brunswick a few years later, leaving his family behind. I know that it could not have been an easy life for my *mé*mère, raising her kids on her own, but I knew her to be a strong, Godly woman, with a very big heart. She had one of those enormous wooden carved rosaries hanging on her living room wall, and a giant picture of the Last Supper in her dining room. She went to Mass at the french church, Église Catholique Sainte Antoine.

Music, fudge, and molasses cookies are the first things that pop into my head when I think of my *mé*mère. She played the fiddle, accordion, harmonica, banjo, and the spoons. She sang along as she played, tapping her foot while us kids danced on the hardwood floors in her old house. Her fudge made our teeth ache, but we couldn't resist it. She knitted us mittens and slippers for Christmas. She dressed up as Santa Claus, and we played along, knowing full well it was her, while we sat at the foot of her overtinseled, flashing Christmas tree, waiting for our name to be called to receive our gifts. She was always happiest when all her family was around.

As I got older, I sensed a sadness about her. She would often lament in broken English through her heavy French accent, about whatever was bothering her; a problem with one of her kids or her finances. She'd had a hard life and plenty of struggles. She lost twins shortly after their birth, and years later, a daughter named Shirley, whom I had never met. Shirley had stayed in New Brunswick when the rest of the family moved to Niagara Falls. She had severe disabilities and lived in a nursing home. Two of her adult children also had less-serious disabilities, but required extra care, and my *mémère* did it all on her own. She always seemed tired. I used to dream about one day having enough money to pay all her bills so that she could have an easier life. Or at least have less to worry about.

Mémère loved to play Bingo, and was more than a little superstitious. If she happened to get dressed in a hurry, making the mistake of putting her shirt on inside out or backward, she wore it that way all day, taking it as a sign that she should go play Bingo. She won now and then, never enough to put her on easy street, but enough to keep her playing. I think most of her worries were financial, and she thought a jackpot would end her troubles. She always had just enough. My *mémère* loved her family, and she told me often that she was happy to have me living with her. She said she wished that she could see my other brothers and sisters more often too. She was well aware of my situation and told me not to worry; she would pray that everything would work out with the annulments and my parents. She assured me that she loved me, that I was her family, and that she would never put me out. Joe felt completely accepted by all of my dad's family. They were warm, loving, and kind. They had their own challenges in life, but they were good to us and made us feel loved.

Joe's divorce had been finalized for several months when he and I drove to Tennessee with my aunt Kathy and uncle Dave to meet Joe's mother and brother Mark. Kathy and Dave took in the tourist attractions while Joe and I visited with his family on our four-day vacation. We had been discussing marriage for months, but it was during this trip in May 1991, at the Rum Boogie Café on Beale Street, in Memphis, Tennessee, that Joe proposed to me. We set our wedding date for March 21, the following year. Joe and I dreamed about our future. There was no doubt about it, we loved each other desperately. We wanted to spend the rest of our lives together, and under the circumstances, we didn't want to wait for annulments. I was ticked off with my parents for being so unreasonable, and placing conditions on us. The only reason we would have considered waiting for the annulments before getting married would have been to please my mother. Hardly the right reason, and at that point, I didn't care much if I had her approval. She wasn't speaking to me and wouldn't let me see the rest of my family either. Joe and I were excited about our future.

SIX

Kiss of the Matriarch

Niagara Falls, Ontario, 1991–1992

I had lived in Niagara Falls my entire life. Joe was well traveled as the owner and operator of his consulting business. My idea of marriage was not one that involved a husband who traveled all the time. I told him that if he wanted to marry me, he needed to find a regular job that didn't involve excessive travel. He agreed. He was tired of traveling and wanted a more settled family life. He made the decision to pack up his consulting business. He didn't renew contracts when they ended, and he didn't pursue new ones. He cashed out his investments and paid his eight employees a three months' bonus. In late July 1991, Joe moved out of his brother's house in Memphis and into the St. Catharines apartment full-time. He immediately started looking for a job. The day he moved into the apartment was the day he gave me my engagement ring. It was now official. We had a ring and a date. I moved in with him.

At this point, I wish to restate my disclaimer. We didn't do things the way we would do them now. I am not at all proud of the fact that Joe and I shacked up before we got married. It's something that I wish we could go back and redo. For the sake of keeping the events of our journey authentic and transparent, I will continue to tell the story from the mind-set that I was in at the time.

Joe and I began planning for our anxiously anticipated March 21 wedding. I missed my family and wanted to share this milestone with them. Anytime I had dreamed of my future wedding, it always included my parents and siblings. I would have loved for all my sisters to be bridesmaids, and my brothers, groomsmen. My heart ached a little each time I thought about walking down the aisle without my dad beside me. I brushed the thoughts away and concentrated on what I felt were the positive things. I received an outpouring of love and support from my friends and many of my relatives. My aunts and coworkers threw bridal showers for me. When I asked my uncle Tony to walk me down the aisle, he graciously said he would. It was a happy and exciting time, tinged with a hint of sadness. I wished that my family could see what an amazing man Joe was. I wanted them to know how much in love and happy we were, but my mother wouldn't give us the opportunity.

Being a practicing Catholic my whole life, I knew that I was not in good standing with the church, and could not receive the sacraments. I still considered myself a Catholic and had no intentions of formally leaving the church or changing denominations. I felt like I was on a sort of sabbatical. Joe had begun the annulment process immediately after his divorce had been finalized, and we planned to have our marriage blessed as soon as they were granted. I never stopped going to Mass, and Joe came with me every Sunday. He was a Christian, raised in the Methodist Church. His grandfather was a Methodist minister. We did not receive communion. My conscience was constantly burdened with guilt over living in sin, knowing right from wrong, but wanting what I wanted. We wanted very much to belong and be in full communion with the church, but we wanted to be together more.

Joe started RCIA (Rite of Christian Initiation of Adults). The priest warned us that the annulment process could be a lengthy one. We still didn't want to wait to get married. Although he completed the program, he wasn't received into the church. I thought often about Gramma Hubbard, who was declining in health. She hadn't been traveling much anymore and was living with my aunt and uncle in Sarnia. I wanted to see her but felt that I must have been a great disappointment to her, living the way I was. I was too ashamed to face her, so I never made the attempt.

I had been asked, along with my sister Bridget, to be a bridesmaid in my cousin Tom's wedding. The invitation had come before Joe and I started dating, so I gladly accepted. At the time, I was excited to be part of the celebration. After being shunned by my immediate, and some of my extended, family on my mother's side, I decided to back out of my bridesmaid duties. Not solely to escape their scorn, even though that was a big part of the reason, but also because I didn't want the drama surrounding our relationship to overshadow my cousin's happy day. I called Tom to tell him about my concerns. I apologized and let him know that I needed to excuse myself from the wedding party. He wouldn't hear of it and insisted that he and his fiancée, Fatima, wanted me in the wedding. He was aware of our situation, having heard the rumors, but he encouraged me not to worry about what other people were saying. He told me that it was nobody's business but my own. Even with his support, I still didn't really feel comfortable about it. I didn't want to put myself in such a vulnerable situation, knowing that my entire family would be at the wedding, a full three-day affair, but I relented. I told him I would be there. I didn't want to throw a curve into their wedding planning or leave them scrambling to find a replacement.

I felt nauseous every time I thought about the day. Dutifully, I took part in all the wedding showers and obligatory rehearsal dinner, smiling graciously and being polite, well aware of the whispers in other corners of the room. My mother had garnered supporters. Either out of loyalty or intimidation, very few of my relatives spoke to me. It was agonizingly uncomfortable to say the least, and I desperately wanted it all to be over. On the day of the wedding, I stood up with the bridal party in my royal purple dress and fulfilled my bridesmaid duties with a smile on my face. I remained as gracious as possible, desperately trying not to attract any attention to myself whatsoever. My only prayer was to get through the day without a confrontation. The wedding ceremony was lovely and incident free. I continued to pray for the courage to make it through pictures, the receiving line, speeches, dinner, and the wedding party dance. Only after all that could Joe and I leave.

After the newlywed couple recessed down the aisle and out of the church, Joe went to wait for me in the car. I listened to instructions about where to meet for pictures. As I walked toward the car, my aunt Betty, who had traveled from Texas for the wedding, called out to me. After being largely shunned by most of my other aunts and several of my cousins all weekend, I was startled that she was actually speaking to me. Already a basket of nerves, my stomach did a flip, having no idea what my mother's sister wanted with me. I cautiously and politely answered her.

"Yes?"

She asked, "Where is he?"

Tentatively, I replied, "Who?"

She inquired, "Your boyfriend, Joe?"

Suddenly panicked, but desperately trying to hide it, my mind raced and my heart began to pound. Why was she looking for Joe? He had been treated like the elephant in the room the entire weekend. No one had been outright rude to him, but other than Tom, Fatima, Fatima's family, and a handful of my cousins, he had been virtually ignored. I couldn't help but be suspicious when I answered my aunt's question.

"He's waiting for me in the car."

What she said next shocked me.

"Gramma Hubbard wants to meet him."

Glancing over my left shoulder toward the church steps, I saw my gramma standing there, holding on to the railing. I noticed her familiar white jacket with the black trim. She looked beautiful, yet frail. Just the sight of her comforted me. I was surprised to see that she had come to the wedding. She had been so ill, and the wedding was out of town for her. It looked as if she were waiting for something. Was she really waiting for me to introduce Joe to her? I nodded to my aunt before quickly walking to the car to tell Joe.

"My Gramma Hubbard wants to meet you."

He looked at me in disbelief as I pointed to the church steps where she was still standing. Looking in her direction, then turning to me, not at all sure that it was such a good idea. Several of my aunts were gathered around my mother at the bottom of the steps, no doubt aware of my gramma's request. I assured Joe that it would be fine. He climbed out of the car, and together we walked back toward the church and up the stairs.

The small crowd of sisters stayed to watch what was about to take place. My mother stood close enough to see and hear me introduce my future husband to my beloved gramma, but stayed back far enough to avoid any contact with me. I knew better than to speak to her. It had been months since I had last seen my gramma. When I looked into her eyes, the disappointment that I expected to see was not there. I saw only love, tinged with a little sadness. Or was it compassion. Quite possibly it was a little of both. She was undoubtedly made aware of the whole situation. I know without a doubt that she had prayed for me all my life, and that she was now praying for Joe too.

She knew better than anyone that I had been praying for a good husband. She had been the one to point me in the direction of St. Joseph, the patron saint to find a good spouse. I had prayed countless novenas to St. Joseph. I don't think it was a coincidence that I found my own Joe. It was also Gramma Hubbard who told me as a young teenager, on more than one occasion, after dating a few young guys my own age, that it was "better to be an old man's pet than a young man's slave." My Joe was fourteen and a half years older than me, and he definitely treated me like a queen.

Her eyes spoke more than she needed to say. I hugged her gently, and she held me tight. Trying hard to swallow the huge lump that was growing in my throat, I introduced her to Joe. She looked up at him, and he bowed his 6'3" frame down to meet her gaze. He extended his big hand gently toward her, but she didn't take it. Instead, she reached her hands up toward his face, placing them on his cheeks, and kissed him. She said, "I am so happy to finally meet you."

A few jaws dropped, and all eyes were on her. The matriarch of the family had just extended a very public sign of peace, love, and welcome to my fiancé. There was no judgment. My heart soared, my knees went weak, and I felt like the weight of the world had been lifted from my shoulders. It was the most perfect act that could have ever been shown, by the person I most respected and admired in the world. It was her way of showing me that everything would be fine, and it was more than I needed to carry me through the rest of the wedding celebration and beyond. With tears in our eyes, I hugged her and thanked her and told her that I loved her before hurrying to join the rest of the bridal party.

The remainder of the day was not nearly as worrisome. We both loosened up and actually started to enjoy ourselves. Joe helped the bridal party with whatever he could, carrying bags, fetching things, and holding doors and umbrellas over the happy couple when the rain started to fall. Even though he was still slightly guarded, I was so grateful to have him there. He told me later that evening that he wouldn't have considered letting me go alone. He wanted to be there for me.

During dinner and the reception, I sat at the head table with the rest of the wedding party. Joe sat with the band. Tom and Fatima no doubt had to puzzle over where to put him. Obviously an awkward conundrum, they wanted Joe to feel comfortable. Putting him with my relatives would have surely caused a rift. My mother undoubtedly made it crystal clear that she didn't want *him* sitting anywhere near her. Joe laughed it off, dubbing himself as the black sheep of the family. The band guys were a great bunch and put him at ease.

There were more than a few good-natured jokes from a couple of my cousins who stopped by Joe's table. They ribbed him about being on "the other side," not worthy of a seat "in holy land." They had been made vaguely aware of the scandal, having heard bits and pieces of the gossip that had been circulating. A couple of them shared their own shunning stories. They told us not to worry about it, it would all blow over in time. Joe was a good sport and enjoyed himself more than either of us expected. We stayed for the first part of the dancing before making a discreet exit. We were more than happy to have my cousin's wedding behind us.

Joe searched the newspapers daily for work. He mailed several resumes off every week, and we waited for the phone to ring. Within a couple of months, he'd had several interviews and received three job offers in one day. He accepted a government job as provincial training coordinator for the Ministry of Labor. Things began falling into place. Because my parents were still not supportive of our relationship, some of our friends and relatives expected us to have a quiet, simple wedding. That was not the case. I was beyond the point of being a shrinking violet, avoiding my mother and her friends. I wanted a big celebration, and Joe wanted me to have what I wanted. Invitations were ordered, the church and hall were reserved, and we met with the Orsinis to plan our reception at the Ramada Suites. Our wedding party was chosen, flowers were selected, the DJ was booked, and our photographer was secured. All the details came together easily.

Joe started his new job. Even though I had only moved into the apartment a couple of months earlier, neither of us felt quite right about shacking up. We didn't want to live together unmarried for another five months. We decided to get married right away in a private ceremony while still keeping our plans for the big wedding and party in March. We contacted Reverend James, the pastor of St. Andrew's United Church, where our big wedding was booked. We explained to him that Joe had just started a new job and had moved to St. Catharines. We told him that we really wanted to be together, but that we didn't want to just live together. We wanted to be married, and we wanted more than a courthouse wedding. He agreed to marry us in a private ceremony the very next week. We had already gone through the required marriage prep course at his church, so there was nothing standing in the way. Joe and I were married in the little chapel at St. Andrew's United Church on November 19, 1991. My aunt Kathy and her husband, Dave, were our witnesses. It was an intimate and simple ceremony, and it made us feel like our union was legitimate. The four of us went out for dinner afterward. It was a Tuesday evening, and we both had to work the next day. We didn't have a honeymoon, and we only told our closest friends that we were married.

Life hadn't changed much, but we were content. We moved out of the two-bedroom apartment in St. Catharines, into a duplex in

Niagara Falls. We continued working and planning for the big wedding celebration in March. I mailed out our invitations, inviting all my family, even the ones I knew wouldn't come—parents, siblings, aunts, uncles, and cousins. It was my way of letting them all know that we were indeed going ahead with our plans.

Although we were already legally married, and the March 21 ceremony was actually a renewal of our wedding vows, it was as close to the dream wedding that I had always wanted. Joe stayed at the Ramada Suites hotel with his brothers, and the bridesmaids stayed at our house, the night before the wedding. The morning was filled with excitement, the house abuzz with hair, makeup, and nails being done. The photographer snapped pictures while we put on finishing touches. Flowers were delivered, and I felt very much like a brand-new bride.

Seeing all our friends, and several more of our relatives than I had expected, filling the church on that beautiful day, made my heart soar. It was a wonderful day. The ceremony was memorable, the reception was elegant, and the meal was delicious. Our flowers were gorgeous, we had a top-notch photographer, a well-known DJ, and an open bar. Everyone had a great time. There had even been an afternoon blizzard. A fitting reminder of our first embrace on that snowy winter night, two years earlier. More than a hundred and fifty guests showed up—family, friends, old neighbors, and coworkers. Missing from the picture were my parents and all my siblings. I wished that they could have been there to see how happy we were. Their absence didn't take anything away from the day, and it couldn't touch our joy. It would have been wonderful to have them in our lives, but we knew that we could still be happy without them.

SEVEN

A Baby Changes Things

Niagara Falls, Ontario, 1993

*N*iagara Falls is a small town. People knew that we were Mr. and Mrs. Joseph Allen. Joe and I were proud of that fact, and we lived freely in the community without any of our previous worries. I continued to work at the Ramada Suites, and Joe carpooled to Toronto to his job at the Ministry of Labor every day. Three months after our big wedding party, I discovered I was pregnant. We were over the moon. We drove to Ottawa with my best friend, Michelle, to celebrate Canada Day 125. It was during that little holiday that the symptoms of my pregnancy hit me full force. Morning sickness would have been welcomed; however, I was sick morning, noon, and night, and every hour in between. I couldn't even brush my teeth without gagging. I was absolutely exhausted. We decided to go to the movies to see *Batman*, Joe and Michelle's pick. I fell asleep after the first fifteen minutes. I couldn't eat. The smells of the food booths in the park sent me running for the nearest port-a-potty, and the boat ride along the Rideau Canal was cut short for obvious reasons. I wasn't much fun on the trip to say the least. I rode home in the back seat of our Honda Civic, letting Michelle ride up front so that I could lie down for the eight-hour drive home.

I spent pretty much all the remaining eight months of the pregnancy on the couch with a sleeve of saltine crackers, a bottle of ginger ale, and a barf bucket. I gained less than twenty-five pounds. I had no idea that pregnancy would be so unpleasant. I wanted nothing more than to have a baby, but the experience was not at all what I had imagined it would be. Throwing up became a normal part of my daily routine. Any day that I felt even mildly well, my appetite was voracious. I ate like I had never seen food, only to have the nausea hit me all over again.

Joe's ten-year-old son, Christopher, came to visit us that summer. After several failed attempts to schedule visits, wasted plane tickets, and court orders, we were happy to finally see him get off the plane in Buffalo. Despite court-ordered visitation, which was next to impossible to enforce because we lived in different countries, our repeated requests to see Christopher were refused or ignored. So were the mandated sharing of school and medical records. Joe had been paying alimony and child support regularly, but in an effort to get his ex-wife to comply with the court order, he quit paying, and we sought custody. The judge was sympathetic to our situation, but determined that it would take time for Christopher to adjust to our new marriage. He said that it may be in Christopher's best interest to live with us in the future, but for the time being, he felt it was too soon. The judge also reduced Joe's alimony and child support to amounts that better matched his new salary. He also stressed to Joe's ex-wife the importance of complying with the custody agreement. This all resulted with us finally getting a visit with Christopher.

Joe's mother and niece flew in from Tennessee at the same time. They hadn't seen Christopher in more than a year, so it was like a mini family reunion. Still very much experiencing nausea at all hours, I wasn't the hostess that I would have liked to be. Joe's mom brought a ham bone and greens with her in her suitcase so she could make him one of his favorite meals. I'm pretty sure we could have found the items in our grocery store, but she wanted to be sure that it was an authentic Southern dish. I hadn't learned to make any of his favorite foods yet, and probably wouldn't have made them right anyway, so I was glad that he would get the treat. Shortly after their arrival, his mom put the bone on to boil, and the smell of the simmering brew brought on violent waves of nausea. I had to run to my room and bury my head under the blanket to escape it.

Christopher stayed with us for a few weeks after my mother-in-law and niece returned home. He and Joe hit all the tourist attractions with my uncle Roger and some of my young cousins. They went fishing and spent time bonding while I stayed home, close to my bucket. Christopher helped me with the dollhouse I was building in the basement. We had BBQs, visited with family, and were invited to dinner with friends. We tried to make his visit with us fun and memorable. We are fairly certain that we succeeded, which was fortunate, because we had no idea that Christopher's first visit would be his last.

Because Joe's ex-wife changed domiciles frequently and refused to disclose where she was living, Joe took the opportunity, while Christopher was with us, to ask him for his address. Christopher broke down into tears, saying that he wasn't allowed to tell us where he lived. Joe and I were not entirely shocked that Christopher had been instructed not to give us his address. We were concerned however about his emotional reaction to Joe's request. He was completely distraught. We didn't press him any further.

Our hearts were heavy when his visit ended and the day to take him back to the airport arrived. Because Christopher was traveling as an unaccompanied minor, an escort had been assigned to him for his flight. Joe was permitted to walk him to his seat onto the plane to see him off. After saying his final goodbyes, Joe met me at the security area, only to be paged back to the gate a few seconds later. He was led back to the plane, where he found Christopher visibly distraught and crying uncontrollably. He said he didn't want to leave. Joe got him settled down before leaving him again and joining me. Our hearts broke. Our resources were very limited, and we didn't have the funds to continue fighting for custody. Joe decided that rather than put Christopher through an emotional roller coaster, fighting to get visitation, and sending him home in tears, he would stop the ride. At the time, we thought we were making the right decision; but over the years, we wished we'd handled things very differently.

My *mé*mère and aunts were really excited that there would be a new baby in the family. We remained close to my dad's relatives, joining them for all their get-togethers, and even going away on camping trips to Northern Ontario. My life should have been full, but there was something missing. Late that fall, I called my mother. I wanted to tell her that I was pregnant and that she was going to be a grandmother. It had been over a year since I last saw her at my cousin's wedding, and more than two years since I had spoken to her. Surprisingly, she didn't hang up on me. I told her that Joe had begun the annulment process several months earlier, and that we were waiting for them to be finalized. I wanted her to know that I hadn't completely abandoned my faith, and that my wish was for my baby to know its grandparents, aunts, and uncles. That phone call led to daily reciprocal phone calls, sometimes several per day. We had a lot of catching up to do. Joe was cautiously pleased for what seemed to be repair work in my relationship with my mother.

About a month before Christmas, we invited my parents over for dinner. Joe made his famous Southern fried chicken. The mood was pleasant, and I enjoyed watching him and my dad make small talk. Joe is a personable guy. I just knew that if my parents got to know him, they would fall in love with him. Before long, we were invited to visit at their house. Slowly I reconnected with my family, and they began to get to know us as a couple. My mother seemed relieved that we were working on getting straight with the church since I had gone ahead and married Joe against their wishes anyway. She still wasn't exactly happy, but things were improving. I was sorry that she was disappointed in me, and I told her so; however, I was not at all sorry for marrying Joe. Joe developed a rapport with my parents, but he remained cautious. Joe had made it quite clear at their initial meeting at the Campaign Life office that he wasn't about to be bullied or controlled, and my mother was very careful about her behavior around him. My dad, always easygoing, got along well with my husband. They drank beer and talked about guy stuff. It was wonderful to see my younger brothers and sisters again. I was amazed by how much they had all grown and changed in two years. I felt like I was slowly earning my family back.

Even as we were building bridges, my mother didn't hide her dislike for my dad's family, or the fact that Joe and I were associating with them. Any time we mentioned them or talked about any of the get-togethers and fun we'd shared, she made remarks that clearly indicated her displeasure. She didn't want to hear about it. I quit talking about them around her. Soon, our visits with my relatives became more sporadic, as our time was filled up with my parents and siblings. I had planned to host the annual Christmas Eve dinner and party at our house that year. I hoped to have our entire family, including all my dad's relatives, together. When I shared my plans with my mother, she announced that she wouldn't attend the party if my dad's relatives were there. I was put into an extremely awkward position. Always the nonconfrontational type. I decided to make what I knew in my gut to be the cowardly decision. I cancelled the party. What I failed to realize then was that that single decision would set the wheels into motion, returning to my mother the power that she thought she had lost when I made the decision to marry Joe.

Aunt Kathy hosted the party at her house, and Joe and I stayed home. We went to bed early, feeling horribly sad and guilty. My baby was due in just a few short months, and I wanted to keep the peace. I am fairly certain that my relatives had figured out the dynamics of my newly reconciled relationship of with my mother. They sensed us distancing ourselves from them. We felt like traitors, but when I weighed the alternative, peace with my mother and contact with my family won out.

I was incredibly anxious to meet the little person who had completely consumed my every thought and action. Not to mention the one who had been making me queasy morning, noon, and night. The nursery had been prepared for months. The ultrasound showed that we were having a girl. I washed all the baby blankets and bedding in Ivory Snow and made up the little rocking cradle we had bought and assembled. Cloth diapers, tiny washcloths, receiving blankets, socks, booties, and bonnets were folded neatly and organized in the changing table. The little wicker basket was filled with bottles of baby bath and diapering supplies, lotions and creams. Tiny outfits and dresses were hung in the closet, and my hospital bag was packed and ready to go. Every day, I sat in the rocking chair that we had bought in a yard sale, looking at all the baby things, and dreamed about the day that we would bring our little girl home.

Two weeks past my due date, I finally went into labor. I had been feeling unusually well and had loads of energy. It was my birthday. After months of dragging and feeling awful, I had forgotten what it was like to feel good, so I took advantage of it. I went through the entire house, cleaning, dusting, shining, and organizing every room, closet, cupboard, and drawer, in preparation of the arrival of our little one. When I got a sudden craving for fried wontons and wings, Joe indulged me. He ordered from the Regency Motel, a complete dive. I never went into the smoky bar. I waited in the car, and Joe went in to order and have a beer while it was being prepared. I had been scheduled for an induction the following morning, but the baby had other plans. By eleven o'clock that night, my labor started. Really regretting my choice of dinner, I called my mother to let her know that we were heading to the hospital. She arrived late the next morning, fully expecting to see her first grandchild, who had yet to emerge. Strapped to a fetal monitor and on a Pitocin drip to speed up my labor, I was exhausted. After fourteen long hours, on March 5, 1993, one day after my twenty-third birthday, Angela Mary Nicole was born. Named after my mother, Gramma Hubbard, and myself, she was the best birthday gift I could have hoped for.

Although she had tried to leave, my mother was present for the birth. Joe asked her to stay, thinking that I should have my mother there. I only saw my baby for a split second when the doctor held her up, before the nurses whisked her to the other side of the room. Joe and my mother watched while the nurses weighed, cleaned, and swaddled her. I waited excitedly, desperate to hold her. Joe was beaming and walked from the baby warmer to my bedside to give me reports. He told me how beautiful and perfect our baby was and how proud he was of me. He hugged me tight and squeezed my hand. The look of love and joy on his face was more profound than I had ever seen before. It was the absolute happiest moment of my life. My mother called over to me from the baby warmer, giggling as she remarked that Angela had a cone head. She began to laugh out loud when she said she looked like Bart Simpson. I was mortified. I couldn't believe that she would say such a thing about my baby, her first grandchild. When the nurse brought Angela over to me, tightly wrapped and pink, she looked at me softly and told me not to worry, that her head was just fine. She said that it was normal, after long hours in the birth canal, for a baby's head to be elongated. She said that babies' heads were designed for that, and that it would round out in the next few days. I could hardly wait to bring her home.

Angela was absolutely perfect. A smiling happy baby, she was good-natured and easygoing. I held her constantly. I sang and talked to her all day long and kept her in her bouncy seat next to me while I showered and cooked dinner. When I vacuumed, cleaned the house, or did laundry, I wore her on my chest in a sling. We went for walks every day, and I changed her outfits like she was a little doll. The cradle in her nursery was hardly ever used for more than her stuffed animals. She never slept in it. I brought her to bed with us instead, nursing her throughout the night in between sleep. I loved everything about being a mother. On the weekends, Joe and I took Angela for long car rides, picnics on the Niagara Parkway, day trips to the zoo, and once in a while, road trips to Sarnia. We spent several hours at my parents' house every weekend.

Joe moved up quickly in the Ministry of Labor, and my role as wife, mother, and homemaker was better than all the dreams I had ever imagined. Our little family was our treasure. We cherished our time together and spent every minute we could with each other. I couldn't wait for Joe to get home from work every night. As soon as he came through the door, he scooped Angela up in his arms and smooched her little face until she giggled, and sang silly songs to her while I got our dinner. The neighbors smiled and waved when we walked through the neighborhood with Angela in the old Peg Perego pram that had been given to us by a man from church. Our evening walks were a part of our daily routine before giving Angela her bath and nursing her to sleep. Life was very simple, but it was equally sweet.

We hardly ever saw my *mé*mère, or my aunts and uncles on my dad's side anymore. I felt a stab in my heart whenever I thought about how they had been there for us during our shunning time. My mother made it clear that she wouldn't participate in anything that they were invited to. She never gave a specific reason, and we never asked. I wanted her approval, now that I was "back in." Even though Joe and I didn't feel right about distancing ourselves from my relatives, I didn't want to jeopardize my newly bridged relationship with my mother, and risk losing my family again. I wanted my immediate family in my life and part of my daughter's life. That meant remaining loyal to my mother at all costs. All the people who had been there for Joe and I in the early days faded away from our life fairly quickly. I had twinges of guilt over the years, but I stuffed them down and tried to ignore them. The more time that passed by, the harder it was to pick up the phone. The years continued to slip away.

EIGHT

Silver Linings

Niagara Falls, Ontario, 1993–1994

*A*ngela turned three months old in June. When I asked Joe what he wanted for Father's Day, he said, "Another baby."

I got pregnant again that very month. We bought our first house and moved in that September. A cute 1950 one-and-a-half–story, three-bedroom house. It was located directly behind St. Thomas More Church, where we had been attending Mass regularly. Joe and I never received communion, but we approached with Angela for a blessing. One Sunday after Mass, Msgr. O'Donoghue asked us how we could fix things so that we could get right with the church. We told him that Joe's annulment process was already underway and that we were still waiting to hear from the marriage tribunal for their decision. It was being handled in Memphis, Tennessee. Msgr. O'Donoghue suggested we write to the tribunal to inquire about the status. He said that sometimes a personal letter might get some attention for our case and move things along. He asked us to keep him posted so that he could get things in motion as soon as possible to have our marriage blessed. Joe also wanted to be received into the church.

Encouraged by Msgr. O'Donoghue's advice and concern for us, we sent the letter the very next day. We told the tribunal that we were expecting our second child, that Joe had gone through RCIA, and that we very much wanted to be in full communion with the church. A couple of months later, we heard from them. Both annulments had been granted. We were free to be married in the Catholic Church. Msgr. O'Donoghue met with Joe and I individually, and then as a couple. At six months pregnant, on December 5, 1992, I went to confession. Joe was conditionally baptized, made his first communion, was confirmed, and we had our marriage blessed. Five sacraments all at once. My parents were Joe's godparents and confirmation sponsors.

Aunt Annie and Uncle Dick drove from Sarnia to celebrate with us. They brought a wedding card for us from Gramma Hubbard. I am certain that she was thrilled beyond words at the knowledge that not only had our marriage been blessed, but that Joe was now a Catholic. I didn't fully consider or appreciate then just how faithfully she must have prayed for us, but I have no doubt she stormed heaven for just that result. I am so grateful today for all her prayers. Not just during the months and years that I was not in good standing in the church, but for all the prayers that she prayed for me over the course of my life. I truly believe they saved not only me, but my entire family. It was our third wedding ceremony and the most important one of all. Sadly, I can't say that I felt any differently that day. I didn't feel like anything had really changed, other than the fact that my mother was satisfied. I was certainly glad that Joe and I could participate in the Mass fully, and that we could receive communion, but more because of my own pride. I didn't like standing out, leaving people to wonder why we weren't receiving communion. We continued to attend Mass every Sunday, but didn't do more than what we thought was required beyond that one hour a week.

Twelve days overdue, Joseph Robert Stanley—named after Joe, my dad, and both my grandfathers—was born after fifteen hours of labor. He was born exactly one year and three weeks after Angela, on March 26, 1994. All our friends informed us that we now had a million-dollar family. We wondered when we would get the million dollars. Everyone wanted to know if we were "done." Angela had spoiled me by being such an easy baby. Joseph made up for it, and then some. He had colic and was painfully gassy. It always seemed to be worse at night. He napped great during the day and liked to swing in his little baby swing, but at bedtime, he screamed for hours. His tiny body would scrunch into a tight little ball, his face turned beet red, and nothing seemed to console him. Taking care of a newborn and a toddler all day was plenty of work, but I loved it and handled it like a pro. Sleep was something that I lacked, and I soon began to wear thin.

I tried everything. I kept Joseph up all day so that he would be too tired to stay awake at night. After giving him his bath, changing, nursing, burping, and rocking him to sleep, I would tiptoe back to our room. After carefully laying him in his crib as quietly as possible, I eased myself—ever so delicately—into bed. The second my head touched down on my pillow, the wailing began. High-pitched screams that penetrated my brain, causing me to leap from my bed. Pacing the floor while tightly holding, bouncing, and patting Joseph's back became a nightly ritual. I was beyond exhausted and honestly thought I would lose my mind. Joe had an early morning commute to Toronto, but he always seemed to be the one who could get Joseph settled. He swaddled him up in his blanket and held him tightly against his chest while he patted his back and sang to him. I told Joe that I could seriously understand what pushed some mothers over the edge to shake or smother their babies. Of course I would never harm my baby, but I could certainly empathize with the mothers who had no support. Parenting is definitely a two-person job. Thankfully that stage only lasted a few months. I discovered that my diet had an effect on how Joseph felt. Salad was my favorite, and that seemed to be what aggravated him the most. Once I made a few changes, he was much happier.

Joe took parental leave for three months that summer. It was a fun and relaxing time for us to bond with our little family. We painted the house, put up wallpaper in the kitchen, ordered draperies for our living room, and decorated the two upstairs bedrooms. I spent weeks painting a Rainbow Zebra mural on the wall in Joseph's room. The inspiration had come from a storybook and quilt that I had bought at the Ball's Falls craft fair with my mother. I brought the quilt with me to the Color Your World paint store where the clerk helped me to match the colors. She mixed all nine into pint-sized cans of red, orange, yellow, green, blue, indigo, violet, black, and white. On the largest bedroom wall, I drew the picture freehand, with a pencil. I painted it in the same rainbow colors as the quilt, carefully outlining everything in black. I then painted the remaining walls in bright indigo. It was the biggest project that I had ever taken on, and it took almost the whole summer to complete.

Baby Joseph spent hours with me in his bouncy chair, conveniently close for feedings and naps. Joe brought me lunch, drinks, and snacks; and he took Angela and Joseph for walks and car rides so that I could work. Being the kind of person who likes to finish what I start, I tend to become slightly obsessive with new projects. I worked steadily and efficiently until it was done. Exhausted by the end of the last full day of painting, I inspected every tiny detail, correcting flaws and finishing touch-ups before going to bed. I could hardly sleep for the excitement, anxious about putting the room back together in the morning.

After feeding the babies and leaving them in their daddy's care, with my cup of coffee, I made my way up the narrow stairwell to the sun-filled bedroom. Straight to work with a smile on my face, I was giddy about how great the room looked, so bright and cheerful, a happy place for reading books and playing with toys. Paintbrushes, rollers, tape, shelves, framed artwork, and all nine cans of rainbow-colored paints were in a giant pile in the middle of the floor. As I scanned the room, I decided to tackle moving the ridiculously heavy, full-sized bed with the squeaky springs, a family heirloom from Joe's great aunt, first. It was the biggest piece of furniture in the room.

Instead of calling Joe to help me get it back into its place, I shoved the bed with the weight of my whole body, budging it only a fraction of an inch with each push. After several heaves, the closet door that I had removed in order to paint the doorframe, and had leaned onto the edge of the bed to get it out of the way, suddenly began to slide down. I glanced down the length of the door and gasped when I saw that the bottom of it had begun to tip over one of the cans of paint. The last can that I had used the night before was the can of black paint. It was practically full because I had only used it to outline the mural. I had worked so late the night before that I didn't want to wake the babies up by hammering the lid back on, so I just left it loosely on top. Standing on the opposite side of the bed, with a mountain of stuff between me and the door, I felt like I was watching the thick black goo spill out in slow motion. Unable to get over the huge pile and across the room fast enough, I must have let out a bloodcurdling scream. I say this because I don't actually remember screaming, but Joe arrived wild-eyed in the doorway within seconds. He told me that he thought that I had hurt myself or that I was being attacked.

I pointed to the huge puddle of black paint. Of course it had to be the black can that got tipped over. Way too much had spilled out for us to ever possibly get it out of the beige carpet. We sopped it up as best we could with towels, but the stain remained. I was devastated. Everything up until that point had gone unbelievably smoothly. The freehand drawing had been meticulously painted in bright and cheerful colors and outlined with precision. The woodwork around the windows and baseboards had been taped and protected, and the ceiling edged with crisp lines. All of that perfection was now tainted by the big, ugly, black, blob on the carpet. Joe saw my disappointment and told me not to worry. He said that the room looked great and that we could hide the spot somehow. Maybe cover it up with a rug. I was distraught. There was no way that I would even consider hiding it. I would know that it was there, and it would haunt me. Covering it up was not a solution. The stain needed to be removed completely. I wanted a new carpet. I didn't even want to try having it cleaned professionally. I wanted a brand-new carpet.

We called my dad. If anyone would know what to do, it would be him. He came over right away to look at it, and when his eyes fell upon the blob, he let out a, "Humph," followed by, "Uh-oh."

Clearly trying to stifle a chuckle, knowing how hard I had worked for weeks on the project. He told me how great the room looked and seemed to think that we could probably have the carpet cleaned, as long as it hadn't soaked into the under pad. I was certain it had soaked all the way down to the subfloor, and was amazed it hadn't leaked through the ceiling as well. My dad pulled up a corner of the carpet along with the under pad to check. Indeed, it had soaked through, but to our great surprise, he discovered that there was hardwood underneath. It was an older home, and there was hardwood throughout the main floor, but we had no idea that there was hardwood upstairs. We were delighted. My dad peeked under the carpet in the bedroom across the hall and found the same thing. He said it would be a really easy job to sand down and refinish the wood. It was wonderful news. It only took Joe and my dad a couple of weeks to refinish both bedrooms. What I had considered a complete disaster became a big blessing and an opportunity for a significant home improvement.

By the end of the summer, we had made the house our own. Cute, cozy, and meticulously clean, inside and out. Rainbow Garden Center was at the end of the street, walking distance from our house. We made several trips each week with Angela and Joseph in their little red wagon to buy perennials and annuals for our rock gardens. Joe mowed and trimmed the lawn and hedges with Joseph in a carrier on his back, while I potted and planted with Angela. The hedges were even, the lawn was lush, and the gardens were bursting with color. Lily of the valley grew prolifically along the stone walkway and beside the garage. My mother came by to dig up the ones that grew behind our shed, filling up bags to plant at her house. Ferns and lamb's ears poked out between the rocks in the backyard, and I filled in the empty spaces with soapwort and pansies. Purple, pink, red, and white petunias mounded up around the spike plants in the island and raised beds next to the garage. In the fall, I planted hundreds of tulip bulbs. We sanded down the rusty wrought iron railing on the front porch and painted it black, a crisp accent to the high gloss gray we painted on the concrete porch. Giant hanging baskets filled with red ivy geraniums framed off the welcoming front door. A tipped-over half barrel mounded up with pansies and purple and white alyssum was a whimsical finish to the walkway leading up to the steps.

We loved spending time outside with Angela toddling around the yard, and Joseph in the stroller or playpen. Joe watched me dig in the dirt, always working, weeding, planting, sweeping, cleaning, and hosing. Neighbors often commented on how beautiful our place looked. We were proud of our little home with the sparkling windows and bright cheerful flowers. Its only spoil was an infestation of mice in our garden shed. We had been given a bunch of vegetable seeds as a housewarming gift, but the mice ate them before we got the chance to plant them. Thankfully they never got into the house. The previous owners had put up a large bird feeder on a pole in the middle of the backyard, and we continued to keep it filled, attracting many different kinds of birds. We loved to watch and hear the songbirds from our sunroom. The feeder also attracted a few pesky squirrels. We thought they were cute until we realized that they were eating up all of the seed, completely emptying the feeder daily. Joe decided to grease the pole with petroleum jelly. That idea provided our little family with hours of entertainment as we watched the squirrels repeatedly scurry halfway up the pole, before losing their grip and sliding to the ground again. We dreamed of one day putting a pool in the backyard, adding onto the house, and building extra bedrooms in the basement. We were sure we'd live in that house forever. We were happy there, and we couldn't imagine that life could ever get any better. Before Joe returned to work in September, his parental leave almost over, I discovered I was pregnant again. We were thrilled.

After three years with the Ministry of Labor, Joe was ready for a career change and more challenges. He put his feelers out, and soon the recruiters were calling. He was offered a Manager of Training and Development position with Toyota Motor Manufacturing in Cambridge, Ontario. He accepted it. It was still a commute, just a different direction. Life was busy for me but in a simple way, and it was everything I wanted it to be. Weekends were our favorite time because we were all together. Yard work, grocery shopping, long drives along the parkway to Niagara-on-the-Lake. We made trips to the Toronto Zoo, the fall craft fair in Ball's Falls, and to visit relatives in Sarnia. During the workweek, we went to bed early, right after the babies went down, and got up even earlier in the morning. Joe had to be up and on the road by four thirty. Toyota had an employee gym, where he worked out each morning before work. He didn't get home until after seven o'clock each night. By the end of the day, we were both exhausted.

My third pregnancy went by incredibly fast, no doubt because I was occupied around the clock with a one- and a two-year-old. With a late spring due date, feeling great and full of energy, I spent the days outside in the yard with Angela and Joseph, playing and gardening. I never really slowed down at all. I was four days overdue when I went into labor. Joe was in Waterloo, over an hour away, hosting a BBQ at the president of Toyota Canada's house, for the Kaizen Circle team. I was annoyed that he didn't have a backup person to take over hosting the party, knowing that I was overdue. I was more annoyed about missing out on a sacred family Saturday. Joe wasn't at all concerned, likely because of my track record of going well past my due dates, and having long labors. The dinner party was a bigger deal for him than I had been aware of at the time. The president had never hosted that sort of party at his house before, so when Joe approached him about doing it, the president told Joe that he would have to be the one to ask his wife. Joe had flowers sent to her with the request. She agreed. Joe was under an enormous amount of pressure during the whole planning process. I wasn't at all focused on the importance of the party, Joe's responsibility in it, or his desire for it to go off without a hitch. I was focused solely on taking care of my little family, my enormous self, and my own discomfort. I was pouty and hormonal. We lived literally minutes away from my parents' house. It wasn't like I was left without anyone to help me in the event of an emergency. I wanted my husband there, at home, with me. June 5, 1995, was a hot day. I pushed our newly purchased Peg Perego triple stroller, with Angela and Joseph buckled in, to my mom and dad's house. My dad BBQ'd, and we sat outside on their back patio all afternoon. Feeling like a beached whale, I watched my sisters play with my kids in the pool from my lounge chair. My dad offered to drive us home, but I declined. I had been feeling contractions all afternoon, and I wanted to keep walking, hoping to bring on a full-blown labor. It would serve Joe right if I delivered the baby while he was away. That would teach him not to leave me in my condition. Yeah, I know, I was a total brat. My labor did continue, and I was quite pleased with myself. One of my sisters walked home with us, and I played out the whole scenario in my head. She could babysit while I drove to the hospital and delivered the baby. Joe could find out when he got home. My plan was foiled because Joe called to check in right after we got home. He sounded upbeat when he told me that the BBQ was almost done and had been a huge success. He said he'd be home soon. I was annoyed at his jovial mood and told him flatly that I would be leaving soon for the hospital. He thought I was joking. My mother, who had driven over when I told her about my plan, assured him that I was serious. He begged me not to leave yet and drove home in record time. I was relieved to have Joe with me but remained somewhat smug, not wanting to give him the satisfaction of knowing that I wanted him there. I was still feeling slighted that he had left me. While I labored and was attended to by the nurses, Joe stayed back out of the way in a recliner, dozing in and out of sleep. A combination of his panicked drive home, nerves, and BBQ food, he wasn't feeling so good.

Patrick Anthony was the easiest of my three deliveries. He was born in record time, only two hours after arriving at the hospital. His easy delivery was overshadowed by the four-day stay in the NICU, a result of aspirating amniotic fluid. It was feared that he might develop an infection, so he was put on oxygen and IV antibiotics. Completely unprepared for such a turn of events, I was scared to death that something could be wrong with my baby. After twenty-four hours in the maternity ward, I was discharged and had to leave Patrick in the NICU. I left the hospital at night, slept at home, showered, and returned early in the morning. I nursed and spent the day rocking and holding him next to his monitors. It was the scariest thing that had ever happened to me. None of the nurses seemed interested in giving me any information. I sat rocking Patrick, listening and observing, hoping to overhear something about his condition. When the doctor finally told me that he could go home, that he didn't have an infection after all, I was elated. He had been in the NICU for four days for nothing, but I figured it was good that they were being cautious. It had been frightening for sure, but I quickly forgot all about it once we got home. Named because I loved the Irish name *Patrick*, and after St. Anthony, one of Gramma Hubbard's favorite saints,

Patrick was a really good baby. Easy and good-natured, he fit right in and fell into step with the flow of our routine. Like our first two babies, we kept him in our bedroom for the first few months. After that, we moved him upstairs into a bigger crib in the Rainbow Zebra room with Joseph. We had two big cribs set up in the boys' room. Joe and I joked that the upstairs bedrooms were big enough to fit three sets of bunk beds and six kids in each.

We drove to Sarnia to visit Gramma Hubbard with our new baby boy. She had been living in a nursing home for a few years, and had also been in and out of the hospital several times. We had visited her a few times each year and witnessed her decline. It was hard to see her so frail. I wished more than anything that I could bring her home with me so that I could take care of her, but it was out of the question. All her doctors were in Sarnia, and she needed around-the-clock nursing care. Frail, but still very lucid, she asked me to lay Patrick down next to her on her bed. I placed him next to her. She leaned her face next to his and curled her arm around him. It was so touching to see her with my baby boy. I wondered how many babies she had held in her lifetime. Not wanting to tire her out, we didn't overstay. We were painfully aware that she wouldn't be with us much longer. Less than two months later, she died. I was heartbroken, but I felt so confident that she had surely gone straight to heaven. I envisioned her reunited with her husband, and some of her children who had died so many years before her, her baby brother Bernard, who had died in her arms, and her parents. It must have been a wonderful reunion. I have no doubt that she met Our Lord's waiting arms. I love the thought of all her favorite saints, for whom she had such affection and devotion, greeting her with choirs of angels singing as she was welcomed into heaven. The first time I ever saw my husband sob was at Gramma Hubbard's funeral. I remember looking over at him in the funeral home during the final family visitation before the funeral Mass. He was hunched over, his big shoulders shaking with tears streaming down his face. Gramma Hubbard had been the first to welcome him into her family. She surely must have realized that day, looking down on all of us, just how much it had meant to him.

NINE

Changes

Cambridge, Ontario, 1996–2000

After three years of commuting to Toronto, and six months to Cambridge, the driving was getting old. Winter driving to Kitchener, Ontario, was treacherous. I worried each morning when Joe left until he called to tell me that he had arrived at work, and again until he walked through the door, safe and sound, usually around seven at night. He hardly go to see the babies during the week because he left the house while they were still asleep and were just going to bed when he got home. Joe wanted to move. I resisted. Cambridge was only a little over an hour away, but I didn't want to move that far from my family. I had never lived anywhere other than the Niagara area. Change was something that I tried to avoid, but after considering the toll that the traveling was taking on Joe and our family, I relented.

The housing market was slow, and it took a few months to sell our house. After several disappointing house-hunting trips, we decided to build our next home. When we finally sold the cute little house that we had poured so much blood, sweat, and tears into, we moved into a rented two-room condo, owned by Toyota, while our new house was being built. I was five months pregnant with our fourth child that July. The whole house-building process was exciting for us. It was fun having the options of choosing our own colors, from the brick, siding, and roof, to the cabinets, tiles, and carpeting. Because we were one of the first to buy in our neighborhood, we got first choice of lots. We picked a large pie-shaped lot with a good grade. It was flat with a small hill along the back. The front yard was tiny, but the backyard was nice and big, and that was the most important for our family. The actual move to Cambridge was bittersweet. I cried the entire rainy drive there, probably more due to pregnancy hormones than sentimental reasons. Cambridge was where I slowly began to unfurl my wings. We were in a completely new place where we knew no one. Even though it was not that far geographically from Niagara Falls, not only did I have to learn my way around our new town, but the town where our condo was, and the ones in between. The condo was within walking distance to a nice park and a Dairy Queen. I walked the kids and our little sheltie, Katie, to the park every day before putting them down for their afternoon naps. In the evening we walked again with Joe after dinner, stopping a couple of times a week for ice cream on the way home. Our temporary home was a good size, with two large bedrooms, two bathrooms, a stacked washer and dryer, kitchen, dining room, and a spacious family room. It was on the twelfth floor. I never saw any other children in our coming and going. The building was mostly occupied by retirees and their pets. We were greeted by them with friendly hellos and comments on how incredible our triple stroller was as I maneuvered it in and out of the elevator. The fact that I was visibly pregnant with baby number four was another popular topic for them to remark on. While the kids napped or were down for the night, I spent my time sewing duvet covers, pillows, and curtains for our new house. I grew more excited about moving as the days flew by. The condo was in a convenient location, but being on the twelfth floor was a drag with three small children, a dog, and baby number four on the way. I longed to open up my patio door and let my kids and dog run out into our own backyard. One very hot day in August, while the kids napped after a nice afternoon at the park, the fire alarm went off. Quickly shaking myself out of the initial shock of the shrill siren, realizing what it indicated, I rushed to grab my three sleeping babies from their beds. They cried and whined as the bell continued to sound, confused and scared about what was happening. I put a leash on the dog, grabbed my keys, and scrambled out the door. Because the elevators were disabled, we had to take the stairs down twelve flights to get out of the building. Now six months pregnant, I carried Patrick on one hip because he wasn't walking yet, and Joseph on the other, because he couldn't walk fast enough, while Angela, crying and scrambling, hung on to the leash attached to Katie as we hurried to the lobby; with our hearts pounding, breathless, the alarm still blaring, babies crying, and dog shaking, we must have looked quite a sight. There was a large gathering of senior men and women, soothing miniature pets in their arms. All eyes were on us as we found a spot to huddle in. I was confused by the lack of panic and the fact that no one had left the building. Where was the fire? Finally, the screeching stopped, and everyone breathed a sigh of relief. One old guy turned to me as he patted his pooch in his arms and said, "That alarm is so hard on the poor doggie's ears."

My jaw dropped as I looked at him. The doggie's ears? Seriously? I ushered Angela and Joseph into the elevator that thankfully was functioning again, with Patrick on my hip. I prayed that I wouldn't go into labor as I dragged the dog back to our condo. There was never any fire. Apparently it had been a planned drill. We never got the memo.

It was nice living so close to Joe's work and having him home every night by five for dinner. It gave us plenty of time to go out and enjoy the summer evenings. Every night we piled the kids into the van to check on the building progress of our new house, getting to know our new neighbors who were all doing the same thing. I needed to find an ob-gyn and a family doctor. We loved our kids' old pediatrician, Dr. Donkor, and I'd had a pro-life ob-gyn who I liked a lot. It was really important for me to find a pro-life doctor in our new city. To my great surprise, I did find one who had been recommended by a friend. Dr. Meenan was a member of Physicians for Life and had a family practice in Kitchener. He agreed to take on our family and also took care of me until my third trimester, when he referred me to Dr. Cescon, who was also pro-life. It was remarkable to me how easily I was able to find these two wonderful doctors, especially when I was so certain that it would be difficult.

Moving into our new house was a huge relief. Of course, it was a lot of work, but it was a treat being the first owners with everything brand-new and clean. Despite a few minor building glitches, it had been a good experience for us. A planned neighborhood with cute cookie-cutter houses, it soon filled up with new families and lots of kids. My dad drove up to see the new place and built us a fence and deck, even before our sod was laid. He also put up a railing around the front porch. We paid for all the materials, but he would only take a small amount for his time and gas. The labor was his gift. Our house was one of the first ones to be completed. Joe and I drove around the empty lots searching for and collecting rocks for our garden. We made countless trips in our blue Aerostar van, with the kids all buckled in their car seats, pointing to the big ones that they saw. At seven months pregnant, I lugged away, excited about our new project. Joe loaded the rocks into the van and wheeled them into the backyard in the kids' red wagon. I arranged each one along the outline we had cut out bordering the fence, until the entire backyard had been trimmed with a rock garden. Our next-door neighbors, John and Jackie, who were expecting their first baby the same time as me, had a giant boulder moved to the middle of our front yard. We affectionately called it Pride Rock. We shared the rock and planted flowers around it for each season. I pored over garden books, picking the colors, plants, shrubs, annuals, and perennials that would attract butterflies and hummingbirds. That winter, I made lists for the garden center trips that I would make in the spring.

Our nest was set up quickly as we anticipated the arrival of our fourth little blessing. I was more than anxious to deliver. I had, what I was told by my doctor, an irritable uterus. Apparently a common thing with third and fourth pregnancies. I was terribly uncomfortable and felt like I was in full labor for weeks. My due date was October 28, but a few weeks before that, convinced that I was in labor, Joe and I headed to the hospital. I was hooked up to a monitor and checked out. After several hours of observation, Dr. Cescon came in to see me. He smiled, patted me on the arm, and told me that I should go home and try to relax. I wasn't in labor yet. Completely exhausted and unbearably uncomfortable, I begged him to induce me. I just wanted to be done, delivered of my child. He shook his head sympathetically and apologized. It was too early. He told me to be patient and rest up. Patience has never been one of my strengths, and I never rested. Joe took me home, pouting and feeling sorry for myself. I couldn't relax or rest, so I did what I do when I'm anxious. I came up with a new project idea. I told Joe to stop at the fabric store on our way home. I bought fabric and patterns to make three Halloween costumes for Angela, Joseph, and Patrick. I pulled out my sewing machine that night after putting the kids to bed, and set everything up at the kitchen table. I was very proud of my first homemade costumes. Lamb Chop for Angela, a fuzzy brown bear for Joseph, and a cute gray mouse for Patrick. I finished them just in time for Halloween. Christina Mary Bridget, named after Gramma Hubbard, and my sister Bridget, her godmother, was born on November 3, 1996. She was six days overdue but a pretty easy delivery. She joined our little clan without so much as a hiccup, easy and content. We set up a rocking cradle in the family room where she napped in the sunshine during the day. She never cried. There was plenty of activity in our busy household to keep her entertained. She watched all the goings-on with her big green eyes, quietly taking it all in. Our family was perfectly balanced with two girls and two boys. We put bunk beds in each of the two small bedrooms, planning ahead for when Christina would outgrow her crib. Again, the ever popular question was asked repeatedly by friends, family, and strangers alike, "Are you done yet?"

Always poring over gardening books, I made lists of the flowers I wanted to add to the backyard. After Christmas, I bought packets of seeds and planted hundreds of pots, hoping to grow enough to fill in all the empty spots in the rock garden. I watered and rotated the seed trays for months, and we all watched them grow. They nearly took over the back doorway. It was like an indoor jungle in our family room. Angela and Joseph were fascinated, and Patrick ate a fair amount of potting soil. All of us were anxious for spring. When the danger of frost had passed, sometime in May, we carried all the plants out and arranged them in the garden. The kids played in the yard with the dog at their heels while I planted and watered. We spent the entire summer in our backyard, watching everything bloom a rainbow of colors. Joe and I built the kids a wooden play structure. It was a kit we bought that included a slide, swings, and a fort. It took us several days to complete because we assembled some of the sections the wrong way and had to take them apart and built them again. It was a labor of love, and once it was finished, our backyard was complete. Beautiful lush green grass, bright and colorful rock gardens, a great swing set for our happy kids to play on, and a little dog chasing them around. We grilled out almost every night on our deck while we watched the kids play. When it got hot, we added a blow-up pool for them to splash in. Bird feeders and a birdbath attracted red-winged black birds, cardinals, and yellow finches, and all my flower selections had hummingbirds, butterflies, and bumblebees buzzing around. The sweet sounds of summer were all around. My dad built us an arbor to complete the red brick and crushed stone walkway that Joe and I had laid. It led from the front concrete driveway to the back gate, and created another opportunity for more flowers. I lined the path with pansies and impatiens, and planted clematis and morning glories on the arbor. Joe indulged me all these things. I loved the projects, and he loved watching me turn my vision into reality. I was always working on something. Neighbors out walking gazed into the yard through the arbor as I watered and weeded. They often stopped to tell me how they loved to look at our yard. They remarked on how inviting it looked, that they could tell we had put a lot of love into it. I even had a lady stop to ask if she could have her picture taken in our walkway with her mother who was visiting from another country. The front yard was as colorful as the back. Pink and white impatiens grew in mounds around the front porch. Bleeding heart, astilbe, hanging baskets of fuchsia, and a bright planter box burst with color against the white-painted spindles that my dad built. It looked like a magazine cover. I put two white chairs with flowered cushions on the porch, and we added a wooden screen door that I painted white. Joe and I sat out on summer nights after the kids went to bed, listening to the crickets, and chatting with our next-door neighbors. Life was simple in that little 1,250-square-foot house. Simple but very very sweet. By the end of that summer, baby number five was on the way.

There was some shuffling of the HR department at Toyota, and Joe decided that it was a good time to move on. He put his feelers out into the recruiting world once again, and very quickly he was offered a position with KPMG in Waterloo, as Director of Human Resources for Southwestern Ontario. I was having some complications with my pregnancy. At around two months, I started spotting. Seeing blood while pregnant is never a good sign. I rushed to see Dr. Meenan, who sent me for an ultrasound right away. He said it appeared that my placenta had torn away in a small spot, but had sealed itself off. He told me not to overdo it, no heavy lifting or straining. He didn't put me on bed rest, but told me to use my judgment when it came to my level of activity. Having four little ones to care for made it difficult to take it easy, but I quit lugging rocks. I vowed not to execute any big projects until after I gave birth. The spotting occurred on a few more occasions throughout my pregnancy, necessitating multiple ultrasounds. They showed that the placenta was still tearing little bits at a time from the same area but, each time, sealing off. I prayed continuously that I wouldn't lose my baby. I had never had any difficulties before. For me, having babies had been easy, almost second nature. This time I was scared. We pretty much hibernated all winter while my pregnancy progressed. That spring, I resisted the urge to dig in the dirt. I longed to spring-clean and plant, but I wanted my baby to stay put more than anything.

Three and a half weeks before my due date, I started bleeding heavily. My youngest brother and sister were staying at our house while my mother was in Chicago with a few of my other sisters at an Irish dancing competition. Because my dad was working, my mom asked if we would babysit. I called our neighbor Joyce, from down the street, at around nine o'clock that night. She came over and stayed with all the kids while Joe drove me to the hospital. I was scared. What was even scarier was that I wasn't in any pain. When we arrived at the hospital and I explained what was happening, they confined me to a bed and strapped on a monitor. Hearing a strong heartbeat was such a relief. They told me not to move from the bed and began doing all sorts of tests. I told Joe to go home, not wanting to leave Joyce with our houseful of kids longer than necessary, as she had two little ones of her own at home. Labor was induced the next morning, and I delivered Grace Rebecca Gerarda, without Joe there. The nurses kept asking me if anyone was coming. I told them that Joe would be coming later on, with a slew of kids. I assured them that I was just fine, I had delivered four babies already. I was more concerned about the little ones at home who were used to having one of us around. I never felt comfortable leaving them with anyone other than family. The nurses seemed surprised that I was okay on my own. I suppose I was calm because I was not completely aware of the gravity of the situation. I didn't know until afterward that I could have lost my baby that night. My placenta had torn away considerably. We named our little girl *Grace* because I just loved the name; *Rebecca*, after Joe's grandmother; and *Gerarda*, in honor of St. Gerard, who I had been praying to for her safe delivery. Grace was the smallest of our babies. At six pounds and three ounces, she was tiny. She had bright-pink skin, piercing blue eyes, and blond hair. We got a lot of puzzled looks because of how fair she was, until her tight corkscrew curls grew in. Joe paraded our other four kids, their eight-year-old uncle, and six-year-old aunt to see the new baby. My parents were completely shocked when they found out that I had delivered so early. My dad drove to Cambridge to visit me in the hospital and then took my brother and sister home with him. Grace was very jaundiced. I had to bring her for blood work every morning to have her bilirubin checked. It broke my heart to take her to the clinic, knowing that she would be getting her heels pricked again. With her jaundice levels staying high for weeks, I had to stop nursing her. The doctor seemed to think that giving her formula might help to flush it out faster. He assured me that I could resume nursing, once her tests were normal. It was emotional, and draining, and disappointing, but we survived it; and I was able to nurse her again. We wanted to have Grace baptized as soon as possible. I had been so worried about her throughout the entire pregnancy, and had prayed fervently that she would be okay. I was grateful and relieved when the jaundice went away, but I wanted her baptized ASAP. We asked our friends David and Anne Packer to be godparents. We had been living in Cambridge for two years, and had gotten to know our pastor, Fr. Phil Sherlock, really well. We felt very much at home in our new parish, St. Clement's, and wanted to have Grace baptized there. All our other kids had been baptized in Niagara Falls, even Christina, who had been born in Cambridge. My mom was disappointed that we wouldn't be coming back home to have Grace baptized in Niagara Falls too. Joe and I had built our own little family, and our parish was a big part of our new life. When I told her the date of the baptism, my mother said that they had a conflict. They wouldn't be able to make it. I got the sense that it was more a matter of our decision not to go back to Niagara Falls, though I never mentioned it. It was more than a month before my mother came to see the new baby, and there seemed to be a change in her. She was distant. Our life and growing family was filled with joy, but she didn't seem happy for us. When I wanted to show her how the garden had grown, and the changes we had made to the house, tiling the back patio door area where the carpet had been, and the new sewing projects I had completed, she was indifferent. I got a strange vibe from her and took it as a clue to shut up. I let her talk about all the things that were going on in her life—her job, Irish dancing competitions and trips, her church activities, and whatever dramas that were going on with her friends and relatives. She only visited our house a few times despite several invitations. If we wanted to visit with my family, we usually were the ones to make the trip to Niagara Falls.

After a year with KPMG, Joe's responsibilities increased. He was given charge of the Eastern Seaboard. A nice promotion. As his responsibilities grew, so did our family. Baby number six would be due in March 2000. Another surprise. We decided it was time to sell our little house and move into a larger one. We started to look at houses in the surrounding area, driving around on Sundays after Mass with our Tim Hortons coffee. We looked at much larger houses in more affluent neighborhoods, and even considered building again. Joe's career was steadily moving in the right direction, our family was getting bigger, and we wanted a house that we wouldn't outgrow. When we showed my parents our blueprints for the house we had designed, my mother remarked that I should focus on my family and not on a house. Everything we did was with and for our family. Building a home that we could settle and stay in for years to come was our goal. We didn't want to keep moving around. My mother's remark stung, but I didn't respond to it. I rolled up the blueprints and put them away. It was becoming very apparent to me that she was jealous of Joe's success and the fruits that we were enjoying because of it.

Our kids had been taking swimming lessons with Robert's Swim School. Their lessons were held at Riverside Park in Preston, with an option of lessons in the private backyard pool of Cindy and Don Nicolson. We absolutely loved the Nicolsons' neighborhood. Its location and the sizes of the homes were exactly what we were looking for. Joe and I wanted a house with a pool. We told our real estate agent about the Nicolsons' house, and asked him to find us one just like it. Cindy and Don were, unbeknown to us, also realtors, and they worked for the same Remax company as our agent Tony. We were amazed at what a small world it was. Tony told us that he knew of a house that would be coming up very soon on the market, on the very same street as the Nicolsons'. He asked us to be patient. Within a few weeks he called and told us that the house was ready for us to look at. When we arrived at the address, we were completely shocked to discover that the house was right next door to Cindy and Don's, and that it had a pool in the backyard. The house was perfect for us. We made an offer on it that night, which the sellers accepted. The house never officially went on the market. It was as if it was meant to be for us. Our closing date was set for December. We listed our house right away, and it sold in four days. The buyers wanted a September closing date because they had a daughter who would be starting school. That left us a three-month lapse between the two closings. We were in a bit of a spot. Not wanting to disappoint the new buyers and risk losing the deal, we agreed. The owners of the house we were buying hadn't found a new place yet, so they didn't want to change their closing date. Our agent told us that he knew of a vacant three-bedroom condo at the other end of town that we could rent until December. It wasn't ideal, but with the sale of both houses so quick and for the right prices, we thought it was a minor inconvenience. We did all our own packing for our move, mainly because we needed to organize things we would need for the three months in the condo. I separated what we would be storing in the basement of the condo. It was a tedious task. We hired a mover to move it all. It was sort of like an extended hotel stay. It was relatively convenient, but it wasn't home.

We had been parishioners at St. Clement's Church from the time we first moved to Cambridge. Fr. Phil Sherlock was the pastor. He had impressed us so much when he remembered all our names by the second Sunday after meeting us, that we knew we were in the right place. Sunday Mass was a big part of our lives. We usually went to the nine o'clock Mass, and were fixtures in our usual pew. We were a bit of an attraction because of the size of our family, and by the fact that we were quite visibly still growing. We were surprised by the attention we got from people who would walk up to us after Mass. They complimented us on our beautiful family, and how well-behaved our children all were, especially for all being so little. We didn't realize we were unusual. We felt like a regular family. People told us that we were a rarity. We were proud of our family, but the attention was humbling and made us aware that people were watching us.

We moved into our new house on December 3, 1999. It had a lot more room than our previous one. There were four big bedrooms upstairs, four bathrooms, a main floor laundry room, attached two-car garage, formal living and dining rooms, family room, and finished basement. It had two fireplaces, an office, and a huge storage area. The backyard was an oasis, fully landscaped with mature trees, flowering shrubs, and perennial gardens. The original owner had been a member of the horticultural society. He had planned the color-co-ordinated landscape to bloom according to color at various times for each season. It was genius. There was a deck, stamped concrete walkway, and outdoor lighting. The icing on the cake was a large kidney-shaped pool and diving board. We hired a fencing company to install a wrought iron fence around it right away to keep the kids safe. We could hardly wait for summer to enjoy our backyard paradise. We immediately began making the house our own, removing layers of wallpaper and painting the entire place. I decorated Joseph and Patrick's room with a safari theme. I painted the walls gold and put up a border with zebras, giraffes, elephants, and lions. I bought cheetah-print faux fur blankets for their bunk beds, and used their already large collection of stuffed animals and decor to finish it off. Angela had a room of her own. We gave her the full-sized bed that Joe and I had used for nine years. I ordered a king-sized bed for our room shortly after selling our house, and had it delivered on our closing day. The reason was that after the people who ended up buying our house saw our master bedroom, the husband said, "Now I know why you guys have so many kids. That bed is tiny."

Funny, at the time, we were expecting our sixth, and went on to have six more, so bed size obviously has nothing to do with it. I stenciled ribbons and flowers on Angela's freshly painted powder-pink walls. Ribbons and bows, dolls and stuffed animals were all part of her little girl room. Christina and Grace shared the third bedroom. We put them in bunk beds, and set up the crib for our next little girl, who had yet to arrive, even though she would be sleeping in our room for the first few months. Painted sea-foam green, I added a teddy bear's picnic border to the walls. Crisp, fresh, and clean, it was a sweet spot in the house. I had the entire place painted by Christmas, just a few weeks after moving in. We set up shelves for all the books and Barbie dolls at the top of the stairs in the loft area. The rest of the toys went downstairs to the full basement, where we had TV and VCR for all the Barney videos. We shopped for new furniture at Leon's, and bought a new floral-print Sklar Peppler sofa and love seat, an accent wing-back chair, carved wooden coffee and end tables, and designer lamps. We had never had a formal living and dining room before. We bought a new dining room suite with a hutch, table, and eight cream-colored tapestry chairs. We kept both rooms formal, and the glass french doors stayed closed except for special occasions. With scented candles and sachets tucked into drawers, it always smelled like vanilla potpourri. It was where Joe and I shared morning coffee after he got home from the gym, and before the kids woke up. Coffee in the living room became our morning ritual. It was where we chatted and dreamed out loud about our life, our family, Joe's career, and our plans.

My role as wife, mother, and homemaker had grown and expanded in every way, and I loved it even more than ever. I loved our home and kept it pristine at all times. I enjoyed cooking and baking for my family, gardening, grocery shopping, and working on projects to feather our nest. I was as happy as I could be. Angela, Joseph, and Patrick continued attending their little Catholic elementary school, Our Lady of Fatima. Even though we no longer lived in the same school zone. They grandfathered us in. They couldn't take the school bus though, so I drove them to and from school every day. That January, Joe traded in our blue Aerostar van for a gold, twelve-passenger, 2000 Ford Econoline. Several of the school parents inquired if I was a shuttle service, and asked how much I charged to transport kids to and from school. They were serious. I was dumbfounded. I got razzed regularly by friends who asked when I planned to paint my van school bus yellow. We got teased about the size of our family, but we never really took offense, we just got more creative with our answers. When people asked us if all those kids were ours, we told them that we loved kids so much that we collected them every time we came across one. When they inquired whether we were done yet, we simply shrugged and said, "Only God knows."

And when they would be so bold as to ask, "You do know what causes that, don't you?"

We replied, "We sure do, and we like it."

We were a novelty, and we didn't even realize it. We didn't feel like we were unusual, but by society's standards, we came to discover that we were. Most families we knew had two, three, and less often, four kids. We were expecting our sixth. We felt normal enough, but people saw us as something of an oddity. We became more aware of the stares when we went out as a family. Our kids were always neat, clean, and pretty well-behaved. I made sure to pay extra attention to detail once I became aware that we were under a certain level of scrutiny. I never wanted to be the stereotypical bedraggled mom with a bunch of kids, so I made a conscious effort not to be her. People were surprised, not because we had so many kids, but because we had so many kids and still seemed normal. I admit that pride was a big factor, but I also wanted people to see that it was possible to have a big family and still keep it together.

Clare Frances, named after St. Clare and St. Francis of Assisi, came into the world on March 16, 2000, one day before her due date. I'd had a doctor appointment that day, and was happy to hear that I could go into labor at any minute. Not one to sit around waiting, I spent the afternoon with the kids and my next-door neighbor Cindy at the Sandylion sticker factory in Markham. We went there a couple of times a year to buy cute stickers for cheap. The kids had fun with them and used them for their arts and crafts. I always let their teachers know when I was going, and they always put in an order. The drive home that afternoon was exciting. Contractions started and continued till Joe and I headed to the hospital. Clare was a delightful baby. I was amazed at how blessed I had been with such good-natured babies, each one seeming to be even easier than the last. Motherhood was an easy, natural state for me. Clare resembled a little Eskimo baby, especially when she was swaddled up tightly in her blanket, with her dark almond-shaped eyes, tanned round face, and fringe of black hair. She would lay like a little sausage roll on the couch, watching all the family antics intently. When she was old enough to sit in a high chair and eat finger snacks, we discovered how much she enjoyed food. She made a "nom, nom, nom, nom" sound whenever she ate anything, so we fed her a lot, just to listen to her little sounds. She was happiest in her chair, eating snacks and watching the other kids color and do homework at the table.

Joe got another promotion. His new title was National Director of HR, and his new office was located in Toronto. Back to commuting.

Very anxious to get the season started, we opened our pool in April that first year. The weather was still very cold, and we were getting the occasional dusting of snow, so we just cranked up the gas heater. The steam rose for months. Cindy used to call out from her next-door window laughing, sharing in our excitement. She said our backyard looked like the hot springs. She loved to see the kids splashing about and our family enjoying our new home. She told us often how happy she was that we were her new neighbors. Our gas and electric bill nearly gave us a heart attack that spring, but it was worth it. The kids swam for a couple of hours every night after dinner, and then ran through the snow into the family room where they warmed up in front of the gas fireplace. After tucking them into bed, Joe and I would sneak out for a dip. We had no idea how labor intensive it would be to open the pool so early, but we soon found out. With the backyard being an oasis of flowering trees and shrubs, every bud, seed pod, and flower petal that fell dropped directly into the pool. It needed constant scooping. The lovely robins and mourning doves that we were so happy to feed and have nesting in our yard deliberately dropped their poop bombs into the pool when they cleaned out their nests. We even had a couple of mallards who set up residence in the late winter and early spring. We thought they were sweet when they showed up and paddled around on the pool cover. We were certain that they would disappear once the pool was opened. We were wrong. Joe threw Frisbees out of our bedroom window to scare them off every morning when they woke us up with their splashing and quacking. Despite all of the nature, we kept that pool crystal clear. Our backyard was our family vacation spot. Sun, snacks, and pool water kept us more than satisfied. By the end of the summer, the kids were golden brown and waterlogged. We enjoyed cookouts, and the kids invited their friends over. They continued taking swimming lessons with Alana Nicolson. Living next door to the swimming teacher, who also doubled as a babysitter, was a definite perk. With the arrival of fall, the yard cleaned up, and the pool closed, Christina joined the school crowd.

TEN

Still Growing

Cambridge, Ontario, 2000–2001

Joe worked from home most Fridays, which allowed me to help out at the kids' school. I volunteered whenever I could, cutting out pages and assembling packets for their teachers, going on field trips, and assisting with school fund-raisers and events. I was asked to serve as secretary of the PTA, and I joined another mother in forming a first-Friday rosary group. Although I still had babies at home, and wasn't available for every activity, I stayed involved with my kids. Helping with homework and projects, and sending in cupcakes to share with their classmates once a month.

Angela began taking piano lessons when she was four, at the Ontario Conservatory of Music; and when Joseph turned four, he joined her. We bought an upright digital piano for them to practice on, and hired their teacher, who lived near us, to come to our house to teach them. We signed Patrick and Christina up to make it worth her while.

Because our house was the biggest, and because we had the most little kids, we almost always hosted the family gatherings. Easter, Thanksgiving, and Boxing Day. I loved baking for Thanksgiving and Christmas. We had a huge cold storage room under our front porch, and we kept it stocked with baked goods, strawberry jam made from the strawberries we picked in the summer, and fifty-pound bags of potatoes. We made a lot of homemade french fries and shepherd's pie. Our fridge and pantry were always full, and we enjoyed entertaining friends and family. We weren't rich, but we were comfortable and enjoyed being at home.

I discovered that I was pregnant again in November 2000, with baby number seven. At thirty-one, I was still young, strong, and healthy. I had no concerns. Joe was more than able to provide for us, and we were thrilled to be expecting again. Dr. Meenan informed me that because of changes in health insurance, Dr. Cescon was no longer delivering babies. Before I had time to panic, he asked me if I had ever considered a midwife. I hadn't, but the question intrigued me. He told me that his daughter-in-law had been very pleased with her experience with her midwife, and he encouraged me to look into it. As soon as I got home, I logged onto our desktop computer and did some research. I discovered that there was a local group of midwives close to our church. After reading the bios of each of the midwives, and the stories of the women who had delivered their babies with them, I made an appointment. I met Alison Lavery, a lovely Irish lady, at her office, which was in a large converted Victorian house. She explained the benefits of midwifery, and I was quickly sold. She was confident that I would be a good candidate, given my history of easy pregnancies and deliveries. I had one ultrasound during that pregnancy and the required lab work. They only did the least amount of necessary procedures, so I didn't find out the sex of the baby like I had with all the rest. We would all have to wait for the surprise. My due date was August 8, our first summer baby. I planned to have a home birth. I spent that summer in a two-piece bathing suit, picking weeds around the pool, floating on a raft with a book, and hanging out with the kids. I was tanned and glowing, and big as a house. I felt amazing.

We celebrated Patrick's June birthday that June with a pool party. He had invited all the little boys from his kindergarten class. All the moms and dads were invited to stay to help watch their kids. Joe grilled hot dogs while the kids splashed in the water. A rope separated the shallow end from the deep end, and I told the kids to stay on the shallow side of the rope. All my kids had taken lessons for years and were good swimmers, but most of the little boys were not. We gave them water wings and blow-up rings to help keep them afloat. All of us moms set our chairs up along the edge of the pool, keeping our eye on the water while we chatted. I noticed that one little boy, who wasn't wearing a float, seemed to be drifting toward the rope. I watched as he began struggling to get his footing. Pointing to him, I asked his mom if he was okay. She froze. I looked at the little boy. His head was above the water, but he had a look of panic on his face, and then he slipped under the rope. It was obvious that his mom was in shock and didn't have the presence of mind to react. She kept yelling his name, "Jake! Jake!"

Without thinking about it, I jumped into the water and plucked him up by his arm. When I carried Jake to the edge of the pool, all the moms were on their feet, leaning over the water with their mouths wide open. The moment of panic was lifted by the other kids' uncontrollable laughter. They hadn't noticed that Jake had slipped under the water, but they did see Patrick's very large, very pregnant mommy jump into the pool. I had been wearing what I called my pink bubblegum dress. It was more like a tent than a dress. When I jumped into the pool, the dress went up and floated on top of the water. They thought it was hilarious that they had seen my underwear. Jake's mom thanked me over and over again and said she couldn't believe how she had panicked when it was her own son who she couldn't save. All the other mothers were just as stunned. They asked me how I had reacted so instinctively. I didn't have an answer. It was just a natural response. I supposed that having a lot of kids may have given me an extra boost of mommy radar.

Shortly after notifying her that my labor had started, Alison came to the house with another midwife, Laurie Rose. They set up the room with all the things we had prepared for the delivery. Knowing that the baby would be arriving any day, we brought my sister home with us after visiting my parents, to help. I called my mother. She wasn't convinced that a home birth was the best decision; however, she didn't want to miss it, and drove to Cambridge from Niagara Falls in record time. Joe was understandably nervous, but I was in great spirits and had no worries at all. I was excited to meet my little baby. While the midwives attended to me, the kids splashed in the pool with Alana and my sister. Labor progressed quickly and was heavy for more than four hours, longer than any of us thought it should have taken. When it looked like the baby wasn't going to come out without intervention, Alison told me that she thought it would be prudent to call the paramedics and head to the hospital. She didn't want the baby to go into distress. I was exhausted. She said the baby's head was tuned just a little bit sideways, and sort of stuck. The birth was not going according to my plan. I wanted to deliver at home. I was too drained to even move, and I definitely didn't want to leave my house.

Joe's nervousness turned into distress. He had paced up and down the hallway for hours, no doubt with regret over agreeing to a home birth. My mother added to his panic as she whispered her opinions about my choosing a midwife over a doctor and a home birth rather than a hospital. I tried to block everything and everyone out of my mind, focusing solely on delivering my baby. Alison kept telling me not to push while she nervously waited for the ambulance to arrive. My mother put flip-flops on my swollen feet while I whined about not wanting to leave my room. I tried to do as Alison told me, but at that stage, there was no stopping me from pushing, the pressure was too much to bear. I don't know if it was sheer will on my part, or if my baby had just finally decided to enter the world. When Alison checked to see what was going on, she exclaimed in her thick Irish accent, "Oh the little rotter! Here he comes!"

One more push, and out he came, kicking and screaming, with the paramedics standing outside my bedroom door, just in case. Alison thanked them and sent them on their way after she made sure that little Callum Peter Francis was healthy and strong. I didn't have to leave the house after all. No longer exhausted, completely elated and reenergized, I was overjoyed and relieved to hold my little boy in my arms. Callum was our biggest baby of all, nine pounds and eleven ounces. Named what we thought was an Irish name, but later discovered was the Scottish spelling; *Peter*, after his godfather; and *Francis* after St. Francis of Assisi. Our little prince after three girls.

Since my sister was there, we weren't planning for my mother to stay with us, but she decided that she would. We figured that the extra help with the kids, dinner, and the laundry wouldn't hurt. It didn't take long before we began to see her controlling side emerge. We had lived in Cambridge for five years, and typically, my mother only visited us on special occasions and holidays. She usually came when my dad and the rest of my family was there. She rarely spent the night because we only lived an hour and a half away. After Callum was born, she stayed for several days, taking charge, and assuming my role as woman of the house. She instructed me to stay in bed and wouldn't let the kids in. She kept visitors at bay and intercepted all phone calls. She came to my room each time a new call or visitor came to bring me her report, and told me how she handled it. She informed everyone that I wasn't accepting calls or visitors because I was resting. Each time my mother entered my room and settled into the wing-back chair to deliver another report, I grew increasingly annoyed. My friends had all been anxiously anticipating Callum's arrival. They wanted to wish me well, not intrude on us and camp out for hours. I felt terrific, better than I had ever felt with any other delivery. I was excited to share our news with our friends, and I resented my mother speaking for me, simply dismissing them, but I said nothing. I told Joe instead. He intervened where he could, bringing the phone to me and sneaking the kids and the odd visitor in. We basically decided to just wait for her to leave before calling everyone back.

Alison returned each day for the first several days to check on both Callum and me. On the third day, she detected a heart murmur. It was concerning enough to her that she sent us to a pediatric cardiologist. I was worried, but didn't allow myself to go into panic mode until I saw the specialist. After consulting with him, we were sent to McMaster Children's Hospital in Hamilton. That's when I panicked. Thinking the worst but praying for the best, I knew it had to be serious for them to send us to McMaster. My mother came with us to Hamilton, where a whole battery of tests were performed—echocardiogram, electrocardiogram, and a complete physical. Once the tests were complete, we met with the cardiologist. He pointed out the murmur and explained the results. His thoughts were that there was no urgency in performing corrective surgery, though he wouldn't rule it out at a future date. The murmur was small, but size wasn't the concern, it was the location. Callum had a subpulmonic ventricular septal defect. In laymen's terms, the murmur, or hole, was below the aortic valve. When the blood circulated through the hole, it created a vortex and sucked the valve into it. The cardiologist said that for the time being, there was no reason to fix it. He told us that we would have to monitor him annually, and that if I noticed any changes in Callum's health, I should alert him so that he could redress the need for surgery. To me this wasn't exactly good news. I wanted to hear that it was nothing at all. Just a simple murmur. Lots of people have them and don't even know it, and live normal lives. The cardiologist told me to take Callum home and treat him like a normal baby. I didn't. I treated him like he was made of glass. I would worry from one checkup to the next that there would be a change. From every, well, baby visit, every cardiology checkup, and every time he had so much as a runny nose. I would live from appointment to appointment, waiting for them to tell me that he needed surgery.

ELEVEN

The Big Move

Cambridge, Ontario, 2001–2002

*C*allum was a happy boy. When he smiled, his whole face lit up with his big green eyes and round cheeks. After three little girls, he was completely spoiled and loved by all of us. Callum was born three weeks before September 11, 2001. Joe was working from home that day in his downstairs office. The kids were at school, I was nursing Callum, while Grace and Clare played in the family room. Whoever Joe was on a call with had informed him about a disaster that had just occurred in New York. He called up the stairs and told me to turn on the television. I flipped the channels to CNN and saw the live pictures of smoke billowing out of the first tower. I ran down the stairs to tell Joe what they were saying on the news, a plane had just crashed into the World Trade Center. It had to have been a freak accident. I went back up the stairs where I continued to watch, with baby Callum in my arms, as people ran in shock. Not knowing where they were running to, just running in a panic, away from the building. Then, horrified, I saw the second plane hit the second tower. In complete disbelief, I ran down the stairs to tell Joe about the second plane. When I got to the doorway, I noticed Joe's glasses lying in the middle of the office floor and the phone hanging off his desk. The person he had been talking to on the phone had already told him about the second plane. Realizing that it had been no accident, but a very purposeful act of terrorism, Joe sobbed in his chair. Tears streamed down my face as I tried to comprehend the horror of what I had just witnessed on the news. I had never seen my husband so visibly upset. Not since Gramma Hubbard had died.

In the weeks and months that followed, we watched numbly, while all the television networks reported on and dissected the story from every angle, inside out. We mounted and flew Canadian and American flags side by side from our garage, in a show of solidarity with our neighbors south of the border. The terror attack had been an attack on humanity, taking the lives of citizens from several countries, on American soil. I felt American by marriage. My kids had red, white, and blue blood coursing through their veins, so that made me American too. I had never considered my patriotism before that point, but two months later, when Joe told me that he was considering applying for an HR position with KPMG in Dallas, I encouraged him to do so.

We talked over morning coffee in our sweet-smelling pretty living room, about the plan. *Our* plan. Joe felt that he had moved up as far as he could in Ontario, and stood a good chance of getting the job. We'd move to Dallas, Texas, where he would work as the director for the HRSC (Human Resources Services Center). After three to five years of gaining valuable US experience, we'd return to Canada, where he would undoubtedly be recruited for a higher-salaried executive position with KPMG, or some other firm. It was an exciting plan. Our kids were at the perfect age. Angela would be entering fourth grade, and we believed that the experience would be invaluable for all of them. We felt privileged for the opportunity. After some serious negotiations, something Joe had become a pro at, he got the offer in writing. He signed it, and on Easter Sunday, he began a three-month commute to Dallas.

Joe returned home pretty much every weekend. Sometimes, every other one, I was on my own with seven kids. I got plenty of sympathy from my friends, the kids' teachers, and other school moms, but it wasn't all that bad really. Our kids were young, and we had kept our life simple, so it was easy to manage by myself. My good friend Kathy Angus came by almost every afternoon with coffee, just in time to help me get the little ones loaded into the van for the after-school pickup. Her thoughtfulness and simple acts of kindness helped me through the weeks. Our neighbors were supportive and let me know that they were there if ever I needed anything. The teachers, staff, and parents from the little Catholic school were excited for our family, but told us that they would miss us a lot. It was a pretty big deal to be moving so far away.

KPMG had arranged all our immigration paperwork with their lawyers, but I had work to do as well. I ordered long-form birth certificates, filled out passport forms, and had all our pictures taken. Kathy helped with all of it. She came along for the ride and helped out with the kids. I also had to gather medical, dental, and school records. There were many tedious details to take care of that I grumbled about, but they kept me busy, which made the time pass quickly. I was anxious to be reunited with my husband.

Joe worked hard at the HRSC, making monumental progress and improving procedures. He gained respect rapidly. We put our house on the market and arranged for a house-hunting trip to Dallas. My mother came to babysit six of the kids. As part of the relocation package, KPMG paid her for child care while Joe and I flew to Dallas with Callum. Only moments after my mother arrived, the evening before Joe and I were scheduled to leave town, our sweet sheltie, Katie, began having seizures. Despite being on anti-seizure medication for several months, she was declining rapidly. She had trouble getting up and moved increasingly more slowly. The medication had been adjusted several times, but each time, it only helped for a little while. After having three seizures in a row, in the span of thirty minutes, Joe and I took her to the emergency vet clinic. The vet gave us bad news. She told us that every time Katie had a seizure, the likelihood of her recovering from it was decreased. She said that it was a certainty that the seizures would continue. When we informed her about our relocation to Dallas, she told us that there was no way that Katie would ever survive the trip. We knew that we couldn't risk leaving her with my mother and six kids while we flew to Texas for five days. We made the heart-wrenching decision to have her put to sleep. She had been a wonderful dog, a sweet and loyal pet, a faithful guardian, and so very obedient. She had always been gentle and protective of our babies, and we considered her a member of our family. Joe and I stayed in the room with her while the vet injected the medication, petting and soothing her as her eyes closed and she drifted away. We drove home in silence, with quiet tears rolling down our cheeks. The new chapter in our lives would start without our Katie dog. We worried about how the kids would react, knowing that we would be heading to the airport hours before they would wake up. Saying goodbye to our Katie was the toughest thing we ever had to do.

Our limo picked us up early the next morning and delivered us to Pearson International Airport in Toronto. Callum was a perfect passenger on the flight. All the attendants remarked on what a good baby he was. His dancing green eyes and beaming grin melted everyone's heart. It was in the baggage claim area of the DFW airport that I heard my very first authentic Texas accent. It was a page for a Ms. Lynne Winters. Hearing the Southern drawl, I giggled out loud. Joe looked at me and asked what was so funny. I repeated the announcement, trying my best to imitate the accent. He rolled his eyes and told me I was silly, that everybody talked that way in Texas. We rented a car and drove to his condo in Turtle Creek, where he had been living since Easter. I was impressed by the luxurious apartment. Much like a five-star hotel, it was equipped with a beautiful kitchen and convenient laundry room. It was a place I wouldn't have minded staying in on my own for three months. Joe excitedly toured me around town, showing me his favorite spots—Luby's, where he bought lunch, and Kroger and Tom Thumb, where he shopped for groceries. The weather was warm and so were the colors. Anything I knew about Texas had come from watching episodes of *Dallas*. What I saw was a pretty close match. I fell in love with it immediately.

We met with our realtor that same afternoon and looked at a bunch of houses, mostly in Southlake. Southlake is an affluent suburban city, about thirty-five minutes from Dallas and only ten minutes from the airport. With seven kids, and knowing how hot Texas summers could get, we insisted on finding a house with a big backyard and a pool. Most of the houses we looked at were beautiful, and all of them were large enough for our family. They all had pools, but the pool took up most of the yard, leaving very little room for the kids to play. After more than a few disappointing tours, I started walking directly to the backyard before even looking at the inside of the house. Our first full day of house hunting was fruitless. We returned to the condo exhausted and went straight to bed. Early the next morning, as Joe and I lay silently, just waking up from a good night's sleep, we turned to each other, wondering if each of us had been dreaming. We both swore that we heard Katie's nails clicking across the floor. A sound that we had heard every morning for nearly ten years. We were sad about our little dog and wondered how the kids were handling the news that my mother would have to deliver.

Our agent had a full schedule of showings for us. When we arrived at Hay Meadow Court, the second or third house of the morning, I immediately liked the look of it. A tasteful red brick colonial, with designer stone trim around the windows and covered doorway, solar screens, and a meticulously kept front yard. The house was on an inside lot on a small, quiet cul-de-sac, one of only eight houses on the whole street. Our agent led us in, and I carried Callum straight through to the backyard, leaving Joe to inspect the main floor. Immediately, I knew it was the one. Lattice covered the large concrete patio, wrought iron fenced the large kidney-shaped pool, hot tub, and fountain. Two giant weeping willow trees grew in the huge fenced backyard. It was private, shady, and cool, despite the already very hot Texas temperatures. I turned to our agent, who had followed me outside, that it was the house. He asked me if I was going to look at the inside. I didn't need to, but Joe and I did anyway. The upstairs had four bedrooms, each with a Jack-and-Jill bathroom between them, with their own sinks, vanity, and walk-in closets. There was a large family room with a loft area, perfect for a computer or study area. The sixth bedroom on the main floor was equipped with a full bathroom that Joe thought would make a great office. There was a formal living and dining room, a huge all-white, eat-in dream kitchen, with double ovens, cooktop, loads of counter space, a walk-in pantry, and a laundry room right next to it. The large master bedroom was on the main floor behind the living room. It had a fireplace, spacious bathroom en suite, and two huge his-and-hers walk-in closets. We returned to the car and told our agent to write up an offer. We drove to his office where he drew up the contract. Not wanting to play games, we offered the asking price, signed it, and it was delivered that night.

Joe and I went to Bob's Steak and Chop house in downtown Dallas for dinner that night to celebrate. Callum, who had been a doll the whole trip, started to get unusually irritable. He'd had two very long days, and I guessed it had caught up with him. I patted and rocked him, and he was happy as long as he was in my arms. Bob's Steakhouse was exactly how I had imagined Texas to be. When we entered, we passed by several gentlemen in cowboy hats and boots, smoking big cigars. I loved the atmosphere in the dark restaurant. The low lights, wrought iron, and heavy wood decor was both rustic and charming. Texas was such a cool place, and we were going to live there. We had just found and put an offer on a perfect house. It was very exciting. We ordered a bottle of wine, toasting our new adventure. Just as we cut into our steaks, Callum started to cry. He had reached his limit. We asked our waitress to box up our dinners, hoping to exit quickly and discreetly before disrupting everyone else's meal. Several of the other diners smiled and wished us luck, telling us they remembered the days when their kids were babies. More than a few ladies sympathetically patted Callum on our way out saying, "Bless his little heart."

The waitress corked our wine, we paid the bill, left a tip, and drove back to the condo to enjoy our meal. While we were sipping our wine, our agent called to tell us that our offer was accepted. I told Joe I wanted to go back and look at the house one more time. The agent arranged it, and we returned the next day. When we arrived, the owners were there, sitting out on their back patio. They were very friendly as we chatted with them. They said they were so happy that a family with small children would be moving in to enjoy the house that they had built. The birds were singing, and the sound of the fountain spilling over the hot tub was relaxing. I envisioned the kids running in the yard and splashing in the pool. The house was spotless inside and out. After taking in every detail, we were more than convinced that the house was going to be perfect for our family. We couldn't wait to move in. Callum cut four molars before we returned home to Cambridge. Thankfully, by the time we boarded the plane, the worst was over, and he was back to his happy smiling self, once again charming all the flight attendants.

We had asked our agent in Cambridge not to show our house while we were away, wanting to spare my mother the headache and inconvenience. When we returned, there was a long list of requests for showings. There was no time to rest after our trip. I jumped into my house selling ritual cleaning, and we got an offer right away. The house had only been on the market for two weeks. We set our closing date for the end of June, right after the kids finished school for the year. We threw one last big pool party to say goodbye to all our friends and then let the movers do all the work.

I bought us all matching Canada Day T-shirts from Old Navy to wear to the airport. All our bags were packed and lined up with handmade personalized tags attached. I was completely organized and felt incredibly accomplished. It had all been quite an undertaking, and we were all excitedly awaiting the big day. The move to Texas was bigger than any of our other previous moves in every way. The distance was greater, the house was larger, our family had grown, and we had acquired a lot more stuff. We could see a pattern developing. Each new job or promotion was followed by a couple more kids and a bigger nicer house. We were living the dream. Our family was happy and heathy, Joe was at a new height in his career, and we were embarking on the most exciting adventure of our lifetime. We arranged for my mother and youngest sister to come with us for the move. KPMG paid for their flights as part of our child care allowance.

TWELVE

Life in the Bubble

Southlake, Texas, 2002–2004

*O*nce the movers loaded the last of our stuff, including our twelve-passenger van, we checked into the Holiday Inn. My dad dropped my mother and sister off so that he could say goodbye. The next morning, two white stretch limos pulled up to drive us to the airport. Joe thought it would be fun for the kids to ride in style. It was the first time they had ever been on a plane. We had a direct flight from Toronto to Dallas, and they were all very well-behaved. We got to the house two days before our movers did. Joe had bought pillows and sleeping bags for all of us, and a couple of air mattresses and patio chairs. We decided to camp out in the house and use the pool while we waited for our truck to arrive. Joe had become familiar with the city, driving from Dallas daily to look at the house after work. He was anxious to take us to his favorite restaurant, Anamia's. We ate dinner there on our first night in town. Joe had been dining there regularly and had told the waiters that his family would be joining him soon in Southlake. When we arrived that night, we were greeted excitedly by a lot of the staff, like we were long-awaited family. They gave us a warm Texas welcome. Seated in what would become our whole family's favorite Tex-Mex restaurant, looking around the table at all my precious children's faces, I suddenly felt butterflies in my stomach. The magnitude of our decision to relocate our family had begun to sink in. I hoped we had made the right decision.

My mother and sister stayed for two weeks. We spent most of the time in the pool and the sun. We did some shopping, took the kids to the movies, and did lots of eating. We ate out, ordered in, and cooked at home. Joe had found the closest Catholic church before our arrival. St. Francis of Assisi in Grapevine would become our new parish. We went to Mass on our first Sunday. It was a modern-looking church, quite a lot different from St. Clement's, but it was well attended and seemed friendly.

The movers arranged all the big furniture for us, but we had tons of boxes to unpack, and closets and shelves to organize. We ordered new beds and dressers for the kids. My mind swam with ideas for decorating their rooms. I was anxious to get the kitchen set up. We had unpacked all the essentials and put things in drawers, but I knew I would change and rearrange things several times before it was exactly the way I wanted it. I knew I wouldn't be able to focus on any of it until after my mother left. She kept telling me how distracted I seemed and how she felt like I didn't want her there. I was certainly distracted. Our family had just made a huge move to another country, into a fabulous new house, in a new city where we didn't know a soul. It was exciting, and more than a little scary. It hadn't been my intention to make her feel unwelcome. I wanted her and my sister to enjoy their vacation to Texas, especially because I didn't know how long it would be before we would see them again. I made a conscious effort to be a better hostess and focus on them and their visit. I tried to suppress the desire to feather my new nest.

Southlake was a beautiful city. A small suburban, planned community where everything was clean and new. There was no such thing as a bad neighborhood in Southlake. Some communities were gated, some were not. All of them welcomed with entryways, planted with native grasses and whatever flowers were in season. Duck ponds, fountains, tennis courts, and neighborhood pools were a normal sight. Every neighborhood had a marquis displaying its name, and they all had their own homeowners association. Pride of ownership was obvious from our initial observations. Properties were well maintained, tastefully landscaped, and lawns were manicured. Almost every house had a pool in the backyard. The hub of the city was Southlake Town Square. City Hall, the Public Library, and the Southlake Department of Public Safety were surrounded by high-end shops, sprinkled with restaurants, businesses, cosmetic dentistry, plastic surgery, nail and hair salons, and day spas. Fountains and park benches attracted young mothers with children in strollers on their morning coffee runs and trips to the library. It was where the tennis players in their cute outfits, and businessmen and women met for lunch. The bandstand and live entertainment brought couples and families out for evening dinners and ice cream. We enjoyed going to Town Square. It had a relaxed and easy feeling with the Texas sun, everyone in light and airy clothing, pedicured feet in flip-flops, tanned skin and fresh faces. It was hard not to notice how beautiful everyone looked, almost flawless, and always seeming like they were having fun. Newer model cars, Hummers, Jaguars, Mercedes, and BMWs were a normal sight and could be seen, all at once, at any given traffic light in town. Most moms drove some variety of SUV to shuttle their kids to and from school and after-school activities. The high school parking lot looked like a car dealership. It was a privileged place to live. The Bubble, as it was dubbed, mostly by nonresidents, was where the elite resided.

The pride of the town was the Southlake Carroll Dragons Varsity football team. Even those of us who weren't sports enthusiasts couldn't help but catch the buzz during football season. Preschool-aged little girls donned miniature Dragon cheerleader outfits and shook pom-poms at all the games. It wasn't necessary to mark game night on the calendar because the whole city turned green when the Dragons played. The whole town showed their spirit. The goal of every little Southlake boy was to one day play on the big boy team. Training began as soon as they could walk and clutch a football. Each little girl dreamed of becoming an Emerald Belle, but they had to train young. Tumbling, gymnastics, and dance classes were the prerequisite if they wanted a chance at making the exclusive team. Daily practices on mats on the front lawn with a group of friends was a common sight, a pastime when the more formal training wasn't underway. Big goals and dreams, but only for the best of the best, the cream of the crop, a select few. I was in awe of it all and also a little terrified that I wouldn't measure up. I wondered if we would fit in or, at the very least, be accepted. I felt more than a little out of place. We were still driving our two-year-old gold twelve-passenger Ford van. None of our kids had been interested in organized sports, and our family was more than three times the size of the average Southlake family.

Carroll Independent School District was why we chose to live in Southlake. A five-star, blue-ribbon school, we wanted only the best education for our kids. They had gone to a tiny Catholic elementary school in Cambridge. We soon learned that Catholic schools in the United States were private and required a tuition to attend. They weren't funded by tax dollars like in Canada. We couldn't afford private school tuition for all our kids. Carroll was a much larger school, more than double the size of their old school. The size of the building and the population of its students wasn't nearly as overwhelming to me as the endless list of required school supplies. We began noticing kiosks of lists in all the grocery stores, pharmacies, and places like Walmart and Target, soon after we arrived in town. When I inquired about the lists, I was informed that the schools expected them to be filled by us parents, and delivered to each child's classroom on Meet the Teacher Day. It was a completely new concept to us. We had never been required to purchase school supplies before. Everything had been supplied. All our kids had to do was show up with their new clothes and shoes, a backpack, and lunch. The very detailed, grade-specific lists included items such as US-brand #2 pencils; ballpoint pens in blue, black, and red ink; low-odor chisel-tip dry-erase EXPO markers; fine and extra fine Sharpies; quart- and gallon-sized ziplock bags; reams of copy paper; scissors; Crayola crayons; washable markers; rulers, both liquid glue and glue sticks; pocket folders with prongs in specific colors; Mead marble composition books; dividers with tabs; Mr. Sketch scented markers; Trapper binders; wide ruled spirals in specific colors; highlighters; and I'm certain I have forgotten several other items, but you get the idea. The lists were a page and a half long; and with four kids in four different grades, shopping for them was a nightmare. I made the mistake of bringing the kids along with the ridiculous notion that it would be a fun outing for all of us. The stores were packed. Unable to fit a shopping cart, much less four excited kids down the school supply aisle, we left the store and went home without buying anything. With a pot of coffee to help with concentration, I made a master list and travelled solo to four separate stores to fill it. It took several hours to find everything, and by the time I was done, I had spent more than three hundred dollars. I shuddered when I remembered they all still needed new shoes, backpacks, lunch bags, and clothes. Meet the Teacher Day was a calendar event for the whole city. Scheduled for just a few days before school started, it was an overwhelming ordeal. I showed up at the designated times with Angela, Joseph, Patrick, and Christina, and our wagon filled with school supplies. Joe stayed home with Grace, Clare, and Callum. After finding the first classroom, we were directed to a row of bins and tables where we were told to put our supplies. I had been under the impression that the supplies I had purchased would go to my own kids. Instead, they were pooled for the whole class to use. I wondered if it was too late to smuggle the rest of the supplies back home. I doubted anyone would notice, but I didn't do it. There was a long line of eager kids waiting to meet the teacher, and we still had three more classrooms to get to. Even more daunting was the paperwork and volunteer sign-up sheets, offering opportunities to be the class mom, party mom, copy room mom, scrapbook mom, lunch room mom, and several other available titles. There was a wish list, just in case we felt generous or were compelled to purchase additional supplies for the teacher. A check writing table where there were more forms to fill out and boxes to check off for teachers' birthday gifts, appreciation luncheons, holiday gifts, end-of-year gifts, class T-shirts, party fees, yearbooks, and a paper fee. The paper fee puzzled me because I had just purchases four reams of copy paper that was required on the supply list. Trying to concentrate on all the forms and sign-up sheets was nearly impossible. My head was swirling. I hadn't brought a checkbook. All I had thought to bring were my four adorable kids in their new shoes and cute school clothes that they couldn't wait to wear. They were all excitedly exploring everything in the classroom and the giant piles of supplies. It felt like the walls were closing in on me. As I looked around the room, none of the other moms looked even the least bit fazed. They had all come prepared, calendars in hand, checkbooks whipped out, writing away, signing up to volunteer, and eagerly discussing which committees to join with their friends. I was frightened to death. I gathered up all the forms and explained to the teacher that I hadn't brought a calendar with me, and that with four kids worth of forms, it would be much easier to fill them all out at home, and let them turn them in on the first day of school. They were truly understanding and put me at ease. They all seemed to know who I was, though I hadn't met any of them yet. Joe had been the one to check out the school before our move, and he told them about our family. I had already been tagged as the lady with all the children. I hurried the kids out of the school, desperate to get into the open air, stifling hot as it was. The kids ran behind me, complaining that they hadn't all gotten to meet their new teachers. I told them that they would be meeting them on the first day of school and would be seeing them every day for a whole year. Then we drove to Sonic for Slushies.

If I had felt overwhelmed at the school, I became annoyed and resentful once I got home. I laid all the packets on the table and filled out the emergency forms and standard information for each kid. Stapled together in each packet was a separate bundle of pages from the PTO. They detailed the various fund-raisers, boosters, and lists of multiple ways to show appreciation for the teachers and staff. Solicitations of cash donations and gift cards for holidays, preferred items to prepare for staff luncheons, and lists of each of my kids' teachers' favorite things. While I thought it was wonderful that there was an abundance of enthusiastic parental interest and involvement, I also thought most of the requests were way over the top and unnecessary fluff. I wanted my kids to get a good education and make some nice friends. While I was not at all opposed to showing my appreciation to teachers who did a great job, I didn't want it dictated to me how I should do so. I might want to knit a scarf or send in a garden plant. I wasn't so sure I wanted to send cash and gift cards to purchase teacher gifts before the first day of school. How did I know if she would deserve it or not? She may turn out to be horrible. I love to cook, but I wasn't prepared to commit to preparing a pot of chili three months before the luncheon. I may be in the mood to bake a pie when the day rolled around. After a lot of muttering to myself and grumbling out loud, I wrote another hundred dollars' worth of checks, deciding to just go with it and not stray from the crowd. I didn't want my kids to feel out of place. It was a relief to tuck the completed packets into each of my kids' new backpacks, and I was glad when the dull headache finally faded. The flyers and newsletters continued to come home each week in their Thursday folders. More cause for grumbling as I leafed through each one, tossing them from folder to recycle bin, advertising for local orthodontics, real estate agents, football camp, basketball camp, hockey, gymnastics, dancing lessons, pottery classes, equestrian lessons, chess club, after-school programs, community events, swimming lessons, and PTO fund-raisers. We chose a few things throughout the year for our kids to do—gymnastics, basketball camp, and show choir. We went to the public library fairly regularly, we found a piano teacher who came to the house for lessons, and the kids went to religious education classes at St. Francis. They stayed active without being overloaded. Many of their friends were in multiple activities and always seemed to be on the go, grabbing Chick-fil-A or Sonic for dinner between practices and lessons. The common chatter among my peers was how busy everyone was. They were always running and complained about not having enough family time. Joe and I resisted the hustle and bustle. We weren't willing to sacrifice our precious family time more than we had to. Birthday invitations came home every week with one kid or another. We declined most and chose two invitations a piece from their closest friends. We spent as much time together as a family as we could. Grilling outside, playing in the pool, tending to the yard and flowers. We watched movies and held our own dance parties in the living room. The kids rode their bikes and played in the cul-de-sac with the neighborhood kids. We went to Sonic for cream slushes or 7-Eleven for Icees as a treat.

Sunday Mass continued to be a constant in our life. Dressed up, hair fixed, clean and polished, we nearly filled up a whole pew. We weren't particularly religious, and we weren't exactly active in our parish, but we felt that bringing our kids to Sunday Mass was important. Anamia's Tex-Mex was a treat we splurged on once a month. The staff had gotten to know our family, and the kids were always really well-behaved when we went out to eat. It was understood that if they didn't behave, they wouldn't get to go out the next time. On one occasion, while we were gathered around the three tables that had been pushed together to accommodate us all, we had almost finished our meal when a lady approached me from behind. She leaned over and handed me five praline treats, a very sweet and rich Mexican dessert made from brown sugar, butter, and pecans. She had purchased them at the hostess counter. I stared at her with a puzzled look on my face. The lady, whom we had never met before, told Joe and I in a voice loud enough for our kids to hear, "My husband and I watched you all come in here. We thought it was incredible to see such a large family with so many small children. We were almost done with our meal when I told my husband that I wanted to stay to watch you all, just to see how long it would take for one of the kids to act up, but not one of them did. I must tell you that your kids are very well-mannered and the best behaved we have ever seen. I wanted to give them a reward for their behavior and to tell you what a remarkable job you are doing as parents, to be able to bring them out to a restaurant and have them behave so well. Some people can't even control one or two children."

My jaw about dropped on the floor, and when I looked at Joe, his reaction was the same. We humbly thanked the lady before she smiled and waved goodbye. Our kids were all smiles, wondering when they would get to taste the sweet treats. It wasn't the first time we had been complimented on our children's behavior in public, but it was above and beyond anything that we had ever experienced. Now don't get me wrong, our kids are not, nor have they ever been, perfect. They are normal kids who fight, talk back, and do a lot of the same crazy dumb things most kids do, but we have always been able to take them out in public without being embarrassed. There have been occasions when we've had to correct them while we were out. I have even left a full shopping cart in the store and carried out a preschooler who threw a temper tantrum back to the car before finishing my shopping. We have loaded the family up to head out for ice cream or an outing, and turned right back around without the treat because they were fighting. I've marched kids out of Mass to the ladies room to give them a stern talking to, or a swat on the behind because they refused to behave properly. We've done all these things only a handful of times. That is why we can go out as a family and enjoy a meal. They all learned early on that we wouldn't tolerate bad behavior. The older kids also stepped up to help keep their younger siblings in line because they knew that one kid acting crazy could ruin it for all of them. Discipline, training, and a lot of love was how we rolled from day one. More and more we were hearing the comments. How beautiful our family was, how much people enjoyed seeing us at Mass, and how well-behaved the children were. All their teachers had only good things to say about them. We felt proud. Our family had always been our number one priority. Everything we did was done with our family's interest at heart. We were becoming aware that other people were watching, looking up to, and admiring us. It was awkward to me because I didn't feel like we were any different from other families, there were just more of us. It was also kind of stressful because I felt like I had to live up to the expectations that other people had of us.

We decided to get a new dog. The kids missed Katie, and we had promised them that once we got settled into our new house, we would get them a puppy. I researched sheltie breeders online. Katie had been a wonderful pet, and we wanted to find one just like her. I found a breeder in Melissa, Texas, somewhere near the Oklahoma border, a much farther drive than we had realized. We turned the two-hour trip to the off-the-beaten-path destination into a family outing. Twix was a sable-colored sheltie whose lineage was very impressive. His father was a blue-ribbon show dog, and we all agreed that his personality seemed the best match for our family. We couldn't wait to get him home. I held his little trembling furry body close to me, while he chewed my fingers with his needle-sharp puppy teeth, all the way home.

Southlake, Texas, had begun to feel like home; but I missed my family, and I knew that they were missing our kids. I wanted my parents to see how happy they were and how much they were growing. We received a big tax return the year after our move, and after paying off our van and credit cards, we decided to take a two-week vacation to visit my family. We flew from Dallas to Buffalo, and then drove to Niagara. We played tourist with the kids, visited Niagara Falls and all the attractions. We stayed with my parents for several days and also drove to Cambridge for a weekend so that we could attend Mass at St. Clement's, our old parish. It was great to see Fr. Sherlock, Sr. Lorraine, and so many familiar faces. We spent a day at African Lion Safari, and visited with old neighbors and friends. We truly enjoyed our first real family vacation.

I had been feeling unusually tired, but chalked it up to the trip and all the preparations that had gone into it, which was no small task. Packing and planning for a family of nine was a big deal all on its own, but managing a sitter to care for our house and pets in our absence, stopping the paper, and making sure all our travel documents and insurance information was in order was a huge chore. I was more than just tired. I was exhausted. After we got to our hotel in Cambridge and I had a chance to settle my brains a little, I realized that my period was late. We had just returned from a day at the African Lion Safari. I left Joe and the kids stretched out on the beds watching television and went across the parking lot to the Shopper's Drug Mart. I bought some snacks for the kids, a gourmet chocolate for myself, and a pregnancy test. I headed back to the hotel room where I dropped my bags and went directly into the bathroom with the test. It took no time for the pink plus sign to appear, much faster than the two minutes the instructions on the box said it should take. Baby number eight, the explanation for my exhaustion. Callum had just turned two, and even though we had never used birth control, or even natural family planning, I was still surprised to be pregnant again. It was the longest span between our kids. Walking out of the bathroom with the stick in my hand, I told Joe the news. He was just as surprised as I was. With his eyes wide, he searched mine to make sure I was certain. I showed him the test stick before a broad grin spread across his face. He shook his head and said, "Oh boy, here we go again."

It took a couple of days for it to sink in, but we were genuinely happy about the little life that had been growing inside me without our even knowing it. We told my family right away. With the timing being what it was, it made sense. They were all equally surprised but very happy about our news. My only concern was that I didn't have an ob-gyn in Texas, and I worried that I wouldn't be able to find one who was pro-life. It nagged at me for the rest of our trip. I'd been fortunate to have pro-life doctors for each of my pregnancies, and I wanted the same for our new baby. I had doubts that I would easily find one in Texas.

Joe and I spent a night at the Ramada Coral Inn while the rest of the kids had a sleepover at my parents' house. Returning to what Joe jokingly referred to as "the scene of the crime," we caught up on some much needed sleep. We had never slept so soundly or uninterrupted for so many consecutive hours. Patrick made his First Holy Communion on the last Sunday of our trip, at St. Joseph's Church in Grimsby, where Fr. Hugh, a priest who was a friend of the family, was pastor. It had been an enjoyable and memorable family holiday, but we were all ready to go back home to Texas.

We had missed a big storm while we were away. The evidence of it had been scattered all over our backyard. Fallen leaves and branches covered our patio and lawn and floated in the pool. The first thing I noticed when I walked inside was the missing corner of our kitchen windowsill. Our dog sitter had come by the house three times a day to walk and play with Twix, but he apparently did not appreciate being left by his family. We had left him gated in our large tiled kitchen where he had access to the doggy door, and freedom to roam the backyard. We figured that the storm must have scared him, and chewing the wood on the windowsill likely relieved his stress. We made a note to call someone to repair it the next day.

The second thing I noticed was the North Texas Catholic newspaper sitting on the top of a huge stack of mail. The bold printed headline caught my eye: NEW PRO-LIFE NFP OBGYN PRACTICE OPENING IN NORTH TEXAS. I snatched up the paper and immediately started reading. There was a picture of Dr. Daniel A. MacDonald, and a write-up about his new pro-life, natural family planning practice. My jaw dropped. I had only known I was pregnant for a week, and was completely blown away by the fact that I was staring at the answer to what had been my biggest concern.

I called Dr. MacDonald the very next day, and we chatted over the phone for more than an hour. I gave him my history and told him about our newest little miracle. We both found the timing of the opening of his new practice to be more than a little coincidental. He told me that he was Catholic and that his conscience wouldn't allow him to prescribe contraceptives or perform procedures that were not in line with the teachings of the church. He had many Catholic and non-Catholic like-minded patients who encouraged him to open up his own practice. God got my attention through that event. There had been several events prior to that one, where God had been trying to wake me up that I had been clueless about, but there was no denying that He had orchestrated the details of finding a pro-life doctor. I mean really! Headlines in the newspaper? Talk about being hit over the head with a brick. Sadly, looking back, I still didn't fully appreciate at that time the magnitude of the miracle. Not to the extent that it changed my life. It hadn't made me consciously aware of the fact that God's hand was in *every* detail of my life, not just the big things. As far as I was concerned, finding Dr. MacDonald was *one* cool event.

I remained as complacent as ever in my faith. We followed the rules of the church, tithed regularly, lived a righteous life, and did our best to raise our kids well. Our charity work consisted of donating toys the kids no longer played with and clothes that didn't fit anymore. We dropped off cans at church for the food pantry when we remembered collection week, usually the stuff that was sitting around that nobody liked. We put a little extra in the special collection at church, whatever happened to be in our wallets. We did what was convenient, never going out of our way to plan or think of ways to give back. We didn't give till it hurt, we gave of our excess. We weren't wealthy compared to most families around us, but we had everything we needed, and our life was pretty comfortable. My faith wasn't what I would have called deep. Far from it. Our life was great, and when people asked me how we did it, how we could have it all—the big beautiful family, a fabulous house, and how we could afford for me to be a stay-at-home mom—my response was always that Joe had a terrific job. I never considered that God had blessed us with everything. Joe worked hard, had a great education, lots of experience, and was driven. I didn't give God the credit for giving Joe those gifts. God was a part of my life, but in an abstract sort of way. I certainly didn't have a relationship with Him. Other than saying bedtime prayers with the kids when I had the energy, I didn't have a personal prayer life. I was too busy to pray. I identified myself as Catholic, but I only halfway paid attention on Sundays.

Joe sent my sister Thérèse a plane ticket so that she could visit us in the fall. What she had planned to be a two-week visit turned into a three-month stay. She loved Texas, and we loved having her. There is a fourteen-year age difference between the two of us, but we bonded a lot during her stay. She was great company for me, was a tremendous help in many ways, and the kids adored her. We went for walks, cooked, and baked; she helped with the kids with their school projects and worked on crafts. She even sent Joe and me out for dinner and a movie once a week, something we hadn't done since our move. We loved her, appreciated her help, and really tried to show her a nice time. My mother called regularly while Thérèse was with us, and we told her all about our crafts and outings. One afternoon, she called to tell us that she and my dad and several of my other siblings were coming for Christmas. We were all surprised, but excited about their upcoming visit.

Thérèse, who loved all things domestic as much as I did, was my partner in crime. We decorated and baked, shopped and wrapped, wanting everything to be beautiful, festive, and Martha Stewart perfect for our company. We baked and built a giant gingerbread house, designed personalized place cards for the table, and tried extra special recipes. We filled the fridges, freezers, and pantry with loads of comfort food and plenty of snacks.

When the evening arrived for my family's arrival, the house looked and smelled like the holidays. Christmas lights glowing, scented candles flickering, and cookies set out on trays for stealing. Thérèse stayed with the kids while Joe and I drove to the airport to pick everybody up. As soon as we pulled into the parking garage, I started to cough. It was a dry tickling cough. We found my family at the baggage claim, greeted and hugged them all. It was the first time traveling to Texas for most of them. When all their luggage came out, we loaded everything and everyone into the van. The coughing persisted, and I was annoyed. I hadn't felt sick at all, but suddenly I couldn't utter a sentence without being thrown into a coughing fit. It progressively got worse as the evening wore on. Over the next couple of days, I began to feel it in my chest. I became exhausted from the coughing. We decided to go to the children's Mass on Christmas Eve, and by Christmas morning, I was barely dragging around.

Grateful for all the preparations we had done in advance, which included homemade quiches we froze for an easy Christmas morning breakfast, we gathered in the living room to open up the mountain of gifts piled under the tree. I wished that I felt better so that I could enjoy the time with my family. There were so many things I wanted to do and places I wanted to show them. I wanted to be the perfect hostess, but the energy was zapped out of me, and I could feel myself getting worse by the minute. I forced myself to keep going, not wanting to miss the kids' excitement and the very first Christmas morning they ever shared with their grandparents. By midmorning, my mother announced that she wasn't feeling well. Her ear was bothering her since the flight. After the gifts had been opened and everyone had eaten, she spent the rest of the day in bed. Joe and my dad grilled ribs while my sisters and I got the turkey and trimmings underway.

Still coughing with a congested chest, my ribs ached and my seven-month pregnant belly hurt from the hacking. Joe told me to forget about the turkey, that we could just eat the ribs, but I wouldn't hear of it. I felt like crawling under my covers and burying my head, but I had a house full of people to feed and it was Christmas. Thérèse and I had put too much time and energy into all the preparations to not see it all through. We arranged our feast on the kitchen island, buffet style. The table was beautiful and festively set with the new holly tablecloth and matching placemats, and Christopher Radko

Christmas dishes, the wrought iron candelabra, wrapped in holly berry garland, and mini Christmas trees in the gold-painted pots that Thérèse had crafted for the personalized place cards, finished it off. Once everyone had gathered in the kitchen for the blessing and we fixed the little kids' plates, Joe insisted that I go to bed. Feeling feverish and completely drained, I obeyed.

The next day, my chest hurt, my throat felt like I had swallowed shards of glass, my ears were aching, and I had a fever. Joe drove me to the urgent care clinic in Grapevine. It was the worst cold I'd ever had, and I was worried that all the coughing and hacking would hurt the baby. As it turned out, it was more than just a bad cold. I had strep throat, bronchitis, a sinus infection, and a double ear infection. The doctor told me that I must have felt like death warmed over. I told her I did. She prescribed an antibiotic and told me I should feel better in a few days. We went directly to the pharmacy to fill the prescription and then straight to bed where I stayed the rest of the day and night, and most of the following day after that. I felt horribly guilty about not being a better hostess and missing out on visiting with my family. Not to mention not being able to take care of my kids or household duties. I rested in the family room when I finally did emerge. I wasn't used to not being in charge, or letting other people take care of things. Between Joe, my dad, and my sisters, the kids were fed and taken care of, and the laundry got done, the visit had not turned out at all the way we had planned. It ended up being quite a disappointment. Thérèse returned home with the rest of the family, with the intention of returning the following month to stay for the birth of our new baby.

Sarah Thérèse Andréa Michelle, named after four of my sisters, was born on February 11, 2004. It was the absolute easiest, almost surreal delivery I'd ever had. After the experience of a totally natural home birth with a midwife for Callum, I opted for an epidural. Never having had one before, I literally giggled through her birth. Dr. MacDonald and the nurses laughed along with us, shocked that I'd never had pain management for any of my other births. Joe was notably less stressed knowing that I was pain free. We made a promise, out loud, that should we happen to have any more babies, I would definitely get an epidural again. Thérèse was a tremendous help while we were in the hospital. It eased our minds knowing that our other kids were taken care of while we weren't there. She was just as incredible while I recuperated. We asked her to be Sarah's godmother.

We invited our priest friend, Fr. Hugh, to be godfather, and we were granted permission by our pastor, Fr. Ken, to allow Fr. Hugh to do the baptism. My mother said she wanted to come, so Joe sent her a ticket, and she and Fr. Hugh flew to Dallas together. Thérèse planned to return home with my mother after her weeklong visit. We were happy and excited about the very special occasion, but it didn't take long for the tensions to surface. My mother assumed the familiar role of woman of the house, correcting the kids in front of us and even handing out punishments. After Fr. Hugh left, she decided to take on the task of potty training Callum, who was two and a half. I had mentioned to her that I wanted to wait until after Sarah was born to start potty training because I didn't want him to have any setbacks while I was in the hospital. I had already bought a potty chair and planned to wait until after their visit was over when there were fewer distractions. Without asking us, she sat little Callum down on the potty seat and told him he couldn't get up until he peed. Callum wanted nothing to do with it. She gave him books and snacks and wouldn't let him up until he did something in the pot. My stomach was in knots, but I didn't say anything to her. Potty training was a job that I had done successfully with all six of my other kids, and I was looking forward to Callum's turn. I was too cowardly to speak up to my mother. Callum was not used to his grandmother. He was still a baby when we moved to Texas, and he'd only seen her twice after that. I understood her wanting to be part of his milestone, but I felt that he would have had an easier time with me helping him. Still, I said nothing. My other kids felt the tension and whispered about how mean she was. They hated to see Callum so upset. I told them that he was okay and that he was upset because it was something new for him. Patrick decided to help his little brother out. When my mother wasn't looking, he poured water from our water cooler into the potty seat bowl and announced that Callum had finally peed. Everyone rushed to the kitchen to see. One of them mumbled, "Finally, now maybe she will let him go."

Callum, who was still sitting on the chair, looked up, red-faced and wide-eyed. When my mother lifted him up to inspect the bowl, he had a red ring around his bottom. She squinted her eyes, directing her suspicious glance toward Patrick. He had been writing lines, the punishment she had given him for some forgotten infraction. She said, "That's the clearest pee I've ever seen, and it's ice-cold!"

We were all amazed by Patrick's plan. He had a heart for his little brother and a mind for deception. My mother added more line writing to his existing punishment. By the end of the day, she gave up on the potty training, declaring that Callum wasn't ready.

Joe and I were the parents, but we always allowed my mother to assume our role while she was around. We could have and should have stepped in, but we didn't. We knew if we did, it would make for bad vibes. Joe poured himself a glass of wine each night after work while she was there. My mother raised her eyebrows, mentioning to me that she thought he had a drinking problem. I didn't tell her that she was the problem or that he was more than ready for her to leave. I resumed the potty training a couple of weeks later, trying to make it as stress free as possible. It took three days and a few accidents for Callum to be completely trained, even through the night.

Sarah was a happy baby. Doted on and spoiled, we dressed her up like a frilly doll. With the early arrival of spring in Texas, we spent hours outside every day, gardening and walking. By June, three months after Sarah was born, I was down to a hundred and sixteen pounds, ten pounds less than my pre-pregnant weight. I felt fantastic. Life was a little busier, but still simple. The kids had made friends at school and in the neighborhood, so there were always extra kids at our house. We monitored who they played with, and limited social activities to kids whose parents shared our values. We spent most of our time together as a family—playing in the pool, day trips to the Fort Worth Zoo, going out to dinner, movies, and walks to Southlake Town Square to enjoy the free music and entertainment on the weekends.

On Independence Day Weekend, we took a road trip to Corpus Christi, Texas, to visit Joe's Uncle Don and Aunt Lilian, who lived on South Padre Island. It was our first time to the Gulf of Mexico, and our first trip to somewhere other than visiting my relatives. An easy seven-hour drive, we were fascinated by the changes in the landscape along the way. The farther we drove, the more palm trees and cactus we saw. Driving across the causeway was incredible. It was almost like we were driving on water. The kids had a ball, wading in the warm Gulf water and picking up shells on the sandy beach. Joseph and Patrick filled their pockets with tiny clam shells, having no idea that there were actual clams living in them until Uncle Don let them know. The older kids all took turns on Uncle Don's paddleboat on the canal behind their house. He and Aunt Lilian were sweet and kind to all of us, and they seemed to really enjoy having all the kids around. They pulled out all their board games, Lilian toured the girls around the room where she kept her doll collection, and let them hold the ones that weren't too fragile. Uncle Don gave Joseph and Patrick some old racket ball rackets, and spent time talking to them about weather patterns and how to prepare for a hurricane. He was a retired Navy Sailor, and he proudly showed us all his pictures, framed knots, and other memorabilia he had displayed in his office. He was the first real live veteran that our kids had ever met.

We bought a family pass for the Aquarium and spent the Fourth of July there. The pass was cheaper than paying individual admission, and it included free parking. We learned about marine biology, explored all there was to see, played at the splash pad, and decided to return later that night to watch the fireworks display. We had no idea how crazy the place would be for the holiday, but it was packed when we returned. Keeping our little family close, we counted our kids over and over again the entire time. The fireworks show over the water was spectacular, but when it ended, it was nothing short of chaos in the park. Everyone wanted to be first to get out. Weaving our way through the crowds in the dark, clutching on to our kids tightly, we found our van. It took more than an hour to get back to the hotel with all the traffic. In the elevator on the way up to our room with our sleepy kids, I counted heads. In a panic, I counted again.

There were only seven. Someone was missing. I listed off each name and stopped at Grace, realizing in shock that she was the one who was missing. Totally freaked out, Joe stopped the elevator and ran down the stairs to the van. My heart pounded as I prayed a desperate prayer that we hadn't left her at the Aquarium. I distinctly remembered counting everyone before we left, but I started second-guessing myself. My brain was in a fuzzy haze, and it seemed like an eternity before Joe arrived at the door, carrying a sleeping Grace. Nearly collapsing with relief, I grabbed her into my arms. By far, it had been the scariest thing that we had ever experienced.

THIRTEEN

On the Move Again

Southlake, Texas, 2004–2005

The dream continued. Our kids grew, we were comfortable, and life continued to move on just a little bit faster. We took pride in raising our kids and made an effort to be good citizens. When I heard about the Red Bag Food Drive, I thought it sounded like a good opportunity to get the older kids involved in a community service project. Red bags were delivered to each house in the city with instructions for residents to fill them with nonperishable food items, to be picked up on a specified day. The bags were then collected and sorted by volunteers. Angela, Joseph, Patrick, and I helped with assembling the baskets. It was a massive, but very well-organized event. Hundreds of people showed up at the White's Chapel Methodist Church parking lot to help. Forming an assembly line, we filled plastic laundry baskets with peanut butter, breakfast cereal, canned fruits, vegetables, tuna, beans, desserts, paper products, toiletries, and candy. Needy families were also provided with milk, a turkey, and bread. The experience had been a meaningful one and had stirred up the desire to do more in the community, though I didn't know quite what exactly.

Joe enjoyed his job at the HRSC. He was good at it, well-respected, and he liked everyone he worked with. He was asked to consider moving into a new role as director of HR Tax for the firm. The tax department had not been doing well, and in fact was a mess.

They wanted him to help fix it. The previous person had left, and they needed someone to step in and turn things around. We had lived in Texas for close to three years. The new role was in New York. As we discussed the possibilities of the new opportunity, we revisited our original plan. The one we had devised over morning coffee in our pretty living room in Cambridge three years earlier. Our plan had been for us to move to Texas, stay three to five years, and then return to Canada, where Joe would move into the ultimate job. This new role added a twist to our original plan, but we could see how it might still end with the same result. New York was much closer to what we considered home, and we looked at it as a sort of stepping stone back to Canada. We decided to go for it. Joe negotiated a much higher salary to compensate for the difference in the cost of living, and accepted the role.

The night that Joe signed the official job offer, I was out Christmas shopping. Because I just had that familiar feeling, I bought a pregnancy test. When I got home, I left the bags of clothes and toys hidden in the van for Joe to carry in the house later, after the kids went to bed. I zipped the pregnancy test safely into my purse before I went into the house. I smiled and waved at Joe and the kids, who were watching television in the living room, and made a beeline to the bathroom, really needing to go. Hearing a lot of excitement in our bedroom, I realized that Joe and all the kids were in there, waiting for me to come out. The kids were dancing around, clapping and cheering, excited to tell me that we were moving to New York. I looked at Joe, who nodded, and said that it was a done deal. The kids were excited that we would be closer to our relatives and old friends. We began talking excitedly about taking road trips to visit. I hugged Joe, congratulating him on his new job, and whispered in his ear that we were going to have a new baby. His eyes grew big, and he held out his arms, pulling me away so that he could look at my face. I nodded that it was true. We celebrated Joe's new career, our upcoming move, and a new baby—all on the same night. The pattern continued— promotion, move, new baby. We couldn't have been happier.

Joe started his new job right after New Year's 2005. KPMG provided corporate housing for him until we found a house and moved our family in March. We discussed waiting till the end of the school year to move, but none of us wanted to be separated that long, so we started looking for a place right away. Joe found a real estate agent and did some preliminary searches of neighborhoods and houses before we made our first family house-hunting trip in January. Because Joe had negotiated a full relocation package, the firm paid all our expenses, airfare, food, and accommodations. They would have paid for two trips, but we only needed one. I bought winter coats for half off at Old Navy after Christmas. The first winter coats we had bought since moving to Texas. We hired a limo service to take us to the Dallas airport. Our plan was to fly to LaGuardia and catch a connecting flight to Buffalo. We planned to drive to Niagara Falls, spend a night at my parents' house, and leave the kids with them for two days while Joe and I flew back to Manhattan, where Joe had a corporate condo on Park Avenue. Our realtor had houses lined up to see, and we hoped to find the perfect one during that trip. Even though it was the dead of winter, I was three months pregnant, and we were under a lot of pressure to find a house, we were excited about a mini getaway. I had twinges of anxiety about leaving my kids with my parents, and us being so far away from them; Manhattan is seven hours away from Buffalo, but I convinced myself that they would be fine.

The kids were excited about being on a plane again. When we arrived at our gate, we noticed some of the other passengers counting them. Although none of them spoke to us, many of them stared. Joe, being a frequent flyer himself, said they were probably dreading a flight with eight young kids and were praying their seats were nowhere near ours. He said he hated flying with loud and unruly children, so he could understand their worried looks. The flight went smoothly, and when we landed, we waited for all the other passengers to get off first, knowing that it would take us much longer to get everyone and all our carry-ons out; we didn't want to hold anyone up. Several people stopped on their way off the plane to tell us how impressed they were with our kids. A few of them told us exactly what Joe had said, how they had been worried about how the flight was going to go with so many little kids. They said they were pleasantly surprised by how quiet and well-behaved our kids had been. Of course Joe and I both had sweated buckets the entire flight, worried that the littlest ones would cry or be scared, but not one of them made a peep. We had planned for everything. We'd brought snacks and books, but the novelty of flying was enough to keep them entertained.

When we finally got off the plane, Joe checked the monitor for our connecting flight to Buffalo. To our horror, all flights had been cancelled. Even worse, we were informed that the airport was shut down due to a major snowstorm. There were news cameras and reporters at the airport, filming and interviewing stranded passengers. Joe went to retrieve our luggage while I stayed with the kids. He found all the bags except for the two Barbie suitcases that contained Christina's and Grace's clothes. I hovered protectively over my little brood in a corner of the overcrowded baggage area while Joe inquired about the missing bags. Finally, after being redirected to several different stations, we all cheered as my six foot three, two hundred and sixty–pound husband made his way over to us with pink Barbie bags in hand. We walked to the car rental area of the airport where Joe waited in a long line to rent a vehicle. There weren't any cars to be had. Every car had been rented out earlier in the day in anticipation of the storm. When Joe inquired about a shuttle, he was told that we would be able to get one once they reopened the roads. No one had any idea when that would be. We were stranded. With our family huddled together along a wall in our own little space, I glanced around at the other stranded travelers. They were all doing the same as us, creating their own little invisible bubbles around themselves. Joe bought us Wendy's from the airport food court for dinner. While we handed out chicken nuggets and french fries to the kids, we discussed the obvious fact that we wouldn't be going to Buffalo. The kids were not entirely disappointed. They told us that they would rather stay with us and look at houses anyway. The event was one that I look back on now and realize was a blessing in disguise.

The roads finally reopened after several hours, and the driver of our shuttle van cautiously navigated us to Joe's one-bedroom condo. To call it tiny would be an understatement. We unloaded our bags and set up sleeping areas in every available space. At either end of the couch, on the small family room floor, in the hallway, and on the bedroom floor all around the bed. After such a long and eventful day, nobody complained about the accommodations. The kids curled up into little balls and fell asleep.

The biggest vehicle available for rent was a seven-passenger SUV. There were ten of us, and we didn't want to rent two cars, mostly because I was afraid to drive in New York City. We doubled two of the kids up in seat belts next to the car seats, and Joseph and Patrick took turns riding in the back in the cargo space. We left early in the morning to meet our realtor. She and Joe had narrowed the house search to the specifications that he knew would fit our needs. A few of the houses were too far of a commute for Joe, and several were fix-er-uppers that needed too much work to bring it up to our standards. A project that we weren't ready to invest in at that point in time. Joe had saved his favorite house for last. Although I wasn't exactly in love with it, it was the best one we'd seen that day. We discovered that no matter where we bought, Joe would have to commute to the city. We chose Central Valley because the commute was reasonable, and the school district was highly rated. The neighborhood was beautiful and the house had a pool, not something that we had been looking for but knew would be enjoyed. The property was covered in a blanket of snow from the blizzard the day before, so we had no idea what the yard looked like. The house had been on the market for a year. We put in an offer, and it was accepted right away. Our closing date was scheduled for March 15, the day before Clare's birthday.

We flew home to Texas and put our house on the market. We had only lived in it just shy of three years. I thought back to the day that Joe and I had walked through it for the first time, remembering how excited we were to have found it. It had been perfect for our family. Now it was just a house that needed to be prepared for show-ing to perspective buyers. Not that it needed much preparing, I had kept it spotless almost to a fault.

We had come a long way from our previous houses in Canada, where we had poured hours of sweat equity into cleaning, painting, and decorating. We had done all the planning, creating, and main-taining of our own landscapes from scratch, and preened over our pool. After moving to Southlake, we got soft. When Joe's mower died shortly after moving in, he hired a crew to cut and trim our lawn. When the front yard needed a facelift, I found a landscaper to design a new look, complete with decorative lighting, river rocks, masonry work, a french drain, ornamental trees, shrubs, perennials, and annuals. Because of the size of our house and the height and angles of the ceilings, I wouldn't attempt painting myself, so I hired a professional. Not just a painter, but an artist, Dore Rodriguez not only painted trim and cabinets, but faux finished, plastered, troweled, and glazed our walls with leather look and Old World finishes.

No longer did I wash my own windows like I had always done, climbing out onto the front porch roof, while pregnant, during a cleaning frenzy in a January thaw. Instead, I hired a couple to clean the solar screens and windows twice a year. I even hired a housekeeper for a short time, but because of my OCD, I cleaned before she came and never thought her work was up to par. Because she needed the work, I kept her on, and we cleaned together. She helped with the kids and cooked some for us. We also ordered a lot of prepared meals once we discovered the Schwann man. We had a pest control service and a pool maintenance service. We didn't even have to go outside to turn on the pool filter, everything was controlled by a keypad at the door. Lights, heater, fountain, sweeper, and hot tub could be activated by the touch of a button. It had taken no time at all to ease into the Southlake lifestyle. We were by no means as well-off as most Lakers. We actually lived in one of the more modest neighborhoods in town by Southlake standards. Compared to where we had come from, we were living the dream. We were enjoying the fruits of Joe's labors, and we viewed the conveniences as a tradeoff for more time with our family.

Joe's relocation package included a guarantee from KPMG that if our house didn't sell within three months, they would take it over at market value. The house showed well and sold within three weeks. KPMG spared no expense, including moving our pets. Our menagerie had multiplied to two dogs: our sheltie, Twix; a golden retriever puppy named Maverick; and our old bunny, Poppyseed. They were scheduled to fly to New York via Air Animals, an elite pet moving service. On the Sunday evening before our movers arrived to start packing, and before Joe was to return to New York, I was doing some laundry just off our kitchen. Callum, who was three and a half, asked me for cookies for the dogs. I took two biscuits out of the bin we kept in the laundry room and handed them to him. I smiled as the dogs sat obediently at his command. Being the second youngest of the family, he enjoyed the authority over the dogs, and they listened to him. Callum handed one to Maverick, who carried it under the table to enjoy it. When he handed Twix his cookie, it dropped onto the floor. He bent down to pick it up, and Twix, perhaps sensing that Callum was trying to steal if from him, lunged at his face. It had all happened so quickly. The growling and snarling sounds that came from him sounded more like a wild beast than our pet. I dropped the laundry that I had been folding and scooped Callum, screaming and bleeding, up to the kitchen sink where I ran cold water over his face. Joe and the kids had been watching a movie in the living room, just off the kitchen. Everyone rushed in when they heard the commotion. One of the kids had put Twix in the backyard while I was tending to Callum. The wound wasn't serious enough for stitches, but it was serious enough for us to question whether we had any business keeping the dog. I felt sick. I had been bitten by a dog less than a year earlier, while walking baby Sarah in the neighborhood. I was horrified that our own dog had bitten one of our own kids. When I considered what would have happened if it had been a kid in the neighborhood, I realized it likely would have been a lawsuit. We were all shaken up. The only words Joe said about it were, "That dog better not be here when I get back."

He flew out the next morning.

While I was relieved that the bite was not serious, I was sick over the fact that I'd always had a feeling that the dog was just a little bit off. We'd owned him for about three years. I had taken him to obedience school, we walked him and played with him every day. He was a good dog, obedient, and walked like a show dog, but he was always unpredictable. We tried to adapt to his quirks. Like when he lunged and snarled at the kitchen cabinets when the sun shone on them in the afternoon, so much so that his gums bled, we put him outside until the sun moved and the shadows were gone. When he chewed the brush and growled when I groomed him, I took him to Pet Smart for his baths. When they complained at Pet Smart that he wouldn't let them brush him, I took him to our vet to have it done. When the behavior continued, they suggested sedation before his baths. He was otherwise a great dog. He loved attention, played well with the kids and with Maverick. One of the reasons we got the second dog was so that Twix would have a buddy. He was a great watchdog, but had never been aggressive with any of our kids before that night. We weren't the sort of pet owners to give up on a pet because he was a little quirky or unbalanced, but we couldn't risk keeping a biting dog. Not with kids, and definitely not with babies.

I called the breeder where we'd bought him, and left several messages, hoping that she could suggest a place that might take him. Not surprisingly, she never called me back. I remembered the trip we had made to Melissa, Texas, where we drove to pick him up at the breeder's house. The breeder bragged about her show dogs and about Twix's bloodlines; his father was a champion blue-ribbon show dog. He certainly was beautiful, but the environment that he came from was far different from the family friendly farm where we had bought our first sheltie, Katie. There, the puppies were handled, cuddled, and loved by the family's children. Twix's breeder lived alone, and the puppies had not been socialized. She picked the best show dogs from the litter and sold the rest. We bought Twix because we were missing our Katie and wanted a replacement, but we soon realized that Katie had been one of a kind. I remembered how Twix had gnawed on my hands all the way home while I petted and tried to reassure him. I recalled his first vet appointment the day after we brought him home. She remarked that he was head shy, demonstrating how when she put her hand near his head to pet him, he flinched. She said that was a sign of abuse and wanted to know where we got him from. I called three Sheltie Rescues, but none would take him when I told them that he had bitten my son. I then called Southlake DPS Animal Control. I explained the situation to the dispatcher and told her that we were moving to New York in a few days and couldn't take the dog with us. She said that we would have to put him under quarantine for the next ten days. We wouldn't have been able to take him out of state even if we'd wanted to.

The next day, two officers came to the house with their animal control vehicle. I greeted them at the door and explained again what had happened. Callum was at my side, looking up at the uniformed men and hugging my leg. I showed them the side of his face where the wounds were still visible, but healing. The movers had been there for several hours already packing things up. I walked the officers through the house to the backyard where the dogs were running around and playing. They had both been freshly groomed only a few days earlier, in preparation for the move. The officers were very sympathetic. It was emotional for all of us, and they understood our situation. Twix was well-mannered when they pet him, and they could see that he had been well cared for. They loaded him into their truck and took him off to be quarantined. One of the officers gave me his card and told me that if we changed our minds and decided to keep him, to give him a call. I told him that we just couldn't risk it. He assured me that he would try his best to find a good home. I gave him the folder containing all of Twix's vet records and papers, hoping that he wouldn't be put down. I prayed that a more suitable family would adopt him.

The move to New York was tougher on the kids than our previous moves. They had made some really nice friends in Texas, and they were anxious about starting, midyear, at a new school in New York. We said our goodbyes over the last few days, promising to keep in touch with teachers, friends, neighbors, and fellow parishioners from our church, and got ready to embark on our next adventure.

FOURTEEN

Detour

Central Valley was still covered in snow when we arrived at our new house on Greenwich Avenue. We had hired a company to paint everything before we moved in, figuring it would be easier on everyone to get the job done while the house was empty. It took us no time to unpack boxes and set up our house. We had donated a lot of stuff to St. Francis Outreach before leaving Texas—clothes, toys, and household items, bringing only what we needed. We had become pretty efficient at moving. We registered our kids for school right away and found our new parish, St. Patrick's Church in Highland Mills. Woodbury Commons, the outlet shopping center; Walmart; and BJ's were all within two miles of our house, so shopping was convenient. Several of our new neighbors stopped by bearing baked goods, to introduce themselves when they saw the kids out playing in the snow. We were warmly welcomed to the neighborhood, and the kids settled fairly easily into their new schools. With just three months left of the school year, they made some new friends. We all anticipated that the start of the following school year would be easier since they wouldn't be the new kids anymore. Patrick had struggled academically from the time we had first moved to Texas. Halfway through the second grade, an independent educational plan (IEP) had been developed for him. We brought his records with us when we registered him in his new school. He continued to struggle in math, and he hated reading.

All the kids made fast friends with the kids in the neighborhood. No matter how hectic our mornings were, rushing them to dress, grab breakfast, and brush their teeth before hurrying out the door, when they joined their crowd of friends at the bus stop, we all relaxed. With coffee in hand, I joined the other moms and dads who had all shared equally busy mornings. We helped each other smile, laughing and joking together, starting the day off on a light foot.

There were more boys than girls in the neighborhood, but everyone got along and played together. When they weren't in school, they were taking over the neighborhood with games like capture the flag, manhunt, and riding bikes. We were like a huge family. We celebrated birthday parties, went to the kids' baseball games, and exchanged treats for all the holidays. It was the closest community we had ever been part of.

St. Patrick's Church in Highland Mills was our second home. We were regulars at the nine o'clock Mass, and Joseph and Patrick began altar serving right away. Our new parish was where we met "Mom Mom Marge," Margaret Duane. A five foot two, spunky lady in her late sixties. She worked as a nurse in the psych ward of a prison. She always sat right behind us at church and told us after Mass that we reminded her of her family when she was growing up. She had a heavy New York accent, and her scratchy voice sounded a lot like Louis Armstrong. It took no time at all for her to show us her heart of gold. She was married to "Pop Pop John," a retired NYPD officer, and they had seven grown children. She instantly adopted us as part of her brood. The more I got to know her, the more I admired her. Always on the go, always helping people in need, caring for the ill and elderly members in her family and in the community, she was courageous and prayerful. Her faith was strong, and her memory was sharp as a tack. She not only amazed us by learning all our kids' names and birthdays, but she reminded them of what saint's feast day fell on their birthday. She always included a holy card with their birthday card, along with her famous two dollar bills and hug coupons. One day, while I was very pregnant with baby number nine, she called to tell me that she was coming to pick up all the kids to take them blueberry picking. She told me how she remembered how busy it was having little ones, and she wanted to give me a couple of hours to take a nap. It was one of the best gifts that I could have ever received. Not only did she take them to pick blueberries, but she brought them home for dinner and a family bonfire. The kids came home tired, dirty, with full bellies and loads of stories. We loved Mom Mom, and we felt loved by her.

One afternoon while folding laundry, shortly after moving into the house, I got a call from a lady with a Texas accent. She told me that she was a dispatcher with the Southlake DPS. She wanted to let me know that she and her fourteen-year-old-son had adopted Twix and that he was doing great. We had all been wondering about his fate. I was so relieved by her call and thrilled that he had found a family and a second chance. She said she wanted to send us his name tag since it had our old address on it. She thought we may want it as a keepsake. Giving Twix up had been bittersweet. We knew it was the right decision, but we still missed him.

Finding an ob-gyn in New York was no easy task for me. I was sad to leave Dr. MacDonald, only four months before my due date. Joe and I even considered flying me back to Texas to deliver but decided that it would be ridiculously impractical, not to mention risky. My pregnancy had been uneventful, and I felt great. After two appointments with two different doctors who didn't impress me, I decided to try one more before giving up. I figured I could always just show up at the hospital when the time came. Thankfully, I did find a great doctor from a completely different network who was a great fit. She was very kind and caring. Once, when I had been detained because of a horrific car accident that had stopped traffic for miles, she waited after office hours for me to arrive. I had called her twice on my way to apologize for the long delay, but she told me not to worry, that she would wait. The accident had been reported all over the country. When I finally arrived at the office, after three hours of stop-and-go traffic in the heat of the summer, she took an unopened water bottle from her purse and told me to drink it all before she would let me leave.

When I arrived at the hospital on the day of my induction, she stayed with me after her shift had ended, and a different doctor had come on. She'd been with me the whole day, laughing and chatting with Joe and me, and she said she didn't want to miss the birth. A couple of the nurses had stayed as well, poking their heads into the room to check on my progress. A few of them found me the next day after I had settled in my room. They told me how much they had enjoyed meeting Joe and me and that they would never forget us. I guess we were something of a novelty. More than a few of them told us that it was refreshing to see a couple who were so in love and who clearly loved their children. It was both flattering and a bit surprising. I didn't realize we were such a rarity. Katherine Mary Anne, named after St. Katherine Drexel, the Blessed Mother, and St. Anne, was born on July 21, 2005.

My mother had hinted that she wanted to come for the birth. She hadn't been to our new house yet. After mentioning more than once that she didn't feel up to the seven-hour drive, I asked Joe to send her a plane ticket. She told me that my youngest sister really wanted to come too, so Joe sent her a ticket as well. Joe picked them up from the airport the day before my scheduled induction. As soon as they arrived, my mother settled herself into Joe's big leather chair, exasperated from her flight. She quickly began voicing her displeasure of the fact that they did not have a direct flight from Toronto to New York, but instead booked a connecting flight from Buffalo. It was less expensive, and we were trying to watch our budget. Joe was traveling less in his new role, and wasn't racking up as many frequent-flyer miles. That event set the tone for the remainder of the visit. She had been the one to insist on being there. We told her that Marge had offered to take care of the kids when the time came. Marge had told us to call her, day or night, but my mother wouldn't hear of it. Once she arrived, she complained about how horrible the flight had been and how they could have arrived quicker if they had driven the seven hours, and would have been less exhausted. I worried whether she would be up to babysitting while I was in the hospital. I hoped that I would be in and out quickly.

Katie was tiny and looked like an exact clone of her big sister Grace. At six pounds and five ounces, she had the same piercing blue eyes and blond hair. Just like Grace, Katie was jaundiced. Three days after being released from the hospital, she was readmitted to go under the lights. It was worrisome for me to return to the hospital, not so much for Katie's sake, I had been through that before, I was more concerned with the rest of the kids who were home with my mother. Once the jaundice levels stabilized and Katie was released, we were all relieved to be home together again. It had been a hot and gorgeous summer, and we were grateful for the pool that we didn't think we wanted. My mother and sister spent most of their visit outside, poolside with the kids. I was sent to my room with strict orders to stay in bed. My mother told me that she would leave if I came out. She said she would consider it an indication that her services were no longer needed. Obviously, I was free to come or go at will. She certainly hadn't chained me to my room, but she laid a guilt trip on me. I just wanted to visit with everyone with our new baby. We were all ready for her to leave, but I didn't want her to know it, so I obeyed. My kids told me later that all they wanted to do was see the new baby and visit in my room, but Grandma wouldn't let them. When she discovered that a couple of them had snuck up, she ushered them out, despite my protests. She even set up a barricade at the bottom of the stairs and sat in a chair so they couldn't get past.

When I heard Mom Mom Marge's distinct Louie Armstrong voice at the front door and realized that my mother was not about to let her in, I sent Joe to intercept. He led her up to our room. She brought little books for the kids and gushed over Katie with tears in her eyes. She told me how happy she was that God had placed us in her life. She only stayed for a few minutes. I'm not sure if it was because she was in a hurry or that she sensed that my mother didn't want any intruders. Several gifts had been left by other neighbors who had come to call with congratulations. I had been through it all before. Rather than get upset, I waited until my mother left to introduce our new baby.

We got to know our neighbors really well over the summer. We held impromptu pool parties and BBQs. We spent time visiting over coffee and drinks. When the weather cooled down, we hosted Friday night bonfires in our backyard. Our concrete patio had an odd square cut out of the center of it. None of us could figure out what the idea behind it was, so we decided to put an iron chiminea in the spot. Our backyard became a gathering place. It backed onto a woods, and was surrounded by trees and fallen limbs, so there was never a shortage of firewood. The kids planned weekly for what had become a sort of ritual, inviting their friends and all the kids from the neighborhood. While the adults sat around the fire enjoying our neighbor Tony's Grey Goose cocktails, the kids played manhunt in the dark. They roasted marshmallows and hot dogs and told stories under the stars. Friday night bonfires lasted up until the first snowfall. The kids snuggled under sleeping bags, sipping hot chocolate, and eating s'mores. None of us wanted them to end. They were, by far, the sweetest memories of our time in New York.

We made our first road trip to Canada six weeks after Katie was born. We attended a family reunion in Sarnia, Ontario. My mother's hometown. The last time that we had seen all of my extended family had been at Gramma Hubbard's funeral, ten years earlier. Joe and I had been married for almost fifteen years and had nine kids. We didn't want to miss the opportunity to show off our family. We wanted everyone to see that we had made it, just in case there were any lingering doubts. The reunion was a fun time. All of us cousins remarked on how much everyone had grown and aged. We introduced spouses and children who hadn't yet met, pondering over how strange a thing time is. How we all thought everyone should look the same as the last time we saw each other. There were some unspoken tensions, typical I suppose for most families, and no doubt more notably in larger ones. There were whispers and chatter about who was in and who was out, and who didn't show up. We avoided it. We spoke to everyone and treated them all the same, and of course, we were much too busy keeping track of our own kids to get involved in any gossip or drama. My mother remained in her comfort zone, surrounding herself with her own kids. She gushed over her grandchildren, mine included. It was not at all typical of how she behaved with them when she didn't have an audience. It was somewhat confusing for my kids, and for me. She had never been the spoiling, doting, granny type. She was more like a sterner version of me. I wanted to believe that she must love my kids in her own way, but she was always so unpredictable and erratic. I went along with her show of affection, happy that she seemed to be enjoying my kids.

After the reunion, we visited with old friends in Cambridge and Niagara Falls. Regrettably, we never went to see my *mémère*, or any of my dad's relatives. So much time had passed. I felt that it would have been too awkward to just show up after so many years, especially after we had abandoned them with no explanation. We stayed at the DoubleTree Hotel in Niagara Falls. The Orsini family had sold the Ramada Coral Inn Suites and Conference Center and opened up the Fallsview DoubleTree Resort. It was great to see them all again. Their family had been a big part of my life. Working for them was how Joe and I had met. Their families had all grown, and the third generation was involved in the business. I admired their family, and it was wonderful to see the fruits of their labor.

We had Katie baptized at Our Lady of the Scapular Church in Niagara Falls, where our priest friend had been appointed pastor, and Christina made her First Holy Communion on the same day. Our trip had been pleasant and memorable, and we decided that since we lived so close, we would return for Boxing Day, the day after Christmas. It had always been the day that our family got together to celebrate. We decided to again stay at the DoubleTree, declining my mother's invitation to stay with them. We knew that we would be more comfortable having the option to leave should things become tense, and we knew from past experiences that the chances were good that they would.

The kids all seemed to be happy in their new schools. Their first full year was a few months underway, and Patrick was still struggling. His teacher seemed to think it was attention related and encouraged us to have him assessed by a pediatric neurologist. We thought that sounded a little extreme. Patrick had never been hyper. He was a typical kid, an active boy who liked to play outside with his friends, riding his bike, and on occasion, played video games. His main struggle was with math, but he was otherwise incredibly bright. The IEP that we had brought from his Texas school had not been implemented in the same way at his new school, for reasons unknown to us. Feeling unsettled, considering the possibility that we may have missed something, we made an appointment with a neurologist. We wanted to help Patrick succeed in school however we could. In the waiting room, we filled out pages of questions while Patrick was assessed by the doctor. Once the assessment was complete, Joe and I were called back for the results and a prescription for Adderall. Patrick had ADD. Joe and I were stunned. I felt sick. We filled the prescription and hoped that Patrick would have an easier time focusing at school. After two weeks on the medication, Patrick felt horrible. He had no appetite, was nauseated, and said that he felt like a zombie. I could see the light going out in his eyes. I threw the pills away. We decided to cut sugar out of his diet and gave him and the rest of the kids a multivitamin. We told Patrick that we didn't care if he got straight As, we just wanted him to do his best and work hard. If he needed extra help, we would be there for him. He seemed to have much less anxiety once we let him know that grades weren't the most important thing in the world and that we cared more about his health and well-being.

FIFTEEN

U-Turn

Central Valley, New York, 2006

Joe was not happy in his new role. In fact, he had begun to regret taking it at all. After realizing that things were not going to work out, I remember him mentioning one of his favorite sayings from a Clint Eastwood movie, "Every good man knows his limitation." So shortly after the new year, he accepted a new role in the firm: National Director for Emergency Response and Crisis Management. Even though it was not an HR job, he jumped at it. It was a role that was born out of a response to 9/11, and there were other benefits, including national scope and the freedom to work in any city where there was a KPMG office, but the job didn't pay as much as he had been making in New York. It payed about the same as he was making in Dallas, so he decided it made the most sense to move back to Southlake.

All our other moves made sense. This one didn't. Not only was I sick of moving, it was not part of our plan. We should have been returning to Canada by that point, not going back to Texas. It was like going in reverse, rather than ahead toward our goal, and it was the lowest point in our marriage. I was not happy. Joe was incredibly stressed out. He had been for pretty much the entire time we lived in New York, but he did a good job of hiding it, hoping that things would improve. We had all made friends and were having fun, really enjoying life. We loved our neighbors, our parish, and Mom Mom Marge. I lay awake many nights, trying to figure out a way to stay. I begged Joe to try to work out some other deal with his boss. He assured me that he had explored every option, and felt that moving back to Texas was the best one for our family. I was angry. I am ashamed to say that for more than a fleeting moment, I wanted him to go to Dallas by himself and leave us in New York. I shudder when I remember how dark that time was.

One day over the phone, I made the mistake of complaining to my mother. It was no secret that I was miserable. The kids knew it, Joe knew it, my neighbors even knew it. My mother and sister Thérèse decided to come for a surprise visit on my birthday. Joe had been in on their surprise. Sworn to secrecy by my mother, he hadn't breathed a word to me or any of the kids. He told me later that he had only agreed to it because he thought it would cheer me up and get me out of my slump. It didn't. When I saw my mother's van parked in the driveway upon returning home from the grocery store, I didn't recognize it right away. After pulling into the garage, my mother emerged from the laundry room door that led into the garage, laughing at my stunned reaction. Not being in the frame of mind to appreciate the humor or the surprise, I wondered how long she was staying. Then I saw Thérèse, and my mood softened a bit. I was not thrilled to see my mother, and I instantly regretted sharing my frustrations with her over the phone. She knew all too well that I was unhappy about our upcoming move. I sensed that she was more interested in getting an inside view of the drama than she was in trying to cheer me up. We had been living in our house for a year. The only other time that she had come to visit was when Katie was born. It dawned on me that my mother only ever came around when there was a crisis or life-changing event. She never seemed interested in coming when we invited her for a visit when life was normal and things were calm and going well.

We had just listed our house on the market. Our real estate agent had come by to put the For Sale sign up on the front lawn the day before, warning us that perspective buyers would be showing up to look at it soon. I had geared myself back into house-showing mode and had a million things to do. There were closets and cabinets to organize and clutter to eliminate. There were things that we knew we wouldn't need in Texas that we planned to donate, like all the winter gear we had just bought—coats, boots, snow pants, sleds, and cold-weather clothing. I made lists of what we would bring and what we would be getting rid of. I tried to be a good host, doing my best to hide my feelings of annoyance at the poorly timed surprise, but my mind raced with all that I needed to do. When the call came a few hours later for a showing, I went into a frenzy. A combination of the stress, brought on by the impromptu visit, and the reality that we were indeed moving, set me into a craze. Knowing perfectly well, due to my OCD, that my house was cleaner and more organized than most, even on a bad day, I still felt compelled to go through the ritual of checking every last detail. I needed to make sure that the house was spotless and meticulously organized, even all the spaces that no one would ever look. There could be no fingerprints or smudges, bathrooms had to be sterile and shining, and all the laundry washed, dried, folded, ironed, and put away. Every drawer was organized. Fridge, freezer, and pantry were cleaned and neat. Floors were washed, furniture was dusted, and vacuum lines evenly spaced on the carpets. Every picture, knickknack, and sofa cushion was put in position. Not one detail was left unchecked. Going through my ritual was not something that I could accomplish while my mother was there. She wasn't about to help me with any of it. I didn't expect, nor did I want her to, but she didn't want me to do it either. Her attitude was for me to just relax. She was on vacation, and she wanted me to visit with her.

"Too bad for them."

Were her exact words when I told her that I needed to get the house ready for the showing. She told me that I shouldn't go crazy cleaning. It was our home, we had kids, and it was lived in. People expected that. What I knew to be a fact was that while she was in the process of selling her house, she cleaned every inch of it every time there was a showing, and even called to tell me everything she had done to get it ready. It was no secret to any of my family how OCD I was about my house. When I insisted that I needed to do what I needed to do, she turned it all around and made it all about her. She told me how unappreciative I was that she and my sister had taken time out of their lives to drive all the way to New York to visit me for my birthday. How they wanted to cheer me up, but I would rather spend the time cleaning my already clean house. Wasn't that nice? They may as well turn right around and go back home. The all too familiar guilt trip. I melted into a crying mess. I was the woman of my house, and there was my mother, coming in to take over again. I did a quick once-over of the house and spent the next two days visiting with my mother and very uncomfortable sister. I couldn't wait for my mother to leave.

I was barely civil with Joe. I had always supported him in his career. Up until that point, things had been working out very well and were going according to our plan. I had been enjoying the ride. Now that things were not going my way, I grew more and more resentful. I was tired of my life being constantly turned upside down because of his career. I didn't like the fact that our plan was being changed. It felt like everything was out of my control. When the time came for us to fly to Texas for our first house-hunting trip, I was not at all excited. I was actually pretty snotty about the whole thing, a Debbie Downer, a real negative pessimist. I told Joe to go pick out a house on his own for us, and he could take the kids with him. Of course I wasn't serious. I couldn't not be involved in such a big decision, and there was no way I would let the kids fly without me. I had such a dark grip on me that I couldn't even utter a positive word to him. The kids were all excited about being part of the search for a new house. They sensed the tension between us, and they sided with Joe, no doubt because I was being such a witch. I hated the way I was behaving. It was like I was outside of myself, watching myself behave badly, but I just couldn't stop. Joe made all the arrangements, and I basically went along for the ride.

We flew to Texas during Easter break and stayed at the brand-new Gaylord Texan Resort in Grapevine. We had reserved two connecting suites, but upon our check-in, only one of them was available. Someone hadn't checked out of the second one. They told us they had an available suite on another floor and that the adjacent one that we should have had would be available the next night. It was just one more irritation for me, another reason to grumble and complain. I didn't even try to hide my bad mood. I complained out loud. As my ears heard my voice, I hated the sound of it, but it just kept spewing out miserable words. It was ugly. I felt ugly. I snatched the room key from Joe, spun on my heel, and walked toward my room, not caring which of the kids were following me. I let him worry about that. I carried baby Katie, and some of the other kids scrambled to keep up. They all wanted to stay with their dad, but half of them came with me. I must have made them feel horrible. Joe and I never fought about anything, and it was making our kids feel torn. One of the suites would have been plenty big enough for all of us. At that point though, I didn't want to be near Joe, and I am pretty sure he didn't want to be around me either. He went to his room with the rest of the kids, and I didn't even say goodnight to him. I ordered room service for us and went to bed. The next morning, we all met for breakfast at the River Walk Café, inside the hotel. I desperately wanted to stop being a downer. A negative energy had consumed me. I was aware of it, I didn't like it, but it was almost impossible to shake. It was trying to divide my happy family. I know now that it was most definitely the devil, but at the time, I was oblivious.

We met with our realtor, the same one we had hired to help us find a house the first time we moved to Southlake. He showed us a bunch of houses. There wasn't one that we liked. More fuel for my grumbling. I was convinced that we would never find a house that I would be happy with. I wanted to go back to the house that we had sold in Meyers Meadow and ask the owners if we could buy it back. Of course we didn't. Why in the world did we ever move out of it in the first place?

We returned to the hotel with plans to meet with the realtor the next day to try again. We picked up the key to our suite, which was finally available, and headed to the restaurant for dinner. As the kids colored their menus and discussed what to order, I looked across the table at Joe. My poor husband had been trying so hard to please me, despite being under an enormous amount of pressure. I was making it worse by being pouty and pushing him away. He looked so tired, and I loved him so much. I was sorry for being such a brat. When our eyes locked, all I saw was love. He wasn't angry with me. He had been waiting for me to work through my snit. I decided at that moment to get with the program and be part of the team that we had always been. We had never fought about anything before that. Any disagreements we ever had were minor and quickly resolved. We loved each other too much to stay angry. I had so much to be thankful for. Smiling, as I gazed around the table at my family, the ice had been broken, and we all relaxed. I didn't want my children walking on eggshells around me. I told them I was sorry and promised to stop being such a grouch. I started to feel their excitement over moving back to our old stomping grounds.

After another delicious breakfast at the River Walk Café, our agent told us about a new listing. An older one-owner home in a part of Southlake that we didn't even know existed. Southview was a mature, secluded, tree-lined neighborhood, within walking distance from Southlake Town Square. It was what one of our new neighbors called Southlake's best kept secret. The house was on a large, three-quarter acre treed lot, with a Walton's-style front porch. A two-story house with dormers and pillars on the front, it was not a typical-looking Southlake home. The covered porch, framed by a hedgerow of Holly and Indian Hawthorn, was shady and cool despite the already warm Texas weather. Heavy natural wood trim took our breath away when we stepped through the front entrance. Our agent told us that the home had been custom built by the owner. The quality and attention to detail was evident throughout. The ceilings in the family room and kitchen were framed with wide oak beams, while the ones in the formal living and dining rooms were recessed. Every room and hallway on the main floor bore heavy crown molding and high baseboards. There were six spacious bedrooms in all, four upstairs and two down, and four and a half bathrooms. The gourmet eat in kitchen was equipped with an island, double ovens, cooktop, side by side subzero fridge and freezer, dishwasher, and ice maker. Sunlight poured in through the large bay window at the sink, the wall of windows in the family room, and the double French doors that led to the in-ground pool. The main floor laundry room was a dream, the largest I had ever seen, with loads of cabinets and counter space. It was right across the hall from the kitchen, and was even equipped with a laundry chute. What we called the West Wing of the house, was a sort of private retreat that could be closed off from the rest of the dwelling. The home office and bonus room, both with their own entrances, one leading to the front of the house and one to the backyard, were separated by their own doors; but they both connected to the master bedroom. The bedroom itself was not the largest we had ever had, but it was definitely cozy and bright, with two large windows on either side of the room. It had built-in book-shelves, cabinets, and a fireplace. It was all the space we needed. The concern we had over where to put our dressers was put to rest when we walked through the huge en suite, into the walk-in closets. There were built-in dressers, shelves, and hanging space for more clothes than Joe and I owned combined. Each bedroom had a spacious walk-in closet with built-in dressers, and all the upstairs bedrooms had window box storage seats in each dormer, and built-in drawers in the wall. The use of storage was limitless. Built-ins, cabinets, drawers, closets, and shelves were tucked in every available space. Even the three-car garage had a drop-down ladder leading up to a storage loft, and there was a climate-controlled dog room with a doggie door. There were two driveways (one in the back and a circular one in the front), outdoor lighting, decorative fencing, and hedges. The back-yard was fenced and private, with loads of space for the kids and dog to run, play, and swim.

The house had been handpicked for our family. Joe and I fell in love with it immediately. It was a little dated, with much too much plaid and striped wallpaper and heavy draperies, and the col-ors were not my favorite, but it had great solid bones. We saw past the cosmetics. The wool carpets were in excellent shape, and there was hardwood and tile throughout the rest of the main floor. It was 4,600 square feet of perfectly-thought-out living space. It was conveniently located to the highway for Joe's commute to Dallas, and the airport, and close to the kids' schools and shopping. We put in an offer, the seller's asking price, and it was accepted that day. A huge relief for all of us. We went to Anamia's to celebrate. We shared our excitement with a few of the servers who remembered us. They were excited to hear that we were moving back. We went to nine o'clock Mass at St. Francis. Fr. Ken and many of our old friends were surprised but delighted to see us back. What were the odds of us returning to the exact same town we had moved from only a year before? It didn't make much sense to us, and Joe and I both wondered why we were being brought back. It was the first time we considered that it might be God's plan, not our plan. And that He had some reason for bringing us back. Some unfinished business perhaps? We had no idea what His reasons were, but we tried to keep an open mind about it, hoping that it would be revealed to us at some point.

Joe's relocation package for the move back to Texas was not the full meal deal like we had enjoyed in all our previous moves. KPMG paid for our house-hunting trip and accommodations, and the cost of our physical move, including flights, pets, and shipping our vehicles. They didn't however guarantee the sale of our house. We weren't terribly concerned. Our house was nice, less than five years old, and sat in a very desirable neighborhood. In the year and a half that we had lived in it, we'd made several improvements. We'd had the whole house painted, hired my dad to pull out the carpet and install hardwood in the family room, and we'd spent thousands of dollars on landscaping. Because everything had been covered in snow when we looked at the house, we didn't find out till spring that there was no grass in the backyard. Our front lawn was lush and green, but the backyard was a much different story. The dirt, weeds, rocks, piles of leaves and fallen tree limbs were revealed when the snow finally melted. The previous owners had installed the pool, concrete patio, and an iron fence, but they had done zero planting. Once it got warm enough, we rolled up our sleeves and dragged out all our garden tools. We raked out the stones, gathered up the tree limbs, and filled more than forty giant bags of leaves. We hired a crew to lay sod and line the side yard with spruce trees. After discovering a fabulous little nursery in Rockland County, I made multiple trips to purchase flowering annuals and perennials. I filled in the enclosed pool area with colorful plantings and covered the wrought iron fence with moonflowers and morning glories. Since the pool area had been fenced in but not gated off from the rest of the patio, we hired a fencing company to install more fencing and a locking gate to keep it safe for the little kids. We tore down the tiny deck and hired a guy to build a Trex deck across the whole length of the back of the house, complete with a trellis for hanging baskets. We moved a flowering cherry tree that had been planted too close to the house, and transplanted it into the circle flower bed in the center of the driveway. We had become experts at home improvements, but we were growing weary of leaving all our hard work behind for someone else to enjoy. It was a good house, and we felt sure that it would sell. We had several showings, and everyone that came through complimented the tasteful decor, beautiful yard, and gardens. They remarked on how clean and organized everything was, in disbelief that nine children lived there.

We finally got an offer. It was way lower than our asking price, so we countered it. They didn't counter back. We were determined not to give our house away, but as time wore on, we grew more anxious. It was the perfect time of year to show. The pool was crystal clear and the flowers were in full bloom. We lived on edge, slaves to the house, always expecting a call, but the showings dwindled. The people who had put in the first offer came back for a second look and made a second one. It was even lower than the first. We were flabbergasted and more than a little annoyed. They must have thought we were desperate. We countered again. There was no way we way we were going to settle that low. We had put so much into the place, improving and adding value to it. We needed to at least break even. I knew they wanted the house, but they didn't counter back.

My mother had told me about the novena to St. Joseph. I loved St. Joseph and had prayed novenas to him in the past, though I hadn't heard about the novena to sell a house before. Mom Mom Marge had given me a little plastic statue, and I accidentally dropped it, knocking off his head. I glued it back on before following the instructions of the novena. Even though it seemed like a superstition, and made me feel a little weird, if not sacrilegious to treat one of my favorite saints in such an undignified manner, I buried him, upside down, on the front lawn next to the For Sale sign. I prayed the novena. We didn't get any more offers. I wondered if it may have been because my St. Joseph had been decapitated. We would have to move to Texas with our New York house still unsold.

Saying goodbye was sad. We had made fast friends with so many great people. We tried to squeeze in as many fun times as we could before we left. When we told our pastor, Fr. Travers, that we were moving, he asked me to write something to put into the bulletin. Puzzled by his request, I asked him what it was that he wanted me to write. He said he wanted me to share our secret about how we always managed to get our family to Mass, on time, dressed nicely, and so well-behaved. He thanked us for being a good example for the parish. Joe and I were incredibly humbled by his compliments. As pastor, he was kind of reserved, and we had no idea that he had taken that much notice of us. I dutifully printed off our note, thanking the parish for being such a wonderful home for our family during our short time in New York. I offered a few words about how we made Mass a big deal for our family and insisted on proper dress and good behavior. The little request from Fr. Travers got Joe and I wondering if maybe God was using our family for something, though we weren't exactly sure what.

When the movers came to start packing, Joe kept the kids occupied while I scrubbed my way out of each room as it was emptied of our stuff. It was the first time we would be moving out of an unsold house, and I wanted to make sure that it was show perfect for the people who would be coming through. I scrubbed and touched up every scuff mark on every wall, and cleaned the few spots I found on the carpets. Before we left, the windows sparkled, bathrooms were sanitized, and floors gleamed. One of the movers who had been packing for two days apparently noticed my cleaning frenzy. He smiled, shook his head, and said, "Ma'am, you are the hardest-working woman I have ever met."

I laughed and thanked him for noticing. We arranged to have the lawn mowed by our regular crew until the house sold, and we made a deal with our next-door neighbors. They could use the pool if they agreed to maintain it till the end of the season. We moved out at the end of the school year. It was the exact same time of year we had moved to Southlake the first time around.

SIXTEEN

Southlake Part Deux

Southlake, Texas, 2006–2007

$\mathcal{J}$oe and I were fairly certain that God must have had some reason for bringing us back to the very same city for a second time. We wondered if there was some unfinished business He had with us there. There was a certain level of curiosity and excitement as we made our journey back. We began looking for clues to solve the mystery. We stayed at the Gaylord Texan again, and both our connecting suites were available the very first night. We watched the Fourth of July fireworks over Lake Grapevine from our balcony, the mood was light, all of us excited about our new house and being back on familiar turf. We still had the New York house hanging over our heads, but we tried not to let it spoil the fun. We decided instead to enjoy the adventure, believing that the house would sell in due time. We spent the days at the new house, letting the kids swim and explore their new surroundings while I cleaned. We took advantage of the house being empty before the movers arrived with our stuff. There was a lot of house to clean. I scrubbed every surface and washed down walls, trim, doors, and light fixtures. I used wood cleaner on all the cabinets and built-ins and lined the kitchen drawers with vinyl liners. I cleaned from top to bottom, scrubbed every floor, scoured every bathroom, and shined all the windows. The house was in good shape, it just needed freshening up. It needed my special touch.

Joe and I decided, upon closer inspection, that it really needed painting. We called a bunch of painters from the yellow pages to see if we could get the house painted while it was still empty. We found one that was available who promised to get the job done before the movers arrived. We let the kids choose the colors for their rooms, and we settled on a neutral color for the rest of the house. Fully anticipating that we would paint again at some point in the near future, our goal was to just freshen things up. Hiring painters out of the yellow pages had not been a wise decision; in fact, it was a small disaster. They had grossly miscalculated the time it would take to complete the job, mostly because they showed up late and finished early each day. They worked slowly, and once the movers arrived, everyone was in each other's way. When they finally finished and returned for touch-ups, they used the wrong paint and had to return multiple times to fix their mistakes. I regretted being so hasty and not doing more research. It was not typical of how I tackled projects. I hadn't been able to find the painter we had hired at our previous Southlake house. Even though the paint job was mediocre, the walls did look cleaner and the house felt fresh. We began enjoying our new place.

Back to familiar territory, we picked up where we had left off. The kids easily reconnected with old friends and looked forward to a new school year. We got a call from our real estate agent in New York, telling us that there was another offer received. Incredulously, it had come from the very same perspective buyer. We had only received three offers, and all three came from the same couple. Their third offer had been even lower than the first two. To say that we were stunned would be an understatement. We accepted the insulting offer with a bitter taste in our mouths and had some pretty choice words and names for the new owners. We had never been the shrewd business type, and we weren't accustomed to dealing with people who were. We sold the house at a loss, but decided that it was better than paying two mortgages indefinitely. The closing date was set for December. We prayed that they wouldn't back out. One morning, as the closing date drew near, we got a call from a lawyer who worked in our realtor's office. I answered, half panicked that the buyers had found some loophole and decided to back out. She said that she'd received a phone call from the buyer's agent, asking if we would be nice enough to allow the new owners to move some of their things into the garage a week prior to their closing date. Laughing out loud upon hearing the request, I told her, "No way."

We were relieved to finally be rid of the house and extra expenses. More than a million dollars of mortgages combined with our new house. It wasn't fun. We certainly weren't rich, and much of our savings had been eaten up.

Katie was sixteen months old when I discovered I was pregnant with baby number ten, around Thanksgiving time. Before Joe and I got married, we'd loosely discussed that we'd like to have five or six kids. We had crept up to nearly double those numbers, but we took it all in stride. There always seemed to be room for one more. People on the outside were always astonished, dumbfounded really, that we were so open to having so many children. We didn't think that much about it. Joe had a great job, earned a handsome salary, and I was lucky enough to be able to stay home with my kids. Note I said *lucky*. That's how I viewed our life in those days. Like it was a mixture of luck and our own doing. We weren't rich and didn't live extravagantly, but we were more than comfortable and had a nice life.

I was delighted to be pregnant again once I got over the initial surprise. I felt fantastic, had loads of energy, and no morning sickness whatsoever. Being that it was my tenth pregnancy, my belly quickly began to grow. I had always been able to lose weight in between babies, but my increased appetite and change of hormones made me ready for maternity clothes almost immediately. I made an appointment with Dr. MacDonald right away. I hadn't seen him since my five-month checkup with Katie before we moved to New York. I knew that he would certainly be surprised to see me back in Texas, pregnant again. It was like old home week when I arrived. He was delighted that our family was still growing. It was fun catching up, and he shared that he and his wife were expecting as well. I took care of getting the blood work done right away. My ultrasound showed that I was five weeks pregnant, a little less than I had calculated. I drove home, excited to show Joe and the kids the ultrasound picture of our new little baby. When you have nine kids, there are no secrets.

It only took a few days for the whole elementary school to find out our news. We didn't care who knew, we were thrilled. The pattern remained consistent. New job, new house, new baby.

Joe worked from home a lot since he wasn't required to work out of any particular office. Now and then he worked out of an empty office in Dallas. He did travel some, but for the most part, he worked from home. The home office was ideal for him. It was soundproof and closed off from the rest of the house. He put in more than eight hours a day. The nature of his new role kept him on high alert, and on call, 24/7. He was responsible for business continuity in the event of storms, power failures, terrorist attacks, natural disasters, and anything that interrupted business. He monitored the news closely for any and all activity in all areas of the country where there was a KPMG office. I enjoyed making his lunch and bringing him coffee, and I loved the convenience of being able to pop out when the little girls napped, knowing he was home. I was able to help out at the school, get my hair and nails done, and have lunch with my friends.

I set up appointments with our old pediatrician and dentist and made an appointment with the cardiologist for Callum's checkup. We were happy to learn that there was a new off-site clinic where he could get his echo and EKG done, in Grapevine. Much closer than the long drive to Cook Children's in Fort Worth. The time between Callum's checkups were always a mixture of worry and relief. I was relieved that he hadn't needed surgery, but at the back of my mind was the reality that eventually he would. Callum was five years old, and had never needed medication for his heart defect. His murmur was apparently quite interesting according to his pediatrician. At his well-check, Dr. Nichols called all the nurses into the exam room to listen to the whooshing sound it made. It wasn't your average, everyday heart murmur.

At the cardiology appointment, Callum was weighed, measured, and had an echo and EKG. He had gotten used to the procedures over the years and, thankfully, wasn't afraid anymore. He was old enough to lay still without sedation like when he was a toddler. Dr. Hess consulted with me after checking all the tests. She didn't beat around the bush. She said it was time for surgery. Because Callum was healthy, and his heart was functioning well, she wanted to correct the defect before things began to weaken. The only symptom we ever noticed was that his legs tired easily after playing hard or being in the heat. Dr. Hess's concern was that the aortic valve was becoming overtaxed. As the blood flowed, the valve got sucked through the hole, instead of simply opening and closing. It had to work twice as hard. Her fear was, if left untreated, Callum would need an artificial valve, and that would require medication for the rest of his life. Dr. Hess was surprised that the defect hadn't been corrected at birth or, at the very least, shortly thereafter. When I told her that he had been born in Canada and that the cardiologist had taken a "wait and see" approach, she wasn't surprised. At the time, Canada's health care system was much different than the United States.

We had nine months to prepare for the surgery. It wasn't an emergency, but Dr. Hess wanted it done within a year. She scheduled it for the following September. We left the office feeling a lot of different emotions. Callum's first reaction was fear. He did not want the surgery. I didn't much like the thought of him going through it either, but I explained to him that once his heart was fixed, he wouldn't have to worry about it not working properly anymore. I put on my bravest face and acted calm and confident, but I felt like melting into a puddle of tears right along with him. I wished I could take his place. I was really afraid. Open-heart surgery was a big deal, not like getting stitches or breaking a leg. Joe was careful with his reaction when I told him, but I saw the concern on his face. We tried to remain positive and matter-of-fact, and we made sure that the other kids didn't get overly dramatic about it either. Callum worried most right before bedtime every night. He told me every night that he didn't want to have surgery and asked me if he was going to die. I did my best to reassure him that everything would be okay, but I silently wondered the same thing. We said prayers together and asked God to help him have a good surgery. We prayed for his doctors and for his heart to be completely fixed. Nine months was a long time to wait, but as the days passed, we became less anxious. It was always at the back of our minds, but we learned to live without obsessing over it.

Christmas was in the air. Decorating, baking, shopping, and preparing was well underway. Our new house was much bigger than any of our other ones, and I decorated every corner of it. Garlands wrapped in clear mini lights, and tied with festive bows, trimmed every doorway. The smell of cinnamon-scented pinecones filled the air. Two Christmas trees, decorated with ornaments that we had collected over the years; the lighted village houses that I painted when Callum was a baby; and the Christmas baubles that had travelled with us and survived so many moves—these were all on display. Curiously, I could not find the baby Jesus that went with my favorite nativity. I hunted and searched every box and bin and sent the kids to the garage to look through the packing paper. I feared that it may have been discarded with the recycling. It was the first Christmas since our move, and all the decorations had been packed up by our movers. Carols played loudly throughout the house for weeks on the television music channel. Us girls baked so many cookies and treats that we could have opened up our own sweet shop. We planned to make it our most festive Christmas yet. We enjoyed the Tree Lighting in Town Square and the concert that our girls sang in with their school choirs. Over the Christmas break, we gathered together on the couch to watch movies, with a bowl of popcorn and treats. For us, there was no better feeling in the world than basking in the glow of our family and the magic of the season.

Joe bought me a baby monitor for Christmas. Baby monitors had come a long way since Angela had been born. We had one for her, but we never used it. Always the gadget guy, the one Joe bought for me had a video camera screen. Laughing at the gift, knowing I most likely would never use it, I loved the fact that Joe was just as excited about our new little baby as I was. After the kids opened up their mountain of gifts and went up to try on new clothes, he handed me a tiny jewelry box. Joe has always had good taste in jewelry and has picked out a few nice pieces for me over the years. I opened the box to find a pair of platinum earrings with diamonds and emeralds. Our first Christmas in the new house had been close to perfect. I had found a mismatched infant to put in the nativity, but just couldn't keep from feeling a little sad that the baby Jesus was still missing.

Since all the kids were still home from school on Christmas break, we decided that we would all go for the car ride to my next doctor appointment. I had another ultrasound scheduled. The plan was for me to go in on my own while Joe waited in the van with the kids. We decided that we would get lunch on the way home and pick up Joe's dry cleaning. My appointments had always been quick, so I knew it wouldn't be a long wait for the kids. I smiled back at the van when I heard Joe crank up the crazy dance music while the kids went wild. I loved my family.

There was no wait at all, and the technician called me back right away for my ultrasound. We chatted about the holidays as she prepared me for the scan. The small talk ceased, and she grew incredibly silent as she ran the doplar over my belly. I tried to stay as still and quiet as possible, without the usual excited giggles and chatter. Sensing that something was not quite right, I stared at the screen and watched the tech's face as she concentrated on her work. I saw the little sac and the tiny form inside, slowly breathing my relief that she had finally found my little baby. She zoomed in to enlarge the image, concentrating intently. The baby was incredibly still. She turned to me sympathetically and told me she was sorry, there was no heartbeat. She got up and left the room to find Dr. MacDonald. I was stunned. No heartbeat? How could that be? Tears ran down my cheeks, but I didn't realize that I was crying. It seemed like an eternity before Dr. MacDonald came in. When he did, he was somber. He did a second scan before turning to me to tell me how sorry he was for my loss. I couldn't speak. It took every ounce of strength I had to keep myself from falling apart. He asked me if I wanted to call Joe. I told him that Joe was waiting in the van with all the kids. Oh God, he was outside in the van with the kids. How would I be able to tell him when I hadn't absorbed it yet myself? I told Dr. MacDonald that I just couldn't understand it. I had felt completely fine. Better than fine. I had no sickness or any pain. I asked him how my baby could have died without me even realizing it? He said he wished he knew. He told me that some women don't have any symptoms at all, and others suffer horribly. He said I was lucky to have been spared the physical pain, because the emotional loss would be difficult enough. He hugged me tightly and told me to call him with any concerns and that I should come back for a follow-up appointment. If the baby didn't pass on its own, I would need a D&C (dilation and curettage). Without stopping to chat with the receptionist on the way out like I typically did, I went right past her desk and out the door. Joe looked at me and knew right away that something was wrong. The lump in my throat choked me, leaving me unable to speak. The kids called out from their seats, "What is it? Did you find out if it's a boy or a girl?"

I quietly told Joe that there was no heartbeat. There wasn't going to be a new baby. He groaned out, "Oh no."

He squeezed my hand and held it all the way home. Angela, who had been sitting in the front row, must have overheard what I told Joe and passed word back to the other kids because there was a series of shushing sounds and multiple, "Just shut ups," before the van fell silent. Joe pulled into the dry cleaners around the corner from our house to pick up his shirts. He asked me if I wanted a coffee from the 7-Eleven, but I declined. I was numb. The life that had been growing inside of me had suddenly stopped, and I had no idea why or even when it happened. I felt empty. When Joe came out with his shirts, I caught a glimpse of the antique christening gown that was hanging with them. I had forgotten that I had asked him to take it in with his shirts. I wanted to have it starched and pressed so that it would be ready for the baptism. It was the christening gown that Gramma Hubbard had bought me for my baptism. All my kids wore it. I burst into tears when I realized there would be no baptism. I could do nothing but cry. I kept myself busy and tried not to cry in front of anyone, saving my tears for the shower or my pillow at night.

School started back, so the kids were gone during the day. Cleaning was how I had always dealt with my emotions. It was an outlet for me. I cleaned furiously, allowing the tears to flow as they came. I dismantled Christmas and packed it away, feeling even sadder about the still missing baby Jesus. Two babies lost at Christmas. I prayed that my little baby was with the baby Jesus in heaven. My heart was broken. I had never felt such sadness in my life. I scheduled the D&C.

Angela stayed home from school to take care of Sarah and Katie on the day Joe drove me to the hospital for the procedure. I decided to have a general anesthesia because I didn't want to be awake for it. Joe stayed with me until they came in and got my IV and sedation going. He was sweet and loving. I know he was just as sad as I was, but he stayed strong for me. I was awake when they wheeled me into the operating room, long enough to say hello to Dr. MacDonald. He smiled and patted me on the arm just before I fell asleep. There is no sense of time when you are under anesthesia, but I was told the whole thing only lasted several minutes. When I woke up in the recovery room, there were nurses bustling around me. They were taking notes, checking vitals, and chatting among themselves and the other patients. My nurse held my wrist, checking my pulse, and asked me how I was doing. I couldn't answer. She busied herself around me, checking monitors, and made small talk. She asked me if I'd had an abortion. If I'd been the least bit groggy from the anesthesia, her questions brought me back to full consciousness immediately. I looked directly at her, horrified, and told her that I had absolutely not had an abortion. I could not imagine why she would ask me such a thing. I had wanted my baby. How could she think that I would kill it? She apologized and said that she'd seen that my chart said D&C, so she assumed I'd had an abortion. I couldn't wait to go home.

Joe helped me to the car and drove me to Wendy's for a chicken sandwich. I hadn't been allowed to eat or drink anything since the night before, and I was starving. I cried all the way home. I cried just about every night into my pillow for weeks. I cried in the shower and every time I was alone. I couldn't sing at church without crying. Having to tell people who asked how I was feeling brought on more sadness for me, and awkwardness for them. When I saw Dr. MacDonald a few weeks later for my follow-up appointment, he couldn't explain why I'd lost the baby. He said that everything looked healthy and explained that it was more uncommon to have had nine consecutive pregnancies and births with no miscarriages, than it was to have several miscarriages. That surprised me, but it didn't take away my sadness. I wanted to give my baby a name. I didn't know if I had lost a boy or a girl, but I sensed that he was a boy, so I named him

Ryan Michael Noel. I had consecrated him to our Lady and found a prayer to baptize the unborn that I had saved from my active pro-life days. I had no doubt that God took my baby into His arms, and I hoped that if I made it to heaven, I would meet him one day. What gave me the most comfort was the thought of Gramma Hubbard, rocking him for me in heaven.

Having a busy household helped me to heal. Spring comes early in Texas, and with that, the urge to plant. Joe and I made multiple trips to the garden center to buy flats of annuals for the front and back gardens. I'd heard that the elementary school science teacher was putting together a garden club. I thought it would be a great opportunity for us to get involved at the school. When I talked to her about it and let her know that our family could work on Saturdays to weed and water, she got very excited. The gardens had become over-grown, and it needed a lot of work to get it back in shape. We put in many hours weeding, trimming, and thinning out plants, clearing the walkways, and sweeping gravel from the pavement. We moved mountains of mulch and spread it under all the plants. We stained the garden shed, picnic tables, and raised vegetable beds, and we organized the tools. By the end of April, we had completed a massive amount of work, and the entire family had been involved in one way or another. Angela was not much for gardening, so she stayed home with Katie and Sarah, who were too little to help. She baked and played with them and helped to tidy the house. It was an invaluable blessing for me because it allowed Joe and I to help at the school with the other kids. We worked hard in the garden and were proud of our family project. We returned home, stopping for a treat on the way, tired and dirty from a satisfying day of work.

When I pulled out the Easter decorations, I found the baby Jesus. He was wrapped up with the baskets and eggs. I was puzzled at how he had ended up with the wrong decorations, but I was thrilled to have found him. I was even more elated to discover that I was pregnant again. Finding the baby Jesus surely had to be a sign. I was completely excited and felt certain that everything would be okay. God had blessed us with another little life, and I could hardly believe it. Joe was just as thrilled. We told no one. We decided that we would wait at least three months before breathing a word. I tried to take it as easy as possible. I felt great, but I didn't want to overdo it. We continued to go to the school garden. All the hard work had been done; we were basically maintaining things like picking weeds, watering, and planting a few flowers every couple of weeks. Joe and the boys did the heavy work. The little kids picked weeds and wheeled the trash to the bins, while I swept off the paving stones and supervised. I made an appointment with Dr. MacDonald. He was excited to see that I was expecting again. He said he had no worries, enough time had passed since my miscarriage, and he expected that the pregnancy would be just fine. The ultrasound showed that I was five weeks, matching up with my calculations. I thanked God for the new little life. I completed the blood work in the next room and made another appointment. I called Joe on my way home to tell him that everything looked great. What a relief.

Two weeks later, I started spotting. Trying not to panic, I called Dr. MacDonald's office. His nurse advised me to stay calm and not to do anything strenuous. I went for an ultrasound that day, and everything seemed fine. Remembering my pregnancy with Grace, I tried to relax as much as I could. I put my feet up and didn't lift anything. Joe and the kids did everything. I begged God not to take my baby. Shortly after Mother's Day, I lost him. The experience was not at all the same as my first miscarriage. With the first one, there had been no signs or symptoms. With the second one, after spotting for a few days, I passed a large clot, containing a still closed sac. It was no blob of tissue. The size of the tip of my little finger, it had a bulging head and little specs of eyes behind transparent skin. I saw the little buds where arms and legs had begun to grow. It was a baby. I was in awe of the tiny creation. It looked exactly like the fetal development pictures I had seen so many times before, and I was holding it right there in the palm of my hand. I was crushed that his little life hadn't lasted longer than six or seven weeks. I had a bottle of holy water, and I sprinkled it over the baby, praying that God would take him to heaven. I placed him in a tiny earring box on top of the little cotton pad that was in the bottom of it. I called down the hallway to Joe. He came right away, and we closed the bedroom door before any of the kids came barging in. I showed him our little baby in the box. He was amazed. It was so surreal. We were heartbroken, but it was a gift to have been able to actually see and hold our tiny baby. We held each other while I cried into his shirt. Always my rock, I was so grateful for his strength and support. Joe took the little box outside and buried it under the big angel statue in the garden. Later that night, I cried into my pillow, wondering why God was punishing me. I tried to think back, retracing my steps, mentally reviewing my actions of the previous weeks. I tried to recall if I had missed taking my prenatal vitamins. I knew I had taken them every day. I didn't smoke, hadn't had any alcohol, and had reduced my coffee to two cups a day. I hadn't overexerted myself. I couldn't come up with one logical explanation. We were relieved that we hadn't told anyone, not even the kids. We wouldn't have any explaining to do. I cancelled my next prenatal appointment. I just couldn't bear going into the office and being surrounded by pregnant women and new babies. I didn't want to face Dr. MacDonald.

A few days after losing the baby, one of the kids left their lunch at home, so I took it to the school office. When I walked in, I was greeted with a heartfelt congratulations by the secretary. She had heard the good news from her daughter, who was in the same class as Christina. I was stunned. How in the world had she heard? We hadn't told any of our kids. I guessed that there was a possibility that Christina had overheard Joe and I talking, but it wasn't like her to mention something like that to her friends without asking us first. We had been so careful not to say anything about the baby around them. I must have looked confused because the secretary apologized, saying that perhaps she had been mistaken. I told her that I had just lost the baby, but that I was surprised that she knew because we hadn't told anyone. She looked horrified and apologized over and over again about blurting it out in the office. There were other people in there hearing our conversation, and they suddenly got very busy with their work. She said she was sorry for our loss. I hadn't meant to make her feel uncomfortable or awkward, but I was dumbfounded. I couldn't get out of the office fast enough. I told her not to worry about it, that it wasn't her fault. When I told Joe what had happened at the school, he was just as perplexed as me. We gently questioned Christina when she came home from school.

"Did you tell someone in your class that I was having another baby?"

It was her turn to be confused. She answered, "No. Why would I say that?"

I told her what the secretary had said to me at the school that morning. Christina told me that she had probably heard about her teacher, Mrs. Allen, who had told the class that she was expecting. It had been our intention to protect the children from the loss, but we found ourselves in a position where we had to explain. I was ready for the school year to be over and the summer to begin. I looked forward to the heat of the Texas sun and the pool water. Healing therapy to soothe my soul.

The time was quickly approaching for Callum's heart surgery. Callum was an August baby, one of the youngest kids in his class. In anticipation of him missing several weeks of school, Joe and I decided that we would have him repeat kindergarten. His teacher supported our decision. The much faster pace of first grade would have been a lot for him to catch up on, and we didn't want him struggling or falling behind. Callum didn't object to the plan, as long as he could have his same teacher. The school promised to arrange it. Summer in Southlake did not disappoint. We spent Saturday evenings at Town Square, enjoying the live bands. We watched the Fourth of July fireworks, went to the movies, and the Fort Worth Zoo. We enjoyed lazy pool days every day and ate BBQ almost every night. By the end of August, we were refreshed and ready to get back to a routine. We shopped for new clothes, shoes, and filled school supply lists. With sun-kissed skin, and hair streaked with golden highlights, the kids returned to school for another year. With Callum's surgery looming, it was even more bittersweet than usual.

My mother and I typically spoke over the phone about twice a month. She knew all about the surgery, and as the date approached, she told me she wanted to be there. Joe sent her a plane ticket. We expected that Callum would be in the hospital for at least five days. We had originally planned for Joe to deliver Callum and me to the hospital, where I would stay until he was discharged. When my mother told us she wanted to help, we decided to take her up on her offer. We knew she would be capable of managing all nine kids, the cooking, laundry, and homework, allowing Joe and I to both stay at the hospital during the time that Callum was in surgery. We hadn't seen my mother in a year and a half, not since her surprise visit to New York. Time and distance had blurred any bad memories. All the kids' teachers were aware that Callum would be having surgery, and they told us not to worry about anything school related. In an effort to make things simpler for my mother, we arranged for them to buy lunch in the school cafeteria. I prepared and froze dinners, and we stocked the fridge, freezers, and pantry so she wouldn't have to stress over meals. The morning after my mother arrived, Joe and I took Callum to Cook Children's Hospital for his pre-op procedures and paperwork. He did surprisingly well through all of it, except for the blood work. That was traumatic. We met with the surgeon, Dr. Erez, who explained to Callum the importance of fixing his heart. While Joe and I signed the insurance forms and releases, Callum watched a video on heart surgery. He watched the entire thing, wide-eyed, in silence. My stomach was in knots. That was a Friday. The surgery was scheduled for the following Monday. We were told to be at the hospital by eleven o'clock. We took Callum out to Kincaid's Burgers for lunch, and did our best to keep the mood light over the weekend. My mother wanted to pick up a few things at Walmart. Knowing that I would be occupied with Callum after the surgery, and likely not in any mood to go shopping, I took her the Saturday before. I was completely preoccupied with worry.

We went to nine o'clock Mass on Sunday, and I asked all our friends and the little praying ladies who I knew to say some extra prayers for Callum and his surgeon. I begged God to fix his heart and let him live a long, healthy life. Knowing how nervous Callum was, all the kids were extra sweet to him. They played whatever he wanted, read him stories, and they all sat, huddled together with him to watch TV. Some of them asked me quietly if he could die during the surgery. The answer caught in my throat. Not wanting to lie, but not wanting them to be afraid, I told them that yes, he could die, that it was major surgery, and we needed to pray very hard that he wouldn't. We prayed for his doctor and nurses too.

We buckled Callum into his booster seat on the day of his surgery, and I sat next to him in the backseat of Joe's Volvo because he was so upset. He had never been so distraught before, but the big day had arrived. After suppressing his emotions for months, they all came flooding out. I blinked back my own tears and stifled my sobs, telling him everything was going to be just fine. He wouldn't feel a thing. Mommy and Daddy would be there the entire time, and he would see us as soon as it was all done. He wailed and cried that he didn't want to have surgery. With tears streaming down his cheeks, and his nose running like a tap, the wails and cries turned into guttural moans after a few miles down the highway.

"I don't want to have surgery. I don't want to have surgery."

Over and over and over. We didn't tell him to stop. We were all feeling the same way.

"Will you be in the room while they're doing the surgery?"

He wanted to know.

"No, we aren't allowed to go in the room, but we'll be waiting in another room right close by."

I answered him as truthfully as possible. Then there was more moaning. I felt helpless, not knowing what more to say or how to reassure him. It was something that he needed. There was no getting out of it.

When we got to the hospital, we were shown into a small room where we waited and went over more paperwork. A nurse checked Callum's blood pressure and temperature. He flinched every time someone came into the room. Someone brought him a teddy bear and put a movie on for him to watch. Time dragged on while we waited. The surgery was scheduled for one o'clock, but when two o'clock rolled around, a nurse came in to apologize for the delay. There had been an emergency, but Callum was next in line. He hadn't been allowed to eat since the night before, so he was hungry and cranky. They brought him a Popsicle. There were more delays, three more in total. Each time, they gave us a new time, it was delayed again, and Callum got another Popsicle. It was difficult to get angry over the delays, knowing that someone else was in an emergency situation and could die. We later learned that some of them had been newborn babies. We never got angry, but we were all weary. Callum was exhausted and beyond anxious. The nurse let us take him to the playroom for a change of scenery. We were pleasantly surprised to see his kindergarten and science teachers walk into the room a few minutes later. They were shocked to learn that he hadn't had surgery yet, but were happy for the opportunity to visit with him and take his mind off the long wait. I was so warmed by their kindness and thoughtfulness. They brought the cards that his classmates had made for him, and a handmade quilt with each of their handprints on the squares. It was a welcomed and much needed distraction. At nine thirty that night, they finally called him back. We were beyond ready, and Callum didn't make so much as a whimper. The long wait had been a blessing. He obediently climbed up onto the big bed with wheels. He looked at the nurse's magic light-up wand, breathed in the happy juice, and was wheeled away in a fog.

Joe and I were relieved and anxious all at once. We had waited all day, and then all of a sudden, Callum was whisked off in a flash. We were led into the surgical lounge area. There was a phone on the wall that the nurse would call us on from the operating room to give us updates. I began to recall all the things that the doctor had explained to us that we didn't want to hear, but that we knew we should pay attention to. The risks and worst-case scenarios. I couldn't get the scary images out of my mind. I had brought some of my devotional books with me to read, but I couldn't concentrate on them. My brain wouldn't stop. I asked God to guide the surgeon's hands, to fix Callum's heart, and give him back to us healthy and strong. Joe and I discussed how Callum's surgery might have been the reason God brought us back to Texas. We took turns going to the bathroom and getting bad coffee from the machine because we didn't want to miss the phone call. After two hours, halfway through the surgery, a nurse called to tell us that things were going well. We relaxed ever so slightly and continued to wait. When the phone rang again, two hours later, I jumped for it. The nurse told me that they would be wheeling Callum out of the operating room. She said that we could wait in the hallway to see him for a few seconds before they took him to the cardiac intensive care unit. We were finally able to exhale. Joe and I hugged each other tightly before hurrying out to the hallway to wait for our boy. Callum was covered up with a blanket when the team wheeled him out on the big bed. His little face was pale and puffy. His eyes fluttered when I spoke to him, not aware of where he was or what he had gone through. I know he recognized my voice when I said, "Hi, Callum."

I was allowed to lean over and kiss his puffy cheek before they whisked him off. Joe walked me to the Ronald MacDonald room where I had to wait until they got Callum set up in the unit. The waiting room was filled with parents and siblings, waiting to see their kids. It had been an incredibly long and emotionally draining day, but it was over, and I was suddenly wide-awake. I told Joe to go home and get some sleep. I had planned to stay in the hospital for the duration of Callum's recovery. Joe would be splitting his time between home and visiting us each day. He needed his rest. We hugged each other with complete relief before he left.

It was the middle of the night. The ICU was dimly lit, but buzzing with activity. Nurses were busily checking, monitoring, charting, and reporting when I finally got to Callum's bedside. I wasn't quite sure where to stand. There was so much equipment all around him. Tubes, wires, and monitor lines were attached to him and running everywhere. I didn't want to lean on anything for fear of disconnecting something vital. He had a breathing tube, a draining tube, three IVs, and wires poking out of his chest, just in case he needed a pacemaker. He looked completely helpless and was very groggy, but not quite asleep. Lulling in and out of consciousness as the anesthesia wore off, he knew I was there. His eyes fluttered, and he tried to focus when I talked to him. I told him I was happy to see him. I was exhausted after being so keyed up, for I couldn't remember how long. The surgery was over, and although I knew Callum had a lot of recovery time ahead of him, I could feel myself beginning to relax. The nurse told me to get some rest. She said that I would need it. I did as I was told but did not—could not—sleep. I closed my eyes every so often, but as soon as any of the nurses tended to

Callum, I watched and listened to everything they said. It wasn't long before the anesthesia wore off and Callum began to really wake up and moan. I don't think he was in any pain. He was on morphine, but he was definitely disoriented. The nurses told us prior to the surgery that he would be given an amnesiac medication so that he wouldn't remember anything about the experience. He tried to talk, but couldn't because of the breathing tube. Every time he moaned, I was up at his side in a flash to reassure him that I was there and wasn't going to leave him. When I heard the newborn babies crying, I thought that it would have been so much better if he'd had his heart fixed when he was first born. He wouldn't have known what was going on. A six-year-old knows what is happening. The look of fear and confusion on his face was the hardest thing to watch. He kept pointing to his mouth. He wanted the breathing tube out, and he was thirsty. The nurse removed it but made him wait a little longer before letting him have a drink, just in case he was nauseated. When he finally was allowed to drink and didn't throw up, he was able to talk. The first thing he said was, "I don't want to have heart surgery. I'm too scared."

I tried not to laugh when I told him that he had already had it. That it was all over and he didn't have to be scared anymore. He just needed to get better. He looked at me, completely confused, and said, "I did?"

I said, "Yes, you did. It's all done. Your heart is fixed now."

He looked down at himself in the bed and saw the wires, tubes, and IVs sticking out of him and connected to monitors. A look of terror came across his face, and he moaned, "But look at me!"

It broke my heart to see him so worried, but it was also a little comical. The amnesiac was great for the surgery, but it wasn't much help in the recovery. He thought he was going to have to live with wires connected to machines for the rest of his life. The nurses smiled sympathetically and explained that it would all be coming out soon. He didn't want me to move out of his sight and wouldn't let go of my hand. I stood at the side of his bed till he closed his eyes. As soon as I thought he was asleep, I snuck away to lay my head down. Before my head touched the pillow, he was wide-awake, calling for me again.

Up in a flash, I rushed back to his side. I didn't want him to be afraid. One of the nurses told me to get into the bed with him because neither one of us was going to get any sleep otherwise. God bless that nurse. That's exactly what Callum and I both wanted.

The next morning, Callum was able to eat a Popsicle. Joe brought me up a coffee and a muffin from the shop in the lobby. Joe, my rock. Just seeing him was a comfort and a relief. We sat there staring at each other, and at Callum in silence. There were no words to describe the emotions we were feeling. Six years of waiting, wondering, and worrying were finally over. All that was left for us to do was to help Callum get stronger. Dr. Erez, Callum's heart surgeon, came in to check on him. He told us that Callum had done very well during surgery and that he expected him to make a full recovery. He told us that the decision to correct his heart defect had been a wise one and that the timing had been just right. He had found fibroids growing on the back side of the aortic valve. If left untreated, together with the defect, Callum would have surely needed an artificial valve. We were astonished and even more convinced that the reason for our return to Texas had to be for Callum's health. Callum's surgery was a sort of turning point. It was when we began to pay attention to how God was working in our lives.

Cook Children's Hospital was a great place to be. Callum got top-notch care. The nurses gradually removed the tubes, wires, and IVs as he recovered. He was still receiving pain medication through his IV, so nothing was hurting him, but he was fearful of anything that the nurses tried to do. They took out the draining tube from his side, the pacemaker wires, the IVs, and later, the leads for the monitors. When he cried or put up a fuss, I told him he would scare the tiny babies in the other beds. That seemed to quiet him down. Once he was released from the ICU and moved to a private room, he was much happier. He had a collapsed lung, so his nurse gave him a bottle of bubbles to blow and showed him breathing exercises. We walked the hallways to the children's area several times a day so that he could switch out games for the gaming system he had in his room. He was in heaven with the video games, and the exercise was good for his lungs. After the last IV was removed, he refused pain medication.

He had never liked to take any kind of medicine. He said it tasted like poison, and would rather suffer than take anything. I couldn't believe that after a major surgery, he wouldn't want something to manage his pain. The medication he had been getting through his IV had long since worn off, but he insisted that nothing hurt. Each time a nurse came in with Motrin, he put up a fuss. When the nurse was finally able to convince him to take some, he immediately threw it up. There was a small sofa in Callum's room for me to rest on, but I got very little sleep. Hospitals are noisy in general, but the pediatric ward is for sure the noisiest. With nurses coming in and out to check vitals every couple of hours, kids crying for their parents, and Callum worried and on edge every time a nurse darkened the doorway, I was weary. Joe came to see us every day, bringing me coffee and took over so that I could take a shower. He never stayed more than an hour or so. The drive from Southlake to Fort Worth was about forty minutes, and he didn't want to leave my mother that long. I called her each day to update her on Callum. She gave me a series of random complaints and infractions that occurred with the other kids. Nothing earth-shattering, just annoyances that I really didn't need to hear about. I had enough on my plate. Joe didn't want to burden me with what was going on at home, but I knew he was tired too. We both just wanted us all to be home.

The day Callum got discharged, we stopped to pick up his prescriptions on the way home. It was a hot September day in Texas. Not having taken his pain medicine, Callum was beginning to feel it. He was weak and worn-out. We had strict instructions not to let him go up or down any stairs or do any lifting. They told him to carry a pillow while walking around, just in case he happened to fall or bump into something. We planned to give him something to eat and put him to bed once we got him home. The kids were happy to see their brother, and relieved that we were finally all back together. They cautiously gathered around to welcome him back. Friends had stopped by with gifts, and several of the neighbors had delivered meals while we were in the hospital. Callum opened his gifts, and we all laughed about the two giant stuffed dogs he got from two separate friends, one brown and one black. My mother sat in a chair at the end of the kitchen table, crocheting silently while the rest of us huddled together, happy to be reunited. Joe unloaded the bags from the car while I got Callum some dinner. He ate very little because he was hurting. He reluctantly agreed to take some Motrin, but within less than a minute, he threw it up, along with his dinner. Everyone froze, staring at the mess, not really knowing what to do. I snapped them to attention, giving instructions and putting them into motion. They quickly fetched supplies, a puke bucket, towels, rags, and a pair of fresh pajamas. I cleaned Callum up and laid him in Joe's big leather chair. My mother didn't move. She continued to crochet silently, watching as the rest of us scrambled. I glanced up at her, making eye contact. I was startled, not so much by the fact that she hadn't offered to help, but because she showed no sign of sympathy and offered no comfort to her grandson. She was completely cold. It had been our intention, since Callum couldn't go up or down the stairs, that he would sleep on the pullout sofa in the family room. He would be close enough for us to hear him if he needed us during the night. After he got sick, and witnessing my mother's indifference, I picked up my boy and carried him back to our bedroom and tucked him into our king-sized bed. The two of us fell asleep almost immediately. Even though there was more than enough room for Joe, he decided to sleep on the pullout. He was afraid of bumping Callum in the middle of the night. He came in to kiss us goodnight. He told me he knew we had been through an ordeal and that we needed a decent night sleep. After five days and nights with virtually no rest, I didn't argue with him.

My mother acted like I had slighted her. She told me that I was behaving the same way as when we had first moved to Texas. She said I was distracted. Not quite sure how to respond, I took it as a criticism. I was troubled that she couldn't understand, even a little bit, what we had all been through. Not only was I emotionally drained, I was sleep-deprived. She was the one who had asked to come to help, but it seemed to me that she wanted to be entertained. She mentioned more than once that she could have, and should really have, been working. She said her paycheck was going to be smaller, but she felt it was more important that she come to help out. The messages I was getting from her were confusing. I was too exhausted to question her about them, much less try to sort them out on my own. Joe dropped her off at the mall so she could do some shopping, and she walked to Town Square on her own a couple of times. She was clearly sulking, and that made me even less inclined to entertain her. I wished that we could have a decent visit just once. No matter what the occasion was, things always seemed to sour, and I had no idea why.

We received an overwhelming outpouring of love from near and far. Neighbors, old and new, friends from church, aunts, cousins, Callum's classmates, our other kids' friends and families, even people we hardly knew showed their concern. Cards and packages came in the mail, meals were delivered for a whole week after we got home, and the moms from Callum's kindergarten class put together a treasure chest of wrapped gifts to keep him from boredom. Phone calls, fruit baskets, prayers, and cookie bouquets warmed our hearts and taste buds. We were incredibly humbled by every act of kindness, however big or small. Never had we felt so cared for. Callum returned to school in October after getting the all clear at his follow-up appointment with the cardiologist. Life soon returned to normal. I found out I was pregnant again. I didn't tell anyone but Joe. We didn't allow ourselves to get excited. We prayed that our baby would make it, but we didn't get our hopes up, and I didn't rush to make an appointment.

Our front porch ran the entire length of the house. It had the potential to be an outdoor living space. I envisioned the look that I wanted, and Joe indulged me. We ordered white wicker-look resin furniture, two love seats, four chairs, and two coffee tables. We chose the biggest, fullest hanging baskets from our favorite garden center. Joe hauled giant planters of lush ferns and placed them at both ends of the porch. I filled our two urns with German ivy, red geraniums, and white impatiens. The tall holly hedges created a natural privacy screen and protected against the hot Texas sun. Even on the hottest summer days, it felt ten degrees cooler in our outdoor room. We hired the landscaping company who had designed the gardens at our first Texas house to soften the straight lines of our front flower beds.

They pulled out the metal edging and used decorative stone to build a meandering border around the perimeter of the house. They filled it with encore azaleas, magnolias, lilies, hydrangeas, and red-tipped photinias. In every empty space, I planted red and white impatiens. The completed project turned out better than the initial vision. We enjoyed our front porch immensely. It was where we enjoyed our morning coffee while we waited with the kids for the school bus, and where we flipped through the mail as we watched for them to return again in the afternoon. In the evenings we listened to the chirping of the cicadas and crickets and watched for the hummingbirds that fed on the flowers.

When the weather cooled down, I decided to make an afghan to wrap up in on cold mornings. With Veteran's Day approaching, and patriotic sentiments in my heart, I bought the yarn and got to work on a red, white, and blue afghan. Imagining how it would look against the white wicker, and dreaming about how I would create an outdoor harvest look for the autumn season, I knitted. Allowing my mind to wander to places of comfort, thoughts of pumpkins and baskets of mums, fall colors, and the smells of spiced breads and pies filled my senses. The magazines in the grocery store with the glossy pictures of welcoming entryways and delicious fall recipes inspired me. I absolutely loved everything about being a homemaker and mother. Creating a home filled with love and comfort was the dream I was living.

No sooner had I finished my afghan and a matching pillow, and debating whether or not to make a second one, I heard about Philip's Wish. It was a charity that was collecting blankets for the homeless. Something stirred in my soul and told me to donate the blanket. I could have easily donated a store-bought blanket, but my gut told me to give up the one I had just made. Stuffing the bulky afghan and pillow into a bag, I whipped up a scarf and some mittens with the leftover yarn. I gathered some toiletries together and brought every-thing to the drop-off spot. Ella Bella Boutique, a high-end specialty children's shop in Southlake. After the kids got home from school, we loaded into the van to make the delivery. With bags in hand, I waited for the salesperson to finish with a customer. Standing to the side while she rang up the order, I noticed a lady come into the store. Something told me she was connected with Philip's Wish, though I didn't know exactly why. I made eye contact with her, and she asked me if the bags I had were for Philip's Wish. I told her they were, and she introduced herself as Cyndi Bunch, Philip's mother. Philip was a little boy who wanted to cover up all the homeless people with blankets to make sure they were warm. We hugged each other, I gave her the bags and left the store. We picked up pizza for dinner from Cici's, just a few doors down from the children's shop, and drove home. The strange stirring in my soul was still there. I knew I had to do more.

SEVENTEEN

Knitterbugs: A Link in the Chain

Southlake, Texas, 2007–2009

The stirrings had surfaced before. The nagging urge to do something meaningful, but never really figuring out what exactly that meaningful thing was. Sometimes the urges were very strong, but I usually grew frustrated, and ultimately suppressed the longing when a revelation didn't present itself. We did the usual things like donating clothing and toys. We sent checks to missions and supported charities here and there when asked. For me, writing checks and bagging up unwanted toys and used clothing wasn't a real stretch. I truly did want to do something personal, but the same old dilemma always remained. I had nine kids, and I couldn't neglect my first responsibility. There had to be a balance. Something that wouldn't take me away from my family but would involve them. Philip's Wish had planted a seed, and an idea began to develop.

When I was about seven years old and in Brownies, one of the moms came in to teach our troop how to knit. We all got a ball of the same thin, lilac-colored yarn, and a pair of long, skinny, metal needles. She taught us the basics. We worked on two or three rows at our meeting, and then we got to bring our supplies home to practice. Most of the other girls tossed their knitting aside, never to pick it up again. I did not. I wanted to learn how to do it. I worked and worked at it but couldn't quite remember the steps to get the stitches from one needle to the other. I tried wrapping and tucking but didn't know which side to hold the yarn on, or which direction to go in. With a bunch of dropped stitches and gaping holes, I grew frustrated and pulled it all out and started again. Gramma Hubbard had been visiting. She watched as I struggled determinedly. Undoubtedly seeing my lack of progress, she told me that she had knitted years ago. She took the needles from me and showed me how to get the stitches off one needle and onto the other. I've met many knitters over the years who all knit in a different style, picking and throwing, English or Continental. Many of them have been puzzled as they watch me work. I guess my style doesn't quite fall into any category, how I hold my hands and yarn, or how I cast on, wrap, and pick. It's what I call the Gramma Hubbard style. She very patiently stood over my shoulder and guided my hands and needles until I had it. I was knitting!

Row after row, I knitted that lilac yarn until it ran out and had grown into a great long strip. Then I ripped it out, rolled it back into a ball and started again. One day while I was working on another long strip, Aunt Mary stopped in after bringing Gramma back from morning Mass. Gramma Hubbard affectionately called her daughter Mary Noreen in her Flying Machine, because she was always on the go. She was one of my favorite aunts, and she was always interested in what us kids were doing. When she came through the door with her Irish eyes shining, singing a silly song or nursery rhyme to the little kids, we knew we were in for some fun. She either got us all giggling or rolling our eyes. I think it was her mission to get a giggle out of us before she left, and she always succeeded. When she saw me in the living room chair with my needles clicking away, she began to chant, "Knit one, purl two. Knit one, purl two."

She noticed that I was only knitting, and asked me if I knew how to purl. Having no idea what a purl was, I must have looked confused. She explained that it was a little like knitting backward. Taking the needles out of my hands, she leaned over to show me how to pick up the yarn from the front of my work instead of the back. I noticed how the stitches looked different. She told me that if I could knit and purl, I could make any pattern I wanted because those were the two basic stitches in knitting. I practiced till I ran out of yarn, and started again and again till the yarn got so frayed that I couldn't use it anymore. I loved it. I had no idea then that the lessons Gramma Hubbard and Aunt Mary had given me would lead to that meaningful thing I had been searching for, thirty years later.

I knitted off and on over the years. In high school I knitted sweaters for friends. While I was pregnant with Angela, I knitted outfits and blankets for preemies and donated them to the Guardian Angels, a charity sponsored by Guardian Drugs Pharmacy. I made baby blankets, sweaters, and booties for my own kids, and for friends and relatives who were having babies. I made loads of mittens, hats, and scarves; and one year, I made matching Canadian Maple Leaf sweaters for all my sisters for Christmas. I suddenly knew what it was that I wanted to do. I wanted to knit blankets for the homeless. It would not take time away from my family. I was knitting all the time anyway. I thought it over some more and came up with an idea to take it a step further. I talked to Melissa Brinker, the guidance counselor at my kids' elementary school, Durham Elementary, and told her about my idea of starting a knitting club. I had already come up with a name for it, Knitterbugs. I wanted to teach kids how to knit blanket squares like the Warm Up America project. Knitting a square was a small enough project for a kid to tackle without much difficulty, and it was something that could be finished quickly. I would then assemble the squares into a blanket to donate to the homeless shelter. Melissa loved the idea. My plan was to meet at our house on Saturdays for four weeks, just enough time to complete an adequate amount of squares for a decent-sized blanket. I was a little apprehensive about opening up our home to strangers. I had the desire to do something nice, but also wanted to protect myself, so allotting a specific time frame gave me a way out if it didn't work out. Melissa was my cheerleader and helped to get the word out by advertising in the school newsletter. Our kids told all their friends, and soon the phone started ringing, and e-mails came in, inquiring about Knitterbugs. In order to keep the blanket squares as uniform as possible, I asked everyone to bring a skein of Lion Brand's Thick and Quick yarn, and size 13 needles. Thick yarn and large needles because I remembered the struggle of the thin lilac yarn and long skinny needles I learned on. Not only would the larger needles and thick yarn make it easier for small hands to learn, it would also work up quickly and make for a very warm and cozy blanket. To keep it interesting, I let everyone pick whatever color they wanted.

Sixteen people showed up on that first Saturday in October. Ranging from second grade to high school, several moms, and a few teachers; I was thrilled by the interest, and more than a little terrified. Thankfully, our family room was very large with a big sectional couch. Everyone found their own space on the furniture, and spilled onto the area rug and into the kitchen chairs that we pulled in. Grateful that my older kids had some experience with knitting, they were able to help the younger kids get started. I moved around the room from person to person after giving a general demonstration. If I had to use one word to describe that first meeting, it would be *intense*. Everyone was extremely focused on learning the craft, and you could have heard a pin drop as they worked. I was sweating as I tried to get to each person to show how to pick up a dropped stitch or get untangled, reminding everyone to be sure to count their stitches. There were a few tears shed by the youngest ones, and some frustrated sighs from the older ones. It was my goal for everyone to feel comfortable with the basics by the end of the two-hour class. We all enjoyed the cookies that Angela had baked, finally exhaling and visiting with each other for a few minutes while we waited for kids to get picked up by their parents. Everyone seemed to have enjoyed themselves, and we were all looking forward to the next meeting. I had survived the first knitting class. Each week became a little more relaxed than the last. As word got out about Knitterbugs, our group grew, with new students joining every week. Everyone was surprised that there was no fee to join and that the lessons were free. The only requirement was that the completed blanket squares be donated. I contacted Cyndi Bunch and told her about our project. She was excited about our efforts, and invited us to the Philip's Wish Blanket Drive kickoff event in December. She asked us to bring the blanket with us. By our third meeting, everyone was knitting with ease. My students had learned to cast on, knit, and cast off. Several of them were working on their second and third skeins of yarn, and were turning in bags of blanket squares, way more than the forty-nine we needed for the blanket. I promised that by our last scheduled meeting, I would have the squares assembled.

My kids dumped the bags of squares into a pile in the middle of the family room floor, and we all got to work arranging and rearranging the squares. Forty-nine squares, each one measuring seven by nine inches; seven rows across and seven rows down, it would be a big warm blanket. I hadn't considered the fact that there would be such a vast array of colors when I left the choice up to each individual. Some of the little girls had chosen dusty rose and baby blue. There were colors that I would never have considered putting together—forest green, red, navy, pumpkin, black, gray, and every kind of variegated combination. There were beiges, taupes, and browns. There was one particular square that one of the middle school kids made and had struggled the longest and hardest to complete. While everyone else made several squares, she only finished one. Her square was huge and misshapen. As we moved the squares around, trying to find the best arrangement, one of my kids held up the odd one and said, "Look how huge this thing is. We can't use it. It's way too big."

I took the square and looked at it, remembering how hard the girl who made it had worked. She had come every week just like everyone else and had done the best she could. I told my kids that we would be using all the squares, including that one. A couple of them rolled their eyes. I decided to put the giant square in the center of the blanket. All the colors, different as they all were, and unlikely as they would be to find in any one project, looked absolutely beautiful together when the blanket was complete. It was a mosaic, a veritable piece of art. I had tears in my eyes when it was complete. I thought about all the little hands that had worked so hard to complete each square. Kids who had never held knitting needles before, who had learned a new skill and made something that would be given away to someone who they would never meet. It was awesome. I could hardly wait to show it to my little group.

Our last meeting was scheduled just before Halloween. We enjoyed Angela's cookies and hot chocolate, and didn't do any knitting. It was a celebration of the completion of our project. Everyone was excited to see the blanket. Each child found and pointed to their own square, while also admiring each other's. My kids later told me that they were glad that I included the giant misshapen one. They realized that the girl who had made it would have noticed if hers was missing and would surely have felt badly. One of the moms came up to thank me for organizing the project. She said she was grateful for the opportunity for her and her kids to work on a community service project together. She asked me if I had plans for another project. I had very much enjoyed the classes and involving my own kids. It had all ended so soon. I had only planned for four weeks. I never expected it to go so smoothly or be so much fun. My students, overhearing the mom's question about future projects, had gathered around to hear my answer. I asked them all if they were interested in continuing our project. It was unanimous, everyone said they wanted to keep meeting. I told them that I would work out a schedule. I had broken out of my shell and stepped out of my comfort zone, opening myself up to others outside of my family. It felt wonderful. I didn't know it then, but life would never be the same.

On Halloween Day, a few days after our blanket celebration, I lost the baby. I knew I was losing him. After Joe left for work and the kids got off to school, I started having horrible cramps and began feeling very weak. I didn't call Joe. I knew that there wasn't anything he could do. He had planned to come home early to help get the kids ready for trick-or-treating anyway. My ob-gyn appointment wasn't for another week. I didn't bother calling the doctor. I didn't want to hear what I already knew to be true. As the morning went on, I was bleeding heavily. Even though I was wearing plenty of pads and a towel for protection, I had to change clothes three times. I felt emotionally numb, but at the same time, tears streamed down my cheeks. I don't think I even realized I was crying. I couldn't understand why it kept happening. It was my third miscarriage in nine months. I had made a grooming appointment for Maverick a week earlier, and I kept the appointment, deciding there was no sense in sitting around feeling sorry for myself. I buckled Sarah and Katie into their car seats in the van, leashed the dog, and drove to Pet Smart. Maverick hated getting groomed. The only time he ever went in the car was to go to the vet or to get groomed, so he knew where he was going. I could feel a gush every time I lifted Sarah and Katie into the shopping cart and struggled with Maverick as I dragged his seventy-five pounds into the groomers. Not in the mood to prepare lunch, I drove through the McDonald's drive-through to get food for the girls and put them down for their naps when we got home. I changed my clothes again, shocked to see that there was still so much blood. I had not experienced anything like it with the previous miscarriages. I didn't have the sense to stop and rest. No doubt in shock, I was on autopilot, just using up nervous energy. I kept going, doing laundry, cleaning, vacuuming, looking for things to organize so I wouldn't have to think about my heartache and grave loss. I got all the kids' costumes together, found their treat bags, and swept out the garage. I was cleaning out the garage refrigerator when I heard the door open up. Joe was home. He instantly knew something was wrong when he saw me. He said I looked really pale. I was beginning to feel light-headed. I told him I had lost the baby. He wrapped his arm around me and helped me back into the house. He said that God must be telling us our baby days were over. Looking back on it now, it was a miracle I didn't hemorrhage to death. I never did go to the doctor. It doesn't matter how many children you have. When you lose one, you know that you have lost a precious life. I mourned that baby and the two I had lost before him. Knitting became part of my healing. Working past my pain and heartache to help people in need, through Knitterbugs, was therapy.

Knitterbugs became part of our whole family's life. We had completed and donated three blankets by the time the Philip's Wish Blanket Drive kicked off in December. Cyndi asked me to speak that afternoon in the Tom Thumb parking lot in Southlake. Several of the Knitterbugs came out. We proudly showed off our blanket and told the story of how we got started. We continued to meet twice a month on Saturday afternoons at my house. When people told me they wanted to join but that Saturdays wouldn't work, I hosted a Tuesday morning class once a month. Soon, more people became interested but said evenings would be better for them, so I added a Wednesday evening at the Barnes and Noble in Town Square once a month. The more that word spread about Knitterbugs, the more it grew. I contacted all the senior centers in the Dallas Fort Worth area, and soon many of them were knitting items to donate. A few of the ladies even joined us for meetings. The Seniors Center in Arlington had a knitting group that met regularly. They decided to start making blanket squares specifically for us, and they called when they had a large collection, sometimes over five hundred squares at a time. I called all of the area of Michael's craft stores. Michael's was one of the drop-off sites for Warm Up America. Many of the stores said that they had received lots of squares, but they didn't have anyone to assemble them into blankets. They were thrilled that I wanted them and welcomed me to pick them up. We drove all over Dallas and Fort Worth collecting squares. The trips turned into family outings, and we often stopped for french fries or ice cream. The kids helped to unload bags and sorted through the squares and organized them into color-coordinated piles. One of the kids' teachers at school took a picture of one of our blankets and wrote up a story for the school newsletter, which led to a story in the *Southlake Times* paper and then the *Star Telegram. Dallas Morning News* sent a reporter and photographer to one of our meetings and did a full-page story on our group. The result was increased interest, more new students, and lots of yarn donations. I started getting calls from people telling me that they had yarn to donate. A lady called and said that her friend had died and left her a bunch of yarn that she could never use up in her lifetime. She wanted it to be put to good use. Joe and I made several trips, bringing back boxes, bags, and bins of yarn while the kids were at school. Some of it was cheap and inexpensive yarn, and some of it was very expensive, imported, fancy, and exotic fiber. There were cakes and cones of hand-dyed angora from France, wool from Germany and England, linen, silk, cashmere, mohair, cotton, and chenille. Yarns that I had only ever seen in magazines, I was able to touch and feel.

One day the kids came in from off the school bus and asked me what was in all the trash bags on the front porch. Puzzled, knowing I hadn't put any bags out there, we all went out to look. We found seven giant black trash bags filled with brand-new large skeins of chenille yarn. Not cheap yarn, running from four to six dollars a skein,

I was blown away. There was no note, so we didn't have a clue who had dropped it off. A week or so later, a lady called to tell me that she had been the mystery donor and that she had more that she had to get sorted out. She said she had heard about Knitterbugs through one of the newspaper stories. She didn't have much time for knitting anymore, but she liked what we were doing and wanted us to have her collection for our project. A few weeks later she delivered six five-gallon Ziplock bags, filled to bursting, along with sixty sets of knitting needles in every size. The lady must have been a serious knitter at one time. I never got the opportunity to meet her because she always dropped it off without ringing the bell. There was more yarn than I had ever seen, and I had no idea where I was going to store it all. I had been asking my students to supply the yarn for our project, but with such a huge donation, they wouldn't have to buy any yarn again. I had no idea, however, what I would do with so many sets of knitting needles. My group was astonished to see all the donated items, and everyone had fun choosing skeins of yarn to work on more blanket squares. We made stacks of beautiful chenille blankets. Joe bought me three Christmas tree storage bins at the Container Store. Even those weren't big enough to fit all the yarn in. Our little pass-through room had evolved from a craft and storage room into a Knitterbugs room, filled to the brim with yarn and finished projects to donate. Knitterbugs Saturdays were always a highlight for our family.

In January, I discovered that I was pregnant again; and on March 16, Clare's birthday, I had my fourth miscarriage. Dr. MacDonald sent me to a genetic counselor. They couldn't find any reason whatsoever for my miscarriages. All my other pregnancies and children had been healthy. I was thirty-eight years old, not exactly in my prime, but I wasn't too old. I began to question whether there was an environmental reason. Maybe there was something strange going on in my house. I was so sad. I had been working on a blue lacy shawl. The same pattern that I had started for each one of my lost babies. Sensing that each one of them had been boys, I chose blue to make the triangle-shaped shawl, with a delicate scalloped stitch in a fine baby yarn. I had lost each baby before completing it. I tore the stitches out after each miscarriage, and started over again with each new pregnancy. Inconsolable with my fourth loss, I stuffed the unfinished project into a bag and threw it away. Looking back, I wish I had completed and kept that little shawl. All the stitches that I had worked so lovingly, with the hope of holding a new little baby in my arms, would have been a sweet keepsake. A memorial for each of the little lives that I had loved and lost. It was much too painful to even look at the partially finished shawl. In one of my cleaning and organizing frenzies, I made the rash decision to toss it. I wrote down each of my babies' names in a book, however, including the date that each one passed, and I prayed that I would see them one day in heaven.

Cyndi Bunch organized a tour of the Presbyterian Night Shelter, a homeless shelter in Downtown Fort Worth. She invited me to come along. A large group of us carpooled. The only places I had been to in Fort Worth were Cook Children's Hospital and the Fort Worth Zoo. I had no idea that there was another side of the downtown. It was a stark contrast from where I had been. The tall buildings and fountains, art museum, and painted murals disappeared as we neared the other side of the tracks or, as the locals call it, the mix master. Dark, dreary, and depressing. Dilapidated buildings lined the streets where trash was strewn about. It was ugly. I saw trash bags lined up neatly along the chain-link fence on Cypress Street. Bag after bag, with the odd mound of what looked like clothing in between. Most shocking was the number of people, mostly black people, standing, sitting on curbs and gathered in small crowds on the corners. I saw an old couple, who looked to be in their sixties, sitting on a sofa that someone had dumped in the middle of a gravel parking lot, amid parked cars. Everything and everyone looked displaced. I was quite simply horrified to see such a sight in a country like the United States. That old couple should have been sitting on a sofa in their living room. I wondered how there could be so many homeless people in one city. Where had they all come from?

There were four of us who rode together. We had chatted and laughed together all the way from Southlake, talking about what a wonderful thing it was and how great it felt to be involved in such a worthwhile cause. Helping homeless people was such a noble thing to do. When we actually laid eyes on the sea of real live homeless people before us, we were speechless. Inside the Suburban, we were silent as we drove slowly down the street while many eyes watched us. We were the ones who were out of place. I had seen homeless people before. You know, the odd bag lady or drunk who wandered around Downtown Niagara Falls. I had never before seen hordes of homeless people, all clumped together in one place. It was April. The sun was shining, but it was a coolish morning. As we were getting out of the SUV, one of the ladies, unsure about bringing her handbag with her, asked one of the others if she would be leaving her purse in the car. Her response, "Heavens no!" And she quickly hit the automatic locks.

We joined the small group that had already gathered in the doorway of one of the shelters, with Heather and Lindsay, the two shelter employees who would be giving us the tour. We all introduced ourselves, and I passed out my freshly printed Knitterbugs business cards to each of the workers. When they read the card, they looked at each other wide-eyed. Turning to me, Heather said, "Wow, this is amazing. We were just talking yesterday about trying to find someone to teach a knitting class to the clients."

My heart stopped. Smiling nervously, all I could choke out was, "Really?"

My initial thought was, "Oh, please, God, no. Don't let them ask me to teach a class." It was a frightening place, and I hadn't even gone inside yet. I had no problem knitting and donating blankets, but it was not the sort of place I wanted to come to on a regular basis. Then it hit me. All the yarn and knitting needles. Was that why they had been dropped off on my doorstop anonymously? It nagged at me all throughout the tour. We walked through four separate shelter buildings. One for the mentally ill, one for women with young children, one for veterans, and one for adult men and women. I was astounded by the fact that there were enough people to fill up four shelters. It was shocking, but I was impressed by how clean and organized each of the buildings were. We toured the kitchen, the dispensary, and the courtyard. There was a nurse's station, a computer room, and offices where caseworkers helped clients with everything imaginable. From locating lost birth certificates and other important documents, matching clients up with services such as addiction help, mental health services, life skills training, job placements, and legal services. The list was endless. I was seeing a lot more clearly how and why homelessness exists, and it was heartbreaking. The camaraderie among the workers, who were—or had been at one time—homeless themselves, and the volunteers, was endearing. The more I saw and learned, the less scary it was. Another startling reality was the numbered spaces on the floor. We were told that the spaces were where the stacks of mats that we had seen piled against the wall would be laid down at night for the clients to sleep on. The clients were not allowed to remain inside the shelter during the day unless they were mentally ill or infirm. Some of them paid a fifty-dollar monthly fee for a real bed and a locker, and were allowed to stay throughout the day. Everyone else was required to leave so that the building could be properly cleaned. By the end of the tour, I was so moved, I just knew I had to do more. I knew for certain that Knitterbugs would continue making blankets and that we would also begin collecting toiletries and other items to donate. I decided to ask Lindsay and Heather what exactly they had in mind as far as a knitting class. They said they wanted someone to teach a class once a week. I told them about all the needles and yarn that had just been donated. They both agreed that it had to be more than a coincidence. I told them that I would think it over and discuss it with my husband.

When I got home, I told Joe about the whole experience. About the trash bag–lined fence, which I learned contained all the worldly possessions of the clients because they couldn't leave them inside the shelter during the day. I told him about the young mothers in the courtyard with the little children and babies, who got their diapers from the dispensary, and about the old couple who sat together on the sofa in the parking lot. I told Joe that I wanted to do something to make a difference if I could. I wanted to help. I could do it on an evening. Tuesday evenings from five to seven. Joe encouraged me to do it and seemed almost as excited as I was. I think he figured it would be a good outlet for me. I was still so sad about losing our babies, but Knitterbugs was helping with my grief.

My new venture was exciting. I planned and organized everything for my shelter class. I bought a bunch of reusable grocery bags and sewed on laminated labels for my new students to write their names. I stuffed a bag full of yarn skeins of every color so that they could choose the one they wanted, and selected the appropriate-sized needles. Angela baked cookies. In an effort to draw more interest, we collected small items and trinkets as door prizes. Paperback novels, hand sanitizers, travel-sized toiletries, and hair ties. Nothing too bulky, just fun and practical stuff. Our first Tuesday meeting was in May. Angela, Joseph, and I drove to the city. I tried to prepare them for the experience so that they wouldn't be as shocked as I was the first time I saw it. My two young teenagers had spent their entire lives in comfortable and sheltered conditions. I don't think anything could have prepared them, but they did a good job of hiding their shock. We signed in at the volunteer desk and made our way up to the meeting room. There were eleven people signed up for the class. Lindsay came up to say hello and to introduce us. Any nervousness that I had initially felt quickly dissipated. They may have been homeless, but they were people. Warm, friendly, and welcoming. I smiled and showed them a sample square and a completed blanket. I told them that if they could learn to make a square, they could make a whole blanket. They all seemed pretty excited about the possibility. I spread out the yarn and invited them to choose whatever color they wanted. They each picked up a set of needles and a bag, and I got started demonstrating how to cast on stitches. The initial small talk grew into friendly banter. The ice was broken quickly, and before the end of the class, Angela, Joseph, and I were laughing and joking along with everyone. We ended with our door prize drawings. Everyone left with something. The big prize was the sample blanket that I had brought. The lady who won it said that it made her feel so happy to have it wrapped around her. That it felt like a big hug because she could feel the love of all the little hands that had made it. It brought tears to my eyes. The little room in the homeless shelter may as well have been my own family room. My new students were a little straggly and rough around the edges with their worn-out clothes, calloused hands, and teeth that hadn't seen a dentist in years, if ever. Their faces were carved with hard lines from addictions, troubles, and tragedies that no one should have to experience, but their hearts were warm, and their eyes became more trusting with each week that I returned.

It didn't take long for the class to grow. Once word got out that there would be cookies and prizes, lots of people showed up. My biggest thrill was when one of the ladies, Margaret, proudly displayed her beautiful knitting. When I returned for the second class, she had knitted her entire skein of red yarn and wanted to know if she could have more. The following week, she had the second skein entirely knitted. I was so pleased to see that Margaret was really enjoying her newly learned skill, that I brought in a giant bag of yarn. That way, if she ran out, she could get more before the next class. Margaret, an immigrant from Uganda, was truly my star pupil. She told me that when she used to ride the bus to Kenya, she would see ladies knitting and wished that she could learn. She was so proud that she finally knew how to knit. After only a few classes, she asked me if I could teach her the language of knitting. Puzzled by her request, I realized that she wanted me to show her how to read a pattern. I went through all my knitting books and put together a packet of patterns, and explained to her what all the abbreviations meant. I gave her the pictures that showed step by step how to make the different stitches. There were thirty patterns in all. By the next class, Margaret had knitted all thirty swatches, one for each pattern. Perfectly. She was a natural. The week after that, she had assembled all her swatches into a blanket. I told her that she could put a border around it. She picked out a fun fur yarn from the bag, I gave her a crochet hook, and showed her how to do the border. I so enjoyed seeing Margaret each week, and she never missed a class. When others came and went, she was always there.

Homeless shelters are transient. Clients leave to live with family or friends, they find jobs and get back on their feet. Others move into transitional housing. The shelter knitting group was ever changing. Only a few of the original students came around, poking their head in to say hello and have a cookie. For many of them, it was more about the fellowship than the knitting, and that was fine with me. I always felt welcomed by them, and I always tried to make them feel welcome, whether they wanted to knit or not. I learned many of their stories; sad, unfortunate, depressing, tragic, and horrifying stories. I felt humbled that they would share them with me, and I did all I could to give them hope. Keeping a smile on my face and offering a listening ear, showing concern and compassion. I wished with all my heart that I could help to fix them all, but I knew it wasn't possible. I prayed for them all by name every night.

I started bringing Margaret the fancier yarns, the angora and fun fur that she loved. One of the girls, Amber, told me that she was pregnant. She had recently married another client. She said she was having a boy. We all shared in her joy as we watched her belly grow bigger. She was glowing. I knitted her a pair of blue baby booties and brought them to her on one of the meeting nights. Amber was friendly and always came up for a cookie, and to say hello. I was surprised when she didn't come up the night I brought her gift. I knew she was around because I heard her voice down below the loft where Margaret and I were sitting. When one of the other ladies came by, I asked her to let Amber know that I had something for her. Amber came up and sat on the bench next to me. She gave me a hug and apologized for not coming up earlier. I told her I was glad to see her and handed her the little bag. She looked inside, and tears filed her eyes when she thanked me. She told me that she had lost her baby a few days before. My heart sank. I just hugged her. I knew exactly how she was feeling. I wondered if part of the reason I had lost my babies might have been so that I could truly empathize with Amber, and so many others who I would come to know who would suffer the same heartache. Amber took the little bag and went back to her friends. Margaret patted my hand sympathetically. I was so sorry for bringing the baby booties. Margaret said it wasn't my fault, how could I have possibly known. She told me she wanted to learn how to make baby shoes. I showed her how to get started that night, and the following week, I brought her the pattern and all the supplies she needed. The right-sized needles, baby yarn, stitch holders, a sewing needle, and a measuring tape. Margaret made several pairs of baby booties. Amber's baby was not the last tragedy that I would share in at the shelter. Rhonda, another one of my students, told me that her son, a soldier in the military, had been killed in Afghanistan. She was completely distraught when she found me in the upstairs loft. She handed me a plastic grocery bag filled with all the blanket squares she had made. They were all coordinated, five different colors, in large, perfectly sized squares, pinned together in the order she had planned to arrange them. She asked me if I would assemble them into a blanket for her. She wanted to give it to her three grandchildren who had just lost their daddy. It was a privilege being part of so many stories and experiences, and I was humbled and inspired by the very people who I thought I was helping. They helped and taught me so much more than I could ever have hoped to help them.

I discovered that I was pregnant in July. I made an appointment with Dr. MacDonald immediately and saw him within two days. He put me on progesterone and mega vitamins and told me that he would be monitoring me extra closely. He assured me that he would be praying for everything to be okay. I was still teaching my knitting class at the shelter, but made the decision, once school resumed, to stop. I knew that the school schedule would keep me very busy, and I didn't want to overdo it. I was sad to leave, and I know that Margaret was disappointed that there wouldn't be any more classes, but she understood. I had shared with her about my miscarriages. I brought her a kit with various sizes of needles and crochet hooks, some pattern books, and lots of yarn. I wanted her to have plenty of supplies to keep knitting. I had been going to the shelter for a total of five months, and the time had flown. I continued to drop off the blankets that Knitterbugs made, along with donations of toiletries, every couple of months. At Christmastime, I asked the school counselor Melissa Brinker if we could involve the entire school in making ornaments to decorate the shelter. A group of us Knitterbugs and some of the school moms helped to display the hundreds of ornaments that the school kids had made all over the shelter. Right before the winter break, we brought a large group of kids to sing carols in the dining hall at dinnertime. I kept in touch with Heather and Lindsay, even though I didn't return to teach. They e-mailed me pictures of Margaret's fashions. She had begun making clothing and purses, all her own designs. I had a dream of bringing Margaret home with me, giving her a room in our house, and helping her to find a job, but I didn't follow through with it. She was a wonderful lady, and I have no doubt in my mind that she was a trustworthy person, someone who I could have welcomed into my family. I wished I had taken that leap of faith. I often wonder where Margaret is now. She had two daughters who were still in Uganda that she hoped would join her in the United States once she got on her feet. I have no doubt that she is still knitting.

Knitterbugs continued to grow and evolve. New members came with new ideas, and we began making more than just blankets. We added baby hats and blankets for John Peter Smith, the county hospital in Fort Worth. We made layettes for Loreto House, a crisis pregnancy center in Denton, helmet liners for the military, mittens for the Pine Ridge Indian Reservation in South Dakota, and scarves for the Special Olympics in Austin, Texas. As soon as there were enough items completed for a donation drop, we would decide the spot, and I would drive to deliver it. Sometimes it was me and a few kids, sometimes it was the whole family, and once in a while, one of my knitting ladies came along. I so enjoyed my group and having them at the house. They were all so dear to me, and our whole family got excited about the preparations on knitting days, baking, pulling in extra chairs, making coffee and cider, and lighting candles. I always decorated for each season and tried to make everyone feel at home. One particular lady, Ginger Roberts, a spunky gal in her late eighties, drove herself and sometimes a couple of her friends to the meetings on Saturdays. She was always working on several projects—baby hats, blankets, and mittens; and she carried everything with her in a big wicker basket, pulling out each item for us to admire when she arrived. She was a real treasure to our group, and we all loved seeing her. At the end of each meeting, she would hug me tight and thank me for having her. She said she loved to come to our house because she always felt so welcome. Her maiden name was Allen, and she often joked with Joe, saying that they must be long lost cousins. She would often call me after she got home to thank me again for giving her a way to feel useful.

I became more aware, as new people joined, that Knitterbugs wasn't just about knitting things to donate. That had been my initial intention, to do charity work, but as it evolved, I realized that it was just as much, if not more, about the fellowship and goodwill we all shared for each other as well as those we were helping. We were all going through our own trials in life. I had lost four babies, there were ladies who were battling illnesses, some who were caring for elderly parents and sick family members. Some were struggling financially, dealing with rebellious teenagers, or had lost a spouse. Knitterbugs was an outlet for all of us, and it allowed us to share with others at the same time. We were all at different skill levels, but I always welcomed everyone. Each one of us was able to contribute in whatever way we chose, stress-free, and it worked very well. One little idea for one project had turned into something of a movement.

My belly grew. I continued holding classes at home and at Barnes and Noble. There were three meetings each month. When I wasn't meeting, I was knitting. I brought my needles with me everywhere—doctor appointments, dentist appointments, and in the car while I waited to pick kids up from various activities. I knitted in the backyard while I watched the kids swim, and on the front porch while we waited for the school bus. There was always a stack of blankets somewhere in the house, and no sooner was one stack delivered, than another stack was started. A bag of hats, a bag of mittens, and bags of squares. The bin that I kept on the front porch for donation drop-offs always had something in it, and more bags were brought to meetings. I carried bags home from Barnes and Noble—pairs of baby booties, baby hats, a sweater, baby blankets, helmet liners; little by little the collections grew, and we delivered them to the right places all over again.

Each doctor appointment encouraged me, and I grew less anxious and more excited. The danger zone period had passed, and I finally felt like I could relax a little. Dr. MacDonald monitored me closely with ultrasounds and more frequent visits. Everything appeared to be going very well. I felt like I was out of the woods with just a hint of caution. My mother hadn't shown much interest in my pregnancy. I had shared with her about my miscarriages, and

I attributed her lack of interest to the possibility that she expected the current pregnancy to end the same way. When I asked, the ultrasound technician told me I was having a boy. A little boy. I prayed that he would stay put.

At one of my appointments, the technician told me that my placenta looked larger than usual. Dr. MacDonald didn't seem to know why. He kept an eye on it and assured me that the most important thing was that the baby was doing great. I soon discovered that he was also breech. Dr. MacDonald didn't seem too concerned because it was still early, and the odds were he would turn on his own. As time went on, my placenta continued to grow, leaving very little room for the baby to turn. If he didn't turn, I would need a C-section. I researched on the Internet about how to get a baby to turn. I went to see an acupuncturist who tried burning moxa sticks next to my little toes. Joseph, our oldest son, came with me to watch how it was done. Supposedly, it would cause the baby to turn. I played soothing music with headphones down low on my belly, because according to the research, the baby would move toward the sound to better hear it. I held bags of frozen hash browns (because we didn't have any frozen peas) on his head, in an attempt to encourage him to move away from the cold. Poor thing probably got a brain freeze before ever tasting ice cream. I did headstands against the wall and pelvic tilt exercises. Nothing worked. I was referred to a fetal maternal specialist, thinking that maybe he could do an external version, which I was warned could be very painful for me, not the baby. I was willing to try anything. The specialist did an ultrasound and said he would never attempt a version because it would be much too dangerous. He didn't want to risk tearing the placenta. He said that it was highly unlikely that the baby would turn on his own because there simply wasn't room for him to move. He said it didn't appear that the baby was under any duress; he had scored well on the nonstress test. The specialist told me that a C-section was the only way to go. He also wanted to inform me that the baby's nuchal folds looked thick. An indicator for Down syndrome. He added that my mature age made it an increased risk factor. I was eight months pregnant; it was the first time I had ever met the specialist. I told him that I wasn't worried. In my mind, I questioned his reason for giving me that bit of doom and gloom mere weeks before my delivery. I gave up the effort of trying to turn my baby around and scheduled the C-section.

When one of my sisters called to ask how I was doing, I told her what was going on. I had decided that I wasn't going to bring up any of the concerns, or the upcoming C-section, to my family unless they called to ask. I still hadn't heard much from my mother. I wasn't thrilled about having to undergo a C-section, but there was no question about the lengths I would go to, to deliver a healthy baby. It wasn't until after my conversation with my sister that my mother called, wanting to know all the details. I was scheduled to deliver at thirty-nine weeks. Without ever mentioning child care for them during my hospital stay, all my kids begged us not to call Grandma to babysit.

"We can watch ourselves."

They informed us. Joe and I looked at each other and thought about it. Angela and Joseph were in high school. The surgery was scheduled for early morning, so we could let Angela stay home with Sarah and Katie. We also had friends and neighbors who had already offered their help when the time came. We didn't invite my mother to come, and she didn't offer.

I hadn't seen Dr. MacDonald for my last several appointments because it seemed that he was either delivering a baby or away on vacation at the same time. I saw his partner, Dr. Pilkington, another pro-life, NFP, and Catholic doctor. Dr. MacDonald assured me that he would be there for the scheduled delivery. No worries. At thirty-seven and a half weeks, on March 30, 2009, at four thirty in the morning, I went into labor. I called the after-hours number, and Dr. Pilkington called me right back.

"I'm the lady with the really large placenta whose baby is breech."

He told me to come straight to the hospital. Joe and I woke up Angela and told her we were going to the hospital and that she was in charge. We told her we would call to let her know how things were going. We got to Presbyterian Hospital in Denton in record time. I was wheeled in, changed into a gown, and a monitor was strapped onto my huge belly. My 5'1" frame had topped out at two hundred and four pounds. Never had I been so large. The baby was still breech, no surprise there, and I was having regular contractions. I didn't need the monitor to tell me that. The nurses were wonderful, lighthearted, and of course, in total disbelief when they found out that it was our tenth baby. Joe showed them pictures when they didn't believe him, and they gushed over how beautiful our kids were. They were convinced that I would be having the baby very shortly. They gave me two shots of some medication to make the contractions ease up, but it had no effect. Dr. Pilkington came in to see me. He did another ultrasound to confirm that the baby was, indeed, still breech. The placenta was very large, and my contractions were not stopping. He told me that as soon as his colleague Dr. Wilson arrived, I would be taken back for surgery. Dr. Pilkington said that he was very concerned about the placenta being so big, and he wanted to be prepared for the worst, possibly an emergency hysterectomy, should I have a rupture. I told him to do whatever he needed to do to deliver my baby safely. He said he would be doing the incision up and down on my belly, not the typical bikini line one. He apologized because he said I had such a beautiful belly. I laughed out loud and thanked him, telling him that it had served me well. It would be a visible reminder of our number ten. Having a C-section was a vastly different experience. I was nervous, and I know Joe was too. Clutching my rosary beads, I prayed for my little guy to be okay. I prayed for the doctors, nurses, and the anesthesiologist. The best part of a C-section is, it only takes minutes, as opposed to hours in my case. Dr. Pilkington asked me what our little boy's name was. I told him, "Ryan."

A few moments later, he held my fresh new baby boy up over the drape and said, "Happy birthday, Ryan."

Tears welled up when I saw my little red screaming boy. I couldn't help but continue repeating, "Thank you, thank you, thank you."

I must have sounded a bit delirious. I was thanking God, so overwhelmingly grateful that He had let me carry the little life to term and bring him into the world. I stayed in the hospital for two nights. I could have stayed for a third, but I was ready to bring my baby home. Dr. MacDonald came in to see me the day I got discharged. He was grinning and shaking his head as he stood in the doorway. He said, "So you couldn't wait for me."

Knowing how many losses I had suffered, he was overjoyed that I was holding my little baby in my arms.

Recovery was painful and slow, but I wasn't short on help. All the girls were right there at every little sound Ryan made, changing diapers and lifting him up for me to nurse. They held him and rocked him while I rested. We were all able to bond with our newest family member. Our bedroom was where we all hung out for the first couple of weeks. The whole family pitched in with doing the laundry, cooking, and tidying the house. Neighbors and friends came by with meals and gifts. It was a time of love, joy, and celebration; and there was absolutely no stress.

Ryan was our little prince. Born only two weeks before Easter, where spring in Texas was in full bloom. We had been asked by our pastor, Fr. Thu, to carry the huge wooden cross in the Good Friday procession. Our whole family carried the cross through the church, up and down each aisle as the choir sang the Stabat Mater. Joe and the big boys lifted it up each time we stopped. I carried baby Ryan with Sarah and Katie on either side of me. It was an incredibly moving experience for us and such an honor to be part of the solemn memorial.

Knitterbugs continued without so much as a hiccup. Ryan was the Knitterbugs baby. He came to all the meetings and was the center of attention. The girls carried him around and passed him to whoever wanted a turn to hold him. He modeled the baby hats, lay on the blanket piles, and got buried in scarves. I brought him with me to the homeless shelter when I made my deliveries. Margaret beamed when she saw him. I was surprised and thrilled to see her. Ordinarily she wouldn't have been inside the shelter at the time I arrived, but she had been hired to work in the commissary, so she was allowed to stay inside the shelter during the day. I would have named my baby Margaret if it had been a girl, and I had told Margaret of my decision months earlier. She wasn't disappointed that he was a boy and was excited to see him, laughing out loud and clapping her hands at the sight of his chubbiness and smiles. I missed her.

Knitterbugs had been a little seed of an idea. A seed that may not have sprouted had it not been for the encouragement of one sweet lady, Melissa Brinker, the school counselor. She was the one who really believed that I could do it. When I got nervous or doubted myself, questioning whether I could pull it off, she cheered me on. I was not sure that kids would be interested, but she was convinced that they would love the idea and that their parents would too. She promoted it, and it was successful. It had taken on a life of its own, evolving into much more than I ever could have imagined. Melissa nominated me for an award. I was very surprised and incredibly humbled when our family was invited to the awards ceremony where I was presented with a plaque.

I was devastated to read an e-mail that I received from the school principal just a couple of months later. Melissa had died. Much too young, an accident had taken her life just days before school was to resume after summer break. I will never forget her. Always kind, always concerned, and always smiling. A compassionate heart, a role model for peace, an encourager, and a helper. Thank you, Melissa.

EIGHTEEN

Blindsided

Southlake, Texas, 2009–2010

Things were busy for Joe at work. He traveled extensively, flying to all the biggest offices in the country. His job was to develop procedures and train employees how to respond in the event of a crisis. A natural disaster, an act of terror, or something as simple as a power failure. Anything that interrupted business. He had implemented the Send Word Now program, a notification system to contact family members and offices in the event of a crisis. We had been back in Texas for just over three years. Joe's job had become increasingly stressful, and he'd had three new bosses in as many years. His latest boss was prickly, to put it mildly. We discussed making another change. The stress was getting to him, and he was on blood pressure medication for the first time in his life. Both of us were convinced that it was job related. Joe kept his eyes open for job postings in Ontario. We thought it might be time to go back home.

KPMG was starting to make cutbacks, and Joe's boss was positioning himself to push Joe out in order to protect his own job. Joe earned one of the highest salaries in Human Resources. They had already made two rounds of layoffs, and things were getting tense. He had worked for KPMG for twelve years and had been promoted and relocated several times. He was well-liked and respected by everyone he worked with. His recent project had flown him from city to city, coast to coast, for several weeks. As he neared the end of his training sessions, he called me after landing in New York to tell me that his boss's boss had sent him a note. He asked Joe to meet him in his office after he finished his training session for the day. Joe told me, somewhat uncertainly, "I'm either getting a promotion or I am getting laid off."

I prayed that it was good news. He said he'd call me after his meeting, which was scheduled for four thirty that afternoon. I prayed nonstop, lit a candle, and could think of little else as I tried to function through my day.

When one of my knitting ladies had stopped by to drop something off, I told her about the phone call. She said she would pray too. At four thirty-five, the phone rang. Joe sounded flat when he told me that he had just been laid off. I was stunned. How could that be? After twelve years with the firm, four relocations, several promotions, and all of his education and experience, it just didn't seem plausible. He told me he was taking the next flight home. He had been scheduled to fly to Chicago and then on to Los Angeles, but he told the big boss, that under the circumstances, he was going home to Dallas. I went into a rant about his jerk of a boss. How it was all his fault, trying to save his own job while making life miserable for Joe. Joe told me that if it was any consolation, his boss had been laid off too. Some of the sting was taken away, but not much. His boss was nearing retirement. We had ten kids at home. Never did we ever expect something like that to ever happen to us. The economy was tanking, and we were in the tank.

I remember Gramma Hubbard telling me when I was a young girl, in a hurry to grow up. Wanting to know what was in my future, where I would go, and what I would do in life. She told me that if we could see into our future, we would most certainly die of a heart attack. We all must go through things in life that are hard, and God prepares us for the hardest things along the way. If we saw the really hard stuff in advance, before we had been prepared, we might just give up. I fully believe, that had I known as a young bride, with all my hopes, dreams, and expectations, that I would have a child with a heart defect, would suffer four miscarriages, or that my husband would lose his job with ten kids to provide for, I would have had an anxiety attack. Somehow though, I didn't panic at all. I was eerily calm and just wanted my husband home so that I could comfort him and assure him that everything would work out okay. I was grateful that he seemed calm as well. I mean seriously, he had not only just received terribly devastating news, but it had been given to him while he was out of state, away from his family. Had he not been of stable mind, he may have jumped off the George Washington Bridge or thrown himself under a subway.

We were all relieved when Joe came through the door. I had already shared the news with the kids. They stayed extra quiet. We hugged him and told him what a jerk his boss was and assured him that he would get an even better job. I had no doubt that once word got out that he was available, he would be sought after. He had a master's degree in human resources and development, with more than thirty years in HR experience, and plenty of other certifications and credentials under his belt. He received a severance package, and we were confident that he would land a new job before making a dent in it. Joe didn't waste any time looking for work. He started scanning jobs as soon as he changed his clothes and unpacked his suitcase. Over the next few weeks, the phone rang constantly. Former colleagues called to tell him how shocked they were. They worried and wondered if they might be next. The employees that Joe had trained were kept on. They only earned half of his salary. It became clear that only the highest paid employees were being let go. Joe has always been a networker. I used to laugh at the boxes of hundreds of business cards that he had collected over the years. I realized how brilliant he was when he dug them out and started going through them, looking people up. He went to focus groups and filled his days searching, meeting, talking, and networking. I brought him his breakfast, lunch, and lots of coffee. I kept the little kids quiet and gave him the time and space he needed to focus and figure things out. I prayed. I told all my Knitterbugs ladies what had happened and asked them to pray. Everyone offered their support and said they would put the word out. People called to let us know when they heard of an opportunity, and they shared their contacts as well as their own personal stories. Everyone encouraged us and were convinced that he would get a new job quickly. He was marketable. We weren't all that worried. We were more injured than concerned. We were proud people, and being laid off had damaged our ego. I did everything in my power to assure Joe of his value and to let him know how much I respected and admired him. I told him that I knew God had the perfect job picked out for him somewhere. I started to pray with a purpose. Every single day I prayed. I knew we needed God to help us.

Two weeks after Joe's layoff, I rushed Ryan to Cook Children's Hospital. I'd had him to the urgent care clinic twice in the same week. He hadn't been himself at all. He'd had a fever on and off, no appetite, and was unusually whiny. At eight months old, I sensed it was more than just teething. The doctor had given him a shot of antibiotics in the office, a first dose of the prescription he wrote for him. He did a chest X-ray and thought he could see a trace of some tiny spots around his bronchial tubes. They were so faint that it wasn't definitive, but he thought it could be the start of bronchiolitis. He didn't think it was that serious. He checked for an ear infection and strep throat, but the test came back negative. Ryan started throwing up. When he didn't get any better, and actually seemed worse, I took him back to the clinic a third time. This time there was a different doctor on, and she did a blood culture. His white count was way up, and his soft spot was puffy, an indication that fluid was building up in his head. She told me to pack a bag and go straight to the hospital. I called Joe and told him to throw a bag together for me. I quickly drove home, less than two minutes away, to grab it from him in the driveway. I told him I would call him when I found out what was wrong. I was frantic. I drove directly to Cook Children's in Fort Worth, parked in the garage, and ran into the emergency waiting area. I checked in at the desk and explained why I was there. The triage nurse came out to where I was sitting in the waiting room and put a red dot sticker on Ryan's blanket. He was getting priority. We followed her into the triage room where I answered a bunch of questions. She got his weight, took his vitals before ushering us to a treatment room, sliding the glass doors closed behind us. Ryan's soft spot was getting puffier, and he was incredibly uncomfortable. He moaned and rolled his head from side to side on me. Usually a very happy, energetic baby with a healthy appetite, he had no energy, could barely hold his head up, and couldn't keep anything down. Nurses and doctors were in and out. They started an IV, drew blood, and said they wanted to do a spinal tap. They covered us both with a huge paper gown tent before they walked us down to radiation for a chest x-ray. I asked the nurse if the tent was to protect him or the other patients. She calmly answered, "The other patients."

Things happened so quickly that I didn't have time to panic. All I could do was beg God over and over again to let my baby be okay. I had not been nearly as worried when Callum had his heart surgery. I had nine other kids who had all gone through plenty of illnesses, colds, flu, fevers, concussion, broken bones, and even chicken pox, but I knew that what Ryan had was clearly something far more serious. I was no doctor, but I felt it in my gut. The doctor told me that they suspected it was meningitis. Meningitis? Kids die from meningitis. The doctors needed to determine whether it was viral or bacterial, which would be a difficult task because Ryan had already been treated with antibiotics. They decided that they would treat him for bacterial meningitis, the most serious form. If it was viral, no harm would be done. If it was bacterial, he definitely needed the medication. They told me that he would be in the hospital for a while, at least a week. My head was spinning. All his immunizations were up to date. At eight months, only half of the meningococcal vaccination had been given. The other half wouldn't be complete until he was eighteen months old. No one could tell me why or how he might have contracted it. He had been teething, and his little nose was running slightly, but it was not a full-blown cold. We were brought to a room where there was a crib set up, but I didn't put him in it. I sat in the rocking chair and laid him on my chest. He was connected to an IV, and I didn't want to risk him pulling it out. I prayed for God to heal my little boy. I couldn't bear to lose him. I told Ryan over and over how much I loved him and sang quietly to him as I rocked him in my arms all night long. The next morning, Joe brought the rocking baby glider chair. Ryan sat and slept on and off as the chair glided and played music. He began to show improvement after two days of antibiotics, and by the third day, his appetite had returned, his fever broke, and his soft spot had returned to normal. The doctor let us go home on the fifth day, convinced that I could care for him at home, with the understanding that his antibiotic treatment had to be continued with a home care nurse for the next five days. He was given big shots, one in each leg. It was torturous, but better than having to stay hooked up to an IV and an extended hospital stay. I was grateful for so many reasons. Having access to an incredible children's hospital once again, and for the return of my baby boy's health. Our next-door neighbors, Cyndy and Greg Duesing, were wonderful. They took care of Katie and Sarah while Joe came to visit us, and Greg drove Joe to the hospital so that he could pick up our car and drive it back home. There had been a neighborhood block party while we were in the hospital, and Joe skipped it, but when word got out that Ryan was sick, all the neighbors rallied together to check in and bring food. Our neighbors and friends were consistently compassionate and caring. Joe and I had almost forgotten about the layoff, or at least we weren't dwelling on it. We realized that we had everything that mattered. Our baby was better, and our family was together. From that moment on, we counted our blessings. We knew that we had a lot to be grateful for, even if everything wasn't exactly perfect.

Joe continued to search for work from morning till night, and he networked nonstop. I asked people from church, and even random people I ran into while out and about, to pray. I started praying novenas, spent time meditating daily, and gave thanks for all that we had been blessed with. It hit me that I had not slowed down enough over the years to really appreciate how blessed we truly had been in our lives. I had taken so much for granted. I had been riding along on the waves of success, enjoying the rise and the climb of the bigger, brighter, and better, but I hadn't given the glory to God. I had barely given Him a thought, and yet, He had given me all of it. My amazing husband, my beautiful children, all our wonderful friends and community. Every single blessing that we had received had come directly from Him, and I hadn't even noticed. I realized that I really needed to pray for my husband. I needed to thank God for him and ask Him to help Joe with his job search. Over the years we had prayed together as a family, some of the time. We went to church every Sunday, we prayed the rosary sporadically, usually during worrisome times, like Callum's surgery, but we weren't consistent. At best, we were luke-warm in our faith. We needed God's help. I began reserving my mornings for prayer time. Sitting outside with coffee before the kids got up. The front porch became my spiritual haven. Hidden behind the holly hedges and the hanging baskets, the Knock Out roses in full bloom, birds singing and butterflies fluttering about, it was peaceful and serene. At first it was difficult. Something to get through, some-what of a chore. I had made the decision to start praying and was committed to sticking with it, even though I didn't feel anything. I couldn't give up. I was desperate. Joe needed a job, and I begged God to help. The more I persevered, the easier praying became, and the more I actually looked forward to it. As the weeks and months went on, I stopped begging God to give Joe a job. Begging was exhausting. I decided to just leave it all in His hands. I slowly became aware, then convinced and fully confident that God had a plan for us. I had no clue what it was, but when I look back on where we had been up till that point, I could see how He had been there all along, providing for us. We were a strong family. We loved each other, we had clung to each other from the very beginning, and together we would get through this. God was with us. He always had been.

Knitterbugs remained a healthy distraction for all of us, espe-cially me. Focusing on helping people who were in real need, much less fortunate than ourselves, instead of our own troubles, gave us a purpose. We continued our outreach full force. We held potluck lunches at the senior center, donated afghans to raise money for a school in Kenya, and for fund-raisers for my mother's parish in Niagara Falls. We donated blankets to St. Francis Outreach at our parish and worked on our ongoing projects for our favorite organiza-tions. Joe remained in a constant state of job searching. He and some other recently laid-off professionals decided to start up a consulting group. As an HR director, Joe mentored unemployed professionals, helped them to revise their resumes, and prepare for interviews. He helped to match them to the right roles, all while still searching for the right position for himself. He spent countless hours helping people, many of whom found jobs, all without pay. It was a way for him to share his knowledge and gifts with others, a lot like what Knitterbugs was for me. As the recruiters called, sometimes three or more a week, and the interviews were scheduled, we stayed hopeful. During Joe's phone interviews, I kept the kids quiet, took them on walks or for a ride in the car. Each call was a potential job. For every rejection, two or three new possibilities replaced our disappointment.

In late fall, we were absolutely certain that Joe would be offered the Director of Organizational Development position for a well-known electronic game company in Grapevine, Texas. They had recruited him at a job fair when he had been applying for jobs with other companies. He happened to stop by their table out of curiosity, mostly because we had kids who played video games. When they asked him about his background, they took his contact information and called him back that same afternoon. After four or more interviews, two psychological assessments, one written, and one with two psychologists, they called him back for two more interviews. They told him that they would be making their decision right after the holidays. All the positive feedback he received seemed to indicate that he would be the chosen one. We were hopeful and confident that he would be working soon. We had a wonderful Christmas. After New Year's, he got the call, letting him know that they had chosen someone else. We were stunned. His investment of time and energy was for naught. It was one of our bigger disappointments, but soon more recruiter calls came in, and hope was renewed. We didn't allow ourselves to dwell on the disappointments.

We felt an overwhelming outpouring of care and concern from our community. Our neighbors, friends, and of course, the Knitterbugs ladies were on constant lookout for opportunities. It was a blessing to have others share our concern, even if only in spirit. We felt their prayers for us. Our kids had been taking piano lessons for several months from Mr. David Platt, their former music teacher from school. He came to the house once a week to teach. When he found out that Joe was laid off, he insisted that we allow him to continue teaching, free of charge. It was incredibly humbling to accept his generosity, but he wouldn't take no for an answer. He told us that he woke up one morning and asked God to put someone in his path who he could help, and there we were. He was not only a kindly and generous teacher, he was an incredibly talented and gifted musician, and a man of faith. He assured us of his constant prayers for our family.

Life was in a constant state of highs and lows. Disappointment came after hope, and the cycle continued. Huge companies called about big roles, and some of them had multiple positions that Joe was considered for. The point of contention always seemed to come down to salary. He was required to disclose his most recent salary. We were in the middle of a recession, and most companies weren't willing or prepared to pay that much. Some companies didn't include relocation, which for us was a big deal. Whenever the interviews progressed to the second or third stage, Joe and I celebrated with dinner and frozen margaritas at Rockfish in Town Square. Joe would excitedly tell me about his interview and how positively he felt that it had gone. We would dream about all the possibilities, anxious for a new start. And then it would all crash. Another opportunity that we fell hard for, and were certain would come through, was in Inuvik, Northwest Territories. A job with the oil and gas pipeline business. It would mean a radical lifestyle change, but we were excited to make it. We researched it and prayed about it, convinced that it was a calling to help minister to the Native people. It would be a life-changing experience for our whole family. It was early April, just before Easter. Joe had several phone interviews, followed by a final one, via Skype. Reminiscent of the previous Christmas, we were as hopeful as ever while we waited for the call to come. Joe was contacted by someone from the company to let him know that his would-be boss was in the process of searching for suitable housing for our family. That gave us reason to be even more confident that he was about to get an offer. After celebrating a beautiful Easter, filled with new hope, we got the rejection call. Their reason was that they didn't feel that we would be happy there. Inuvik is in the Arctic Circle, two miles from the

Arctic Ocean. They were afraid that we would hate it once we got there. They never gave us the opportunity to make that decision for ourselves. We were disappointed, and a little insulted. They had no idea how adventurous our family could be, and how we had psyched ourselves up about it. Our kids were just as bummed out as we were. Once again, we tried to let it go, accepting the fact that it wasn't God's plan. There was a tug-of-war going on in my heart, and head, and soul. A constant state of praying for God to take it all, and not being willing to give up, trying to control what we had no control over. Trying to tell God what we wanted, and waiting for Him to give us what we needed. The battle continued while there were more job searches, more recruiter calls, more interviews, more margaritas, and more disappointments.

I found myself pregnant again. I kept it to myself. Filled with mixed emotions—from panic, to joy, to stress, to excitement—I decided to keep it a secret until I couldn't hide it anymore. After a couple of weeks, I was just itching to tell Joe, but I didn't want to give him any reason to stress or worry. I continued to wait. I prayed to St. Thérèse the Little Flower. I prayed that if I should tell Joe, I would receive a rose. It didn't matter what color. A few days after starting the novena, I went to Walmart for groceries. The entire time I shopped, I saw several female employees carrying long-stemmed roses of every color. There were roses everywhere I looked. They were walking through the store with roses, standing at their checkouts with roses, and some, having finished their shifts, were leaving with roses tucked into their bags. I watched as an employee stood near the floral display, handing out roses to other employees. When I asked the girl who was checking my groceries what was up with all the roses, she said that they were giving them out to all the mothers in honor of Mother's Day. I thought about my novena, wondering if the roses were some sort of a sign from St. Thérèse, but I still didn't tell Joe about the baby. No one had actually handed me a rose, though I secretly wished someone would. I really wanted to tell him. I lost the baby the very next day, Mother's Day. When Joe saw me sobbing in the office, he asked me what was wrong. I told him about the baby, and about the roses, and how I had wanted to tell him but didn't want him to stress out. He told me that I should never worry about stressing him out, that we could handle anything. Of course I already knew that, but we were under so much stress as it was. I had dreamed of the perfect scenario, and played it over and over in my mind, how Joe would land the perfect job, and how thrilled he would be when I told him I was pregnant again. We didn't get either. It was getting discouraging. We wondered when we would get a break.

Before the end of the school year, Joe met with an investor. An incubator who got him thinking about going into business with her to start up a company. She would invest the money, and he would invest the sweat equity. It seemed like a great deal and a plan that would work. The concept was to teach unemployed and underemployed professionals how to consult and start up their own consulting businesses. She wanted Joe to teach the courses. This new venture gave us more hope than ever. Joe had already owned and operated his own very successful consulting business, so I was confident that this was the answer. We believed that it was only a matter of time before he started making some serious money. We finally relaxed a little, and although Joe never completely gave up his job search, he wasn't as aggressive about it.

NINETEEN

Eyes to See

Southlake, Texas, Summer 2010

$\mathcal{A}$ family that we knew from church, Barb and Armen Fraser, were going through a similar unemployment situation. Armen had lost his job several months before Joe. Barb owned and operated a drapery business out of her home, and was looking for some help a couple of days a week. She offered to pay me ten dollars an hour. I told her I'd love the job. It was summer, and I could easily work five hours a day, twice a week. Though I wasn't a professional seamstress, I did have a little experience. I enjoyed working with Barb. Not only did I learn a lot about making draperies, but the two of us quickly developed a friendship, based mostly on our shared Catholic faith. Since being humbled by Joe's job loss, and feeling more vulnerable than ever, my faith was my hope and consolation, and it had begun to grow. I prayed on my way to work, for my family, for Armen and Barb and their family, and for all the other people who needed jobs. I thanked God for all our blessings and that I would be a light to others. I prayed that in everything we did as a family, we would be an example of hope. People asked me how I could have such a bright smile and positive outlook with all that we had on our plate. I was beginning to see that it was all God, not me, getting me through each day. The more Barb and I shared our faith and prayed for each other, the better we both felt. We inspired each other, and our faith and friendship grew.

Joe and I made the decision to homeschool our kids. Homeschooling was something that I had wrestled with from the time Angela started kindergarten. We felt like it was time. We wanted a Catholic education for our kids, but sending them to private school was absolutely not in our budget. After talking with other homeschool moms, and researching curriculum, we decided that we wanted the flexibility and freedom for our kids to learn at their own pace. All the core subjects, as well as those of our own choosing, would have a solid Catholic foundation. Homeschooling would allow for more family bonding time, baking, cooking, sewing, building, exploring, playing, swimming, and relaxing. We would turn chores like grocery shopping, pet care, yard work, cleaning, and running errands into real-life skills learning experiences. We were growing weary of the rushing around and hustling of the school year, leaving precious little time to be together as a family. Several of my kids had asked over the years if they could be homeschooled. Tempted as we were, we never took the plunge. While we felt that homeschooling was the best option for all our kids and our family, our son Patrick was the one we felt would benefit the most. He had been active in seventh grade with football, had made some nice friends in the neighborhood, and was a happy-go-lucky kid. But by eighth grade, he seemed to have lost interest in sports, and despite our encouragement, he didn't want to play. He had gone for a couple of weeks' worth of cross-country training in the summer before high school, but decided it was too hot to run. Living in Texas, where the summers were oppressively hot, we couldn't blame him. Ninth grade had started out fairly well, but quickly became challenging, even despite his IEP. His teachers loved him and always commented on how well-mannered, polite, and well-liked he was. They were concerned that he wasn't completing his assignments or homework and never studied for tests. When he did happen to finish an assignment, he forgot to turn it in. By the end of the year, he was missing the bus regularly. Patrick seemed to look forward to being homeschooled, mostly because he could sleep in an extra hour if he wanted to and because it would be a self-paced curriculum. A couple of the girls grumbled about the new plan, but mostly everyone was on board. I ordered the materials and lesson plans and anxiously awaited the shipment. My heart was excited about forming my children's minds with wholesome lessons and experiences.

Our ice maker leaked. We knew when we bought the house that it wasn't working, but it hadn't been an issue for us because there was an ice maker in our freezer, so we never bothered to fix it. It was just sort of there, built in with the cabinets. What we didn't realize was that it was still plugged in. It was turned off, but the seal that prevented the water from filling it up wore out, causing it to fill and leak on our hardwood floors. When we saw the puddle of water on the floor, we assumed it was our dishwasher, so we quit using it and called our repair guy to check it out. He told us that the dishwasher was fine. It was the ice maker that was leaking. Once the floor dried out, the boards curled up and lifted off the concrete slab. We called a floor guy to come look at it. He suggested we call our insurance company because he didn't think the floor could be repaired. The house was more than fifteen years old, and that matching the wood and stain would be next to impossible. The insurance agent agreed, and we began the claims process, something we had just gone through with our roof after damage from a hailstorm. We had never made an insurance claim in our entire marriage, but within six months, we had made two. Realizing the magnitude of the mess that would be created by ripping out, sanding, and staining floors, we decided to make it worth our while. We pulled out all the carpets on the main floor in the living room, dining room, hallway, office, two bedrooms, and the stairs, and replaced them with wood. We knew the process would not be fun. It would actually be a lot like moving. Everything would have to be taken out of the house and put into the garage, but we had no doubt it would be worth the inconvenience.

I continued to enjoy my workdays in Barb's drapery room, cutting, pressing, pinning, and sewing. She was very skilled and patiently showed me how to measure, hem, and sew on trim by hand. I loved seeing all the beautiful fabrics that came in. The draperies were ordered, designed, custom-made, and hung in million-dollar homes, exclusive clubs, and condos. Barb sewed for fabric stores who contracted her out to work. She was a wonderful boss, friend, and sister in Christ. Some days she invited my kids to come with me, and her daughter Rachael took them roller-skating or swimming at the community pool. Some days, Armen baked bread with them. Once in a while they all worked on crafts or played video games. They were always kind and generous with my kids. It was a blessing to be part of their life. When the kids didn't come with me, they helped out at home. Each of them had their own chore list, and they all helped out with the little kids. I kept on top of the laundry and cleaning, and surprisingly, I felt extraordinarily organized and clearheaded. Even though I was only working five hours a day, twice a week, I managed it all as a working mom of ten, and I felt confident and proud. When I got home around one thirty, the kids and I enjoyed a treat and a swim. Most of my earnings went toward the Bread Outlet, where I bought discount bread and pastries. Now and then, I splurged on craft items to keep the kids busy. Joe continued networking and worked at growing his business.

One August morning on my way to Barb's, in Lewisville, I stopped at the CVS pharmacy. My period was late, and I had been feeling unusually tired. I bought a pregnancy test and two vigil candles with pictures of saints on them. Never having seen them sold anywhere before, I was excited to find them. When I got to Barb's house, I let myself in through the front door and walked down the hall, straight to the bathroom. The two lines on the test stick instantly turned pink. The positive result rendered me light-headed and slightly overwhelmed. I was about to embark on my first ever homeschooling adventure, the curriculum had only arrived a few days earlier. Our floors were scheduled to be torn out in a couple of weeks, and my parents were coming to visit us shortly thereafter in September. On top of that, we were experiencing concerning behavioral issues with Patrick. We had recently learned that he was sneaking out of the house at night to hang out at Town Square with some new friends. Joe's business wasn't taking off as we had hoped. Thankfully, we weren't struggling financially. We had some savings, and much of the severance package left. We also had a decent 401K as a cushion. I was concerned that our mortgage and bills would eat through our savings, but Joe was confident that it was only a matter of time before his business picked up.

My head was swimming as I walked up the stairs to the workroom. After greeting Barb, who had already begun to work on a new order, I tried to shake the fuzziness off and get busy. Utterly distracted, I attempted to measure a three-fourths seam, but found it impossible to focus. Noticing my lack of presence, Barb asked me if everything was okay. Feeling awkward about not telling Joe first, I had grown close to Barb, and really needed to share my news with someone, so I told her. She knew all about my previous miscarriages. We had shared a lot with each other over the short amount of time that I had worked with her. Barb stopped what she was doing, walked around the cutting table, and hugged me. She prayed out loud, asking God to watch over and protect my little baby, that it would be safe and healthy. Then she sent me home and told me to rest. I called Dr. MacDonald's office on the way home and told his nurse that I was pregnant. I asked her if she would call in a prescription for progesterone and super vitamins because they seemed to have worked for Ryan. She excitedly told me she would do so right away and made an appointment for the following week. Famished, I stopped at McDonald's for a supersized Quarter Pounder with cheese and french fries. After dieting for several months, I had reached my goal weight, but I suddenly realized that I was really hungry. I picked up my prescription and told Joe my news that night. He was tentatively excited. Always at the back of our minds were our lost babies. We prayed that our baby would make it. After all, we'd been blessed with Ryan. I immediately slowed down, and we told the kids right away, mostly because we needed everyone to pitch in with housework, laundry, and vacuuming. More importantly, we wanted all of them to pray. Each one of them was excited about a new baby, and they all willingly helped out. They helped with little Ryan, lifting him in and out of his crib, and came with me to the grocery store to put all the heavy items into the cart, and loaded them in and out of the van. They enjoyed the added perks of picking out their favorite snacks and treats, so I never had to beg for a helper. We rewarded them for all their help with mini outings, special lunches, or shopping for little things that they needed. Having so much support from my whole family was incredible blessing, and it was heartwarming to see their excitement for their new little sibling. I only worked for one more week with Barb, just until the crew started on our floors. She understood that I needed to guard my baby and not overdo it, and with summer almost over, my need to prepare for homeschooling.

The work crew showed up for the demo of the old floors and removal of the carpets, and to move all the furniture into the garage. We hung out in the backyard while they banged away. It was a loud and dusty job. Home improvements are rarely glitch free, and ours was no exception. After spending an entire day on the demo, the crew never showed up at all the following two days, nor did they call. I made several phone calls, helping the flooring store owner to understand that we wanted our job completed in a timely manner. She assured me that the job would be complete in two weeks, as promised. She explained that they had run into some problems with another job. Once they got back to work and the sanding and staining process began, we checked into the Hilton Hotel at Town Square to avoid the dust and fumes. We booked three rooms for our ten kids and two dogs. Joe and I stayed in the connecting rooms with all four of the boys and the two youngest girls, and the four oldest girls stayed in a room across the hall with the dogs. I brought along a few of the homeschool books as a sort of a soft start, planning to dig in deeper when we were settled back into the house. The kids took turns walking the dogs, and we drove back and forth to the house regularly to check on the progress of the work. The hotel was two minutes from our house, but we pretended to be on vacation, walking around Town Square and going out for dinner. When the work was finally done, we met with the flooring store owner for our inspection. The results were more than disappointing. For the most part, the floors looked absolutely beautiful. The color, a rich antique mahogany, was classic and exactly what I had chosen. The finish was smooth and clean, but there were multiple areas where the stain hadn't taken, and the boards were void of color. They had a sticky, uncured finish. The owner agreed that they would need to redo them. She called a meeting with her wood supplier to try to figure out who was to blame for the defective boards. We didn't care whose fault it was, we just wanted it fixed. Our main dilemma was that my parents would be arriving the very next day for a five-day visit. The owner had guaranteed that all the work would be completed at least a week before my parents' arrival. That was one of the reasons we had chosen her company. She decided that they could move most of the furniture back into the house so that we could clean up and get ready for their visit. After they left, the workers would return to move everything out again and refinish the floors. It was not ideal, but we didn't have any other option.

My appointment with Dr. MacDonald was like old home week. He and all his staff were convinced that our new baby would be just fine. They believed in those super vitamins. With blood work complete, and my ultrasound looking great, Dr. MacDonald told me that he planned to monitor me extra closely. Feeling fantastically delightful with all the classic pregnancy symptoms, fatigue and constant hunger, I felt a deep sense of awe and wonder at the knowledge that I was carrying a newly created life within me. I was overcome with joy.

It was the first time my parents had come to visit us together in our new house. I hadn't seen my mother since Callum's heart surgery, and I hadn't seen my dad since the Christmas before we left New York, four years earlier. I had spoken with my mother fairly regularly over the phone, once a month or so, and we e-mailed each other almost daily. When I told her I was pregnant, she seemed genuinely happy. The distance seemed to have been good for our relationship. After hearing about my knitting classes at the homeless shelter, she sent some reusable bags that she had bought, with my sister, to give to my students. I told her about our Knitterbugs projects, and she reminded me that it had been her idea for me to knit blankets for the babies in the hospital, after reading a newspaper story about the need for them when we had first moved to Texas. On several occasions, she asked me to make baby blankets for her coworkers and friends. I happily did so and shipped them to her. When she let me know that she was once again organizing the Irish Festivities fund-raiser for Development and Peace at her parish, I made an afghan, a knitted baby dress with booties and a teddy bear for their raffle, and shipped those as well. Our relationship worked because of the distance. A part of me wished I could be involved with all the family gatherings with my siblings, but when I got the phone calls afterward about the latest drama, I was relieved that we weren't part of it. Families have drama. Large families have even more drama. I often listened uncomfortably as my mother vented about the most recent saga and who was in the doghouse. I tried to remain neutral, always figuring that there had to be another side to her stories. We looked forward to my parents' visit, and I prayed for it to be peaceful. On the surface, it was, for the most part, pleasant. There was no obvious drama, and everyone got along. My dad, not surprisingly, fixed a few things while he was there. I enjoyed watching him do what he had done in every other house we had lived in. He walked around, jiggling handles, and eyeing up doors, checking how aligned things were, adjusting and tightening anything that was loose or askew. Always a worker, never one to sit around, he sized up our house, and I could tell he approved. I told him of our plans to stain the rest of the heavy wood trim and cabinets to match the floors.

We went on a shopping trip to Walmart to buy new bikes for the little girls. The old hand-me-down ones had seen better days. My dad fixed the training wheels and helped them to ride. We spent time in the pool, Joe grilled out on the patio, and we enjoyed coffee on the front porch while we watched the little kids play. My parents' visit was relaxed, except for the off side comments about our plan to homeschool. My mother informed me that my father didn't think it was a good idea.

"Your father thinks that kids should be in school."

My response to her was that our kids had all been in school for their entire education, and we were going to try something different. My father never voiced the opinion to me himself, nor did my mother mention it while he was present. She made the announcement while he was sitting on the back patio, working on a crossword puzzle. Not wanting to make him uncomfortable, I didn't question him about it. I didn't want to feed into the drama that I sensed my mother was trying to create. Another comment that sent shivers down my spine was made while we were all in the pool. The kids were all splashing and playing, and I was sitting near the edge on the step. My mother casually asked me if we had spoken to Christopher, Joe's son. She had never once mentioned his name before that time, ever. I was stunned and wondered why, all of a sudden, she chose to bring up the subject at that particular moment, with all my kids around. It was beyond bizarre to me. What should have obviously been a question for Joe, she asked me. Joe was at his office at the time. I told her that no, we hadn't heard from him and that she needed to be discreet because we hadn't discussed Christopher with our kids. I stared directly at her. The look in her eyes was cold and dark, her mouth was tight, almost smug. She dropped the subject, but I was left with a very uneasy feeling in the pit of my stomach.

Joe and I took my parents to Rockfish for dinner. I ordered tea, no margaritas for me with my little bun in the oven. We walked around Town Square, looked in some shops, and stopped for ice cream. It was a pleasant evening with just us grown-ups. Not surprisingly, there were no questions or opinions discussed about homeschooling or children from previous marriages. On their day of departure, we had coffee on the front porch while the kids played in the front yard and rode their bikes. We took pictures together, and my mother asked all the kids to write her a letter. We waved them off as Joe drove them to the airport. Immediately after the van was out of sight, Patrick began listing all the reasons he should go back to public school and why homeschooling him would not be a good idea. He had been the one who was happiest with the whole homeschool idea, but all of a sudden, he didn't want to do it anymore. We told him that while his opinion was interesting, we had already made the decision to homeschool, because as his parents, we felt it was in his best interest.

The flooring crew returned the day after my parents left. Once again, they cleared out all the furniture, and we checked back into the Hilton, into the same three rooms with the same ten kids, and the same two dogs. The owner assured us that the floors would be fixed and that we would be back in our home in four or five days.

I went back to see Dr. MacDonald for my twelfth-week checkup and ultrasound. I loved the relaxed and welcoming atmosphere in his office. Everyone was always cheerful and friendly. Being in the middle of a stressful renovation gone wrong, and after a very strange visit from my parents, I welcomed the peaceful space. I brought along my knitting, and got busy working on a pair of socks that I had started a couple of days earlier. Smiling and waving back at the nurses and office staff when they winked their excitement about another baby on the way, I followed the ultrasound technician back to the little room. Feeling relieved to have made it to twelve weeks, out of what I believed was the danger zone, I marveled at my little baby on the screen. I saw arms and legs kicking and moving, and a tiny beating heart. I thanked God. When the scan was complete, I waited in the exam room for Dr. MacDonald. He scarcely looked up when he came in, his nose in my chart, he was intently looking at the ultrasound pictures. Not his usual good-natured jovial self, he was incredibly serious. I was taken by surprise because I had never seen that side of him. He told me that he had some concerns. The baby's head looked larger than it should for twelve weeks, and the ventricles were also very large. I stared back blankly at him, questioning what it all meant. So my baby's head was big. Was that a problem? Joe was a big guy. Some of my kids had bigger heads when they were born and grew into them. Dr. MacDonald said that he was concerned that there could be fluid in the ventricles. I still didn't quite understand, and I was too afraid to ask. He wanted me to see a fetal maternal specialist to make sure that there wasn't anything serious going on. He smiled sympathetically and told me not to worry, that he just wanted to rule out any concerns. I was worried, but remained hopeful. He hadn't given me a diagnosis, he was just being cautious. I couldn't imagine that there could be anything seriously wrong, I had just seen my baby swimming around on the ultrasound with my very own eyes. Kicking its legs and waving its arms, its heart was beating. It was alive. I didn't cry. There wasn't any need to. Dr. MacDonald wanted me to see a specific specialist, not the one I had seen when I was pregnant with Ryan. He wanted me to see a specialist who shared his pro-life views and wouldn't counsel me to have an abortion. That startled me. Dr. MacDonald knew that I would never have an abortion, but he didn't want me to have to deal with someone who might pressure me that way. I agreed to see the specialist he recommended. I cried on the way home. Not sobbing cries, but tears of worry over the possibility that something could be wrong with my baby. I prayed that God would let my baby be okay. When I shared the news with Joe, he said there was no sense in worrying until we had something to worry about. I tried to put it out of my head and just pray. As they say, ignorance is bliss, and it was. Well, sort of.

We checked on the workers several times a day. The company who had been contracted out by the flooring company to adjust our doors couldn't finish their job until the floors were done. We had real concerns with them. They broke the locking mechanism on our garden doors, and none of the other three doors had been sealed properly. The way that they had been cut left big gaps at the bottom where light and rain and bugs could get in. They showed up at the house every day but never seemed to accomplish anything. They sat on the back of their truck eating donuts or walked around the front yard on their phones, killing time. Everything about them seemed fly by night. The flooring owner told me not to worry, that they had been using that particular company for years. She assured me that the doors would be perfect. The second attempt at redoing the floors was a bust. Instead of resanding and restaining the entire floor, they sanded only the spots that hadn't cured. That resulted in large splotches of different shades of stain, with distinct border lines where they tried to fix the original mistakes. I was thankful that we had withheld half the payment, despite having been asked for more money by the owner, prior to the first failed attempt. I was beside myself, and Joe was not very happy either.

The kids were beginning to go stir-crazy living in the hotel, and the dogs weren't used to being confined. I didn't think any of us could have handled a third three- to four-night stay. The night before, our last one at the Hilton, Patrick had snuck out of the room. Joseph had woken up and noticed that he was gone, so he and Joe went out looking for him. Joe talked to a police officer who was on patrol. He gave the officer a description and told him that Patrick had snuck out of our room. He also told him that he'd been caught sneaking out of our house more than once. While they were talking,

Joe spotted Patrick in a car, driving around with some kids he didn't recognize. Joe yelled out to him, and Patrick knew he was caught. He got out of the car, and Joe grabbed him by the collar of his shirt, right past the officer, and back up to our room. No sooner had we all settled back into bed, drifting off, hoping to get some sleep, did the fire alarm go off in the hotel. It was almost midnight. We bolted out of bed and woke up our sleeping babies and kids. The older kids, startled, met us in the hallway with the dogs, and we all made our way down the stairs and out onto the street where all the other hotel guests had gathered. Thankfully it had been a false alarm, but needless to say, we'd all had enough of the hotel.

I met with the flooring owner at the house the next morning and told her we'd had enough. They had tried to save time and money by only patching the flawed areas, making the floors look even worse. We were not happy, and we were all exhausted. She told us that she would foot the bill for a final hotel stay. She knew people who owned a hotel who would give her a discount rate, but it was in another city. The whole reason for us staying at the Hilton was because it was close to home and Angela's high school. Being a senior, we had given her the option of either finishing up at Carroll Senior High School or being homeschooled. It would have been much too inconvenient to drive through morning traffic across two cities, to get her to school on time and back every day. We declined the offer and made a trip to Bass Pro Shop, where we purchased a large, nine-person tent and an air mattress. We set it up, along with the smaller tent that we already had, and camped out in our backyard until the floors were fixed. Our kids had their first homeschool lessons on the back patio that October. All of us gathered around our fire pit, sipping hot chocolate while we studied our catechism. It was not how I had planned it, but it was creative, and the kids didn't seem to mind. They actually enjoyed it. It was part of the beauty of homeschooling. The owner of the flooring company hired out a guy who apparently was a fixer. She had called him out on occasion to fix the mistakes her crew made. Shaking his head as he surveyed the mess, I could see that he clearly wasn't happy. He told me that the owner regularly hired unskilled workers who she could pay less, because she thought by cutting corners, she would get a higher return. Instead, it always ended up costing her more.

We were relieved to finally have someone who seemed to know what he was doing. He and his crew sanded down all the floors and began restaining that day. Our air conditioner died. In order for the stain to cure properly, the air conditioner needed to be running. I called our repair guy, and he came out right away. He shook his head, realizing what the problem was, and told us that he had seen it all before. The dust from the sanding had clogged up the filters, causing the units to seize up. He checked all three of them. Yes, we had three air-conditioning units in that big house. He changed all the filters and told us that we would need to change them again in a few days. He said that the ducts were filled with dust and recommended we have them cleaned out after the floors were finished. He said that any reputable flooring company would have sealed all the vents before doing that much sanding, and they would have also used a bag sander. They did neither. Not only did we have the added expense of the air-conditioning repairs, we were spending more money on food and gas because we couldn't go inside the house. The new flooring guy told me that he would be waiting a full day in between coats of stain and sealer to allow it to cure properly. He wasn't taking any chances.

TWENTY

Total Surrender

The fetal maternal specialist office was about an hour away, in Allen, Texas. I had to wait two weeks for the afternoon appointment. I was invited by my neighbor, who was also a parishioner at St. Francis of Assisi Church, to a Magnificat prayer meeting that morning. I had shared with her the concerns of my doctor, and she offered to pray for me and my baby. She'd also asked her prayer group to pray. I had never been to a charismatic prayer group before. It was very different, but I felt a sense of peace. The ladies in the group prayed over me, blessed me with holy oil, and prayed for my baby to be healed of any problems or illness. I left the meeting and drove to the appointment by myself, leaving Joe at home with the kids and the workers. He tried to do what business he could from his makeshift office in the tent. We hadn't much discussed the possibilities, but we both silently worried about what the specialist might find. I prayed the rosary my entire way there. I had made every effort not to worry or dwell on anything negative. I had told Barb, my next-door neighbor Cyndy, and my mother about Dr. MacDonald's concerns, but no one else. None of my knitting ladies even knew that I was pregnant. The office was a long drive but easy to find, and parking was convenient. I found the office without any trouble, checked in, and filled out the paper-work that the receptionist gave me. There was one other woman in the tiny, remarkably silent, and clinical waiting room. Reality began to set in that something could be seriously wrong with my baby.

When the ultrasound technician called me back, I followed her to the unusually oversized room, and got set up on the table. The screen on the wall was huge, the biggest one that I had ever seen, and I watched as she scanned my belly. My baby had grown quite a bit since my last ultrasound, and I searched for anything that looked unusual. I saw a beating heart, and arms and legs moving all around. Paying particular attention to the head, it looked perfect to me. I'm not a doctor, but I didn't think it looked that big at all.

The technician was polite but professional. She asked me if it was my first baby. I told her no, that it was my eleventh. On cue, she did a double take. Of course, she was amazed and commented on how you don't hear of big families like that anymore. She asked how I managed it all, noting that I must be very organized. I politely went along with the small talk, praying that everything was looking okay. Surely, if there was something seriously wrong, she wouldn't be so chatty. She asked me what brought me to the specialist, which surprised me. I expected that Dr. MacDonald must have sent a memo with my referral. I explained what Dr. MacDonald had told me, how he had been concerned that the baby's head and ventricles were larger than they should be for twelve weeks. She measured the baby's head and said that it didn't look that overly large. It was on the big side, but still within the normal range. I breathed a sigh of relief. I knew it. Everything was fine. Dr. MacDonald was just being cautious. We would have a good laugh after I socked him in the arm for worrying me half to death. Then she said, "Oh. Now I see what he means."

That was the end of the chitchat. I wanted to scream, "What!" "What do you see?" "What does he mean?"

But I couldn't speak. My throat was closed. She quickly left the room, and I waited alone, still on the table for what seemed like an eternity, until the doctor came in. He walked around the table and sat in front of the monitor. He introduced himself and shook my hand before resuming the scan. It didn't take him long to find what he was looking for. He turned to me and said, "Mrs. Allen, I am very sorry. I have no good news for you."

He pointed to the screen and showed me the outline of my baby's head. He said that the size of the head wasn't the biggest concern, the real concern was that the ventricles were very large and filled with fluid. He pointed to the inside of the head and said that the area inside should appear white on the screen. Even I could see that the space was completely black. He pointed to a brain stem and told me that he could not see a brain. His prognosis was severe hydrocephalus, or most likely, holoprosencephaly. I wasn't sure what that was. I knew that it meant water on the brain, but I had no idea what it would mean for my baby. He soon informed me of the possibilities. He said that more than likely, my baby would not survive the pregnancy. That it had a brain stem but no brain. No messages could be sent to the organs; therefore, the baby would have no organ function. There would most definitely be severe facial deformities. If by chance the baby did survive, it would certainly not live long; several hours, possibly days at the most. If it turned out to be severe hydrocephalus, which he doubted, the baby could survive, but would live in a vegetative state and have severe mental retardation.

I felt like I was in a dark tunnel. How could this be happening? I couldn't speak. I just kept gulping back the lump in my throat that threatened to choke me, while tears silently rolled down my cheeks. The doctor handed me a tissue, then asked, "Given all this information, how would you like to proceed with the pregnancy?"

His question brought me back to the room. The words *abortion* and *termination* were never used, but I knew what he was getting at. Dr. MacDonald had sent me to this particular specialist, confident that I wouldn't be counseled into an abortion, but the doctor was hedging around it. I didn't ask him to clarify what he meant. I already knew. If I had told him that I wanted out of my situation, that I wanted to terminate my pregnancy, I have no doubt that he would have given me that out. I was resolute. I wanted to make it perfectly clear how I wished to proceed. I looked directly at him and informed him with a shaky but assertive voice, through tearful sobs and choking gasps, that I had ten beautiful children at home, and that God alone would decide whether my baby lived or not. I told him I would proceed with my pregnancy the same way I had with all

217

the others. He smiled, patted my hand, and told me that he would see me in four weeks. Before he walked out, I asked him if he could tell if I was having a boy or a girl. I knew that it was still very early, but he was a specialist, and his equipment was far more sensitive than regular ultrasounds. He took the Doppler once again and scanned my belly. He said that he was fairly certain that I was having a boy. I named my baby Michael before I left the room.

I pulled myself together and walked out to the receptionist's desk to make my next appointment. I walked to the car and called Joe. Barely choking out the words, I told him that it was not good news. He told me to hang up the phone and come home. Through my sobbing tears, I drove the hour-long trip home, not knowing what to think. Not able to think. I wasn't even able to pray. Completely numb, all I could do was groan. I think I must have been in shock. Certain that it must be the worst day of my life, I miraculously made it home safely to our tent city. My little kids rushed to greet me when they heard the car. Stone-faced and completely drained from sobbing all the way home, I had no tears left. Or so I thought. Walking through the gate with the kids trailing behind asking questions, "Is it a boy or a girl?"

I couldn't answer. Afraid to open my mouth, knowing that attempting to utter a single word would cause me to crumble again, I didn't want to fall apart in front of my kids.

It was late afternoon. All I wanted to do was lock myself away in my bedroom and cry into my pillow, but I could not enjoy that luxury. We still couldn't walk on our floors. I wanted to be alone, to close my eyes and block out the world. Joe sent the kids out of the tent so that I could tell him what the doctor said. I explained as best I could, the facts that I had been given. We did our best to keep our voices down, but it was next to impossible to have a private conversation, being that we were living in the backyard. Tents are not exactly soundproof. The look on Joe's face was grave but loving. As much as he tried, he couldn't hide his own fear when he told me not to worry, that we would be okay, and that God would help us through. Our kids are nosy. They were in tune to the fact that there was something wrong with the baby. They overheard bits and pieces of our conversation, and they questioned us about what was going on. Not wanting to alarm them, but realizing we couldn't hide it, we told them we all needed to pray for the baby because there was something wrong with his brain. Sensing that I needed to be by myself so that I could attempt to absorb it all, Joe loaded the kids into the van and took them somewhere.

My mother had known about the appointment and was expecting me to call her with a report. I didn't want to talk to anyone. It felt as though I had a watermelon lodged in my throat. I simply could not speak. Knowing that she would be waiting to hear from me, I quickly typed out an e-mail to tell her what the doctor said, and told her I wasn't ready to talk to anyone yet. Immediately after sending the e-mail, the phone rang and continued to ring, multiple times. I recognized her number on the call display but didn't answer. I turned the ringer off and lay on the blow-up mattress in the tent, trying my best to block out everything.

When Joe and the kids returned, one of them quietly came into the tent and told me they had bought me a present to make me feel better. It was a scented candle. I didn't believe that I would ever feel better again for the rest of my life. The phone rang again, and one of the kids ran into the tent to hand it to me, calling out, "It's Grandma."

Knowing I couldn't avoid her forever, I took the phone. Trying to remain quiet and calm, I quickly erupted into blubbering sobs. I told her I didn't want to talk, that I was much too upset and distraught. There was so much going through my head, I didn't want to even think about anything. My mother refused to hang up and continued to ask questions. I told her I had already e-mailed her everything I knew, that I felt numb and had no idea how I was going to get through it all. I had no idea how it was going to turn out. The doctor had given me no hope. Every possible scenario was grim. Utterly drained, I told my mother I needed to go, and I hung up the phone.

My Barnes and Noble Knitterbugs meeting was that evening. I contemplated sending out an e-mail to cancel, but it was already late, only an hour before the meeting was scheduled to begin. Most of the ladies wouldn't get the message in time, and I definitely wasn't up to calling anyone on the phone. None of the ladies knew I was pregnant, so there wouldn't be any baby questions. I could pretend like everything was fine. I decided to go. I pulled myself together, put on some fresh makeup, and drove to Barnes and Noble. I made my way up to our regular meeting spot and put on my cheeriest face. I sat in one of the big comfy chairs and knitted and chatted as usual. No one had a clue that I had just received the most devastating news of my life.

The kids were all asleep when I got home. I sat in one of the patio chairs and called Barb. Ever calm and reassuring, she told me that she would pray. She reminded me that God's plan wasn't always our plan, but His plan was always perfect. We needed to trust Him. Barb said just exactly what I would have told her if she were the one going through what I was. I knew she was trying to comfort me, but my faith was being tested. Words were simply words. I had talked the talk plenty. Suddenly, I was being asked to walk the walk, and I was shaking in my boots. In the dark, I made my way to our tent, exhausted and drained. Feeling a rush of emotions, I was unable to fit them into their own compartments, they just melted together. I desperately wanted to organize all the information, thoughts, and fears that were beginning to consume me so that I could figure out how to move forward. Sleep was what I craved, but my mind refused to allow it. I quit taking the progesterone that I had been prescribed. I had taken it for three months, but figured there was no point in continuing, the baby probably wouldn't live.

All the miscarriages I'd had, had occurred with no warning. Some I had been able to see very early on with an ultrasound before they were gone. Others, I had lost even before my first doctor appointment. I had been heartbroken with each one of their lost lives. I had not expected them to die, but when they suddenly did, I had no option but to accept the fact that they were gone. This baby was further along than any of the others. He had a clearly visible form, a beating heart, and arms and legs. He was active and very much alive. I had seen him, a boy. Michael. If he wasn't going to survive, when would he die? Where would I be? Would I know? Would my body just expel him like a miscarriage, or would I have to labor and deliver a dead baby? I was terrified. The thoughts played over and over again in my head as I tried to sleep. There was no rest to be had. What if he did live? What if he were like the horrifying pictures I had regretfully researched on the Internet? How would I ever manage to care for a baby with severe deformities and disabilities, when I had ten other children who needed me? Having babies had been easy, almost second nature for me. My other miscarriages had been heartbreaking, but I felt like a miscarriage would be a blessing; I wanted God to just take my baby, right then and there. I asked Him, out loud, to just let me have a miscarriage. The moment the words were spoken, I immediately took them back, feeling incredible guilt and disgust with myself for even considering such a thing. I wanted to at least see my baby. To have the chance to hold him, even for only a moment and kiss his head. To tell him that I loved him and that he was wanted.

The floors had cured enough to walk on, so I was able to use our shower in the master bathroom. It was a piled-up mess of furniture and decor. Because we had to move everything out of the bedroom and office, the workers stacked a lot of it in the bathroom. I managed to shift some stuff out of the way, just enough to wedge myself into the shower. I was grateful for the opportunity to lock myself away and release the stored-up groans and tears that I had been holding in. I let the hot steamy water soak into my head, penetrating my brain, trying to wash away all the pain and anxiety. I had played every possibility over and over inside my head. I was dizzy, on an emotional roller coaster, with no idea when it would stop. I wanted to get off, but God was controlling the ride. I had no idea why He was being so cruel. I decided to have a bold conversation with Him that morning. Stepping out of the shower, I wrapped myself in a towel and stood in front of the mirror, scarcely recognizing the reflection looking back at me. Puffy red eyes and strained face, the dull ache in my head and heart weighed me down. Despite the extra long very hot shower, every muscle in my back, neck, and chest still ached from sobbing. I told God that He could fix my baby, and I demanded that He do just that. I told Him that we had been faithful to our wedding vows. We had gratefully and lovingly welcomed every life that He had blessed us with. I wanted Michael to be healed. I prayed that if it was not His will that Michael be healed, that He would give me the grace to handle whatever the outcome might be. I thanked Him for the gift of Michael, and I returned him to God that day. I entrusted my unborn baby boy to Him with complete and total abandonment. Remarkably, a complete sense of peace—that I have never experienced before, or since—instantly washed over me. It was powerful, liberating, and absolutely surreal. I felt free to live. To continue with my pregnancy, however long it might last, without being chained to fear and anxiety.

I began to pray specifically and exclusively for Michael. Joe's job was nowhere near as important as our baby. While I knew that God could easily cause multitudes of miracles, simultaneously, I didn't have the energy or capacity to focus my prayers on anything but Michael. I had never prayed so intensely for anything in my life. Nothing else had ever been that important. The more I prayed, the calmer I became and the less anxiety I had. I prayed novenas to multiple saints, promising to honor them by giving Michael their names as middle names. I prayed day and night, offering up every little thing I did as a prayer—laundry, cooking, and schooling the kids. I prayed as I drove and shopped, knitted and ironed. When I woke up in the middle of the night, I prayed. As I drifted back to sleep, I offered up every breath I took and every beat of my heart as a prayer. I knew God was hearing me, and I believed He would answer.

With our floors finally finished and our house put back together, life returned to a new normal. I had only told a handful of people about my pregnancy, people who I knew would pray. A few of the regular Knitterbugs ladies, some friends from church, and my next-door neighbor, Cyndy Duesing. She had become a prayer partner and was a tremendous support to me. I called Cyndy after each of my appointments to let her know how things were going so that she would know how to pray. We prayed the rosary faithfully every night as a family. It was precious to see our other kids praying so fervently for their baby brother. We didn't know what God's plan was for baby Michael or our family, but we were able to live peacefully, one day at a time.

222

We decided to paint the house. The whole flooring experience had been a disaster. Not only had it taken more than a month, and three attempts to get it right, we had to hire a professional door guy to come and repair the mess that the original ones had made. The floor guys had scarred up walls with their sander and splattered stain on every wall, trim, and door, including our outside pillars on the front porch. In an attempt to cover the damage, they touched up the stains with the wrong-colored paint. We called Dore Rodriguez. Not just a master painter and plasterer, but an artist. He promised to get the job done. We had hired Rodriguez painting when we lived in our first house in Texas, so we knew from experience that he was a man of his word. His crew was quiet, courteous, and skilled. When they completed a job, they left no trace of a mess anywhere. We picked out colors and decided on textures and special finishes. Dore said that he could also stain the kitchen cabinets and all the wood trim, built-ins, and ceiling beams to match the floors. They started the job the week of Thanksgiving while we were in South Dakota.

Not a vacation, but more like a Knitterbugs mission trip, I had been in touch with the Red Cloud Indian School on the Pine Ridge Indian Reservation, in Pine Ridge, South Dakota. I had arranged to visit the school, Sacred Heart Outreach, and the Pine Ridge Hospital. Knitterbugs had been busy for months, knitting, sewing, and collecting items to donate. We had over four hundred and fifty pairs of mittens, hundreds of hats, scarves, baby blankets, large blankets, baby sets, toiletries, and clothing. We crammed every inch of space in our twelve-passenger van with knitted items. The kids and I had sorted and labelled everything for each charity, school, and individual classroom. Our kids had made and attached little handmade ladybug tags on each pair of mittens. We told the kids that they could each pack three changes of clothes for the trip. We filled up a cooler with drinks and snacks for the eighteen-hour drive.

We boarded the dogs in a kennel and left the house keys with Dore and his crew before we hit the road on a Friday night. A few of the people that I had shared my pregnancy news with thought that we would have canceled our trip, but I wouldn't hear of it. We all needed the distraction, and our kids had really been looking forward to it. We had intended for it to be more than just an educational experience. We wanted to take them out of their bubble and open their eyes to real hardship and poverty. Pine Ridge, South Dakota, is one of the poorest places in the United States. That was the main reason we chose it as a charity. We had made and sent seventy five pairs of mittens there the year before. When I told Mom Mom Marge about it, she shared stories with me about a trip that she had made to Pine Ridge with her kids when they were little. She was thrilled to hear that we were making the same trip with our family. She told me to be sure to visit the Crazy Horse Memorial.

The drive to South Dakota was long but remarkably easy. We stayed at cheap motels, renting one room, sharing beds, a cot, and floor space. We wanted our kids to get a feel for what it was like to sacrifice some comfort. They were used to living in a big house with plenty of space, a big yard, pool, access to a kitchen, clean laundry, showers, and whatever else they needed. The idea was to experience a glimpse of how life is for some people in our own country. The little taste they would get wouldn't even come close, but it was something. They complained about how the rooms smelled and how ugly they were decorated. They grumbled about sharing beds, the cramped quarters, not being able to bring more clothes with them (though I did laundry at every hotel), and how little room there was in the van with all the bags of knitted donations. We responded by telling them that they needed to be grateful. That the whole purpose of the trip was to help them to appreciate all that they did have and to help those who had far less. We made it to Rapid City late Saturday night and went straight to sleep. We went to Mass at St. Thérèse the Little Flower Church the next morning. While planning the trip, I chose that particular church because St. Thérèse is my patron saint, and I intended to pray there for a miracle. The little church was so packed that our family couldn't sit together. Joe sat somewhere in the back of the church with some of the kids, while I went up to the choir loft with the rest. When Mass finished, I lit a candle and prayed by the beautiful statue, asking St. Thérèse to intercede for my baby boy. We spent the day doing some sightseeing—the Crazy Horse Memorial, which was spectacular; Mount Rushmore, which we didn't get to see because of such dense fog, but we did see some pretty cool mountain goats. We went to a drive through wild life preserve called Bear Country, where we got up close with wolves, bears, bison, and wild cats. We took the kids to Chili's for dinner before going back to the hotel to squeeze into bed. It was a really enjoyable and much needed family day. Most of the grumbling had subsided, and we were all bonding in a new way.

Our visit to the Red Cloud Indian School was scheduled for the following day. The plan was to make our way back to Texas after delivering all our donations. I was super excited to be visiting the school, outreach, and hospital. That particular Knitterbugs project had been a real labor of love. After many months of knitting and preparing, I couldn't wait to give it all away. Joe got up first to shower and dress, and was about to get coffee for us when he called for me to come look. He was standing in front of the window, holding back the curtain. I made my way through the maze of bags, beds, and cots to see what he was looking at. The kids, beating me to it, jumped up and down, singing, "It's snowing!"

Our van, which was parked directly in front of our hotel window, was completely covered in a thick layer of snow, and the huge fluffy flakes were still falling steadily. Barely able to see the rest of the parking lot, Joe seemed to be uneasy about the trip ahead of us. Being a Canadian girl, I wasn't afraid. It was the last day of school before Thanksgiving break, so we had to make our delivery that day, or the kids wouldn't get their mittens. I finished getting ready and packed up our things while our kids danced around excitedly. We told them not to play in the snow because they didn't have the right gear, and we didn't want them sitting in wet clothes on the trip back. Our instructions fell on deaf ears. When I made my way out to the van where Joe was clearing the snow and loading up bags, I noticed the guy who had been shoveling the entrance had a big smile on his face. He was leaning on his shovel, watching Grace make a snow angel, right in the middle of the parking lot. Glancing over at our Texas license plate, he asked us if our kids had ever seen snow before. We told him that it had been a long time since our kids had seen that much snow. He told us we shouldn't have any trouble on the roads, since snow is no big deal in South Dakota. He was right. The roads had been plowed, but visibility was not great because it was still snowing heavily. It reminded me of the night Joe had kissed me for the first time.

As we drove through the city, our kids were astounded by all the bundled-up students, waiting for school buses. They were shocked that school hadn't been cancelled because of the weather. Joe and I laughed, explaining to them that it was just a normal winter day in South Dakota. We got worried when we didn't see any road signs for the reservation. We definitely didn't want to get lost or stranded in the storm. As we scanned the street, looking for a place to stop for directions, an Ogallala Sioux Transit bus turned in front of us. We realized we were heading in the right direction, so we continued to follow the bus. It was a two-hour drive from Rapid City to Pine Ridge, under a heavy winter sky. The closer we got to the reservation, the more the sun seemed to break through. First, it was a heavily filtered light that got brighter and brighter the closer we got. When we arrived at the Red Cloud School, I remarked to the principal about the peculiar weather, and how the sun hadn't appeared until we got on the reservation. She smiled broadly and said, "That's because you're in God's country now."

She invited us into the school, and the boys unloaded the bags. We visited the primary classrooms where our kids handed each student a pair of mittens. It was touching to see the children's smiles brighten as they chose their pair and immediately tried them on.

One of the most memorable moments was when we visited the huge kindergarten classroom, a cheerful sunny place, filled with children's artwork. The teacher had her students sit in a circle on the floor mats. She told her students that usually, when people buy a pair of mittens from the store, they don't ever get to know who made them or even where they come from. She explained that the mittens we brought for them had been made by us and our knitting group and that we had driven them all the way from Texas to hand-deliver them to the children personally. She showed them on the map how far we had driven. The kids beamed and were thrilled with their new mittens. The principal told us that the first snow of the season had fallen that morning. We were glad that we got the delivery in before the Thanksgiving break. We left a big bag of extra mittens, just in case any of them got lost. We delivered hats and scarves to the neighboring high school before making our way to the hospital, to deliver the baby items.

Pine Ridge Hospital was new and beautiful, and the waiting area was filled with people. I wondered if many of the people weren't there because they were sick, but it was a place to keep warm. We were relieved to find such a nice hospital, because we had driven past the old one by mistake, and were distressed to find such a dilapidated, abandoned-looking building. We were told that it had been the former hospital and, shockingly, was still being used for other services like addiction counseling and Head Start programs. Our attempt at opening our kids' eyes to life outside their comfort zone was successful. As we passed by dozens of ramshackle homes, trailers, and run-down shacks with broken-down cars and trucks, we were well aware of the fact that they had to be bitter cold during the long, hard Dakota winters.

We drove around in search of Sacred Heart Church Outreach and passed by it several times before realizing that what looked like a storage building was actually the church. We showed up without any notice. Despite several attempts to make contact prior to the trip, I was never able to get an answer. We found the door at the back of the low, flat-roofed building, and I rang the bell. That's when we met Angie, the lady who ran the place. I explained why we were there, and she invited us to pull our van around to a different door, where she met us with a shopping cart. Joseph and Patrick unloaded all the rest of the bags, filling the cart, and we carried what wouldn't fit. Angie was surprised that we would make such a long drive. When I explained that we had been in contact with the school and had arranged the trip months earlier, she welcomed us warmly and invited us in for a tour.

I called out to Joe and the rest of the kids to come in. Angie showed us the center. We met her son and daughter in-law, who were busy sorting the food pantry, and her grandchildren, who played in the empty dining hall. She explained that the multipurpose room was used for community events and dinners. She answered calls in the rectory and greeted a couple of people who had come in to get some clothing, in between showing us around. It was clearly a busy place, and she was obviously efficient at her job. There were two ladies sorting through donations in the outreach room, and Angie explained that with the weather turning cold, many people would be coming in to find warm coats and boots. She took us into their church, a simple but reverent place. There were no pews, only chairs set up in front of a humble altar. It was plain, but clearly a cherished and respected space. She said that the doors were kept locked unless Mass was being said. I was drawn to a beautiful statue of St. Kateri Tekakwitha. Angie said that it had been rescued and donated to their church. We told her that the outreach center was our last stop before heading home to Texas. She loved all the handmade items we had brought and said that she would use many of them for their Christmas baskets. I told her about the Knitterbugs ladies who had come together, along with other people from our community, to donate their time, talent, and treasure in order to make the project possible. She remarked, "You all made them specifically for us, *and* drove them here?"

I laughed when I told her we had. She invited us to return for their powwow in August the following year. Joe and I promised her that we would come back one day. We said our goodbyes and headed south. Driving until it got dark, we stopped for the night in Nebraska.

The trip had been better than we had imagined. The weather had cleared up completely, and after a quick breakfast, I took the wheel. Making only the necessary stops for gas, food, and potty breaks, I drove the entire trip back to Southlake. Each time we stopped, Joe offered to take over driving, but I was on such a high from the trip, I didn't feel tired at all. We arrived home a day earlier than planned.

The painters were still hard at work, plastering, faux finishing, staining, and glazing, so we camped out upstairs to stay out of their way. I typed out my Knitterbugs newsletter to share the details of our trip with everyone while it was still fresh in my mind. Feeling a sense of joy and hopefulness, I typed up a second e-mail to tell them about Michael. Up until that point, only a few people knew that I was pregnant. I asked everyone to pray. Everyone was excited to hear about the trip and to see the pictures we had taken, and the response to my prayer request for Michael was overwhelming. It was a huge comfort to me, knowing that there were others praying for us and for our baby.

I felt remarkably well. I had moments of anxiety, and I got butterflies before each doctor appointment, but I was, for the most part, very much at peace. I was monitored very closely, with ultrasounds every two weeks, either with the fetal maternal specialist or with Dr. MacDonald. I continued to pray, never ceasing, always increasing, as I drove, as I did my daily chores, morning devotionals, evening rosaries with the family, and each time I awoke in the middle of the night. My prayer was always the same. "God, please heal Michael. Don't let there be fluid on his brain. Make all his systems and organs work. Let him be able to see. Don't let there be any chromosomal abnormalities. Let him be healthy, strong, and as beautiful as all my other children. Give me courage and grace to persevere and help me to accept your will." I prayed novenas to St. Thérèse, St. Joseph, St. Gerard, St. Jude, St. Raphael, St. Anthony, Blessed Pope John Paul, St. Michael the Archangel, and the Blessed Virgin Mary, asking them all to intercede for me. To pray with me for Michael's healing. As soon as one novena was complete, I began another. I believed my prayers were being heard, I knew they would be answered, and I continued to pray. Mom Mom Marge mailed me a plastic novena prayer card of St. Gerard. I tucked it into the waistband of my pants so that it would be close to my belly. I traced the sign of the cross on my belly every day with the St. Joseph's holy oil that had belonged to Gramma Hubbard. I bought a Benedictine Crucifix at a Parish Mission that we attended, and had it blessed. I slept with it resting against my belly every night. Sometimes I woke up with the imprint of the crucified Jesus on my skin. I wasn't being superstitious, I truly believed that my baby would be healed.

Knitterbugs continued to be my outlet, and renovating the house was a distraction. The timing of our decision to homeschool our kids proved to be a blessing. It was much less stressful for our entire family than public school. The older kids worked through their lessons independently, at their own pace, while I helped the younger ones. They all worked ahead, all except for Patrick. He continued to rebel, refusing to get out of bed, complaining that it was all pointless, that he wasn't going to learn anything anyway. He told me that I was wasting my time. His math program included a computer disc tutorial, which worked through every single problem in his textbook. He pretty much sat in front of the computer with headphones on, copying down the work. When I turned my back, I saw him checking a Facebook account that I didn't even know he had. I told him that he was only hurting himself by not putting in any effort. I couldn't force him to learn. He snuck outside to smoke cigarettes and refused to tell us where he got them from. It was clear that he was still sneaking out at night. Whenever we discovered that he wasn't in his bed, we took the car out to look for him. He always showed up a few minutes later with the same story, that he had just walked to a 7-Eleven to buy a drink or a candy bar. He always smelled like cigarettes. We told him that he was not allowed to leave the house that late at night. He was fourteen years old. We had no problem with him walking around the corner to 7-Eleven during daylight hours if he asked us permission first. We had a big problem with him sneaking out of the house, leaving the garage door up, and the back door unlocked, especially late at night. He never asked us to go anywhere in the light of day, so we suspected that he was up to no good. Our house was equipped with an alarm system that we hadn't been in the habit of setting. We began using it every night.

The first Wednesday Barnes and Noble Knitterbugs meeting after our South Dakota trip, and after sending out my prayer request, was in December. It was the most well-attended meeting I'd ever had. People who had been on my e-mail list, but hadn't actually come out to meetings, showed up. People who only came now and then were there that night. Everyone was excited to look at the pictures we had taken and hear about the trip. Many of them offered words of support and comfort, and some shared their own stories of difficult pregnancies. They all reassured me of their prayers. One of the ladies that came out that night was Nanette Mazzuca. She was quietly working on a blue blanket when I greeted her. I hadn't remembered meeting her before. She said that she was a parishioner at St. Francis Assisi, where we went to church, and that she had seen our family at Mass. The meeting left me feeling uplifted and energized. I'm not sure if it was out of curiosity, or the desire to be supportive, but the meetings continued to bring new people out. I soon began receiving e-mails from people who had heard our story, offering us encouragement and prayers. Knitterbugs had become a sort of prayer chain, and I learned that our family had been added to several other prayer lists, connecting across several other states and countries. Rosaries and Masses were offered up, candles were lit, and novenas were prayed. I felt enveloped by God's grace, a direct result of the multitude of prayers.

Each moment that I carried Michael inside of me, I felt humbled and incredibly grateful, knowing that I may not get a tomorrow with him. Every single day was a gift, and I was consumed with love for him. When the first tiniest flutter tickled my insides, I trembled with joy. Michael was alive, and I felt blessed and privileged to carry him so close to my heart.

With each doctor appointment, the reports got slightly more encouraging. One of the specialist's greatest concerns had been the possibility of poor organ development and lack of organ function. A fetal echocardiogram showed that Michael's heart was perfectly formed, and that there was no murmur. Ultrasounds monitored and measured all his organs and showed that they were all functioning normally. Michael's head was still large, but his body was catching up. The fluid seemed to be less than what had originally been measured. Most encouraging of all, his brain looked like it was developing normally. He had a brain. Not just a brain stem as originally reported. I kept my prayer warriors updated with the news from each doctor visit and begged them all to keep praying. Their prayers were indeed working. The e-mails offering encouragement and prayers multiplied, keeping me on a high. A miracle was taking place, and not only was our family witnessing it in real time, but so were hundreds of other people, friends and strangers alike. I praised God for all of His mercy and power and thanked Him for the hope He was giving us. I still had no idea how things would turn out, nothing had been promised, and there were no guarantees. The specialist remained guarded and hadn't shifted from his expectation of Michael being born with disabilities, but I stayed hopeful.

Just before Christmas, I received a card in the mail from Nanette Mazzuca. Inside, I found a pretty silver cross bookmark and a note, thanking me for the Knitterbugs project. I was touched by her sweet and thoughtful gesture as I recalled the quiet lady who had come to work on the light-blue blanket at Barnes and Noble a few weeks before. I mailed her a thank-you note.

TWENTY-ONE

An Epiphany Miracle

Southlake, Texas, January 2011

I had heard about a new Canadian saint. St. Brother André Bessette had been canonized on October 17, 2010. I remembered visiting St. Joseph's Oratory in Montréal, while on a high school French trip, and standing in awe of all the hundreds of canes, crutches, leg braces, and walkers that hung in the church. People had come from miles with their crippled and sick children and family members in hopes of a miracle. Brother André encouraged everyone to pray for the intercession of St. Joseph, to whom he had great devotion. Countless people were healed.

Brother André had wanted to become a priest, but because of his frail health, he was refused. It was thought that the rigors of the priesthood would be too much for him. Brother André had been frail his whole life. A sickly baby and child, he was the eighth of twelve children, and orphaned by the age of twelve. His lack of strength and coordination made it difficult for him to keep a job. Because of his holiness, he was made the doorkeeper of the congregation of the Holy Cross. His job as porter, one he held for 40 years, greeting visitors and praying with them for their infirm family members, many of whom had been miraculously healed, was quite a fitting role for him. When he heard someone was ill, he visited to bring cheer and pray with them, and would rub them lightly with oil taken from a lamp burning in the chapel. Word of healing powers began to spread, and when an epidemic broke out at a nearby college, André volunteered to nurse. Not one person died. Sick people began to flood the doors, but André took no credit for any of the healing; he attributed it all to St. Joseph. Although there are no documents on record, founding the oratory in honor of St. Joseph is what St. André is remembered for. I talked to my mother about the wonderful news of a new Canadian saint, feeling a connection, having visited the very place he had founded. She told me she had some novena cards and said she would mail them to me.

Joe plugged away at his business, Empowered Voyage. We were still in a decent place financially, between the severance package from KPMG and unemployment, but he still wasn't drawing an income from his business. We cashed out our 401K retirement savings in order to complete our home renovations. We were confident that Joe's business would take off any day, or that he would land the perfect job. He always kept one eye open on the job market. The home renovations were something that we hoped to enjoy ourselves, but we kept in mind that it may be necessary to sell. Having things freshened up and updated could only help. We were anxious at times, but we weren't really afraid.

Christmas has always been one of our family's favorite times of the year. With the house renovations complete, we excitedly prepared for the holidays. The girls and I picked out festive fabric and sewed holiday aprons before diving into our marathon baking. Christmas carols and movies played while the house filled up with delicious smells. The kids decorated gingerbread houses, made Christmas cards and decorations, and we all felt incredibly hopeful.

I recognized the fetal maternal specialist phone number on the caller ID when the phone rang one morning. The receptionist had called to tell me that she needed to change my December appointment. There were no openings until after New Year's. I was disappointed to have to wait an additional week, but she offered me the earliest available appointment at a closer office, with the same specialist. I marked the time and date on my calendar, January 6, the Epiphany. Smiling, I thought it seemed like a nice date for my appointment. Exactly nine days before the Epiphany, the box of St. Brother André Bessette novena cards, which my mother had sent, arrived in the mail. I began praying it that very day.

Joe's office was in Irving, Texas, not far from the specialist's office. I signed in and chatted with the friendly receptionist. The atmosphere was much more relaxed than the one I had been going to. The ultrasound technician called me back. At six months through my pregnancy, I had lost track of how many ultrasounds I'd had. They had become so routine, I felt less anxious with each one. Still, before and during each scan, I prayed for even the slightest positive improvement. Less than a minute into the scan, the technician announced, "Wow! That head looks so much better."

My heart skipped a beat. Incredulously, I asked her, "It does?"

She said, "Yes, I don't see any fluid at all."

I'm not sure if she was supposed to report her findings to me, but she didn't act like it was a secret. She had a big smile on her face, and her eyes were shining when she left to get the specialist, Dr. Predanic. My heart was beating out of my chest, and I could hardly contain my excitement while I lay on the table in the tiny room.

My initial fetal maternal specialist had been Dr. Rosnes, but after my first visit, I was followed exclusively by Dr. Predanic. I liked him. He was professional, but as my pregnancy progressed, he seemed less clinical. I had told him, right out of the gate the first time we met, that we were praying for our baby. That lots of people were praying for Michael. At first, he had looked at me skeptically, somewhat sympathetically. I assumed he feared that I was getting my hopes up and was setting myself up for a big disappointment. He had been witnessing the gradual improvements and encouraging results from each of the tests. Michael was growing and thriving. All his organs were functioning normally, something both he and the first specialist had predicted wouldn't happen.

Dr. Predanic came in and began the scan, confirming what the technician had announced. He told me that he was very encouraged. There was no fluid on Michael's brain. I asked him where it went. He looked directly at me and said, "I don't know."

He said that Michael's head was still large, but not as out of proportion as it had originally been. The third ventricle was still larger than it should be, and he wasn't sure why. He told me that in his entire career, he had only seen three cases like mine, mine being one of them, where the prognosis had improved rather than progressed. To say that I was elated would be an enormous understatement. That joy, though, was bittersweet for me because I instantly wondered how many of the other babies with a similar prognosis had been allowed to improve, and how many of them had been aborted instead. Dr. Predanic spent twenty minutes cropping several 4-D ultrasound pictures for me to take home to show Joe and the kids. His demeanor was light, and his smile was kind as he explained all the different parts, outlining and giving me the best pictures he had taken. We were both very excited. I reminded Dr. Predanic before I left that Michael had hundreds of people praying for him. He smiled genuinely at me and said, "Keep praying. It's working."

I knew in that instant that Michael had touched my doctor's life. He was touching many lives, and he wasn't even been born yet.

I pulled out my novena card and said the prayer in thanksgiving for the incredible news that I had received. Indeed, St. Brother André Bessette had interceded for me, and my prayers were being answered. I saw something on the card that I hadn't noticed before. When I got to the end of the prayer and moved my thumb, I read the date printed at the bottom. January 6. St. Brother André Bessette's feast day. It was January 6, 2011. My heart stopped. How had I missed it? I called Joe to tell him the news and then drove directly to his office. He was standing in the parking garage waiting for me when I pulled in. I could see the relief on his face as I approached. We nearly collapsed into each other's arms. We had no doubt that we had just experienced a true miracle. With his big arm protectively wrapped around me, we rode the elevator up to his floor where we were greeted by his colleagues, with whom he had already shared the news. They were all waiting to hug us and hear the story again. Everyone had tears in their eyes when I showed them the ultrasound pictures. They gladly accepted the St. Brother André prayer cards I handed out. Only one of them was Catholic, but no one argued that the amazing turn of events was a miracle. I typed up an e-mail to my Knitterbugs ladies, sharing the miraculous news with them. They too were of all faiths, even one who was an admitted agnostic. It made no difference to me. I wanted them all to know that their prayers were indeed working. I begged them to please keep praying.

I supposed it may have been due to scheduling changes, or perhaps vacation plans, that I only saw Dr. Predanic one more time. Dr. Rosnes, my original specialist, saw me for my last appointment. Dr. Predanic had been on the journey with me, following all Michael's progress and improvements, so I was a little disappointed when I didn't see him for my next appointment, but I was glad that Dr. Rosnes got the opportunity to see how his original prognosis for my pregnancy had changed so drastically. He was genuinely happy about how much Michael had improved. I hoped that it might make a difference in how he delivered difficult prognoses in the future; I prayed he could use Michael's example to give hope to other mothers who were in similar situations.

Just like Dr. Predanic, Dr. Rosnes was still puzzled by the large size of Michael's third ventricle. He recommended that I have a fetal MRI. He also asked me if I had considered the possibility that Michael may need to have surgery at birth. He said that if I delivered at Presbyterian Hospital in Denton, where my ob-gyn, Dr. MacDonald, had privileges, Michael may need to be care flighted to Cook Children's in Fort Worth. Because it had already been decided that I would deliver via C-section, I wouldn't be able to travel to another hospital until after I recovered. This added a new twist to everything. Dr. Rosnes told me that I should consider finding an ob-gyn at one of the Children's Hospitals to do the delivery.

With only five weeks from my due date, I went directly home and searched the Internet for a new doctor. That search led me to Northlake OB-GYN, at Medical City Hospital in Dallas. There were several practicing obstetricians, more than ten, both male and female. Some were young, and some were middle-aged. I scrolled from top to bottom and then back to the top, stopping at *Dr. Bruce Roberts*. By far, the oldest of all the physicians, in his early seventies, there was something about his profile picture that told me I would be in good hands with him. I called the number, and after explaining my situation to the receptionist, she told me that someone would get back to me. Dr. Roberts's nurse called me back right away. After once again explaining why I was in need of a new doctor, she asked me if I was Jehovah's Witness. Perplexed by her question, I told her I was a Roman Catholic. Chuckling, she said that Dr. Roberts was Catholic too. When I asked her why she wanted to know, she said that Dr. Roberts had a very low incidence of blood transfusions and that he was often requested by Jehovah's Witness patients who were having planned C-sections. That was comforting news for this Catholic girl too. The nurse told me that she would share all my information with Dr. Roberts and that she would let me know promptly whether or not he would agree to take me on as a patient. I said a prayer, but didn't have much time to worry about it because she called me back within minutes to tell me that Dr. Roberts would take me on. She made an appointment for the very next morning. After hanging up the phone, immensely relieved, I returned to the Northlake OB-GYN website to read Dr. Roberts's full biography. When I read that his oldest son's name was Michael, I smiled at the coincidence; but as I read further, I realized that there was much more than just a coincidence in names. On top of Dr. Roberts's many degrees, accolades, and his impressive title of captain in the US Air Force, he was a member of the American Association of Pro-Life Obstetricians and Gynecologists.

In my frantic search for a new doctor, I didn't think I had time to do the research to find one who was pro-life, but God knew that it was important to me. I went on to read through every single profile of each of the other ob-gyns in the practice. Not one of them was listed as being pro-life. God had handpicked him for me, and I told Dr. Roberts so the next day at my first appointment. As he sat, not across his desk from me, but knees to knees, face-to-face, listening to the journey that Michael and I had been on, tears filled his clear blue eyes. He thanked me for sharing the story of how God had chosen him, and he told me that he believed everything would be just fine. He sent me down the hall for an ultrasound, and when I came back, he didn't seem concerned at all with the results. He asked me if I would consider switching to a fetal maternal specialist at Medical City, to make the sharing of medical information more timely, and also to cut down on travel time. I could see both doctors on the same day. It made perfect sense to me.

Dr. Roberts was like the calm in my storm, and my stress level dropped instantly. Before leaving his office, I'd had an ultrasound, a complete exam, lab work, both of my next appointments were scheduled with Dr. Roberts and my new specialist, Dr. Weiss, and my C-section had been scheduled. Dr. Roberts remarked to me, after I told him about the request for the MRI by my previous doctor, "You must be about doctored out by now."

Letting out a long sigh, I told him I was, but that I was truly hopeful that everything would turn out okay. He assured me that he felt the same and told me to go ahead with the MRI appointment. He said it wouldn't do any harm and might provide some answers.

Throughout my entire pregnancy, my next-door neighbor Cyndy and my dear friend Barb were a source of constant support. They lifted me up in prayer and encouraged me from one appointment to the next, through Joe's unemployment and each and every job interview. When I told them about the miracle of Dr. Roberts, they were as amazed as I was; but like me, they weren't surprised at how God had worked out every tiny detail. Barb was the one who drove me to my MRI appointment. It had been scheduled on my birthday, March 4, exactly one month before my C-section was scheduled. She brought me flowers and a little cake, and we had made plans to have lunch together after the appointment. Joe's first Empowered Voyage training session was scheduled that day, so he wasn't able to come. I would have been fine to go on my own, but we were both grateful for Barb's offer to drive me.

The MRI wasn't terrible, but it wasn't exactly fun. It was more than a little uncomfortable being so very large and pregnant, and having to lay completely still for such a long time, confined in a tiny space. The techs did a great job of propping up my big belly on pillows as I lay on my side. Even with earplugs, the clanging and banging was extremely loud. I kept my eyes shut tight and prayed Hail Marys for the forty-five minutes that the scan lasted. Barb was chatting with another expectant couple when I got back to the waiting room. She introduced us, and for a few moments, we encouraged each other as we shared our stories. They too had been given a terrible prognosis, but were holding out great hope. They were on a similar journey with their little girl, who would, unbeknown to any of us at the time, be delivered only a few days later. She would be born prematurely, undergo multiple surgeries, and have a lengthy hospital stay.

I didn't have to wait long before I was called back to the radiologist's office for my results. She told me that the reason Michael's third ventricle was so large was because of a condition called ACC, agenesis of the corpus callosum. She explained that the tissue that connects the left and right brain, the corpus callosum, was missing. The defect could be a symptom of a genetic condition or syndrome, or it could have been something that happened during the development, with no known cause or reason. She noted that Michael's eyes were wide set, hypertelorism, which gave her reason to suspect that he may also have septo-optic dysplasia, an underdevelopment of the optic nerves, which affects eye-brain communication. She explained that there were vast ranges of symptoms for these diagnoses, from very mild to very severe. We wouldn't know the severity until Michael was born, and most likely, not until he was months—or even years—old. She said that Michael could be dyslexic or that he could be a switch-hitter in baseball. Only time would tell. She also explained that there were many documented cases of people who had lived most of their lives perfectly fine, without even knowing that they had ACC. The defect was sometimes only ever discovered after a sports or other type of head injury that required an MRI. The radiologist wasn't an alarmist, but I had mixed feelings after the appointment. Now that there was some definitive reason for the large third ventricle, I found myself speculating on the level of severity of the potential side effects. I had to remind myself that God had it covered and that Michael seemed to be healthy in every other way. Barb and I discussed the doctor's findings over lunch at a Mexican restaurant. She assured me that it was all good news and reminded me that we had been lifting Michael up in prayer from the moment I learned I was pregnant.

The evening of my birthday, I found a small gift bag in the Knitterbugs donation bin on the front porch. It was from Nanette Mazzuca. Inside, I found a little brown chenille baby blanket with blue satin trim. Embroidered on the corner was this verse: "For this child, I have prayed. (1 Samuel 1:27)"

I was moved to tears. I really didn't know the lady that well. She had come to a couple of meetings at Barnes and Noble and had mailed me the pretty bookmark around Christmastime. Her thoughtfulness had really touched my heart. I wrote out a thank-you note right away, but being so caught up in the emotion, I also sent her an e-mail to thank her. When I read her reply the next day, she said that I may not realize it, but there were other people that I didn't even know who were praying for Michael. She said that her friend Cathy was one of them. She said that she hoped that I could meet Cathy one day soon, but she was going through cancer treatments and wasn't up to having visitors quite yet. I began praying for Cathy right away. Nanette sent me another e-mail, telling me that she really wanted to help out when I went into the hospital, but that she and her husband would be out of town. She explained that he travelled extensively on business and that they had a lot of frequent-flyer miles saved up. She told me that because she often accompanied him on his trips, the last thing they wanted to do in their free time was travel. Through conversations at Knitterbugs meetings, Nanette knew that all of my family lived in Canada. She told me that she wanted to send a plane ticket to someone that we would like to come help us when Michael was born. I was stunned. I barely knew the lady, but I was quickly seeing her heart, and I found her thoughtfulness and concern remarkable. I told her that I didn't know how to thank her, but I knew that my mother would no doubt want to come. I called my mother to tell her about Nanette's offer, and of course she was thrilled. I gave her Nanette's e-mail information so that the two of them could make the arrangements. The next day, I sent flowers to Nanette and her husband, Bob, on behalf of Joe and I and my mother.

Over the next week or so, with my delivery date quickly approaching, I got my nest prepared to bring my baby boy home, cleaning and organizing the house from top to bottom, inside and out. I even planted some flowers. Early one afternoon, while I was sitting on the front porch, supervising Joe as he hung some new flower baskets, Nanette stopped by. She brought with her a giant bag of hotel soaps and toiletries that her friend Cathy had collected for the homeless shelter. Cathy had also sent a very generous McDonald's gift card. She thought it might come in handy when my mother came to help. Nanette said that Cathy wanted us to know that she was keeping us all in her prayers. That was also the day that Nanette revealed to me that her husband, Bob, was the CEO of Boy Scouts of America. It made perfect sense to me. They were certainly doing very thoughtful and generous deeds.

My first appointment with Dr. Weiss, my new fetal maternal specialist, was scheduled on the same day, but just prior to my appointment with Dr. Roberts. As comforted and at ease as I had been with Dr. Roberts, I experienced the exact opposite with Dr. Weiss. The nurse brought me back into the exam room and set me up on the table before leaving me to wait for the doctor. A man of short stature, he entered the room, barely glancing up, staring intently at my chart as he approached the ultrasound machine, sat down, and began typing. Without looking up, he asked me if I planned to have any more children after this pregnancy. Stunned, I told him that I had no idea, that my husband and I would leave that up to God to decide. It was at that moment that he finally raised his eyes up to look at me. I instantly got a bad vibe from him, but I remained calm and composed. He told me that Dr. Roberts had called to ask his opinion of Michael's large third ventricle. Dr. Weiss informed me that he told Dr. Roberts that he had no doubt that it was agenesis of the corpus callosum. I looked directly at him and said, "Wow. You knew that without seeing the results of the MRI?"

He said, "Oh, yes."

I remarked incredulously, "That's incredible. I've been followed by two ob-gyns and two fetal maternal specialists, and none of them had it figured out."

He smiled smugly and assured me that he had complete confidence that that was the reason behind the large third ventricle, without even looking at my chart. I didn't believe him, and I didn't like him. He began the ultrasound scan and, right away, exclaimed, "Wow! That's a big head!"

After having been told how much better Michael's head had been looking, and how much more in proportion it was only two weeks earlier, I was startled by his announcement. I worried that it had suddenly grown larger. I asked him, "How big is big?"

His reply, "Trust me. You don't want to know."

I so badly wanted to hit that smug little man. I was so insulted by him, but I said nothing. Against my better judgment, I made my next appointment before proceeding to Dr. Roberts's office, which was on another floor.

With such a stark contrast in mood and atmosphere between the two offices, I was grateful to be seeing Dr. Roberts last. I didn't tell him specifically why I didn't want to see Dr. Weiss again, I just asked if there was someone else I could see. I'm pretty sure that Dr. Roberts knew what Dr. Weiss's personality type was, just by his response and the sympathetic look in his eyes. He remarked about how sometimes these young specialists are so knowledgeable and highly educated that they forget that they are dealing with human beings. He asked me if I could just tolerate him for a few more visits, for convenience's sake. I agreed, solely as a favor to Dr. Roberts. My next appointment was even worse. The receptionist and nurses were sweet and friendly when I checked in and had the nonstress test done. However, as soon as Dr. Weiss entered the room, my ire grew. He glanced up from my chart when he walked in and immediately began the ultrasound.

"Yup. That head is still big. It's pretty safe to say he's not gonna be the smartest kid in his class."

I was close enough to scratch his eyes out, but I restrained myself. Looking directly at him, very calmly and emphatically, I informed him, "That's not our first priority. We have been praying for this baby from the moment we knew he existed, and we love him no matter what his IQ score might be."

The hurtful and insensitive remarks ceased, though the doctor proved to be quite pushy. He was insistent that I see a genetic counselor and that I book a tour of the NICU prior to Michael's birth. He was adamant that Michael should have genetic testing done and was convinced that he would be spending time in the NICU after birth. He said he wanted me to be prepared. While his recommendations may have been well-intentioned, I politely declined. I told him that I would cross those bridges when and if I needed to. I wanted to enjoy the final weeks of my pregnancy without adding to my appointment schedule. I also didn't want to borrow worry over hypotheticals. He, however, did not respect my wishes. He went ahead and called both the geneticist's office and the NICU to schedule appointments. When they called me to confirm, I politely thanked them, but told them that I wouldn't be needing the appointments. They were very understanding and told me that I could always schedule again if I changed my mind. I couldn't get over how pushy this guy was, but I was feeling my backbone. A younger me would have gone along, just to keep the peace. Life was teaching me how to stand up for myself.

TWENTY-TWO

God's Thunder

Southlake, Texas, April 2011

Joe picked my mother up from the airport on a Saturday, two days before my scheduled C-section. We decided to invite Bob and Nanette for a BBQ on the evening of her arrival so that they could all meet each other. It was also the first time that Joe and I met Bob. Joe grilled a feast, and the girls and I baked up a storm. Nanette brought homemade goodies and treats for the kids, and she gave me a beautiful hand-knitted baby blanket for Michael, the one I had seen her working on at our meeting at Barnes and Noble. She also gave him a big teddy bear with a matching blue hand-knitted sweater, with Michael's name knitted in red. I was glad that my mother would get the opportunity to meet the lovely couple who we barely knew, who had done such a thoughtful thing for our family, out of the clear blue.

The next morning, we got up early for Mass. We had changed parishes at the start of the year and were attending Our Lady of Lebanon, a Maronite Catholic Church. My mother didn't make any comments about it, but judging her expression at Mass, she didn't look comfortable. After Mass, we went to the hall for coffee and donuts while our kids attended their religious education classes. Barb and Armen had been looking forward to meeting my mother and invited us to sit with them when they saw us. Joe and I had asked Barb and Armen to be Michael's godparents, and Barb was giddy with excitement that our little boy would be coming into the world the very next day. When I introduced my mother, I took note of her body language. The all-too-familiar cool, tight-lipped, obligatorily polite, but not-too-friendly greeting. I instantly tensed up. Barb was her usual warm and friendly self as she told my mother how excited she was to meet little Michael and how much she loved and admired our family. What should have been a moment of shared excitement over her new grandchild and pride for her family, my mother remained stiff. I could sense that Barb was picking up on the tension. She changed the subject, asking my mother how she liked the Maronite Mass. My mother answered in a matter-of-fact way, "It was fine, but I wouldn't want to attend it every Sunday."

Barb told her that it took some getting used to, but that we had grown to love it. My mother told her that she wasn't interested in getting used to it. Barb glanced at me. I looked back sympathetically, feeling very uncomfortable. I had no trouble standing up to my pushy doctor, but I couldn't stand up to my mother. A few other parishioners came by to give us their good wishes, which thankfully took some of the tension out of the air. Once the kids were done with their classes, Barb hugged me tight and told me that she would see me the next day to meet her godson. My mother stared coldly. I had been hoping that she wouldn't find out. I had told Barb that she was welcome to come to the hospital. She had been a huge part of my journey. Once we got in the van, the remarks started.

"I don't think it's appropriate for her to come to the hospital. It's a private time for you and your husband."

I explained that Barb wouldn't be there for the actual delivery, she would be coming after Michael was born. She still wasn't keen on it.

After we got home, I overheard my mother's conversations with our kids. Some of the little ones mentioned how Barb was like a grandma. Barb had grandchildren the same age as my kids, and she was indeed a grandmotherly figure in the sense that she genuinely cared about and loved our kids. She showed them kindness and was generous with her time, but she by no means ever tried to be their grandmother. Clearly, my mother felt threatened. After more disap-

246

proving remarks, I spoke up and told her that Barb was my friend. I loved her and had invited her to come to the hospital. I didn't care if she liked it or not, but I didn't want to hear one more negative word about it. And I didn't want her discussing her opinions with my kids either. That evening, Barb called me and apologized for over-stepping. She said she meant no harm, she was just so excited over Michael's much-anticipated and long-awaited birth. She sensed that perhaps she was intruding and told me that she would wait for me to call her before coming to visit. She didn't want to step on anyone's toes. I told her that she was not intruding at all and that she was welcome. I wanted her there. I explained that my mother tended to be a bit jealous and controlling with people. She had been that way with my friends and neighbors my whole life and that she shouldn't take it personally.

My C-section was scheduled for 7:30 a.m., but we had to be at the hospital by 5:30 a.m. Joe and I set our alarm for 4:00 a.m. to give us enough time to shower and make the drive to Dallas. Angela, Joseph, Patrick, Christina, Clare, and Callum were all up as Joe and I were heading out the door. My mother and the rest of the kids were still fast asleep. We hugged them all and told them to be helpful. Joe promised to send them pictures just as soon as Michael was born.

The weather was wild. Torrential rains, crashing thunder, and bolts of lightning that split the sky. Joe and I looked wide-eyed at each other, both of us wondering if we would make it to the hospital in one piece. There was no one on the road at such an early hour. Joe gripped the steering wheel while I gripped tightly onto the door handle, my other hand holding my belly and my rosary, praying that we would arrive safely. The storm didn't let up at all for the entire trip. There was so much water on the highway that the van actually split it in two, like the parting of the Red Sea, as we drove through it. The thunder continued to crash and roar, and the lighting struck the road in front of us in spectacular illuminated flashing bolts. I felt like God was showing us His mighty power, right before our eyes.

Joe dropped me off at the door and parked the van. We made our way up to the Labor and Delivery floor, where I was prepped for surgery without delay. Dr. Roberts came in to see me before the rest of the team and asked me if I'd slept much. I told him, "Not really."

He said he hadn't either. He patted my arm, smiled with his clear blue eyes, and told me he'd see me in a few minutes. Once Joe was suited up in his coveralls, a nurse brought him in. Smiling his big smile, in his usual way, he said, "Hi, honey!"

Like we were just hanging out, no big deal, putting me at ease. I know he was just as nervous as I was. Neither one of us knew what the outcome would be. Our lives would be forever changed, but we both knew, with God, we could handle anything together. He kissed me on the forehead and sat behind me, holding the hand that clasped my rosary. I watched the busyness around me and was filled with so many emotions. The big day had finally arrived. I had enjoyed my pregnancy, and I knew that Michael was healthy and safe inside. In mere minutes, he would be out, and I had no idea what life would be like on the other side. I prayed that God would help me through whatever it was He was about to hand me.

Dr. Roberts told me not to be concerned if I heard him and his associate, Dr. McClintock, talking about their weekend or other random things. He said that they did C-sections all the time, and they could almost do it with their eyes closed. I wasn't worried. I closed my eyes and tried to pray my rosary while they did their job, only managing to utter partial Hail Marys because I truly couldn't focus. I heard Dr. McClintock exclaim, "What an overachiever! Trying to scream, and you aren't even all the way out!"

I wished Dr. Weiss had been in the room to hear that. I heard my baby boy's cries. Dr. Roberts beamed as he held him up for me to see before the nurses took him to the warmer to do their thing. Joe squeezed my hand and kissed me. I thanked God over and over and prayed that Michael was okay. I told Joe to go look at him and tell me how he was. Dr. Roberts said he thought he looked just great and that he saw people walking around with heads like his every day. He said we didn't have anything to worry about. Michael scored perfect on his APGAR. He was beautiful. Eight pounds and three ounces strong, but his overachieving scream before his complete birth had caused him to aspirate fluid into his lungs. When he started to make grunting noises and had trouble breathing, the nurses took him back to the NICU for oxygen. I wasn't able to keep him with me in my room, which was terribly difficult for me. I wanted to hold him and nurse him and look at every part of him, but I wouldn't be able to do that for several days.

Once I was stitched back together, I was wheeled to a recovery room where Barb was waiting. I sent Joe down to the NICU to find out whatever he could from the doctors. I was grateful to have Barb there to share the excitement, and the worry. She assured me that Michael would be just fine, reminding me again how he had been covered in a multitude of prayers. I told her to go down to the NICU to see Joe and meet her godson. She promised to continue praying for Michael.

Before the nurses brought me to my room, they wheeled me to the NICU on my gurney so that I could see my little boy. That's when it really hit me. He was all swaddled, hooked up to a CPAP (continuous positive airway pressure) machine and a monitor in his Isolette. I hadn't even gotten a chance to hold him, touch him, kiss him. I couldn't bear to leave him. The NICU doctor said that an x-ray showed he had fluid in his lungs. He would have to stay on the oxygen until the fluid was gone. They had inserted a feeding tube, because nursing him or giving him a bottle could cause him to aspirate more fluid. The doctors said that because of the concerns about fluid on his brain during the pregnancy, they would be ordering an MRI before releasing him, just in case he needed a shunt. Because Michael would need to be sedated and breathing on his own for the MRI, they couldn't do it until after his lungs were clear and he was off the oxygen. The doctor couldn't speculate how long it would take for his lungs to clear. We just had to watch him and wait. I was sad that I couldn't have my baby with me, but grateful that he would get the care he needed. I prayed that he would get better quick so that I could take him home.

My hospital stay was emotional to say the least. The NICU was filled with babies who were in much more serious situations. Babies that had been born much more prematurely who had already endured multiple surgeries. Some had been there for months, some for more than a year. I felt guilty about being so emotional when some of the mothers had to leave their babies every day, after only visiting for a few hours, because they had to return to work and care for other children. The toll that it must have taken on them, I simply could not imagine. I felt blessed that we would be going home within days, and I began praying for all the other babies and their families.

Once I was allowed out of bed and able to move around freely, I spent every possible moment with Michael, sitting in the very uncomfortable rocker or up on the tall stool next to his Isolette. I wished that there had been some sort of recliner to put my feet up on, but there wasn't. I shifted positions a lot and tried propping them up on whatever I could find. My ankles got terribly swollen, and my feet looked like balloons with fat sausages sticking out of them. I knew that I should be resting, I'd just had major surgery, but I didn't want to leave my little guy or miss any new updates from the doctors. I stared at Michael in awe, stroking his head and delighted at the tightening of his tiny hand around my finger. After four days, I was allowed to change his diaper. Just being able to hold his pacifier when he lost it was a privilege. Whatever little ways I could find to care for him while he was still connected to the oxygen and wires, I did with joy. I rubbed his back while he slept, I whispered to him and told him how much I loved him. I prayed the rosary while I stood next to him, drinking in the awesomeness of his very being. I prayed in thanksgiving for the great miracle that he was. I traced the sign of the cross on his head with the same blessed oil I had used while he was in my belly and prayed that the MRI would come back normal and that he wouldn't need a shunt. Michael's lungs improved every day; and each day, the oxygen he was being given was reduced. He developed a little jaundice, so they put him under ultraviolet lights. The only time I left his side was to go to the pumping station to pump breast milk.

I brought some baby yarn and knitting needles with me. While Michael slept, I knitted baby hats for the babies in the NICU. Each time I finished one, I handed it to one of the nurses who would deliver it to the baby of their choice. Once word got out that I was making hats, a few nurses came in to give me a heads-up, letting me know that another baby had arrived and what color I should make.

Knitting baby hats kept me from worrying about Michael. I prayed as I knitted, turning each stitch into a prayer for Michael and the babies who would be wearing them.

One evening, a female doctor walked into Michael's little pod and introduced herself as Dr. Shirley. I recognized her name as the geneticist that Dr. Weiss had asked me to set up an appointment with. She told me that Dr. Weiss's office had let her know that I had delivered my baby. She wanted to come by to talk to me. I must admit that I was annoyed that Dr. Weiss had once again pushed his way in, but I decided to humor the doctor. She was friendly, and I answered all her questions. She went through the standard ones about family health history for Joe and myself, which are actually quite unremarkable. None of our kids had any health issues, other than Callum's heart defect. I am fairly certain, and I am no expert, that if there had been a genetic issue, it would have presented itself with one of our other ten kids, but it had not. Dr. Shirley seemed to feel the same way. She asked me if I had any photographs of our other kids. I always carry a photo wallet with me. I pulled it out of my purse and showed her the kids' most recent pictures. She commented that two of our kids looked different than all the rest, and remarked that neither of them looked like Joe or I either. Her comment sounded utterly ridiculous to me, Joe, and everyone that I later mentioned it to. Some of the other kids overheard when I was telling Joe about her observations, and they wanted to know which one of them she was talking about. Dr. Shirley asked me if there was any chance that Joe and I could be related. I laughed out loud and told her there was no chance. She assured me that it was a standard question. She also wanted to know if I had any grandchildren yet. Growing weary of her questions and wanting our impromptu consultation to end, I told her that no, I did not have any grandchildren. She apologized and said that it was not out of the realm of possibilities and that I would be surprised how many women were grandmothers at my age.

As Dr. Shirley wrapped up her consultation, Michael began to cry. Despite my patting him on the back, holding his little hand, and giving him his pacifier, he grew increasingly upset. I think he must have sensed my anxiety during the visit with the geneticist. I had not been allowed to hold him, and I was afraid to do anything that would interfere with his oxygen and monitors. All the nurses seemed to be busy with other babies, and none of them were close enough for me to call to them. I continued talking, patting, and soothing, but nothing helped. Michael looked up at me with his dark eyes. He was mad, and he wanted to be picked up. I was about to pull the nurse's call bell when Dr. Shirley asked me if I wanted her to go find Michael's nurse. I told her yes. She left and returned shortly, telling me that his nurse would be right in. She seemed puzzled as to why I wouldn't just pick him up. I told her that the nurses had told me that it was best for Michael to stay in his Isolette so that he would get the proper flow of oxygen. I was a rule follower, so I didn't question or protest their authority. I can tell you that if I were in the same situation today, I would definitely have just picked him up, and probably would have picked him up much sooner. Dr. Shirley said that Michael looked pretty robust to her, and she couldn't imagine why I hadn't been allowed to hold him yet.

Michael's little roommate's nurse came into the room when she heard the screaming. She observed me trying to soothe him, laying my face close to his, covering him so that he could feel like I was holding him. She shook her head, walked over to his crib, picked him up, and handed him to me. She rearranged the wires, tucked them up under his blanket, and turned the volume down on the monitors. I think she figured it was about time I got to hold my own baby. She muttered something about how big and strong he was, that he just wanted his mama. I thanked her over and over again, with tears streaming down my face. Every ounce of stress and anxiety that I had, seizing up in my neck and shoulders, instantly melted away. I was finally holding my sweet boy. I forgot that Dr. Shirley was still there until she spoke up. She was smiling when she told me that Michael looked great. I thanked her. I realized that while her just showing up unannounced had been annoying initially, I would have not been given the chance to hold Michael that day. A God wink. Dr. Shirley said that she didn't see any point in doing genetic testing right away. She said that she had no concerns.

"Just watch and see who he becomes," was her recommendation. That was excellent news to me when Michael's nurse came in, she stopped cold in the doorway. She had a surprised look on her face when she saw me sitting up on the stool with Michael in my arms. I really didn't care. I know my smile was huge, and I couldn't contain my joy. She came over and checked the monitor and said that the alarms would probably go off with me holding him. I told her that I wouldn't be bothered by them. I was holding my baby, and I wouldn't be putting him down. Michael and I sat and rocked. He kept his little dark eyes fixed on mine, finally getting a good look at his mommy. I gazed at his sweet face while he slept. I kissed and stroked his head and looked at his perfect little fingers. I had waited and prayed for so long. I was finally holding my miracle, and it felt like a dream.

Joe came to visit in the afternoons. Once I was discharged, (Dr. Roberts had shown mercy on me and allowed me to stay for a fourth night) he came to visit in the evenings, and we left together after Michael's night feeding around eight o'clock. We would go home to shower, sleep, and he would bring me back the next morning to spend the day with Michael. Joe went to the office for a few hours after he dropped me off, still trying to make his business profitable. The kids missed me and wanted to know when we would be bringing the baby home. I sensed that the tensions were beginning to grow with my mother there, by the body language and pained looks in the kids' eyes. They remained silent, not wanting to burden me with their complaints. Joe seemed to be a little more on edge as well, his nerves beginning to fray. The hospital gave me a pump to use at home, since my milk supply was high. I had never used a pump before, and I felt like I could feed several newborns with all the bottles I filled.

Michael stayed on a feeding tube until his oxygen was completely removed. For the most part, all the nurses in the NICU were amazing. Some were better advocates than others. I especially loved the older, more experienced nurses, the seasoned ones who trusted their instincts. I was so anxious to nurse Michael on the day that his feeding tube was removed. The little Slavic nurse told me that she wanted him to take a bottle first, before I tried to nurse him. She said that he probably wouldn't nurse right away because it would be much harder work for him. She fed him a four-ounce bottle, and he still seemed hungry for more. She said, "Go ahead and try to nurse him, but don't be disappointed if he doesn't take to it."

The minute I put him to the breast, he nursed instinctively, like he'd been nursing all along. The little nurse laughed out loud and clapped her hands in disbelief, exclaiming, "Look at that!"

She told me he was a big strong baby, much too big to be in the NICU. She said it was about time for him to be going home.

The MRI was scheduled for Monday, eight days after Michael's birth. No longer on a feeding tube or oxygen, he was only connected to the leads on the monitor, measuring his oxygen, blood pressure, and heart rate. The nurses measured his head every day and rechecked his blood work to make sure the jaundice was gone. Everything looked normal. Because he would be sedated, he couldn't eat for two hours before MRI. He was not a happy camper. I had been nursing him on demand, and he didn't like suddenly being starved. The nurses unplugged all the leads so that I could walk him around the room, free of the monitors. It helped some, but he was hungry, and there was a two-hour delay in the MRI schedule. The nurse who had come to our rescue the night that Dr. Shirley was there, the one who had plucked Michael up and handed him to me for the first time, was once again his roommate's nurse. We chatted while I rocked and soothed Michael, and she took care of the baby girl in the next crib. I told her Michael's story. She was thrilled to hear that we had kept the faith and had not given into fear at the doctor's prognosis. I told her all about Knitterbugs, the work we had done, and how so many people had come together to pray for Michael. She told me that all the nurses had been talking about the baby hats. She said that just that small act of kindness had touched so many people—moms, dads, and nurses. I told her that knitting was therapy for me. She remarked on how cute the two little hats were that I had knitted for Michael's roommate. She said that she believed in prayer and that Michael was indeed a miracle. Through our conversation, I learned that she was Catholic. We talked about our children and spent two hours sharing our faith while we waited to be called down for the MRI. It not only helped to pass the time, it was uplifting for both of us. She told me to keep the faith, that everything would be okay with Michael. God wouldn't abandon us after bringing us so far. I told her that I just wanted the MRI to come back with no surprises. I didn't want him to undergo surgery. Everything had gone so well. Michael was strong and seemed so healthy, but the delays and the extra caution of the doctors insisting on the MRI was making me doubt. She gently admonished me and told me to give it up to God. He would take care of everything. I felt blessed to have been given those moments with that nurse. I needed to be set straight, and she was the one that God sent to do the job. Once again, God had placed in my path the person that I needed, at the moment I needed her.

I noticed a pattern. It had been happening more and more often. Any time I felt weak or afraid, another human angel showed up. The hospital chaplain came in and prayed over Michael. He told me not to worry, that Michael was one of the lucky ones, that he would be going home soon. Finally, Michael's nurse popped her head in and said they were ready for him. We wheeled Michael through the halls and down the elevator to the basement in his little crib, screaming all the way. When we got to the MRI area, everything moved very quickly. I was able to stay with him while he was sedated until he fell asleep, which was almost instant. Before I left Michael's side, I looked directly at the anesthesiologist and told him to take care of my baby boy because he was an absolute miracle. Without breaking eye contact with me, and with a gentle smile, he assured me that Michael would be in good hands. Joe met me in the little waiting room with coffee, and we sat quietly together. I knitted and prayed for the forty-five minutes that the MRI lasted, and when they wheeled Michael out, they called me over so that he would see me when he woke up. We all went back up to his room, all of us fully expecting him to be released that afternoon.

It was a relief to be back in Michael's pod, with the MRI done, the final test that we had all been waiting on. The nurses reconnected him to the monitors and told me to go ahead and nurse him since he had gone for hours without eating. It calmed him down instantly. Joe and I sat anxiously awaiting the NICU doctor or head nurse, or anyone, to poke their head in to give us the results. Joe had installed the infant car seat in the van; we had all our bags packed up and ready to go. We talked about how great it would be to finally go home with our little boy. How excited the kids would be to finally meet their new baby brother in person. After a couple of hours, Joe asked our nurse when we would hear something. She told us that she thought we would have heard something by then and that she would check for us. A few minutes later, the NICU doctor came in to tell us that she was trying to locate the neurosurgeon on call because he would have to be the one to read the MRI before Michael could be released. Michael's roommate's nurse came in to ask how everything had gone. We told her that the MRI was done, but that we were waiting to hear the results. She calmly said, "Remember what we talked about. You have to have faith!"

I smiled and told her I was really trying.

The head nurse returned several minutes later to tell us that the neurosurgeon had left to go to another hospital to perform a surgery. Unfortunately, he would not be back until the next day. We were completely deflated. I really wanted to cry, but I kept it together. We were so close, and yet still so far away. Like being one number off on the lottery. The nurse kept apologizing. She knew how desperately we wanted to go home. Trying to reassure us, she said that she had looked at the MRI herself, and that from what she could tell, it didn't look like there was any fluid on Michael's brain. She reminded us that she wasn't a neurosurgeon and that she didn't have the authority to sign off on the MRI. She could discharge us, but if we left the hospital and Michael did have to return for surgery, it would be in a less-sterile environment. He would have to be admitted to Pediatrics, and she assured us that we didn't want that. She said it would be much better for Michael to stay put for just one more night. She promised us that we would be first on the list to talk to the neurosurgeon the next morning. It was already five o'clock in the evening. I told her that I was not leaving. I told her that we wouldn't discharge Michael until after talking to the neurosurgeon, but I wanted to stay in his room with him that night. I just couldn't bear to leave him again. She smiled and told me that she could arrange it. Michael was doing so well, I had been with him around the clock, leaving only at bedtime. I was the one caring for him, nursing, bathing, and changing him. The nurses did their checks and reports, but he was totally thriving, strong, and healthy.

The head nurse came in and said that they had a room on the other side of the NICU, reserved for families, that she would assign to us. The room was tiny, like a long narrow shoebox. It had a twin bed, a chair, and a shower. It was exactly all that we needed. She said that after the shift change, one of the nurses would bring us down and get us set up. I didn't have any toiletries or clothes with me. We had been expecting to go home that night, so I wasn't prepared to stay. Joe's colleagues had given us a two-hundred-dollar Target gift card, so we ran to the store and picked up some toiletries, a change of clothes, and some snacks for our little party in Michael's room. Joe and I ate dinner together before he dropped me off for the night. Kissing me goodbye, he told me to have fun. We both wanted to be driving our little guy home, but being allowed to spend the night with him was the next best thing.

I went back up to Michael's little pod and waited patiently for the nurse to move us to our private room. I picked up my sweet boy and nuzzled his face and told him we would be rooming together for the night. I was giddy with excitement, and I couldn't wait to snuggle with him. When worry and doubt about the MRI results crept in, I tried my best to pray them away and just enjoy my baby in my arms, but it wasn't easy. The fear kept nagging me. What if there was a problem? What if Michael did need surgery?

Hours went by. It was a busy night in the NICU. Michael's new nurse came in, one I hadn't met yet, apologizing for the delay. Twins had just been born, and she was getting their pod ready. I told her I was in no rush, that I would be spending the night; and as long as I was rocking my baby, I was happy. Around eleven o'clock that night, a different nurse came in to tell me that she would be taking us to our room. She apologized, saying that it was an unusually busy night with new admissions, so Michael's nurse asked her to get us settled in. She was very sweet and kind. A short, round, African American nurse, younger than me, she shared in my excitement of moving out of the NICU. She told me that she mostly worked the night shift and that she had helped out with Michael a few times when his nurse was on a break or busy with another baby. She told me how great she thought Michael was doing and how strong and healthy he was. She wheeled his crib into the tiny room and brought me some towels and more diapers. She went over the list of phone numbers to call if I needed anything and told me that I could order breakfast in the morning. She let me know that Michael's nurse would probably come in to check his vitals once things slowed down on the floor. She smiled a big bright smile as she walked toward the door. Before stepping out, she said, "Now if you need anything at all, just call the desk and ask for me. My name is Faith."

Goose bumps instantly sprung up over my whole body, and a huge lump caught in my throat. I choked out a thank-you, just before she closed the door behind her. The sound of my voice surprised me as I spoke my thoughts out loud, "Wow, God! That was amazing!"

I didn't get much sleep that night. I held my sleeping baby boy while I listened to the news, his head nuzzled under my chin. I kissed his cheeks and breathed in the scent of his sweetness. No more wires or monitors, just his soft sweet body in the little monkey sleeper I brought for him to wear. I wanted to curl up with him next to me in my bed, but didn't, for fear of getting scolded by his nurse. I could hardly wait to get him home. It was very late when she finally came in to check his vitals. She told me that if I needed to leave the room or take a shower, I should bring Michael down to the nurse's station. I didn't tell her that I wasn't planning to let him out of my sight under any circumstances. That night I nursed him every time he made a peep, and I prayed every waking moment that the MRI results would be normal.

I woke up before six the next morning, filled with energy despite very little sleep. I didn't bring Michael to the nurse's station while I showered. Instead, I wedged his crib into the bathroom doorway. I showered and dressed quickly, ordered breakfast, put on my makeup, and fixed my hair. I got Michael bathed, dressed, and fed as soon as he woke up and said my morning prayers. It was just before seven when I heard a knock on the door. My heart thundered in my chest as I leapt to my feet to open it. Three smiling females entered, introducing themselves as neurosurgeon fellows. They squeezed into the tiny space between Michael's crib and the wall. Each of them remarked how cute he was and how great he looked. One of them spoke up, saying that they had all reviewed the MRI and that they concurred, there was no fluid on Michael's brain. My knees almost gave out. I exhaled. She added, "We don't anticipate that the fluid will return or that he will need a shunt in the future."

She told me to follow up with our pediatrician and watch his milestones. They wished me luck and told me we could finally go home and enjoy our baby. I wanted to embrace each one of them but held myself together and thanked them before they left.

Michael's roommate's nurse, the one who had reminded me to keep the faith, walked into the room right after the neurosurgeons left. She smiled as she hugged me and said to Michael, "What a happy day it is!"

She told me how glad she was to be his nurse on our going-home day. She had all his discharge papers with her. The only instructions I got were to follow up with our pediatrician and a pediatric urologist regarding Michael's undescended testicles. She saw my blue pieta prayer book on the side table and told me what a good girl I was, saying my prayers and keeping the faith. She asked where I got the book because she wanted to get one for her daughter. I told her that I'd had it for years. It had been given to me by Gramma Hubbard. Our church had recently put some on their bookrack, and I just happened to have two in my bag. Strangely, I still don't know why I had them, but I gave them both to Michael's nurse. She was thrilled. We both agreed that God had obviously placed us in each other's path.

I called Joe right away and told him to come get us. He said he was already on his way and arrived at the hospital a few minutes later. Our nurse wheeled me down the NICU hallway in a wheelchair, with Michael in my arms. Smiling nurses lined the hallway, waving goodbye as we passed them. They wished us well and congratulated us on our release. It was another day of work for them, caring for all the babies who couldn't go home yet. Along with all the babies and their families, I added all the nurses and doctors who took care of them around the clock to my prayer list. NICU nurses will forever hold a special place in my heart.

We drove home in the bright hot Dallas sunshine. I sat next to Michael, who was bundled in his car seat. I stared at his beautiful face as he slept, tightly gripping my finger all the way home, feeling more like we were floating than driving. The kids crowded around when Joe carried Michael into the house, trying to get a look at him in person. None of them had come to the hospital to visit. They had only seen the pictures that Joe texted them from his phone. Each one of them took a turn holding their new baby brother, whom they had all prayed so hard for. They were seeing the proof of their answered prayers. What a testimony Michael was. My legs were swollen up like balloons. A result of not keeping them elevated or getting enough rest after all the IV fluids. Finally home and able to calm down and relax, I propped them up on big pillows. I laid my head back on the sofa and closed my eyes, absorbing the sounds of my family all around me. We were home. The kids had all made cards, and the house was tidy. We crowded together on our huge leather sectional couch, snapped first pictures, and breathed sighs of relief. The kids filled me in about all the neighbors who had brought meals and pizza gift cards. It was a relief knowing my mother didn't have to worry about cooking.

Joe decided to work from home the next day, and I had decided not to resume homeschooling until after my mother left. We were decompressing and celebrating. My mother came into our bedroom. Joe and I had been awake for a while, marveling at little Michael, tucked between us in the bed. She sat in the wooden rocking chair with her tea. She told us that she had peeked in earlier, planning to sneak the baby out, but that I had my arm around him. She knew there was no way she could take him without waking me up. I picked Michael up and handed him to her. The rest of the house was still quiet, something we all knew wouldn't last long. My mother began to tell us everything that had happened at home while I was in the hospital. I had been expecting it and had tried to mentally prepare myself. She told me all the picky, normal, kid things that happened day to day. Nothing earth-shattering by any stretch, but she reported it like we weren't disciplining our kids enough. Ryan, who had turned two a week earlier, was too demanding, bossing the older kids around to get what he wanted. Sarah and Katie had left toys and clothes on the floor in their room. Angela was so loud in the morning while she got ready for school, banging and crashing drawers and doors, turning on lights, waking her up each day. She told us that she made Clare open and close the door, ten times quietly, to remind her not to slam it. She informed us that Christina had a real attitude problem. She had no idea what her problem was, but she said she wouldn't give her the time of day. Anytime my mother asked her something, she claimed that Christina gave her a dirty look and wouldn't speak to her at all, and spent most of the time upstairs trying to avoid her. The report about Christina was the most surprising to me because she was one of my most helpful kids, especially with Ryan. I listened to all the petty criticisms, nodding along, humoring her, when what I really wanted was to give her a big eye roll. I resisted. I smiled, bit my tongue, and allowed her to go on. It wasn't important. Baby Michael being born healthy and finally home—that was what mattered.

My mother proceeded to tell us how wonderful Patrick had been, what a great helper he was, and how he really aimed to please her. He had offered to help dry the dishes anytime she washed them and fixed her cups of tea all day long. Joe and I exchanged knowing glances. She had been duped. We didn't say anything. Again, we simply nodded and smiled. She told us that there had been one incident with him, however, but they had an understanding. They had reached an agreement with each other. We asked her what happened, but she said she couldn't say. She had promised Patrick that she wouldn't break his confidence. The little hairs stood up on the back of my neck. That was not going to fly with us. Right off the bat, I told her that if they'd had an understanding, and if she'd promised not to break his confidence, she should have kept it to herself. Since she hadn't, I insisted, as his parents, she needed to tell us. I found it curious how she had no problem telling us about all the petty insignificant stuff that the other kids had done. Obviously, whatever Patrick had done had to be serious if she wouldn't say anything. It didn't take that much convincing for her to cave. She told us that forty dollars had gone missing from her purse. She said that she questioned the girls about it, and that Grace told her she should ask Patrick. My mother told her that she never would have guessed that Patrick would have been the one to take it, given how helpful he had been. Grace insisted she ask him. My mother told us that she did ask him, but in such a way as to trip him up. She said, "I called Patrick over and told him that someone had stolen fifty dollars out of my purse."

She said that Patrick looked shocked and said, "Fifty?"

Because it was forty dollars that went missing, not fifty. She said she knew then that it was him because of his reaction. She said he didn't admit to it right away. He told her that he would try to find out who had taken it. Later on that afternoon, she said she pretended to cry, telling Patrick that she didn't have much money and that my dad had given her the forty dollars for her trip. She said that was when Patrick finally admitted that he had taken it. He told her that he owed his friend money and had already given it to him.

It was then that we realized that the situation with Patrick was more serious than just sneaking out to hang out with friends, going to parties, and occasionally drinking. It suddenly occurred to us that he could be using drugs. We couldn't be sure, but why else would he owe his friend money and be willing to steal from his grandmother? Of course we were not at all happy to hear of the event. Joe told my mother that Patrick had taken advantage of her. His helpfulness and hospitality was his way of manipulating her, and she had fallen for it. We reminded her that we had warned her of Patrick's behavior and trouble with the police when she first arrived. Seeing the concern on our faces, she then told us that the paddle had better not come out while she was there, or she would be taking the next flight home. Joe told her that in his house, if he felt that there was a need to use the paddle, he would; and if she didn't like it, he would be happy to drive her to the airport. Joe never used the paddle except for when we caught Patrick sneaking out, but we wanted her to know that she was not running the show. There was something about her look that gave me the feeling that she believed Patrick's acting out was somehow our fault. We told her that we wouldn't say anything to him until she left, but we most definitely would deal with it. Joe gave my mother forty dollars, assuring her that he would be working it off with plenty of extra chores.

After being home for two days, I noticed that Michael's soft spot, which initially had been very much sunken in, was puffed up. I thought it may have been because he had been lying down. It seemed to go down a little when I sat him up, but I kept my eye on it. When it happened again the next morning, I grew concerned. I called the pediatrician's office, and they told me to bring him in right away. Dr. Nichols checked him out from head to toe while I gave him the history of my pregnancy and all the concerns about fluid on his brain, up to the MRI that showed there was no fluid there. He listened to everything and told me that he didn't have any concerns. He said that it wasn't unusual for the fontanelle, soft spot, to be either puffy or sunken. We should be concerned if it became rigid, which it was not. I felt much better. His soft spot never did sink back in. It always remained soft and puffy, and was actually quite large compared to all my other babies'. His head wasn't a typical shape. It was large and looked like he had a dent in his forehead. Dr. Nichols assured me that it would eventually close up, round out, and look quite normal.

I wanted to visit Dr. MacDonald's office to show off my little miracle boy. He and his entire staff had been praying for Michael. My mother seemed apprehensive about the impromptu trip, but agreed to come along for the ride. The kids piled into the van, and we drove to Denton. My mother and I took Michael into the small waiting room. It was lunchtime, so there weren't any patients waiting. Dr. MacDonald was at the hospital, called out on a delivery; but his nurse, Michelle, was there. Her eyes welled up when she saw us. We stood huddled in a circle in the waiting room while she held and marveled at Michael, believing that she was holding a little miracle. She had been there the day Dr. MacDonald saw the first worrisome ultrasound, and continued to be there for the remainder of the pregnancy. She'd heard about the improvements and hoped and prayed with me that everything would turn out okay. She said that

Dr. MacDonald would be disappointed that he missed us, but she would tell him about our visit.

We drove back to Southlake. When I pulled into the garage, my mother began acting very strangely. She told the kids to wait in the van and not go into the house until I went in first. She had been acting weird the whole morning, and I soon found out why. Walking in the back garage door and down the hallway, I was stunned to see someone standing in my kitchen. It took me more than a minute for it to register that it was my sister Thérèse. I was completely surprised. My mother had talked her into coming, and Thérèse's boyfriend had bought her the plane ticket. Joe picked her up from the airport after we'd left for our trip to Denton. I later learned that Angela had known about the surprise visit. She told me that she wasn't feeling well that morning, so she stayed home from school; but in reality, she wanted to be there for Thérèse's arrival. I was thrilled to see my sister. None of the other kids had been in on the surprise, but they were all happy that she had come. It was a reprieve for all of them. They had all been giving me looks, speaking volumes without uttering a word. I knew they had plenty to tell me, but they were waiting until they could speak freely. Anytime one of the little ones complained about something that my mother said or did, I made excuses for her and told them to just behave and not give her any reason to get annoyed with them. Looking back, that is exactly how I had lived my whole life. Always avoiding confrontation, even when I knew she was wrong.

I had booked Michael's baptism while I was still in the hospital. It was scheduled for the following Saturday night. I wanted to have him baptized as quickly as possible. My mother changed her flight so that she could be there. Because it would be a late night on Saturday after Mass and the baptism, we planned to have a little lunchtime celebration on Sunday, the day after. We ordered a tray of sub sandwiches, and Barb told me she would get a cake. I prayed that there would not be any drama. I didn't want my mother making Barb feel bad, but I was prepared to say something if she did.

Before the Saturday evening Mass at Our Lady of Lebanon, Joe and I waited out in the foyer of the church. We processed in, carrying Michael in my arms, with Fr. Assaad. Once we arrived before the altar, Fr. Assaad took Michael from me and placed him on the altar. The moment was so moving. One that I will never forget. I had been praying only the Joyful Mysteries for my entire pregnancy. Joining myself and my baby to each one of them. The Annunciation: I was thrilled at the discovery that I was carrying a new life. The doctors had announced that there was a problem, serious and devastating prognosis, but there had also been many encouraging and hopeful annunciations as my pregnancy progressed. The Visitation: Barb and I had shared the very first moment, praying over Michael as soon as I saw the positive test at her house that morning. I had visited with my neighbor Cyndy, the Knitterbugs ladies, and my praying friends. We had traveled to South Dakota and shared our story with everyone we met, asking for prayers. The Nativity: I begged God for Michael's nativity, that he would be born, and He had allowed it. Michael was alive and well. At that very moment, we were witnessing his Presentation. Michael was laid on the altar. I had returned Michael to God while he was still in my womb. After the devastating news that he most likely wouldn't survive the pregnancy, God had healed him. He had given me the opportunity to once again present Michael to Him. The tears rolled down my cheeks, overcome with joy at the sight of my baby boy on the sacred altar. The baptism was beautiful and ceremonial in the Maronite rite. Our whole family—Armen and Barb, Michael's godparents, and everyone in attendance along with Fr. Assaad—walked out of the church, and reentered with Michael, a newly baptized child of God. We headed back to Southlake, but instead of going home, Joe pulled into the Anamia's parking lot. He said this was by far our biggest celebration yet, and Anamia's was where we went for the big ones.

The next day, Armen and Barb arrived at lunchtime. My mother was gracious. She made tea and took on the role of hostess. I was cautiously pleased, always on alert should something go awry, but thankful when it didn't. She made a big display of presenting Michael to his godmother to hold and made small talk with our guests. Barb and Armen bought a double stroller so that I could take both Ryan and Michael for walks. Their visit was short and sweet. Sensing that

Barb did not want to overstay, I told her that we would catch up and visit later on.

Joe drove my mother and sister to the airport the next day. We were all more than ready to get life back to some sense of normal. He pulled out of the driveway, and the second the van was out of sight, the floodgates opened up. Each of the kids took turns, purging all of what had been building up over the previous two weeks. They had been miserable. They all wanted to know why I had given the ticket from Bob and Nanette to my mother. Why couldn't I have given it to anyone else? Christina was the first to tell me how horrible it was. She believed that my mother hated her. *Hated* her. I told her that was ridiculous. She didn't hate her. Christina asked me, "Well, then why would she accuse me of stealing money out of her purse? What did I ever do to her?"

That was a part of the story that my mother had left out. According to Grace and Christina, my mother had first asked Grace if she had taken the money. After Grace told her that she hadn't, my mother told her that she bet Christina had taken it. Christina said that after her accusation, she avoided my mother for the rest of her visit. She told me that my mother had picked on Callum the entire time and that he was in tears most of the time that I was in the hospital. Callum chimed in and stated that she hated him too. Christina said that she stayed in Callum's room with him for the whole two weeks. One by one, each of them told me about their own injustices. She had taken all the housephones and kept them with her in her room so that no one could answer the phone but her. They said that she was really annoyed by the fact that Joe had texted pictures to Angela's and Joseph's cell phones, but not to hers. Joe hadn't done so to keep her from seeing the pictures, he simply didn't have my mother's number saved to his phone. He texted them to our two kids who had phones, fully expecting them to show everyone, including her, which they did. The problem was that she wanted to be the first to see them. She had made sarcastic comments about Barb showing up to see the baby at the hospital before her. When she saw the video that Joe had taken when my friend Tracy had come to visit in the NICU, a video that they had made for me because I couldn't get out of bed to go see him myself, she questioned who she was and why she was there. All the kids had the same things to say about Patrick, who had remained curiously silent during all the venting. Patrick had been her little pet and acted all helpful and sweet. He and my mother had spent hours sitting out on the front porch in deep conversation, not allowing the rest of them to take part. She made the rest of them stay inside. If she went outside to the backyard, she locked the doors, kept the keys, and wouldn't allow anyone in the house. Some strange friend of Patrick had come asking for him. An older guy that they said looked shady with piercings and dreadlocks that none of them knew. We later found out that he had gone to the high school, but had been kicked out of school and his house. He was eighteen, and a druggie. Patrick grinned through the recant and said he thought it was great that Grandma liked him. He seemed really pleased with himself about having pulled one over on her.

We all knew full well that Patrick was a charmer. He had always been a likable kid, polite, respectful, and well-socialized. We had always received great reports and feedback from every one of his teachers, coaches, his friends' parents, the youth group leaders, and our friends. We had raised him well. What we were also discovering is that he was a sneaky, manipulative liar and a thief. He had so many good qualities, gifts, talents, and abilities. It was extremely frustrating, discouraging, and disappointing to watch him put so much energy into negative and destructive things. He had fooled us for a long time, but we were onto his game, and we weren't going to make it easy on him. It would be a couple more months before we discovered just how bad it actually was.

I let my kids talk, and talk, and talk. I had been stifling them for far too long. I wondered just how long I had been stifling them. As I recalled each of my mother's visits over the years, there had always been an element of conflict or drama that I swept under the rug. It had gone on for my entire life. I had just learned to adapt. It happened when my kids were babies, but the drama usually involved other people—her friends, her relatives, my dad's family, my siblings. I would listen to her rantings, nodding in agreement, always her loyal ally, even when I knew she was wrong. As my kids grew and we moved away, it became more subtle. Our contact was not constant, and our relationship was long-distance. When she visited, I tiptoed around her in an effort to ensure that her time was pleasant and enjoyable, fixing nice meals, baking, treating her out to dinner, always buying or making a special gift. She'd often spend the night or several nights, depending where we were living. Once the kids were old enough to see through her, it was more difficult to make excuses for her behavior. I found myself telling them to just lie low and not give her reasons to get upset, that she'd only be there for a short time. I taught them to be respectful.

I could no longer ignore their feelings. I couldn't make any more excuses. How could I tell them to be respectful to someone who was so mean, unfair, and hurtful? They vented for several days, remembering things. I had knots in my stomach. Joe was cautious of his words around the kids, but we had plenty of conversations about it when we were alone. He had known that the kids weren't happy while my mother was there. He said that they always came back to our room to hang out with him when he got home from visiting Michael and I in the hospital. I told him that I really wanted to believe, that considering the circumstances that we were in, she would have been less like herself and more like a grandmother. I just wanted her to be a grandmother to my kids. Just once. Joe said, "A zebra doesn't change its stripes."

It was very disappointing. My heart ached, and I felt guilty that I had left my kids at her mercy. What should have been a joyous time for our whole family had been tainted by miserable frustration. The only consolation was that my kids all had each other for support.

Things quickly returned to normal. We all reconnected and felt that our family had become stronger than ever, after experiencing such a tremendous miracle. Michael was held and carried around constantly. We never put him down, and he was never left alone. Joe walked him around outside, the kids took turns holding and loving him, and I rocked him and sat outside with him, marveling at him. He slept between Joe and I in the bed, surrounded with love.

I shared all the wonderful news with my Knitterbugs family. I had sent them pictures and updates from the hospital. They all agreed that Michael was a true miracle, and they expressed how thrilled they were to be part of it. Although I had only attended that one Magnificat prayer meeting before my first appointment with the fetal maternal specialist, I went to another one shortly after Michael was born, and I brought him along. I wanted the ladies who had prayed for him to see how perfect and beautiful he was. None of them seemed surprised. They'd had complete faith that he would be just fine. After we had all prayed and they blessed Michael with holy oil, one of the ladies went back in her prayer journal to the day that I had attended the first meeting. She read aloud what she had written. She had heard God speak to her, telling her that we shouldn't be concerned, that my baby would be healthy. There had been countless prayers offered up for Michael by more people than we would ever know. To us, that was a miracle in itself. God had been so faithful. I have no doubt that the miracle of Michael touched numerous lives and changed hearts.

Joe became increasingly concerned about his business venture. He still hadn't made any money. It was a start-up that had plenty of potential; he was putting in tons of sweat equity, but he wasn't making much more than connections in return. It seemed like he was helping everyone else get matched up with potential jobs, and a lot of them did get hired. He was always volunteering time and effort to help others reach their goals, but he still didn't have an income. He still believed that Empowered Voyage would be profitable eventually, but we didn't have the luxury of time. Our mortgage was more than four thousand dollars a month, our utility bills were high, and our savings were quickly being eaten up. I walked into Joe's home office one morning where he had been sitting at his desk, crunching numbers. He swiveled around on his chair and looked at me with strained eyes. He said he hated to have to say it, but he really thought we needed to sell the house. We would run out of money otherwise. I sat across from him with Michael in my arms and looked into his eyes. I told him to call the realtor. I don't think he expected me to be so calm about it, but I was. I told him it was just a house. We had just come through a life-altering journey. I got my miracle. If God could fix Michael and allow us to have him, He could take care of everything else—a job, a place to live, whatever our family needed. I wasn't worried. My journey with Michael had been a turning point for me without a doubt. I had discovered something that I prayed I would never forget. It hadn't been easy, but it had worked. Surrendering everything to God had saved my sanity, and prayer had caused a miracle. We both agreed that by the end of the month, we would put the house on the market.

TWENTY-THREE

Human Angels

Southlake, Texas, Spring 2011

anette called to invite our family out to dinner at their favorite restaurant, Vinny's, with Cathy and Al. She said that it would be their treat, to celebrate Michael's birth, and Cathy, who was cancer free. It would be our first time meeting Cathy and Al. We humbly and gratefully accepted. The invitation, unbeknown to us at the time, would also be the beginning of an incredible and unbelievable journey of love and unwavering friendship.

Bob, Nanette, Cathy, and Al were already waiting for us when we arrived and filed into the restaurant. Several tables had been pushed together to make one very long one, with Bob, Al, and Joe at one end, and Nanette, Cathy, and I at the other, and all the kids in between. The conversation was lively, happy, and a breath of fresh air for all of us. Cathy was the star of the night. The absolute sweetest lady that any of us had ever met, she took a genuine interest in each and every one of our kids. She engaged each one of them, asking them about themselves, making each one feel special. She had a twinkle in her eye. A lady in her early seventies with blond stylish hair, bright-pink lipstick, and an even brighter smile, she was infectious, upbeat, and natural. I found myself in awe of her energy. Just having gone through a major ordeal, two bouts of cancer, no one would have believed she had ever been sick. All my kids took to her instinctively.

Nanette was as sweet as ever, giggling along with Cathy's antics. She nudged me, pleased with the fact that she knew we would click. She enjoyed watching Cathy interact with the kids.

Nanette held Michael and marveled at how perfect he was. She said she had prayed for him from the minute she found out about him, and lit candles for us while she and Bob traveled. The guys talked about Joe's job search and offered some advice and tips. They promised to help him network. We discovered that Al had also worked for the Boy Scouts, in Human Resources. The three of them seemed to hit it off and have a lot in common. We swapped stories and laughed the whole night. Bob hugged me on the way to the car, thanking me for sharing our miracle with them and for being a great example of family. I was humbled. They had all been incredibly generous to our family, yet he was the one thanking us.

With boxed-up leftovers, and the dessert that they insisted the kids order, we left full and happy, talking all the way home about the kindness that we had been shown. I couldn't wait to write thank-you notes and to have the kids write their own as well. They were all amazed at how much fun they'd had. They admitted that when they first learned about the dinner invitation, they expected it would be kind of boring hanging out with old people. They were pleasantly surprised that our new friends were seriously cool, and some of the nicest people they had ever met.

I talked to Cathy and/or Nanette practically every day after that. The two ladies were incredibly supportive and upbeat, and they each took turns calling to check in on us. They complimented us on the job we were doing with our kids. I laughed and told them that we were a work in progress. I shared with them that we ran a pretty tight ship and that our family was our number one priority. They said they could feel the love. We chatted about lots of things, our interests, our chores. They wanted to get a sense of how we managed to keep it all together so well. We laughed about funny things the kids said and did. We shared stories, recipes, worries, and our faith. We were all Catholic. I shared with them that we had decided to put our house up for sale. Joe had revamped his resume, and although he was still doing some Empowered Voyage things, he was full-on, back in job search mode. He had never quit looking, but he had become extra choosy about what jobs he would apply for when he started his business. We really didn't have a plan. We just wanted to get out from under our huge mortgage.

One morning, Cathy called to ask if it would be okay if she and Al came to pick up a couple of the older girls, Christina and Grace, to take them on an outing. I told her they would love it. When I asked them, they raised their eyebrows. "Where are we going?"

I told them I wasn't sure. Something about visiting a horse. That was even more puzzling to them. They felt slightly awkward, but agreed to go. Cathy and Al came to pick them up and told me they'd be back in a few hours. Christina and Grace left politely quiet and a little uncertain, but returned smiling, giggling, and very much at ease. They excitedly told us all about visiting the little rescue horse named Taco. They had stopped to feed him carrots before heading to the mall. They brought home bags of candy from the candy store. I was shocked to see how much they had, giving the girls a look, hoping they hadn't been greedy. Understanding my look, they explained, "We couldn't help it, Cathy kept telling us to get more, and she told us to pick out everybody's favorites so that we could share." Always thinking of others, never wanting to leave anyone out, Cathy was kindhearted. It was an enjoyable time for all of us. I called to the girls on their way up to their room, to be sure to write out a thank-you note. Before I could finish my sentence, they both called down to me, "We know!"

Cathy called regularly to check in, especially when Bob and Nanette were traveling on business. She invited us all out for dinner again, saying that I shouldn't have to cook on Mother's Day. She told me she had invited Bob and Nanette too. Joe and I were blown away. The kids were totally excited to be invited out again just a couple of weeks after our first treat. Our next dinner was just as fun as the first, a happy time with laughing and sharing stories. Everyone was relaxed, and the kids were very well-behaved. Joe and I could not believe how our new friends had taken us under their wings. We agreed on the way home that we needed to invited them over to our house for dinner. We couldn't afford to treat everyone at a restaurant, but we wanted to show them that we appreciated their kindness. We wanted to do something nice for them. When I told Cathy and Nanette that we wanted them all to come for dinner, they said they would love to. We decided that the best time to plan it would be when Bob and Nanette returned from a trip they were taking at the beginning of June.

A few days after Mother's Day was Grace's birthday. That morning, I caught a glimpse of a car pulling around our front circle driveway, but when I got to the door, it was gone. I figured it must have been someone just turning around. A few seconds later, the phone rang. It was Nanette. She told me to check the front doorstep because Cathy had just dropped something off for Grace. Cathy and Nanette were a tag team. They had asked for all the kids' birth dates, not just out of curiosity, but to celebrate them. Grace smiled all day long after finding the gift bag with the Charming Charlie's gift card. She couldn't believe what they had done and was excited to go shopping that afternoon. When I called to tell Joe, we again marveled over the thoughtfulness of the folks we had only just met. It seemed as though they were on a mission. They were a team, performing acts of kindness to keep us lifted up and encouraged. Not wanting to leave anyone out, more outings were planned with a different set of kids each time. Movies, lunch, and rides at the mall. Each day, Cathy called with another idea or invitation. We were overwhelmed by the generosity and didn't want to continue accepting without giving back. Cathy insisted that they appreciated us allowing them to be part of their lives and sharing our family with them. She and Al had never had children, and they very much enjoyed being around ours. I told her we really wanted to have them over for dinner. She said that Nanette's birthday was coming up, and we could plan it for then. She suggested throwing a surprise birthday party for her. I loved the idea. Joe would grill, and the kids and I would bake. Cathy said that she had decorations and party games for the kids. She said Nanette would love a kid themed party, but I knew the real reason was that Cathy wanted the kids to have fun. We talked and planned it out and cleared it with Bob's schedule.

During all that time, Patrick continued sneaking out of the house. Despite our efforts to keep him in, being on constant vigil, monitoring his movements throughout the day, checking and rechecking that windows and doors were locked. We knew that the weekends were his preferred days. Friday and Saturday nights were when all the action happened. Typically, he would show up at the door, early in the morning after a night of partying, but on one particular night, he didn't. We had lost track of how many times he had snuck out. In the beginning, our initial reaction was panic and fear for his safety, but after many times of the same old story, we just got plain mad. We questioned how he could be so insensitive to cause us so much stress and worry. As the afternoon wore on and he still hadn't returned home, I began to really worry. I called the police. When the police officer arrived, I gave him a photo, and he took down all of Patrick's information. When Barb called to chat, I told her what was going on. She told me she would pray. I prayed my head off and couldn't concentrate on much else. Barb called again to see if Patrick had come home. When I told her that he hadn't, she told me she and Armen and their daughter Rachael were coming over, and we were all going to search for him. Angela stayed home with the little kids, while Joe and I, wearing Michael in his baby carrier, Joseph, Christina, Grace, and Clare headed to Southlake Town Square.

We had been out to Town Square for dinner on many occasions. We'd seen the clusters of teenagers hanging out, groups of friends going to the movies and having ice cream. They had seemed innocent enough, despite having heard reports that several businesses and their patrons had complained of kids being a nuisance. What we saw on that Saturday night was an eye-opener for us. I was very surprised to see very young teenagers, some as young as our girls, twelve and thirteen years old, just loitering around. There was a visible police presence. We approached an officer and told him why we were there. We told him that we had already spoken to an officer earlier that day about our missing son. He said that he would be on the lookout and that we should check on the top of the parking garage, a popular hangout spot. Joe, Armen, Joseph, and Rachael went up to check while Barb and I stayed in the square, talking to kids, asking them if they'd seen Patrick. Michael was one month old. The police officer was very sympathetic. He shared with us that he and his fellow officers referred to Town Square as the Playpen, because parents dropped their kids off to hang out on the weekends while they went off to do their own thing. Some of them weren't even Southlake residents and came from neighboring cities. Parents were under the impression that it was a safe place to let their kids socialize. The police basically babysat until curfew. We told them that we only lived a five-minute walk from there and we never allowed our kids to just hang out. On occasion, we drove them to meet a friend for a movie and picked them up as soon as it was over, and that was usually during the day. He was impressed that we were there with a search party, looking for our son. We told him the lengths we had gone to up till that point. He said it sounded like we were doing everything right and urged us not to give up. He said he wished more parents were as vigilant. I couldn't help but feel like a failure. If we were doing everything right, why was Patrick still continuing with his behavior?

Barb was not shy about walking up to kids to ask about Patrick. After a few conversations, she found someone who knew him. The kid was a wealth of information, and he led us through a chain of people who eventually got in touch with him. Patrick had apparently been at Town Square earlier in the evening. He actually saw us when we arrived and took off with some friends before we noticed him. We kept the police informed of all the details we were getting. The police went to the location that we had been given for Patrick. Not considering the level of sophistication that the teenager operated under, they all had cell phones, we felt confident that the officers would drive up with Patrick at any moment, but someone had tipped him off, so they fled. Barb and I made our way up to the top of the parking garage where we were met by what seemed to be the more hard-core partiers. They looked at us like we were intruding on their turf. I was very suspicious of their activities. Joe and Armen were in a heated argument with one of the kids who said that we were way too overprotective and that we really should lay off. Joe got very much up in the kid's face and told him he needed to keep his mouth shut and mind his own business. He told him that he was Patrick's father, and if he had a father who cared, he would do the same thing. I think Joe must have hit a nerve because the kid shut up and backed away. We later learned about several of the kids who hung out up there, and pretty much all of them were troubled on various levels.

We got home around eleven o'clock after talking with John, a friend of Patrick's who we had met and had even been to our house. He and his girlfriend listened attentively as we expressed our grave concern. He said that he would find Patrick. I have no doubt that John was a partier as well. He was a few years older than Patrick and had his own car. I could tell that he had a conscience and he cared about Patrick. Barb, Armen, and Rachael went home. I lay awake in bed nursing Michael, praying the Joyful Mysteries of the rosary, begging God to bring my son home. Shortly after 1:00 a.m., I heard the doorbell ring. It was John and his girlfriend, and they had Patrick with them. Patrick came in looking like he hadn't slept in days. He was glassy-eyed, his clothes were rumpled, and he looked exhausted. I hugged him and told him to never do that to us again. Then I called the police. They needed to know that he was safe at home.

Three officers showed up at the door. I invited them into the living room where we all sat down. They told Patrick he shouldn't be hanging out with the likes of the kids he was hanging out with. He said, "Man, look around you. Look at your parents. They care about you, and you had them worried sick. Your mom was out with your newborn baby brother looking for you tonight. You can't do that to your parents. Look at this house and all that you have here. Clearly your family loves you. Your brother and sisters were out looking for you, their friends were out looking for you. Those kids who were hanging out on the parking garage, trying to keep them from finding you, sending us on a wild goose chase, they aren't your friends, and they don't care about you. Most of them come from broken homes and have addicts for parents. One of those kids got kicked out of his house because he wouldn't follow the rules. We found him asleep in a garbage dumpster one night. He goes around from rooftop to rooftop, sleeping in different places every night. I know that's not the kind of life you want."

I was in tears listening to the officer talk to my son, heart to heart. Patrick looked almost too exhausted to listen, but he sat nodding his head in agreement. We thanked all the officers for their help and for their time. They told us that it was their job and not to give up. When they left, Joe called Patrick into the family room. He had the paddle in his hand. Patrick stood looking at Joe. Joe grazed the paddle across his backside before grabbing him up into a bear hug. He told him through sobs that he loved him. The only reason we were so hard on him was because we loved him.

We put our house on the market. We immediately got calls for showings. The stress of never knowing when the phone would ring kept us on edge from morning till night. When the call came in, whoever answered would announce, "Showing!"

And everyone scrambled to pick up, polish, sweep, and mop before quickly exiting the house so that the realtors and clients could walk through without our whole family underfoot.

One afternoon while Bob and Nanette were traveling in Pennsylvania, somewhere around Pittsburgh, Nanette called me. She had mentioned to me that Bob would be retiring as CEO of the Boy Scouts of America in about a year, September 2012. She said that they had plans to retire in Pennsylvania. They had lived there once before when their son was in high school, and it was where they had made some of their best friends. They'd kept in touch with them over the years, and many of them still lived in the same area. It was where Bob and Nanette wanted to return. Their plan was to find some property on which to build a house. They had made a few trips to find just the right spot, but hadn't had any luck, so they decided to look for existing homes on the market. The day she called me, I could hear the excitement in her voice. She told me they had just put an offer on a house, and it had had been accepted. She went on to tell about the area, in detail, and what a great place it was to raise a family. It was a small town with a great school district. Aware of the fact that we homeschooled, she told me that there was also a great cyber school, PA Cyber School, where a friend of hers worked. She said that Western Pennsylvania was only a four-hour drive from Niagara Falls, where my parents and most of my family lived. It sounded to me like she was trying to sell me on the area. I had to admit that it did sound like a wonderful place. I congratulated her and told her that it all sounded terrific. Then I said, "I'm going to tell Joe to start looking in the Pittsburgh area for a job."

Nanette replied with an excited, "Yes! And then you guys could house-sit for us!"

It struck me as an odd thing to say, but then I figured that if we both lived in the same area, we could house-sit for them when they traveled and take care of their many cats. So I replied, "Sure, and you guys could house-sit for us too."

Thinking that if Joe did find a job there, we would more than likely make some road trips to visit family. I hung up the phone feeling excited that Bob and Nanette had found their retirement home. There was a little twinge of sadness that they would be moving away, but also a newfound hope that maybe Joe would find a job there. Things would be falling into place for them. They had been incredibly kind and generous with our family, and I was genuinely happy for them.

That same week, Cathy and I exchanged several phone conversations and finished planning Nanette's birthday party. It was scheduled for the day after Bob and Nanette returned from Pennsylvania. The kids worked on gifts for her, painted birdhouses, flowerpots, and a picture frame with the picture of all of us at Vinny's restaurant from the first time we had dinner there. They made cards and posters, I knitted some dishcloths and baked a key lime pie, Nanette's favorite. They were simple yet heartfelt gifts, and we knew that she would appreciate them. When the day of the party arrived, we were in full festive mode. The kids were all on board, blowing up balloons, hanging decorations and a piñata. The kitchen was abuzz with the preparations—scalloped potatoes, veggies, and chicken for frying. The coolers were filled, and the house was clean and shining. Cathy insisted on baking the birthday cakes. Midway through it all, we got the dreaded call, Showing! We took it in stride and didn't allow it to upset our festive mood. We didn't leave the house as we normally did, we just let the real estate agent and her clients come through while we continued to get things ready for the party. They didn't seem to mind at all; they actually remarked how delicious everything smelled and asked if they could stay for the party.

When Cathy and Al, and Bob and Nanette arrived, we got right to it. Joe and Joseph started frying up the chicken, and the food smells drew everyone in. The fun, laughter, and excitement were contagious, and there was action in every corner of the house, a bingo game, pin the tail on the donkey, and Cathy's famous bubbles that didn't pop. Nanette opened her gifts, and the kids busted open the piñata on the front porch.

Our For Sale sign had gone up a week or so before the party. Upon noticing it, Bob asked us where we planned to go once the house sold. We told him that we didn't really have a plan, we just wanted to get out from under our huge mortgage. We said we were thinking of finding a place to rent until Joe found a job. We told him we were leaving it in God's hands. His reply puzzled me.

"Be careful what you ask for, you just might get it."

Both Bob and Nanette seemed slightly distracted. We attributed it to the fact that they had been traveling and were no doubt a little tired. On top of that, they had just bought their retirement home. They excitedly described it to us in detail, and it sounded wonderful. Bob was thrilled that he had negotiated a John Deer riding lawn mower and some office furniture with the deal. Bob told us that in all the years that he worked for Boy Scouts of America, he and Nanette had moved some eighteen times, to several different states. They had bought a lot of very nice houses. Bob liked some more than Nanette, and vice versa, but this was the first time they both really loved the same one. Bob's retirement was still a year away, but they were relieved to have found a place.

The day after the party, we got the house cleaned up again, just in time for an early morning showing. The showings were a huge annoyance, but we knew it was an unavoidable part of the process. Being on high alert at all times was stressful for all of us. When the calls came in, it was all hands on deck. For the most part, the house was always maintained and in good order, but there were extra showing details that needed attention. I kept a mental checklist, shining fingerprints off windows and appliances, floors dust free and polished, every surface clutter free and clean. Vacuum lines on the upstairs bedroom carpets, kitchen, laundry room, and bathrooms spotless. Lights turned on, books, toys, and clothes organized and lined up. Garage clean and swept out, front porch and patio hosed off, outdoor furniture arranged and clean, lawn mowed, and pool crystal clear. OCD doesn't even come close to describing the rituals I went through each time the phone rang, before putting the dogs into the dog room and exiting the family through the garage. We drove around the corner to wait on the prospective buyers and their agents to walk through. The most frustrating part was that sometimes they didn't even go inside the house. On occasion, clients would walk in and out in less than five minutes. We would later get feedback that the buyers thought the neighborhood was too old, or they didn't like all the trees because they would be too much to maintain. We were frustrated by the lack of research on the agents' part in finding out their clients' needs, prior to scheduling the showing. We were emotionally invested in our home, and knew what a treasure it was, and we took it personally when it was simply brushed off and not even looked at. Selling a house had never been fun for us, but selling that particular house was probably the most emotionally draining of all.

We'd had multiple showings and no offers. Our agent arranged for a company to come in and stage the house. I was quite confident that the two ladies who showed up would have very little to do once they arrived and saw what a beautiful place they had to work with. I had taken great pride in decorating our home. It was tasteful and impeccably clean. I was not prepared for their recommendations. They used fear tactics to do their dirty work, telling me that potential predators could be coming through my house. If they saw all the photos of our beautiful children, they could start stalking my family. I was horrified. Never before had I heard such a thing. Immediately, I began collecting all the pictures that I had so lovingly displayed in the family room and our bedroom, while the ladies collected all the collages of family photos from the walls. They rolled up the designer area rugs that I had ordered, because buyers might think we were trying to hide something, even though the floors were perfect. We thought they made the house welcoming and added to the decor, but the stagers said they had to go. They not so delicately informed me that all religious articles should be removed. The prospective buyers may not share the same religious beliefs as us. We wouldn't want to risk a sale because they were offended by our Catholic statues and crucifixes. That was going too far. I told them that the crucifixes stayed. I would be willing to move my twenty-four-inch painted statue of the Immaculate Heart of Mary to our bedroom, but it would remain visible. They tried to convince me that they were experienced stagers, and they couldn't guarantee that our house would sell if we left the articles up. They said they would be informing our agent that I was noncompliant. I informed them that we had just received a miracle in our family and told them about Michael. Then I let them know that I would not hide my faith over a real estate deal. They finished their work and left the pile of unworthy items in the foyer for us to dispose of however we wanted. I was completely distraught, and so were the kids. Joe wasn't home, and Joseph begged me to give him permission to ask the women to leave. I wished I'd had the nerve to tell them to get out myself, but I didn't. Once they were gone, we brought the boxes out to the garage to be taken up to the loft for storage.

Nanette had forgotten a few things from the party, so after the showing, I gathered it up to take to her. I had never been to her house before. I knocked on the door and brought the items in when she greeted me. I noticed that she had put the birthday poster that the kids had made on her mantle, and she had set up the little birdhouses around her kitchen. I was touched to see that she had obviously appreciated them, simple as they were. When she walked me back out to the driveway, she stopped and said that she and Bob had been talking something over. They wanted Joe and I to consider house-sitting for them. I was confused. She said they didn't want their new house to sit empty for such a long time. Bob wouldn't be retiring until the following September, and they would need to stay in Texas, where the Boy Scouts Head Office was, until then. She said they would need a house sitter, and she reminded me that we would be needing a house. She told me that we could live in their house, rent free, for ten months. She said it was their hope that our house would sell and that Joe would land a job in Pittsburgh during that time, hopefully giving us the break that we needed to make up for what we had lost. I am pretty sure my jaw fell right there on her driveway. I know I hugged her and practically collapsed in her arms at the thought that she and Bob would even consider such an offer.

I don't remember driving home. I'm fairly certain I floated there. When I got to the house, I walked directly to Joe's office and shut the door, locking it behind me. Joe was sitting in his leather chair, intensely scrolling through job sites on his laptop. He turned around and leaned back when I walked in. He looked so tired. It seemed that there was a permanent furrow on his brow lately. In a matter-of-fact voice, I told him about Nanette's offer, still not quite believing it myself. He looked at me in disbelief and made me repeat what I'd said. I told him again.

"Bob and Nanette asked us to consider moving into their house in Pennsylvania, rent free, until they move in, sometime in June of next year. They don't want to leave it empty, and they don't want to live in separate states. They need someone to house-sit for them, and they would like us to do it."

Joe's shoulders instantly relaxed, and he exhaled deeply, laying his head on the back of his chair. He said that he had been praying for some relief, some sort of answer, but that Bob and Nanette's offer was not something that he ever would have imagined. I told him that God always seemed to have an incredibly creative way of doing things in our lives. Joe agreed that it must have been the answer he was looking for. We never even discussed it. We looked at each other and decided that it wasn't all that far-fetched. We had nothing to lose.

The timing couldn't have been better. The closing on Bob and Nanette's house was in August. We had two months to plan and organize our move. Joe immediately began searching for jobs in the Pittsburgh area, and I called Nanette. I told her that we still couldn't believe their offer, but if they were serious, we would take them up on it. I think she was surprised that we had made a decision so quickly, but she sounded relieved. She said that they would have had to find a house sitter otherwise, and that we were really helping them out. We were helping them out? That was incredulous to me—to us. They were saving our butts.

Bob and Nanette invited us out for lunch to discuss the details with them and to sign a lease. They needed one for insurance purposes, and according to their lawyer, they had to charge us rent. Our rent was set at one dollar a month, which Joe promptly paid with a ten-dollar bill. It was an emotional day. Things had happened so quickly that we could barely absorb it all. We wouldn't be homeless. We had been praying for an answer to our situation, and God had handed it to us in His not-to-be-outdone, creative way. It was more than a little overwhelming.

We researched various moving options, calculating all costs, and decided on PODS. Essentially, moving ourselves seemed to be the most cost-effective method. Joe made multiple trips to buy boxes and packing supplies, while I got busy sorting, purging, and packing. Between having a yard sale and donations to St. Francis Outreach, we eliminated major amounts of clothing, shoes, toys, holiday decorations, home decor, furniture, electronics, patio furniture, and pool toys. Even with the huge amount of purging, we still managed to fill up four PODS with the stuff we either needed or couldn't part with. The PODS were delivered one at a time, filled, and picked up, before a new one was left in its place. All the while, we continued to have regular showings, so we had to maintain constant order in the house, keeping boxes neatly stacked and floors swept and clean.

Cathy and Al stayed in constant contact with us and arranged outings for our family—lunches, movies, dinners, trips to the Aquarium and the mall, even shopping for clothes and shoes for the kids. Their generosity was endless. They gave of their time and concern, as well as their treasure. The kids welcomed the fun and distractions, and it helped reduce the stress of our entire situation, not to mention the whole moving process, which was no small undertaking. All the while, Patrick continued to be a concern. We kept him under constant watch, which was a tremendous drain all on its own. Joe kept him close, having him help with loading the PODS and moving heavy items. The minute we had our backs turned however, he was out of sight, sneaking a cigarette or disappearing altogether, reappearing with a questionable explanation as to his whereabouts. Joe and I were on constant high alert and so were the rest of the kids. They found his clothes hidden under the hedges, in the garage, inside not-yet-full packing boxes, in the pool equipment bin, and other random places. Chewing tobacco and cigarettes were confiscated, and so were the iTouches that we found on him. They didn't belong to him, and he refused to give us a straight answer as to how he had obtained them. It was clear to us that he was using them to plan his schemes. His bad behavior and rebelliousness escalated to a new level, making us anxious to get out of town and away from the temptations that he obviously had no self-control over.

One day, when the Culligan man arrived to disconnect our water-softening system for the move, Patrick disappeared. He had been in the garage when the technician arrived and had seized the opportunity while we were distracted to disappear. I was signing the service invoice when Joe went out to the garage to look for him. He didn't answer when Joe called, so he asked the other kids if they knew where Patrick was. The Culligan man, hearing the exchange, spoke up, "Are you looking for the teenaged kid who was here a little while ago?"

Joe said, "Yeah, we are."

The Culligan man replied, "I just saw him get into an orange Jeep with his buddy."

Red flags instantly went up. The orange Jeep was not where he was supposed to be. We had been learning more and more about the kid with the orange Jeep, and that he was a delinquent, much to our dismay, like our son. He had gone through a teen court program and had served community service hours on some of the same assignments as Patrick. I called the kid's house and spoke with his mother. When I introduced myself to her, she told me how wonderful Patrick was, so polite and respectful. She was so happy that Patrick was friends with her son. I thanked her and told her to please tell Patrick to come home immediately since he was grounded and did not have our permission to leave the house. She put Patrick on the phone. I told him to get his ass home. He got home a few minutes later, not at all happy that we had made such a big deal out of him leaving with his friend. He was embarrassed that I had called his friend's house, but I really didn't care. He muttered under his breath about how stupid it was, that he wasn't doing anything wrong and wanted to know why we had to be so annoying about everything. We ignored his displeasure, reminding him that his behavior was the reason he was under house arrest. We remained on high alert. Only a few weeks from our move, Patrick seemed to be spiraling more and more out of control. We knew that the move would be a big change for all of us, especially the kids, but he was the one we were the most worried about. He was the one who continued to act out in a negative way.

We tried to get as much of the big stuff packed, and the more labor-intensive jobs done early on. Moving is one thing, but managing a multistate move and actually doing all the work yourself is huge, especially with a large family. We started breaking down some of the beds during our last week, so the kids slept in sleeping bags in their rooms, which, for most of them, was fun. Angela claimed the couch in the family room. We were down to the bare bones, with only one POD left to finish loading. Being on high alert, we checked and double-checked all the doors and windows, making sure that the screens were in place and that there were no magnets on the security contacts. We had discovered that Patrick figured out how to sabotage the alarm system by sliding a thin magnet over the contact, so that he could open a door or window without the alarm sounding. We kept our eyes open for stashed clothing and our ears tuned for unusual sounds. We had almost developed a sixth sense. It was the kind of training that we learned on the job, in a very short period of time. We didn't enjoy it, but it was necessary. We remained observant of every detail and placement of objects, and all movements. I have no doubt that we thwarted several escape attempts, but as vigilant as we were, Patrick worked just that much harder to stay a step ahead of us. Joe, having once worked in a correctional facility, remarked more than once that Patrick had a criminal mind. It made me cringe to hear him say that, but it became clear to me that it could be true. Joe began guard duty, sitting in a chair at the back door that led to the garage. A vantage point that gave him a clear view of all exits and enabled him to hear any movements from the boys' bedroom, directly above him. We were completely exhausted physically, emotionally, and mentally.

On the same night that the Culligan man clued us in on Patrick's whereabouts, Joe went to bed, worn out from days of packing and loading. I stayed up to organize the kitchen one more time. The cabinets and drawers had been emptied and washed out, and the dishes and utensils that we were using for the last few days were organized on the counter. I finished some laundry and made mental notes of what we had left to do. We would be driving both vans, so we would pack up the last of our things, along with our clothes, and take them with us on the road trip to Pennsylvania. Worn out and desperate for sleep myself, I decided to set up a chair at the base of the stairs. I tipped it, just so, so that if anyone came down the stairs in the dark, it would come crashing down, making enough noise to wake up the house. We were all sleep-deprived, and I was weary of playing night watchman.

At around eleven o'clock, Christina, having heard something, came into our room to tell us that Patrick was gone. Because it had been going on for so many months, my initial feelings of anxiety, worry, and fear had been replaced by anger and frustration. I got up and followed her out to the main foyer area of the house. I disarmed the security system and checked all the windows and doors in order to figure out which one had been compromised. I noticed that the laundry room screen was missing. Our fatal mistake had been succumbing to our exhaustion and going to bed. Patrick had managed to take advantage of any and every opportunity; our stress, distractions, and sheer exhaustion were all weaknesses in our armor. I glanced toward the stairway, noticing the chair, still tipped and untouched on the bottom step. I got into the van and drove around the same old spots, 7-Eleven, Southlake Town Square, and up to the top of the parking garage. There were a few shady characters hanging out, but Patrick wasn't one of them. I called his friend's house, the one with the orange Jeep. The kid's dad answered the phone. I apologized for the late-night call, told him who I was, and asked him if his son was home. He assured me that he was indeed home and had in fact been sleeping for hours. I told him that Patrick was missing and that I suspected that he and his son were together. I informed him that they had been together earlier that day and asked him if he could please check. He said, "He's asleep. We set our security system, and no one has gone out."

At that point, I couldn't help but shake my head and think how naive this dad was. We had been in la-la land for a long time ourselves. I told him I was sorry for disturbing him and drove home to call Southlake Police. An officer quickly arrived at the house. I was past feeling any emotion. In a very matter-of-fact manner, I told the officer about what we had been dealing with over the last year. I told him that it was not the first time we had called the police. Patrick was a minor, was out without our permission, and that we were pretty certain that it was more than just teenage rebelliousness. We suspected that he was using drugs. I told him about the incident earlier that day and how the Culligan man had seen him get into the orange Jeep. As soon as I mentioned the orange Jeep, the officer's eyes lit up. He looked up from writing in his little black book.

"Orange Jeep? I just saw that jeep turning out of this neighborhood a little while ago."

He jumped up from his chair, and as he walked toward the front door, he told me that he had followed the Jeep for a while, but the driver hadn't given him cause to pull him over. I told the officer that I had called the kid's house and spoken with the dad, but he swore the kid was asleep and couldn't have possibly gotten out because their security alarm was set. The officer shook his head and rolled his eyes. I gave him the kid's name and phone number. He said he would call me when he found Patrick and that he had an idea where he might be.

I knew that it was not a coincidence. I had no doubt that God was watching all the events and the timing was His. I prayed the Joyful Mysteries of the rosary every time Patrick went missing, asking, pleading, begging our Blessed Mother Mary to intercede for us and ask God to send our son home. She knew what I was feeling. Her Son too at one time had gone missing. Obviously my son was not missing for the same reasons. Her Son was going about His Father's business, ours was being a delinquent. Nevertheless, she knew my anxiety. Within thirty minutes, the officer was back, looking none too pleased. He told Patrick in no uncertain terms that if he got one more call about him, he would not have an easy time of it. He wished me luck with our move and told Patrick that he was lucky to have parents like us. He said that if he was smart, he would make a fresh start in Pennsylvania and stay out of trouble. From that night on, Patrick spent the rest of his nights in our Southlake home, bunking with Joe and I on a pallet on the floor in our bedroom. We pushed our air mattress in front of the door, and Maverick, our golden retriever, slept by the window. Oh, Patrick was not at all happy with his new accommodations, but we were all finally able to get some much-needed sleep at night.

Joe and I were heartsick. We could not understand why our son was doing the things he was doing. We were sad and terrified about the path he was on, the damage he was doing to himself, and the dangers that he was putting himself in. We were grateful that we would be leaving his contacts. It made moving that much easier for us. The house, as much as we loved it, was nothing more than bricks and mortar. Our son was priceless. If we could just get through the last few days, we could save him. I couldn't help but wonder if that was the reason we were moving. To save Patrick. God's plan was in action, and we were seeing it quite vividly.

One afternoon while I was out on the front porch getting rid of the hanging baskets, hosing down the potting soil and dust, and giving the windows one last wipe, I had Patrick, under much duress, cleaning out the van. I had grown accustomed to his argumentative, condescending attitude, and it took every ounce of self-control to maintain calm and unshockable composure. Inside, I was crumbling. Patrick divulged my worst nightmare. He told me that he indeed had been using drugs, and what was worse, he said he liked it. I was horrified. I told him that when we moved to Pennsylvania, we would be putting him into a treatment program. He needed help. He told me he wasn't addicted. He didn't need rehab. He could quit if he wanted to, it wasn't a big deal. I didn't believe him. He had been smoking pot and had tried ecstasy, speed, and listed off a host of other pills that sent my head spinning. He shouldn't know about all those things, and I should have known more. I don't know how much of his confessions were sensationalized for shock value. It was hard for me to know for sure because it seemed that he enjoyed shocking me. He said that he had started experimenting his first year of high school, some months after Joe got laid off. I do know that whatever it was he was doing, he seemed to have been functioning normally, aside from his out-of-character ugly attitude. He hadn't acted the way I would have suspected a druggie to act, not that I had been around many, if any, to really know, but he definitely wasn't zoned out. I am convinced that had we stayed in Texas, his behavior would have most definitely escalated, and he may well not have survived. We tolerated living with his angry attitude, and it got very ugly indeed, no doubt due to withdrawals. We could see the light at the end of the tunnel with only a few days before we left town. We kept him in sight, day and night.

I shared what was going on with Cathy. I was so worried, but also felt guilt, shame, and embarrassment. I wondered how it had happened to our family. Where had we gone wrong? How had we missed the signs? What would people think of us? Cathy assured me that we were doing the right thing and that our move was going to be a step in the right direction. She told me that she would be praying for all of us and for Patrick especially.

Katie's sixth birthday was July 21, and Cathy and Nanette said they wanted to plan a Hello Kitty–themed birthday party for her at Vinny's. It would be the last time we would all be together before our big move. Bob and Nanette would be traveling again, and we wouldn't see them until closing day at their new house in Pennsylvania. They wanted us all to have one last big celebration in the place where we had all met that very first time, only three short months earlier. Once again, we were humbled by their love, thoughtfulness, and generosity. It was a festive night for sure, the most festive night we'd ever shared together. The kids had all been busy making posters and gifts. They had spelled out each of Bob, Nanette, Cathy, and Al's names in acrostic descriptions for each of them. Our children had grown to love and admire the four wonderful figures in their lives. They had become great role models of friendship, kindness, compassion, support, and generosity. They had cared for each and every one of our kids, celebrated their uniqueness, and recognized all their individual gifts and talents. They got to know them all personally in such a short time frame because they made a point to. They were genuinely interested, and they truly cared. None of it was for show, and they expected nothing in return. Our children appreciated and looked up to them. The kids made their own individual cards, and we worked on a giant flowerpot for Al's birthday, which was also coming up. The kids put their painted handprints on it, and we potted a Knock Out rosebush in it. We had learned that Al had a green thumb and a great love of gardening. His yard bloomed vibrantly and was always neat as a pin.

Not only had Vinny's restaurant been transformed into a Hello Kitty haven of balloons and pink and white decorations, after a great meal, a giant cake was carried out, and the gift exchange began. Katie opened all the wrapped-up things that Cathy and Nanette had picked out, Al was thrilled with his painted flowerpot, and everyone loved their personalized posters. There wasn't a dry eye in the place. It was bittersweet for all of us. Nanette bought each one of us girls necklaces with our names on them. She also bought dog tags for Maverick and Scamp with our new address so they wouldn't be lost, just in case they got away. Bob gave us all Steelers ball caps since we would be living near Pittsburgh, Steelers country. The restaurant staff joined in the fun, taking pictures for us and giving us a whole section of the restaurant. Unbeknown to any of us, Joseph had written a speech. He stood up and read what he had written, outlining how much we had all felt loved and cared for by each one of our new friends. They had stepped in during a very stressful time in our lives and made things easier to bear. He told them how much we would love and miss them all. More tears flowed. We drove home with mixed emotions. The last three months of our time in Texas had been more jam-packed with more love and friendship than all nine years we had lived there combined.

Another tough goodbye was my last Knitterbugs meeting at Barnes and Noble. The group of ladies had become a huge part of our journey. They had made so many outreach projects, both near and far, possible. When I asked them to pray, they prayed. Not only was Michael with us, healthy and beautiful, but he was the link in the chain that started our friendship with the Mazzucas and the Morins. The Knitterbugs' prayers had been heard, and God had answered them in incredible and unexpected ways. Our journey and upcoming adventure to Pennsylvania was one of those ways. I began to see clearly that God had been answering all our prayers, in ways that I could never have dreamed up, and He was using other people to do it. People who were paying attention to what was going on around them. It was very apparent that our friends were always listening, waiting and looking for opportunities to help. The Knitterbugs ladies were all excited about our new adventure, and they wished us well. They made me promise to keep them posted about how things were going along. One of them agreed to keep the group going, to be the drop-off spot for donations. She said she would continue delivering the completed items to our various charities. Nanette didn't come to the last meeting. She had given me permission to share the story of their offer of their house, and I was glad that I didn't have to keep it to myself. I wanted to share our incredible faith journey as a witness of God's incredible power and mercy. Nanette didn't want any attention though, and she joked that she didn't want everyone to be mad at her for taking me away from the group. She didn't want any recognition or praise. On my way out of the meeting, my cell phone rang. Nanette and Cathy had come into Barnes and Noble, incognito, hoping to catch me on my way out. They wanted to invite me to the Cheesecake Factory to celebrate my last Knitterbugs meeting. Of course I couldn't turn them down. It was a great way to end the night. I wished I'd had more time with those wonderful ladies.

Once the last POD was picked up, it was just us and our bare essentials. Al and Cathy surrounded us with help and kindness. Not only did they continue to pick up and treat all of us to lunch and movies, they brought over a TV and a folding table and chairs. They picked up our laundry and delivered it back, clean and folded. Cathy insisted that we were not allowed to refuse. She said that it gave them joy to help. I learned to stop protesting and graciously thanked them for all they did. They brought snacks, drinks, breakfast foods, and treated us to a pizza and sushi party at the house. They brought games and things for the kids to do to keep them entertained, and they even brought special treats for the dogs. On our last night, Al and Cathy took us out to Anamia's for dinner. We later learned that they had quizzed the kids to find out what everyone's favorite things were. They actively worked at doing kind things. They put time, effort, and thought into every single thing they did. At the end of our meal, they gave each of the kids a gift. The girls each received a pretty butterfly necklace, and the boys got a flashlight. Each one of them also received an envelope with twenty dollars in it for the road trip, to buy treats and snacks along the way. They gave Joe and me each a hundred dollars. We were, as always, astounded at each and every turn. They never wanted us to make a fuss over what they did. They simply wanted us to enjoy it. Joe and I shook our heads. Why us? How and why had they picked us to adopt and care for? We simply couldn't figure it out. We decided to make it our mission, should we ever be blessed enough to help another family the way we had been helped, to do so.

Many of our friends and neighbors came by to say goodbye and wish us well. Our friend Tracy Korschun came by one day with a box. She said we weren't allowed to open it until we got to the house in Pennsylvania. We had become friends through our sons, who were friends and schoolmates. Tracy was an inspiration to me, a Christian lady with a strong faith, she was my sister in Christ. I had made such beautiful friends in Texas, all of them sharing a common thread—their love of God and spirit of goodwill. Not all of them were Catholic, but they each had a solid faith, and I loved them all equally. They were the treasures that I would miss the most.

We loaded up as much as we could into the vans the night before moving day. I worked late into the night, cleaning and vacuuming the upstairs, making the kids sleep downstairs to keep it all from getting messed up. We needed to make sure the house was neat and clean before we left, early the next morning. I was stressed about the house not being sold, knowing there would be showings. Cathy told me not to worry about anything, that she would come by and make sure that everything was perfect. We left our extra keys with her and Al. They planned to check in regularly to make sure that lights were turned off after showings and that everything stayed dusted and tidy. It was a great relief and comfort to us, and we trusted them completely.

We were up at four thirty on the morning of the move, showering, dressing, rolling up sleeping bags, and deflating air mattresses. We collected the last of our personal items and crammed them into both vans. Our next-door neighbor Greg Duesing came over to say goodbye. His wife, Cyndy, had sent him over with a box filled with things to keep the kids busy during our long road trip. Another faithful sister in Christ, Cyndy had been like a surrogate mother to me during Joe's layoff and my pregnancy with Michael. She was one of the first phone calls I made after each of my appointments, and every time a job prospect looked promising for Joe. A wonderful woman of God and a blessing to me, I would miss her dearly. The enormity of our move began to sink in. We loaded up the kids, the dogs, and the bunnies, turned out the lights, and locked the doors. We pulled out of the driveway and didn't look back. With one last trip to 7-Eleven to fuel up and get coffee, we received more well-wishes from the employees that we had gotten to know. Our kids reminisced about their treat trips after yard work and chores, rewards earned after their hard work. All fueled up, we hit the road.

TWENTY-FOUR

The Winding Road to Beaver Falls

August 2011

$\mathcal{W}$e watched the sunrise as we traveled along the highway out of Texas. We drove eleven hours straight the first day, through Arkansas and into Tennessee, stopping for gas, snacks, potty breaks, and lunch. I drove our fifteen-passenger van with nine of the kids, and Joe took the twelve-passenger van with the other two kids, both dogs, and two caged bunnies. One of our biggest concerns while contemplating renting a house was whether or not we would be allowed to have pets. Nanette and Bob were animal lovers who insisted that our pets were welcome in their home. Joe's van was smelly, and mine was loud, and neither of us wanted to trade with the other. I nursed baby Michael at each of our stops. He was a wonderful little traveler. For the most part, the trip was uneventful, and frequent stops made it bearable. The dogs got walked at each stop, and we had plenty of snacks and activities to keep the kids busy. Music and changing scenery helped to pass the time. Angela took pictures and sent them to Cathy and Bob as we traveled along, keeping them updated about where we were. Cathy called us every few hours to check on how we were doing. They were very much part of the trip, in spirit, and we felt them with us.

We had some concerns about hotels allowing our menagerie of pets, but Joseph had done the research and discovered that the Red

Roof Inn allowed them. It wasn't fancy, but we weren't exactly on a luxury vacation. Our first stop for the night was the Red Roof In in Nashville, Tennessee. I had been leading the way all along, with help from our GPS of course. Once we got to Tennessee, I let Joe lead, assuming that since we had arrived on his old stomping ground, he would have some favorite place to stop to eat. Apparently a lot of things had changed over the twenty some years since he had last been there. Nothing looked familiar to him, so we didn't bother stopping for food. We decided to just go straight to the motel.

Pulling into the parking lot, I instantly felt eyes watching us. I wasn't the only one. The kids told me that there were people staring at us. Glancing up as we started unloading bags, I noticed several people standing along the second-floor balcony, smoking cigarettes, drinking beer, and watching us intently, like we were some sort of freak show. I don't know if they were having a party, but they were definitely interested in us. I have no doubt that we must have looked a sight. I tried to put myself in their shoes, imagining what they saw. Two huge vans pulling into the parking lot, emptying out with not only eleven kids of all ages and sizes, but two big leashed dogs and two caged rabbits. Yeah, we were kind of a freak show. I rolled my eyes and didn't blame them for staring.

Joe stayed in one room with Joseph, Patrick, Callum, and the dogs. I stayed with Sarah, Katie, Ryan, and Michael. Angela, Christina, Grace, and Clare took both bunnies to the third room. The kids helped to clean out the cages and walked the dogs before we crashed for the night. We were beyond exhausted. All the weeks of planning, packing, and loading the PODS, stressing about Patrick and tying up loose ends, gathering paperwork, medical records, and saying goodbye to friends, was still so surreal. More than once I asked myself, "Are we really doing this?"

It didn't take long for us to fall asleep, and morning came quickly. After a quick trip to McDonald's for breakfast and coffee, and gassing up for the second leg of our trip, we were back on the road. We had heard that there was a bad storm heading our way, and Joe wanted to beat it. It was Sunday morning, and I wanted to go to Mass. There was a church nearby with a nine o'clock Mass, but Joe didn't want to wait. He wanted to get on the road before the storm. I felt uneasy about missing Mass, and the kids were shocked that we weren't going either. I prayed God would understand. We still needed to get through the rest of Tennessee, Ohio, and finally, the Red Roof Inn in Cranberry, Pennsylvania. Our second day of travel was much like the first; we took more pictures along the way and sent them to Bob and Nanette, who were in China, and Cathy and Al. I told Angela to send some to my mother as well. I knew she would be curious about the trip. She was very surprised to hear about Bob and Nanette's offer of their home and was planning to visit us the week we moved in. With more phone calls and encouragement from our friends, the excitement mounted with each passing mile. Our nerves were also more than a little frayed. Joe and I were the only drivers, so we had no relief. The crazy wild storm that Joe had been hoping to beat in Tennessee caught up with us in Ohio. Sheets of rain poured down, thunder crashed, and a bolt of lightning struck the road directly between both our vans. I saw it in the rearview mirror, and Joe watched it through his windshield. I had a Pieta prayer book stored in the console, one of several copies like the one Gramma Hubbard used to use daily; I told Angela to open it up to the page with the prayer against storms and to read it out loud. She read it through once, and I told her to read it again. Louder. As soon as she finished reading it through the second time, the storm instantly stopped. All my kids were wild-eyed at the power of the prayer. The moment it stopped, Christina snapped a picture of a cloud in the sky that had appeared in the shape of an angel. Callum said, "We should have gone to church."

I vowed that I would never miss Sunday Mass again for any reason, short of being bedridden. We were all quite sober after that, until we saw the signs for Pittsburgh. We had been watching the signs intently, counting the miles, and calculating how much longer we had to drive. Seeing the city of Pittsburgh over the highway was impressive. I wished that I could have been in the passenger seat to enjoy the view, but I had to keep my eyes on the road. The landscape was vastly different from the flat roads and wide-open Texas skies that we had grown accustomed to. The hills and tree-lined roads were beautiful for sure, but they were challenging to maneuver.

Arriving at the Red Roof Inn in Cranberry, we went through the same drill. Three rooms, same roommates, dogs walked, and cages cleaned. If there were gawkers, we didn't notice. We were too tired to care. What an adventure it had been. We were almost at our final destination. Joe and I exchanged a few words before we retired to our own rooms. He'd had enough of the smelly pets, and I'd had enough of the kids' whining, though we still wouldn't have traded. Patrick had actually been quite pleasant during the trip. We guessed partially because the drugs had worn off and also because there was nowhere for him to sneak off to. It was a stress we were glad to be free of.

The next day was closing day on Bob and Nanette's new house. They had flown into Pittsburgh, from China, the night before. Nanette hadn't gotten much sleep because of all the excitement, but when I spoke to her that morning, she said that she felt like she could climb a mountain. We made plans to meet them in the Walmart parking lot in Chippewa after they finished signing paperwork, and picked up the house keys. We were all too excited to stay in the motel, so we loaded up the vans and drove to Beaver Falls to take a peek at the house.

The drive from Cranberry to Beaver Falls took about forty-five minutes. The winding roads and rolling hills made it that much more exciting. It was like a roller-coaster ride, anticipating the next dip and turn, until arriving at the end. We couldn't wait to see the house. It was still too early to meet Bob and Nanette, so we decided to do a drive-by. Still leading the way, I followed the GPS instructions up a ridiculously winding mountain. We had no idea that the house would be so high up. The kids hung on tightly to their seats, bracing themselves as we wound ourselves higher and higher, at every turn, looking slightly terrified over the edge of the road at just how high we were. The guardrail seemed just a little too flimsy for protection. When we finally reached the top, the sky opened up. The houses were spread out with large fields in between. It was peacefully pictur-esque with rolling acres, a red barn, and grazing horses.

We actually passed right by the house the first time. Hidden from view, the long driveway was framed with ornamental shrubs, mature trees, and flowering perennials. There was still a moving truck parked out front, so we didn't linger around. We drove back down the hill and took the kids to McDonald's for an early lunch. Chippewa was a small town, but it had a Walmart, so we knew we would be set. We pulled into the parking lot to wait, all of us wearing out Steelers hats. Bob and Nanette were beaming when they arrived. It had to be such a happy day for them. We were excited too, but it was still very surreal and slightly frightening. After hugging each other hello, Bob tossed the keys to Joe and told the kids to go pick out their new rooms. He and Nanette headed into Walmart to buy supplies for the housewarming party they had planned for that night, and we drove back to the house.

The property was huge and seemed to go on forever, roughly six acres. The plantings were beautiful and abundant. Every inch of space was landscaped, every level, nook, and cranny was a new space to explore. The kids scrambled out of the van. There were pathways, walkways, and secret stairways leading up to grassy flat areas and down to wooded retreats. Fire pits on the side yard and up on the multilevel back deck. Squirrels, chipmunks, birds, and butterflies scrambled, swooped, and fluttered about. There was even a swing set. The place was like a resort, alive with movement and color. The inside was spacious and bathed in sunlight from huge unobstructed windows and skylights. It was exactly what we needed at that very moment in time. A place to be away from the world, to commune with nature, and each other. A place to reconnect and to figure out where we were going. There were three large bedrooms upstairs, each with its own bathroom. The huge master suite was on the main floor and had a sitting area with sliding doors to a private deck. In all, there were six bathrooms, a huge family room, formal living and dining rooms, eat-in gourmet kitchen with a desk area and a huge pantry, office, large foyer, and loads of storage space, three fireplaces, and a main floor laundry room. The basement was unfinished but was huge and open. A perfect place for playing and riding bikes and skates on rainy days. To top it off, it had a three-car garage, an extra-long and wide driveway and basketball goal. It was a nine-thousand-square-foot house. By far, the biggest place we had ever lived in.

Our PODS were scheduled to be delivered the very next day. We had plenty of furniture to fill up all the rooms. Joe and I discussed what furniture would go where while the kids picked out their rooms. The four oldest girls got the biggest room, the three oldest boys got the next largest, and Sarah and Katie shared the smallest room with Ryan. Michael would bunk with us in the sitting area in the master suite.

When Bob and Nanette arrived, we helped them unload their supplies and set up chairs for the party. They had invited all their friends, not only to help them celebrate their new house and return to Beaver Falls, but to introduce them to us. They wanted us to have a list of people we could call if we needed anything. They also thought it would be a great way for Joe to network. Their friends had lived in the area for years, and they thought the contacts would be helpful. Everyone wanted Joe to find a job. Just before the party began, Joe took a call from a recruiter in Bob's new office, and Nanette tied black-and-gold balloons, Steelers colors, to the mailbox, to help her guests find the driveway.

Bob, Nanette, Joe, and I sat on folding chairs in the family room, taking it all in. None of us could really believe that we'd actually made it to that day. We called Cathy and Al and sent them pictures of all of us in the new house. We wished that they could have been with us. Cathy was still under her doctor's supervision and wasn't able to travel. I know she would have been there if she could have. We heard the front doorbell chime. It was the next-door neighbor, Romaine Smith. She had seen the balloons out front, and the vans in the driveway, and wanted to come by to introduce herself. She said that she was happy to see new neighbors after the house being empty for almost a year. The previous owner was a doctor and had moved out of state. Romaine told us that she had recently lost her husband to cancer, only a month earlier. She said she didn't so much mind living alone, but liked the reassurance of having someone nearby, just in case anything happened.

We introduced Romaine to our kids and explained the situation to her, informing her that we weren't the new owners, that Bob and Nanette were, and that we would be house-sitting for them temporarily. Romaine was happy to see that we had teenaged sons. She said that she maintained her own lawn, but that now and then she needed help moving the large tree limbs that sometimes fell. We assured her that our boys would be more than happy to help. She told us that she was a professor at Geneva College, which was in downtown Beaver Falls, and she asked us if any of our kids were of college age. We told her that Angela had been accepted to the University of the Incarnate Word in San Antonio, Texas, to study music, but with us moving to Pennsylvania, she decided not to attend because she didn't want to be so far away from family. Romaine told us to let her know if she was interested in applying to Geneva. She said they had a great music program and that she would be happy to introduce her to the head of the music department and give her a tour of the college. We were once again amazed. Romaine was friendly and outgoing, and it seemed to us that she would make a wonderful neighbor. I was sorry to hear about the loss of her husband and hoped that we could help her out any way that we could. We thanked her, and Nanette invited her back for the housewarming party.

The party was a lot of fun. Nanette had invited my parents to attend, but they declined. They planned to come a few days later, which was actually a relief to me. We met several new people, and knowing that I would never remember all their names, Nanette made up a set of flash cards for me prior to the party, with photos of each of her friends, including their names and descriptions of them on the back. She left no detail unfinished. We felt welcomed by everyone. Joe chatted with several of the guests, sharing his background with them. They all said that they would keep their eyes and ears open for opportunities. They left us with a list of all their contact information.

Most of Nanette and Bob's friends were Catholic and attended Our Lady of Fatima Church in Aliquippa. Nanette said that most Sundays, when they lived in Beaver County years before, they all went out for breakfast after Mass. She hoped that we would join them sometime. We decided that we would start going to their church. If Nanette loved it, we figured we probably would too. Bob and Nanette would be flying back to Texas the next morning, and we weren't sure when we would see them again. They thanked us for taking care of their home. We hugged them both hard, thanking them for giving us not only a home, but hope. There was loads of food, snacks, and treats left over from the party, enough to last us a week. The kids unrolled sleeping bags and threw down pillows, I set up the pack and play for Michael, and Joe filled the air mattress. We went to sleep, anticipating the arrival of the PODS the next day. There was much work still left to do. We wouldn't be getting any real rest just yet, but we felt much less stressed.

Joe and I were awakened early. Our air mattress had sprung a leak. Every bone in our bodies ached, and there was a dull fog in our brains. Still, we felt incredibly grateful, and the quiet peacefulness of the setting was soothing. I couldn't find the cord to my coffee percolator, not a huge disaster because whoever had brought the coffee maker for the party, had left it behind. I put on a pot for Joe and I while we waited for the PODS. The kids were still asleep. I walked around the main level of the house, soaking in the sunshine. There were so many windows and patio doors, three sets of doors on the main level, and two more in the basement. We walked out onto the deck and sat in the chairs with our coffee. I wondered if we would ever feel settled. My emotions were running wild, and I prayed that we had made the right decision. We had hope, and yet we still had doubts. We were emotionally fried, but we could not give up. There was still so much work to be done, and we had to hold it together for the kids. We didn't dare speak of what we had already been through, but Joe and I were both thinking the same thing. Our minds were flooded by all the ups and downs we'd had over the last, almost two, years. We'd been through hell, and at the same time, we'd been incredibly blessed at every turn. It was almost too much to take in.

The PODS arrived, and although we knew that meant a lot more backbreaking work, we welcomed it. The busier we stayed, the less time we had to think. Unloading the PODS and unpacking the boxes went a lot faster, and we were much more efficient than we had been packing and loading them. We got it all done—unloaded, unpacked, and boxes broken down, in record time. Having a lot of kids really comes in handy when there is a job to do. Joe and the boys did all the heavy unloading and carrying, and the rest of us kept busy unpacking and directing where to put things. Romaine arrived at the back door with a tray of subs from Subway. She told us that she had seen the PODS and was impressed by how all the kids were pitching in to help. She again told us how great it made her feel to see a big family next door. She said she figured we could use some lunch. It was such a heartwarming and neighborly gesture. She left quickly, mentioning that she was on her way to visit her mother. We thanked her. The tray of subs, the kids' favorite lunch, was quickly devoured. Angela got the kitchen organized while the other girls got their rooms set up, and kept Ryan and Michael entertained.

By the time my parents arrived, late in the evening a couple of nights later, we were pretty much finished. Other than losing the screws to the bunk beds, it looked like we'd lived in the house for years. The screws turned up in a random box, and Patrick was able to build the beds. There was some fine-tuning to do, but all the furniture was where it belonged, and the boxes had been emptied. We found the box that Tracy had given us, with strict orders not to open until we arrived. Everyone was excited to see what was inside. Gathered around while I pulled off the tape, the kids all groaned and rolled their eyes when they saw the big stack of yellow knitted blanket squares. Tracy had taken them home after a Knitterbugs meeting, with the intention of assembling them into a blanket to donate, but never got around to it. There was a card inside, with five hundred dollars, "to help us with groceries." A huge help indeed, and a huge blessing. We were so grateful again that God had gifted us with such generous and thoughtful friends.

TWENTY-FIVE

True Colors

Beaver Falls, Pennsylvania, August 2011

*M*y parents and sister arrived around nine o'clock in the evening
in my dad's new pickup truck. We visited with them for a short time
that night before heading to bed. Early the next morning, we gathered in the kitchen to fix coffee and prepare breakfast. I didn't anticipate any drama, given the fact that Joe and I would both be around,
and that my mom tended to be better behaved when my dad was
with her. I was pretty sure that the visit would be pleasant, but the
kids remained cautiously optimistic. Their last experience with their
grandmother was still fresh in their minds. They were, however, less
concerned knowing Joe and I would both be there close to home. It
had only been four months since Michael's birth. I was glad that the
big moving-in party that my mother had tried to plan, for all my
brothers and sisters to come help, hadn't materialized. I felt that it
was way too soon and would have been much too overwhelming. I
intended to invite my family over after we were settled in, possibly
for Thanksgiving or around the Christmas holidays.

As we sat around the table drinking coffee, we talked about
how incredibly generous Bob and Nanette had been to share their
house with us, rent free, for close to a year. My mother, instead of
understanding our overwhelming gratitude for the people who had
inserted themselves into our lives, for what seemed to be the sole pur-

pose of lifting us up, questioned why anyone would want to retire in such a huge house. She remarked, "It isn't like they had a big family or anything," and "Most retiring couples downsize."

She said that she wouldn't want the maintenance of a house that big. Stung by her response, I told her that Bob and Nanette loved the house and that we thought it was beautiful. I told her that they had a lot of friends and planned to entertain and enjoy it. I was annoyed that she would say such a thing. It wasn't her business. She had that look in her eye again, the tight-lipped disapproving look simply because I didn't agree with her. I changed the subject. I talked about the housewarming party and the thought behind it, an opportunity for Joe to network and giving us a circle of support. I told her how Nanette had even given me a stack of pictures with her friends' names on the back so that I could put faces to their names, and about her friend who had given us the information on PA Cyber School. We hadn't yet decided on whether or not we would choose that route, but it was an option we were considering. My mother made it clear that she was not a fan of the idea, and informed us that we needed to put our kids in regular school. I let her comment slide without responding. I told her about our neighbor Romaine, that she was a professor at Geneva College, and had offered to help Angela. She offered no comment.

At every turn and topic of conversation, I was met with opposition or indifference of some form, and it was exhausting. She seemed to resent any effort made by anyone who showed us kindness or was helpful. I couldn't understand why she couldn't see how thoughtful and kind so many people had been to us, her own daughter and her family, who happened to be going through a very difficult time. I hoped that she would share in our gratitude. I am certain that if someone had showed my children the kindnesses that we had been shown, I would appreciate it and feel incredibly grateful. We told them about how wonderful Cathy and Al had been before we left, making our transition easier. Helping with the laundry and bringing by meals and a table and chairs for us to use. Thinking of things that we were just too tired to consider, and acting on it. They were things that any woman, any mother, could relate to. But she said nothing.

305

I wasn't telling her about it for any other reason than to share my amazement and gratitude at how God had worked such a fantastic miracle through all the people He had placed in our path.

The kids took turns talking and sharing stories. The conversation seemed to revolve around all the fun things that they had done with Cathy and Al, the dinners and treats, movies and shopping, the sleepover that Sarah and Katie had at their house. Katie showed off the birthday gifts, a little Hello Kitty toy and a book that she'd received at her special party at Vinny's. Callum excitedly shared that his birthday was just a week away and that Cathy had promised to mail him a package. He showed off his Bumblebee remote control car, just like the one from Transformers, that Al had bought for him after taking him to see the movie. As the kids smiled and laughed, recalling all the fun and excitement that was still fresh in their minds, it was obvious by the glances my parents exchanged, and their deafening silence, that they were tired of hearing about it. I think the kids picked up on it because they slowly left the table one by one. It pained me that my children couldn't share freely the joy that they had in their hearts. They truly admired and looked up to the people who had been so kind and genuine. When my mother remarked, "Well, it must be nice to have lots of money to do all those fancy things."

I got it loud and clear. How sad. I didn't have the courage to stand up to her to tell her that it was so much more than the things that they gave, and bought, and provided. It was about the spirit that they had done it in. They hadn't done it for recognition or notoriety. They were not showing off. They were showing kindness and compassion, and they did everything with a spirit of love and friendship. They knew we were going through a tough time, and they tried to help by being our friends. I wished I had spoken up, but again, I felt like the little girl intimidated by her mother.

We needed to get groceries. I told Joe that I was going to head out to Walmart for some supplies. My mom and my sister wanted to come. Even though I would have preferred going alone, but I knew that it would save any drama from occurring at the house in my absence if they were with me. I filled up my shopping basket with all the regular items that I knew we needed, but anticipated it would take multiple trips to get the kitchen stocked the way we were used to. I shopped on my own while my sister and mother went in a different direction, finding things that my sister needed for college and whatever else they decided to buy. My mother was aware that there was no sales tax in Pennsylvania. She told me that she intended to do some shopping when they were planning the trip. I suspected that her visiting us was more about a free place to stay, along with being the first to get a look at the house. Nothing had changed much. My heart was already sinking, and they hadn't even been there twenty-four hours. I was grateful that her visit would be short and that I would be home for it all. My kids wouldn't be left at her mercy.

As soon as we got home and unloaded the bags, Joe and my dad went out to pick up our new dryer. Our old one was gas, and on its last legs. Bob and Nanette's house was wired for electric, so we decided to wait till after the move to buy a new one. We also needed a new grill, since our ten-year-old one hadn't been worth moving. After my dad installed the dryer, he and Joe went out to buy a cheap barbecue at Walmart. While they were gone, I got to work organizing the master bathroom, and my sister helped the little girls set up their room. The older girls had already finished setting up their room, and my parents and sister were staying in it, so they played with Ryan and Michael. My mother was in the kitchen washing some dishes. I hadn't been back in our bedroom long before Joseph sprinted in, out of breath, and said, "You need to get out here quick! Romaine is at the door, and Grandma won't let her in."

Surprised by my son's exasperated entrance and his concern for our new neighbor, I started to make my way to the other side of the house. I asked him why he didn't tell my mother to let her in. He said, "I did. I told her she was the next-door neighbor, but she's blocking her in the doorway."

Annoyed, I picked up the pace and quickly walked back to the kitchen with Joseph at my heels. I saw my mother's back. She was standing in the tiny entry just off the laundry room, her hand on the doorframe, not about to let anyone pass. I had witnessed the security guard stance many times before. I called out cheerfully over my mother's head, "Hi, Romaine! Come on in!"

Take note. This was *the* turning point of the visit and the cata-
lyst for the dramatic course of events that would follow. My mother
spun on her heel, glared through me with a wicked look, and walked
back to the sink, returning to the dishes without uttering a word.
Romaine came in, alternating her glance from me to my mother's
back and walked a few steps toward the kitchen island. I don't know
for certain if she sensed what had just taken place, but I felt a knot
in my stomach. I smiled as she set down a bag of tomatoes on the
large island counter. She said that she had picked them while she was
visiting with her mother. Her dad had passed away, but her mom still
kept the garden that he had started years ago. She told us that she was
thrilled to have someone to share their tomatoes with because they
always got so many. I thanked her, telling her how nice it was to get
fresh garden tomatoes. We hadn't had much luck growing a garden
in Texas with it being so dry. Romaine only stayed for a minute,
explaining that she was on her way to pick up her granddaughter,
who would be riding with her on the Lance Armstrong bike tour.
This piqued my mother's attention. She quickly turned around and
spoke up, "Oh, I'm riding in the MS bike tour."

Romaine congratulated her and said that she would be riding
in memory of her husband who had just died of cancer in June. My
heart stung, hearing it once again. Romaine's loss was still so fresh.
My mother then asked Romaine where a good place was to buy a
new bike. No condolences were offered, she was simply interested in
where to find a good deal on a bike. That, as it turned out, had been
the main reason for her trip. She had come to buy a bike. Romaine
told her that Snitger's was the place to go and where it was located.
After Romaine left and the door was closed, my mother looked down
at the tomatoes and said, "Those are overripe."

I looked directly at her but said nothing. The knot in my stomach tightening painfully. Then she said, "She tried to push her way
right into the house."

Of course I didn't believe that for a second, though I didn't say
it. I looked at my mother and said flatly, "It doesn't hurt to be nice
to the neighbors."

Her response was an icy, "She's not *my* neighbor."

With that, I walked back to my room. I knew that it was all going to be downhill from that point. I didn't like my mother. If she wasn't my mother, I wouldn't have anything to do with her. I had been surrounded by kind, sincere, and genuine people. People who cared about me and my family. People who wouldn't think of hurting others. My mother was mean and hurtful. I didn't want it to escalate. I wasn't about to feed into it. Of course my dad wasn't around to witness the whole thing, and neither was Joe, but my kids were. Joseph followed me into my room and said, "What is her problem?"

I told him that I really didn't know, but that I believed she was sick. I avoided her for the rest of the day.

After Joe got back and my dad got busy building the new grill, the front doorbell rang. Joe answered it this time. My mother was busy putting books and knickknacks into our antique bookcase in the dining room. A job that I had always insisted on doing with every move, but I said nothing about it and let her work, knowing that I would rearrange it all after she left. It was the next-door neighbor on the other side. He came by to introduce himself and to give us his number, just in case we needed anything. He shared with us that he was a property manager, and his wife was an ob-gyn. They had just returned from his son's graduation from medical school. Joe told him we were house-sitting for the next year and that he was in between jobs, hoping to find something in the Pittsburgh area. The neighbor told us that the schools were great and that he was sure we would like the area. My mother didn't say a word while the man was at the door. We thanked him for coming by and told him that we were sure we'd see each other around. The minute the door closed, my mother spoke up.

"He sure does like to hear himself talk, doesn't he?"

Wow. She just couldn't help herself. Joe said, "I thought it was nice of him to come by to introduce himself."

We had moved around a lot. Bob and Nanette's house was the eleventh place that we had lived, from the time we were first married. In every place that we had lived, including the transitional condos in between houses, we had met our neighbors. We always introduced ourselves to new neighbors who moved in as well. It was a normal thing for us to do. My mother, however, for some unknown reason, had a problem with it. I still didn't have any idea why, but she always seemed suspicious of everyone she met, and she always wanted to be in control, even when it wasn't her house. I walked away. Joe looked at me like, "What was that all about?" I told him what had happened earlier with Romaine. He didn't say much, but I could tell by his reaction that he wasn't happy about it. Romaine had been nothing but kind and neighborly. Neither one of us appreciated my mother's rudeness toward her.

My mother called Patrick upstairs to his room, much to his dismay, where she had begun organizing the boys' clothes. She complained about how Joseph and Patrick had way too many clothes. In reality, they didn't have that many clothes. What they had was a bunch of clothes in various sizes, that were still in very good shape that didn't fit them anymore, that I was saving for Callum, who was much younger and smaller. Mostly khaki pants, jeans, and polo shirts, some dress pants, and dress shirts. Nothing that would be out of style when he did finally fit into them. We had moved from a house that had giant walk-in closets and built-in dressers, with more than ample room to hang up all their clothes, and then some. My mother was having a hard time fitting all the clothes into the much smaller closet in Bob and Nanette's house. It was something that I would have dealt with later, but she decided to take on the job without being asked. Instead of just figuring out a solution, she decided to be condescending and insulting, and all but called me a clothes hoarder. I regularly donated bags and bags of clothing, among other things, several times of year. I was simply being practical and frugal. There was nothing wrong with the clothes, and saving them for Callum would save us money. She made a big production of sending down a giant box of clothes, announcing that they certainly didn't need them. I didn't bother trying to explain my rationale for keeping them to her. I knew that it would have just created another confrontation, and I didn't want to deal with it.

While she finished up her organizing, the rest of us went outside to sit on the back deck. It was a great deck that stretched the whole length of the back of the house. The built-in fire pit was right in the center of it at the back of the house. I sat holding Michael, visiting with my dad, sister, and some of the older girls on the corner section of the deck, just off the kitchen. The fire pit was not clearly visible from where we were sitting. We looked through photos on my sister's computer, and I explained how to make cake pops, something the girls and I had learned to do that summer. The kids asked to have a bonfire. We'd had regular fires out on our patio on cooler evenings in Texas. Patrick came down from his room, complaining about feeling trapped.

"Every time I tried to leave, Grandma called me back, and she wouldn't stop asking me questions."

I guessed that it was no doubt due to the fact that they had been so tight when she came for Michael's birth, but I didn't remind him. It was obvious that he was annoyed. Patrick gathered wood and built it up in the fire pit, a job he had always enjoyed. The kids asked if they could roast marshmallows. I had bought lots, knowing that we'd have plenty of bonfire nights. The fire wasn't lighting because the wood was wet, so Joe put some lighter fluid on it to get it started, and then walked past us into the house to put the lighter away up in the kitchen cabinet. While he was doing so, one of the kids brought out a bag of marshmallows, and they all started putting them on their skewers, getting ready to roast them on the fire. When Joe came back outside and saw them all roasting their marshmallows, some of them starting to eat them, he yelled, "Is anybody watching these kids? I just put lighter fluid on this wood, and they are eating marshmallows!"

He snatched up the skewers and told them they couldn't have them because they would get sick from the lighter fluid. He then walked past us again, shaking his head, muttering under his breath, something about being self-absorbed while the kids were eating poison. I looked up at him. I knew he was just about at the end of his wits. He'd had enough. I'd had enough. All the stress and anxiety that we had been holding in was starting to bust out.

We have always been a loud family. Yelling is not uncommon in our house, even in the best of times. Mostly, quite simply, in order to be heard, we need to be loud. Secondly, there are times when we just have to yell to get the attention that the situation calls for, and the situation was a pretty big deal. I yelled back. I told him that I didn't know that he'd put the lighter fluid on the wood. I never saw him do it. He was the one who'd decided to start the fire, not me. It was not my fault. I didn't tell him that it was his fault, even though I thought it was; I just told him that I had not been involved in the fire situation at all. Then I got up and went to bed, walking past my mother, who had finally come down the stairs and was getting ready to join us, just in time to witness our heated exchange.

It ended up being an early night for everyone. The little kids went to bed, and Joe followed. He apologized to me for the blowup. I told him it was fine, that all our nerves were frayed. He was ready for my parents to leave, and so was I. We just wanted to get on with some sense of normalcy. We held each other tightly, soaking in what was left of each other's energy. Together we would be okay. We always were.

The next morning I got up early to put on coffee. I had decided that I would clean the patio furniture and hose down the deck. It was dusty and moss covered in some spots. Joe connected the hose and the new nozzle he bought for me. The girls came down and said that my parents were gone. I thought it would be just like my mother to up and leave without a word, but the truck was still there. They had gotten up early to go for a walk. I was well into hosing and cleaning when they returned, and neither one of them came out to say good morning. I didn't go inside either. Hosing and cleaning was therapy for me. Something about the water washing away the dirt and grime was healing. I just needed to be alone. My parents left again, this time taking the truck, not telling anyone they were leaving or where they were going. They just simply left, taking my sister with them. It was fine with me. I hoped they were going home.

Several hours later, after I had finished with the deck and patio furniture and we were busy getting supper ready, they came back. My mother was all smiles and giddy with excitement, a totally different person. I stared at her, baffled and a tiny bit frightened at what might have caused her demeanor to change so drastically. She told us she had bought a new bike. She was absolutely gushing about it. It was exactly the one she had wanted, and it was on sale for only five hundred dollars. I couldn't tell you what color or what brand name it was, I never went out to look at it. It wasn't that important to me, but it had certainly made her happy. They also brought me a coffee maker. I had mentioned more than once, while searching through boxes, that I needed to find the cord to my percolator. I knew it was around somewhere because it was one of the last things we had packed into the van. I took the coffee maker box from her and set it on the counter.

It was Saturday night. My mother informed us that she had done research and that she wanted to go to Mass at Divine Mercy Church. She had found the Mass times online. We had already told her that we were planning to go to Our Lady of Fatima in Aliquippa, where Nanette's friends went to church, but we didn't press the issue. I was annoyed that my mother had once again taken control, but I let it go. They would be leaving the next day, and we could go to whatever church we wanted to later. I believe she wanted to avoid meeting Nanette's friends. It worked out for the best because I honestly didn't want her to meet them anyway. I didn't want to run the risk of her insulting them. The rest of the evening was polite. My mother did some laundry, and my dad commented on how nice and clean the patio furniture looked. My dad seemed very guarded to me, not his usual self at all. He was much more reserved, almost like he was watching for something and seemed to be following my mother's lead. I didn't press him.

We used our GPS to find Divine Mercy Church on Sunday morning. It was not easy to find, but when we finally did, we were confused. The sign on the church said St. Mary's, but there was a sign out front that said Divine Mercy. We later learned that the church had changed names several years before. My mother had the Mass times wrong. We were very late for the first Mass, and the next one wouldn't start for more than two hours. I smiled smugly to myself. I told Joe that we may as well go to Our Lady of Fatima in Aliquippa. The first Mass was at eight. We wouldn't make it to that one, but surely there would be one we could go to. We drove all the way to Aliquippa, a good thirty-minute drive, and discovered that the ten o'clock Mass had already started and the next Mass wouldn't be until noon. We went back to Beaver Falls. My mother rode along with us in our van, pleased with herself that she would get her wish after all. The boys rode with my dad. Mass at Divine Mercy was very nice. The priest who celebrated was filling in for the pastor who was away. He was an older priest and wore a Pittsburgh Pirates stole. I think he said he was the chaplain for the team. It was obvious that he was a big fan. My parents declined coffee when we got back to the house, saying they would be heading straight home. We were all relieved.

The minute the truck pulled out of the driveway, the kids started venting. The main topic of discussion was the night of the bonfire. They said that after Joe and I had gone to bed, my mother held an inquisition, questioning each of them about whether Joe blew up and yelled like that regularly. They told her that he yelled if there was good cause and that he was obviously worried about the little kids eating marshmallows with lighter fluid. They said that she continued to press them, fishing for information, as they described it, and she told them that he shouldn't yell like that. They told us that she had made it out to be a much bigger deal than they thought it was, and when she kept on, they decided to just go to bed. Joe and I were ticked off that my mother would put our kids in that kind of situation, but we were not at all surprised. She had undermined us in the past. We wished that they had told us what she had done before they'd left, but we knew that it would have been awkward for them. I knew that my kids were feeling the way I had felt many times, and it made me sick. Relieved that they were gone, we all began to relax.

Bob and Nanette's house was a safe haven for us. Joe and the kids walked the trails in the woods behind the house, each time going a little farther, exploring the beautiful and abundant nature. The kids walked the dogs several times a day because there wasn't a fenced yard. They spent the remainder of the summer outside, playing, exploring, riding bikes, and just being kids. We felt safe and secure, grateful to have such a beautiful roof over our heads, but always at the back of our minds was the fact that Joe still needed a job. Our main focus was searching for work.

Joe and I were extremely concerned about not having health and dental insurance. We had an insurance plan while he was working on his consulting business, and it cost over two thousand dollars a month. With no real income being generated from the business, we couldn't afford to continue paying for it. With eleven kids, we couldn't risk not having insurance either. Nanette told us that in the state of Pennsylvania, there was a health program for kids, and she was certain we could get some sort of coverage. After doing a little research and making some phone calls, we were pointed into the direction of Beaver County. The Welfare office. Our stomachs sank. Welfare office? How had it come to that? We only needed medical insurance, not Welfare. I had tried unsuccessfully to fill out all the forms online, but I kept getting timed out, no doubt crashing the system because we had so many dependents. We decided to head down to the office. We piled everyone into the waiting area where I filled out the paperwork and Joe and the kids waited. Joe had a file folder containing all our legal documents—birth certificates, social security numbers, lease, and whatever other required proof of residency we needed. It was a long wait. After an hour or so, the kids got antsy, and the little ones were hungry and cranky. I decided to take the youngest ones out to the van, leaving Joe to continue the wait with a few of the older kids. It was an incredibly humiliating and humbling experience for me, but I know it was a whole lot worse for Joe, being such a proud man. He had never depended on anyone to pay his way or support him, and had always been the one to help other people out. For us to have fallen to that level had been a real ego crusher.

While meeting with the caseworker and discussing the situation, Joe said that she looked at him from across her desk and asked him how we had made it that far. Other than getting four hundred dollars, minus taxes every two weeks from Texas unemployment insurance, we had no other income or investments. The little we had in our bank account was quickly being eaten up by our mortgage and van payments, and our house still had not sold. Joe told the caseworker that we had been blessed with good friends. She told him that we indeed would qualify for medical and dental benefits, as well as food stamps. Food stamps? It had never occurred to us. We were actually poor. We were living in a nine-thousand-square-foot house

315

on a six-acre lot, but we qualified for food stamps and Medicaid. The caseworker gave Joe an EBT card, a kind of debit card, and told him to program in a PIN number. The card could be used to buy food. She said that we would soon receive ACCESS cards in the mail, which we would present for medical and dental appointments. She said that we didn't qualify for Welfare, not that we had asked for or even wanted it. Other than our mortgage and van payment, insurance, a few credit cards, cell phone, and the utilities for our house in Texas, we didn't have any other bills. It gave us some relief, but it was bruising to our psyche.

There was a certain stigma attached to food stamps and Medicaid. We didn't think that we were in that class. We knew we needed it for our kids, and we were grateful for the help, but we hoped we wouldn't be on it long. Our goal was to get off as fast as we could, and Joe was even more determined to find a job. He had, throughout all his years of employment, undoubtedly paid more into the system than we would ever take out of it, but that didn't make us feel any better about using it. We definitely didn't want anyone to know about it.

Angela decided that she wanted to attend Geneva. She had looked up the courses online, submitted her application, and got accepted two days later. Romaine was thrilled. She said that she would be more than happy to give her a ride to school on the days that their schedules were the same, which worked out to be two or three days a week. Wanting our kids to meet people and hopefully make friends, we decided to enroll them into the Blackhawk school district. We drove to each of the three schools to register them. Bob, Nanette, Cathy, and Al never missed a beat. They were happy to hear that things were falling into place and that we were settling in. They sent packages for the kids and generous gift cards to purchase back-to-school supplies, new shoes, and backpacks. When they heard that Angela would be starting at Geneva, Bob and Nanette sent her a laptop. We were overwhelmed, yet again, by their continuous thoughtfulness. They always seemed to be in tune to our needs without us ever even saying anything. They called us regularly, tag teaming with each other, keeping us lifted up and giving us hope. I had not heard a word from my mother since their visit. She didn't call or e-mail, and neither did I.

I sent out an e-mail update to my entire e-mail list, all my Knitterbugs ladies, and many of our friends who had been asking about us and the move. I told them all about our journey from Texas to Pennsylvania, from start to finish, and how incredibly blessed we had been by the kindness and generosity of our dear friends. I shared how they had lifted us up and cared for us, more than we had ever been, by anyone else in our whole lives. I also added that I hoped that each one of them would know the love and support that we had been shown, and reminded them that we could all be that for someone else.

My youngest sister had been included in the e-mail and took offense to it. She fired off an angry reply to me, pointing out that my family had come to help us move into the house. She wanted to know how I could say that our friends had been even more supportive than my own family. She said that she had been excited about coming to see us, but her visit had been ruined after Joe hollered the night of the bonfire. She told me that she had felt more like an intruder than a guest. I shared her e-mail with Joe and our older kids. I told them that I had no intentions of responding to it, but they all insisted that I needed to reply. I waited a couple of days before e-mailing her back. I told her that I made no apologies for my e-mail and reiterated that our friends were absolutely genuine and had shown us more love and support than we had ever experienced in our entire lives. That had been the God-honest truth. I also told her I had indeed felt intruded upon by their visit, mainly because of my mother's behavior. That was the gist of the e-mail exchange, and it was also the end of our communication. She didn't respond, and I didn't hear from any of my other siblings or my parents. I had no doubt that their version of the story would be circulating among all my other brothers and sisters. I had witnessed it with my other siblings and relatives many times, this time I guessed that my family would be the main characters of the drama.

TWENTY-SIX

Bob the Bus Driver

Beaver Falls, Pennsylvania, September 2011

Due to construction, the bridge on Achortown Road was out, and because the school buses were unable to maneuver up the steep winding road on the other side of the mountain, the kids were picked up by a large school van. On the first day of school, the high school kids—Joseph, Patrick, Christina, and Grace—were the first to be picked up at the top of the long driveway. At 7:35 a.m., the same van returned for Clare, who was in middle school, and Callum, who was in intermediate school. The driver, a small white-haired man, donning a Steelers ball cap, returned a third time for the elementary kids—Sarah and Katie. I introduced myself to Bob, whom I guessed to be in his late seventies. He proudly told me that he had been driving for McCarter Bus Lines for many years. He had retired, but being the kind of man who liked to keep busy, he returned to work for the bus company part-time.

With the bridge being out, he had been asked to drive the school van. He admitted that he was a little disappointed about driving the van, preferring to drive the big bus, and was a little insulted when they told him he was too old. I sensed that his pride was hurt, more than he was disappointed about driving the van. I smiled sympathetically and told him that I was glad to meet him and very happy that he would be driving all my children to their schools. Bob noticed

318

the For Sale sign that was still standing at the edge of the property and asked if we were moving in or moving out. I told him that we had moved in the month before and that we were house-sitting for the new owners until they moved in the following summer. I told Bob briefly about our situation and how Joe hoped to find a job in the Pittsburgh area. He told me to send him over to the bus barn, because John McCarter was always looking for new drivers. He said to tell them that Bob Javens sent him. I thanked him and waved to the girls as they drove off before hurrying back inside.

Joe was on his laptop, intently searching for new job postings when I told him about my conversation with Bob. He got up, put on his shoes, and went directly to the bus barn. He told them about my conversation with Bob Javens that morning, and they hired him on the spot. He filled out a bunch of paperwork, had a background check and drug screening, and started his training a couple of days later. He rode along with one of the more experienced drivers to learn the route and was driving on his own by the end of the week. He drove a large van, much like ours. He left the house at five thirty each morning and was assigned to driving the problem kids, who attended the alternative schools, in Pittsburgh and Zelienople.

The drivers joked that Joe's large size, and the fact that he was an experienced dad of a bunch of kids, made him a good fit for the assignment. They had trouble keeping drivers for that route. The kids were tough, and he had his work cut out for him. Joe gained a new appreciation for the great kids we had. Anything our kids did paled in comparison to the boys on his route. They were foulmouthed, verbally abusive, and violent. One of the boys was threatened regularly by another kid, and Joe had to frequently pull over and stop the van to reprimand them. He was very concerned for the kid who was being bullied, and he informed Mr. McCarter about it. He felt that the kid who was being bullied should be assigned to a different bus for his own safety, believing that it was only a matter of time before he got seriously hurt. The boy's mom was grateful that Joe had taken the initiative to look out for her son, who was much smaller and more vulnerable than the bully.

Joe didn't particularly enjoy the route. It would have been much less stressful had he been assigned to a regular school route with kids who weren't so troubled, but he didn't complain. He was grateful for the work, and he began to see it as an opportunity to be a positive role model for the boys, who were all missing fathers in their lives. He tried to mentor the little delinquents as best he could. I don't know how much he got through to them, but he did try. He told me about the conversations that they had. When they complained about how unfairly they'd been treated by everyone at home, at school, and even with the police, Joe tried to help them find different ways to make improvements. He told them that people would respect them if they respected themselves. Joe had worked in a corrections facility in Memphis after graduating from University of Tennessee, so he had some experience dealing with their type of angry and hostile behavior. He only had a small window of time each day to interact with the boys, but gradually they developed a rapport. If nothing more, the boys respected him and seemed to appreciate his interest in them.

Our family began praying for the boys every night when we said our rosary. When the weather turned cold and Joe noticed that one of them wore nothing more than a T-shirt, we went through our boys' closet and found a warm jacket and a hoodie to give him. Joe said that the kid didn't say much when he gave him the jackets, but he put the hoodie on right away and wore it every day after that. Whenever I did any baking, which was pretty often, I sent treats for the kids on Joe's route. I wanted them to know that we cared about them. They may have been troublemakers, and hard to get along with, but they were still God's children. McCarter's called Joe to do extra runs whenever they needed a driver, on top of his regular run, so he was able to put in a few more hours now and then. The job paid ten dollars an hour, and he only worked between four to six hours a day. It wasn't much, but it got him out of the house and made him feel like he was doing something. He never stopped his job search.

I enjoyed chatting for the few minutes each morning with Bob when he picked up Sarah and Katie. After a few weeks of driving our kids to school, he complimented me on how well-behaved they all were. He shared with me that he and his wife, Peggy, had four children, several grandchildren and great-grandchildren. It was quite obvious that he loved and was very proud of his family. He said that even though he hadn't been happy about it at first, being assigned to driving the school van rather than the big bus had been a blessing. Bob said that his wife hadn't been feeling well. She'd recently been diagnosed with chronic fatigue syndrome and fibromyalgia. She had always been very active in her church, playing the organ, and in the community, with meals-on-wheels. At that time, she was not able to do any of it. Bob shared with me that he was grateful for his new assignment and part-time schedule, because it gave him the flexibility to take Peggy to her appointments. Her doctors were working on finding the best medications and dosages for her condition. It was easy to see that Bob was very concerned about his dear wife. I sensed the pain he felt at not being able to help her.

I told Bob that I would have dinner ready for him and Peggy that night. He put his hands up to protest, saying that I had much too much to do with so many children to take care of, but I insisted. I told him that it would be no bother at all. I always cooked extra, and it would make me feel great to pack something up for the two of them. I can't remember exactly what I made for dinner that night, but from that night on, I sent dinner and dessert home with Bob fairly regularly. He returned the bag and containers when they were done; sometimes they would have enough left for a couple of days, and I would send out another meal.

After several weeks, Bob was in better spirits. It seemed that the doctors had found medications that worked well, and Peggy was feeling much better. She sent me a note, thanking me for all the meals. She said they had been a great help to her and that she was feeling good enough to cook again. She said that it was humbling for her to be on the receiving end, after so many years of being the helper. That was certainly something I could relate to. Bob told me that I was a lot like Peggy. I was flattered, but I wouldn't find out how great of a compliment it truly was until several months later. He said that Peggy had been a seamstress, using her talents to help others. I told him that I was a knitter and that I was hoping to get a Knitterbugs group started in Beaver Falls. It never worked out, but I kept on knitting.

The school routine was well established within a few weeks, and the kids all seemed to be fitting in easily. From what I had noticed, Beaver Falls was a very small town. Everybody seemed to either know or was related to everyone else. Most families had lived in the little town for generations. It became hysterically obvious when we went out to the first Blackhawk Cougar Football game. I listened while two mothers, who were sitting behind us, talked about their daughters who were cheerleaders at the game. The mothers reminisced about their own cheerleading days on the same football field, cheering for the same school. Not only had they been classmates and cheerleaders, they were filling each other in on all the latest news about their other former classmates. I listened as they went through their class list, discussing who had married whom and who worked where. From what I was hearing, more than a few of them had become teachers at the high school. My girls and I giggled and rolled our eyes while we eavesdropped. Christina told me, "See, I told you. All the kids in my class are related to each other, and all the teachers too."

Our family had moved so many times over the years, that I hadn't given much thought to the fact that there were people who actually stayed in the same town for their entire lives. I was sure there must have been pros and cons to it, but at that moment, it was endearing to me.

Patrick joined the football team. He had played football in seventh grade in Southlake, and although it took some heavy encouragement from us and from the school counselors, he decided to try out. He had always been strong and athletic, and we really wanted him to be involved in something. Joe met with the coaches, and they saw to it that he was able to get a scholarship to play. We were thrilled that Patrick would be part of something positive and hoped that he would make some nice friends and enjoy his high school experience. I insisted that he repeat the tenth grade since he had completely blown off his entire homeschool year. Joseph chose to repeat eleventh grade. He could have easily jumped right into his senior year; he was a smart kid and had always done well in school. He was a well-rounded student, but he wanted to make friends and become involved in more than just academics, so we didn't protest. Football practice was every day after school, and the games were on Friday nights. We loved cheering in the stands and being part of it all. It gave me joy to see Patrick proudly wear his uniform. Christina and Grace came home daily with stories about girls giggling and talking about how cute the Allen boys were, rolling their eyes at the awkwardness of it all. Apparently there weren't many new kids who enrolled in the school, so our kids were almost instant celebrities. Things seemed to be going well for all of them, and we were grateful that they had been so warmly received.

Even before our move, I had begun writing what Cathy called *my epistles*. A sort of weekly journal of what was happening in our lives. I called the updates Tales from Beaver Falls. Our friends had invested so much time and love in our family that I wanted them to know how things were going. I tried to keep them as upbeat and lighthearted as possible, telling them about each of the kids, how they were doing in school, what activities they were involved in, and new friends that they had made. I told them about the house, the wildlife we saw, the cardinals that clung to the bedroom window screen every morning, funny things that the kids said and did, and my trips to Walmart. It was sort of a private blog. Sometimes the epistles were emotional. It was an incredibly emotional time for our family. I never wanted to burden my friends, but they wanted to know what was going on and encouraged me to continue writing. They wanted to know how to pray for our family. I trusted them completely, and I bared my soul when I needed to.

Our Texas house still hadn't sold, but we were confident that it wouldn't be long before it did. There were more frequent showings after we switched to new real estate agents with Ebby Halliday. They were big on marketing, advertised in popular publications; they hosted several open houses and even held a realtors breakfast. Cathy and Al had been the ones to suggest the new agents, and they worked with them, keeping us posted on how things were going. They did regular drive-bys and got feedback from the agents whenever they could. They were the go-to team. Texas was in a drought, and the water restrictions and scorching heat had taken a toll on our grass and shrubs. Al tried to keep things alive by watering in the evenings, hoping to save our shrubs and azaleas. Cathy made sure the floors were dusted, the toilets were flushed, and the cobwebs were kept at bay.

Joe had decided to start studying for a Farmers Insurance agent certification. We'd been Farmers customers for years, and he had been solicited by an agent to take the course. Figuring that there was nothing to lose, and keeping himself open to every possibility not knowing what God might have planned for him, he signed up. In between bus runs, he studied and listened to the cyber instructors for hours, did online quizzes, and read through pages of insurance jargon. It was painfully boring for him, but he forced himself through it. He told me that he had to do something to provide for his family; driving the bus wasn't enough to support us. Between the driving and studying, he continued to search, using what little free time he had, for a real job. I watched him grow wearier and wearier before my eyes, regularly finding him asleep in his chair, chin to his chest with his laptop still on, fingers resting on the keyboard, completely exhausted. Daily, I begged God for relief.

We had been attending Mass at Our Lady of Fatima in Aliquippa every Sunday. It was a bit of a drive. Romaine had mentioned that there was a much closer church in Chippewa that she sometimes took her mom to. We thanked her, but we told her that we were happy going to Our Lady of Fatima. We had driven past Christ the Divine Teacher one day. It wasn't a very attractive building, kind of stark and modern looking. We decided that it would be a good alternative if the weather got bad in the winter, but we liked Our Lady of Fatima. It was a nice church, but our kids began to complain that there weren't any kids their age who went there. The music was not as familiar, but the homilies were usually very good, and we began to get used to it. After several weeks, the faces became familiar, and we started to feel welcome as people smiled and greeted us. Our biggest challenge was getting out of the house on time. We tried to go to the early Mass at eight o'clock, which meant we had to leave the house by seven fifteen. Joe and I hate to be late for Mass, primarily because we think it's disruptive and disrespectful, but also because with a family the size of ours, it's impossible to find a seat together unless we arrive early.

On a couple of occasions, despite rushing the kids along and going a little over the speed limit, we walked into the church during the first hymn. We informed our kids, who preferred attending the early Mass, that if they weren't ready on time, we would start going to the later one. The following Sunday morning, Christina woke up with both her eyes swollen shut. It seemed to be some sort of allergic reaction. I told her that she would have to stay home. She'd previously made plans to go to the movies later that afternoon with a friend from school, and I told her she would have to cancel those plans as well. The rest of us were all up and dressed, and after several time checks, Joe was hollering up the stairs, "You have twenty minutes!"

"Fifteen minutes!"

"Ten minutes!"

Always very annoying, but it works. We piled into the van at exactly seven fifteen. Everyone except Angela, who was eighteen. We waited for two minutes, honked the horn, waited another minute, then left. By the time we got to the bottom of the hill, my cell phone buzzed with a text from her. She couldn't believe that we had actually left her behind. She had been straightening her hair, applying makeup, and trying on different outfits when we pulled out of the driveway. I texted her back, informing her that we were not turning around because it would make us late. I told her that I would drive her to Christ the Divine Teacher at noon. She wasn't happy about having to go to church alone. We figured that it would not only be a good lesson for her, but also for the rest of our kids who were witnessing the consequences.

When we got home from Mass, the kids changed clothes and prepared to have lunch and enjoy the rest of the day. Angela was dressed and waiting, ready to go to church. After taking a hot shower and a dose of Benadryl, the swelling had completely gone from Christina's eyes. She asked me if she could still go to the movies with her friend. I told her that she could, but that she would have to go to Mass at noon with Angela first. I drove the two of them to the church, which was only three minutes away, once we got to the bottom of the hill. I spent a quiet hour by myself, sitting in the van, knitting in the sunshine. I felt a slight twinge of guilt over not going in with them, but I selfishly savored the quiet time alone.

The hour passed quickly, and when Mass was done, I watched as Angela and Christina walked back to the van, chatting and smiling happily. They gushed as they climbed in, telling me that we absolutely had to start going to that church. They said that the priest was young and his homily wasn't boring; they actually knew the hymns and recognized kids from school. After hearing their excitement, I really regretted not going in. I felt their enthusiasm, and it was refreshing after the recent grumbles. We told Joe when we got home, and he agreed that we should at least check it out.

The following Sunday, we didn't have to leave the house until eight thirty, and we were still early for the nine o'clock Mass. Just as the girls had reported, the priest was young, the hymns were familiar, and Fr. Schreck had knocked it out of the park with his homily, which just so happened to be a strong pro-life message. There was no doubt in our minds that we had found our home parish. We introduced ourselves to Fr. Schreck on our way out, telling him that because of our daughter being late the week before, we had discovered his church. He laughed out loud and didn't seem surprised at all. With a twinkle in his eye, he told us that's usually how the Lord works. We thanked him and told him that we felt like we were home. The van buzzed all the way home as we talked about how amazing Mass was. The whole experience had been incredibly uplifting. The inside of the church was modern looking but had a reverent feel, the priest's homily was very strong, and the music was familiar. The kids even recognized several of their classmates and friends, which made a big impression on them. It made perfect sense to all of us to make Christ the Divine Teacher our new parish. When we got home, I immediately went to work writing a letter of introduction for Fr. Schreck, telling him about Michael, Knitterbugs, Joe's layoff, and how we ended up in Beaver Falls.

Each Sunday at Mass, I felt as though Fr. Schreck was reading my thoughts. Whatever it was that was going on, my worries and concerns, or even the little blessings that had occurred, he hit the nail on the head. Of course I knew that it was the Holy Spirit working through him. I felt like I was really plugged in. Feeling at home in a parish is a rare gift, and we felt very connected and incredibly blessed to be there. All our kids felt the same way. Beaver Falls was indeed a small town, and Fr. Schreck was well-known. Not only was he the pastor at Christ the Divine Teacher, but St. Rose of Lima as well. What struck us all was that despite his young age, how unwaveringly Catholic, traditional, and straight as an arrow on the truth he was. He maintained a wonderful sense of humor while he taught the deadly serious lessons. He connected with his flock, young and old, stirring everyone into action, waking us up and challenging us all to live out the Gospel.

I began to attend Mass on Wednesday evenings once in a while and, now and then, on Friday mornings. I tried to get there as often as I could. Gas prices were high, and with our two big vans, it wasn't cheap. We were driving a lot with pickups from practices, after-school activities, and grocery shopping. Going to Mass was a luxury to me, and I wrestled with guilt over the cost of gas and the added driving. I didn't get there as often as I would have liked to, but I had a great desire to go to Mass and adoration. The Blessed Sacrament was exposed for one hour before each Mass. The more I went to adoration, the more I desired to go, and I tried to get to the church for the full hour when I could. We registered as new members of the parish and signed the kids up for religious education classes. We were warmly welcomed and felt very much like we belonged.

We were almost out of money. We paid the most important bills first—van payment, insurance, utilities, and the mortgage on our house in Texas; and we left the credit card bills at the bottom of the pile. Joe made partial payments for our cell phone. He couldn't risk canceling it because it was his contact number for all his job applications. We called our real estate agent and told her that as of October 1, we wouldn't be able to make our mortgage payment. We would have to foreclose. We had no idea how long it would be before our bank took possession of the house, but we were pretty sure it would be soon. It was the lowest, most desperate feeling we had ever experienced. We were powerless and out of ideas. I told Joe that I didn't know exactly what God was trying to show us, but we had no other option than to leave it all in His hands. God had led us to Beaver Falls for reasons we had yet to understand. Patrick seemed to be in a much better place, and Angela was enjoying Geneva College. We couldn't help but wonder if coming to Beaver Falls was for our kids' benefit. Losing our house was not as important as losing our child to drugs and alcohol, or a fatal accident. We honestly believed that Patrick was spared a life of addiction, or quite possibly a tragic fate, by moving to the tiny town. I told Bob and Nanette and Cathy and Al, in my next epistle, that we'd run out of options. Joe had been burning the candle at both ends, driving bus and studying for the insurance certification, all while still searching for jobs online. They assured us of their prayers.

Callum brought home a flyer from school, inviting him to join the Boy Scouts, and he said he wanted to join. Joe and I told him that we thought Boy Scouts would be great for him, and we promised him we would look into it. I was excited to tell Bob and Nanette and Cathy and Al since they were all part of the Boy Scouts family. Not surprisingly, they were thrilled. Being who they were, Bob and Nanette arranged to have Callum outfitted as a Webelo at the Scout store in Pittsburgh, and they footed the bill. Joe took Callum into the city where the store was, and the two of them were treated like royalty. Joe brought Callum to his meetings and stayed to help out. They enjoyed spending the time together. We felt that Boy Scouts was a great organization to be part of, especially judging by the example that had been set by our friends.

On one of the several nights that Joe and Callum were out selling popcorn, a big Boy Scout fund-raiser, a large envelope was delivered to our door by FedEx. The foreclosure notice from Chase bank had finally arrived. We had been expecting it, but it still came as a shock. We had been holding out hope that Joe would be offered a job at the eleventh hour, sparing us from foreclosure, but it wasn't to be. My head was dizzy while I waited for Joe to come home with

Callum. He knew what the envelope contained without even opening it. Neither one of us knew what to say, so we didn't say anything,
we just held each other. I had a sick feeling in the pit of my stomach,
and my head was in a fog. I gave it up. There was not one thing we
could do. We were not in control over what was happening. We had
done everything in our power to help ourselves, but it hadn't been
enough. I told God to do whatever it was that He had to do. I trusted
that He had a reason for all of it.

I went to bed and typed up an epistle. It was therapeutic for me
to write, and I needed to get so much off my chest. Within a couple
of hours of hitting the Send button, Bob called to talk to Joe. He
wouldn't hear of us losing our house. Bob was confident that it would
sell; it just needed a little more time. He didn't want us to suffer the
devastation that a foreclosure would cause for years to come. He told
Joe that he would call his banker in the morning and would trans-
fer twenty thousand dollars into our account, enough to cover our
mortgage until the end of the year. It was a loan that we would begin
paying back as soon as Joe got a job, which Bob also believed was
just around the corner. They drew up a contract, and everything was
taken care of within twenty-four hours. We were absolutely stunned.
Once again, we had been saved. God was providing for us in unbelievable ways, and He was using the Mazzucas and the Morins.

Cathy and Al and Bob and Nanette began a new mission. They
teamed up with our realtors with renewed zeal to get our house sold.
The Texas drought had destroyed most of our landscape. Our friends
rallied together and hired their own landscaping crew to give our
property a facelift. They pruned our trees, pulled out all the dead
shrubs and ornamental plants, and mulched the entire front and side
yards. They organized, paid for, and supervised the entire project,
which lasted two full days. They continued to encourage our real
estate agents, bringing them treats and gifts, keeping them motivated
to go the extra mile to find a buyer. Our friends had invested in us.
We were not only dumbfounded by their overwhelming generosity
of funds and time, we were completely startled that they had come
up with the very idea to do it at all. It was incredibly humbling, and
there are no words to describe the gratitude that we felt.

Just to keep things off balance, that very same month, we were contacted by the IRS. It seemed as if the balls would never stop dropping. Joe had cashed out his 401K a year earlier in order to continue paying our mortgage, bills, and to generally provide for our family. At the time that he cashed it out, he fully expected to land a job and have it payed back, well before accruing interest, but that was not how it worked out. We owed over forty thousand dollars in taxes, and the interest had already begun to be added on. We had no idea how we would ever pay it back.

We had giggled for years at the infomercials for the debt-resolution companies, Ronnie Deutche and Patrick Cox, when they came on TV. I suggested to Joe that we should call one of them; it certainly couldn't hurt. He looked them both up online and put in a call to Patrick Cox's tax attorney office, Tax Masters, and scheduled a telephone appointment. We felt like we were doing something. If nothing else, it would get the IRS off our backs, and as long as we were negotiating a resolution, the IRS wouldn't harass us.

We lived moment to moment. Each day brought us another roller coaster of emotions, worries, and trials. Joe steadily received calls and e-mails from recruiters, setting up first, second, and even third interviews, which gave us sustaining hope. Every single call was a potential job, and we found ourselves dreaming and planning around whatever it was, researching the city, and checking out housing costs. I am convinced that it was God's way of keeping hope alive for us, always giving us a thread to hang onto. Despite our best efforts to not get our hopes up too high, they always managed to get away from us, only to come crashing down violently. Rejections and promises of follow-up calls that never came, deflated us. And then days later, new possibilities—sometimes three and four calls on the same day—started a new cycle of hope. There were always two or three "in the hopper," as Joe would call it. It did my heart good to see him excited about each new prospect, believing that surely he would get one of them, and it pained me deeply when the rejections came. I prayed for the roller coaster to stop.

School was the one constant routine for all of us. The kids were happy, and we tried to keep life as normal as possible for them. They were aware that we were in a financial crisis, but it hadn't affected their physical life. They were part of an intact loving family, had plenty of food, and quite a nice roof over their heads. They had been warmly accepted in Beaver Falls. They understood that Daddy was searching for—and needed to find—a job, and we prayed a family rosary every evening that the job would come. We did our very best to hold it together emotionally for them. The youngest kids were less aware of the situation than the older ones, and we tried to keep things real without scaring any of them.

My days were quiet but busy while the kids were at school. I stayed home with Ryan and Michael, reading to them and playing while taking care of the household, cleaning, cooking, baking, and buying groceries. Even when everything was clean and the laundry was done, I found things to keep busy with, knitting or weeding the gardens. I filled the time to escape from the worries. The days flew by, and even though I was heavy at times with fears, I loved my life and counted the blessings that we had. Bob and Nanette's house continued to be a haven of peace for me. I loved cleaning it, and cooking and baking in the big bright gourmet kitchen was an escape. There was so much space for the boys to play. Michael spent almost all of his time on a big sheet on the floor, creeping around and playing with toys, while Ryan built elaborate Lego structures and floor puzzles. We had set up all the children's books on a bookcase in the large front closet, and Ryan chose from our large collection, book after book, carrying them to Joe and me to read to him.

I had always loved being a wife, mother, and homemaker. Despite all the stresses that we had been bombarded with in such a short amount of time, my feelings had not changed about any of it. Other than the grocery shopping. Grocery day had always been an exciting day for me. It meant buying all the foods for the new recipes I wanted to try, fun snacks and treats for the kids, fresh produce, and loads of BBQ food for Joe's famous cookout meals. That was before food stamps. I found it to be incredibly humiliating and embarrassing to shop for groceries with a food stamp card. I was ashamed. I was always careful to keep the green-and-yellow card hidden in my hand. I kept it out of view of the people standing in line behind me, but I couldn't hide it from the checkers. They always knew. Most of them didn't react in any way, but there were a few, who after I swiped my card and selected the EBT Food button on the PIN pad, glanced up at me, checking me out like they were surprised that I was on food stamps. It may have been all in my head, but it was a gut feeling I got, especially from one employee in particular. She would scan the end of my receipt each time I went through her line and actually circle the balance at the end of it, showing me how much I had left on my card. I had no doubt that she was more curious about my balance than she was trying to be helpful. I avoided her line at all costs, even waiting in much longer lines rather than feel the humiliation. I didn't feel like I was the type to be on food stamps. As if there was a type. I had so much pride. I didn't want to be one of them. I felt like I was better than that. We were just going through a hard time; we weren't lifetime Welfare cases.

I found myself regularly preparing for the actual checkout process, well before swiping that awful card, justifying my reasons for having it. I explained to the checker how we had just recently moved to Beaver Falls and how my husband was looking for work because, sadly, he'd been laid off from his job after a twelve-year career. I wanted them to know that he wasn't a loser, a deadbeat. He was educated and wanted to work. He wasn't at all happy about needing food stamps to feed his family, and he was spending every waking moment trying to get off the system. The checkers were sympathetic and immediately chimed in about the poor economic state and the fact that there were so many people out of work. I told them that Joe had a master's degree and years of experience and that he had applied for close to two thousand jobs in two years. I did all the explaining so that they wouldn't think less of me for having an EBT card. I hated that card. Joe hated it even more. We were ashamed to be on food stamps, but we needed it. I absolutely believed that food stamps were necessary for people who had a real need to be on them—disabilities, illness, job loss. But I also knew full well that there was plenty of abuse of the system. That many people had become complacent, taking the help with no real motivation to work toward getting off of it. I wanted to make sure everyone knew that it was a temporary situation for us. I didn't want to be judged.

As time went on, I found myself looking at the shoppers in front of me in the line, mentally picking out the ones who I thought were on food stamps, looking for "the type." I was shocked by how many people had that same little green card. A lot of people had them, and many of them didn't look the type at all. Most of them didn't seem concerned about hiding it either, they just whipped them out and didn't care who was looking. I was sick with pride, but I never stopped trying to hide that card. Besides food stamps, our kids got free lunches at school, and they told us that most of their friends did too. Although I found it shocking, it didn't make me feel any better; actually, it made me feel worse. There had to be something very wrong that so many people needed government food assistance, but I had no clue what it was that was broken.

Beaver Falls was a fairly depressed area. When the steel mills shut down, lots of people were left unemployed and the economy began to fail. The downtown area had crumbled drastically. There were skeletons of once very impressive and affluent homes and a vibrant town. Boarded-up windows and dilapidated wraparound porches, overgrown yards littered with riding toys and kiddie pools, and barking dogs tied out front. Once-stately homes owned by doctors and lawyers were now converted into group homes for the mentally ill and rehab patients. Low-income and government housing were all located in Downtown Beaver Falls, and a large percentage of the population was black. Having always lived in middle- to upper-middle-class areas, our kids had been incredibly sheltered. Other than my volunteering days at the homeless shelter in Fort Worth, we never entered that kind of territory. We were essentially desensitized to the fact that there were poor people living not so far from us. Whenever we drove to that part of town, Joe and I always said to each other, "That could have been us."

We hoped and prayed that it would never be us and that a job would come before we had to move out of the Mazzucas' house.

I began to spend more time praying. I had somehow lost the intensity in my prayer life, and I really wanted to get it back. Prayer had given us Michael, a huge miracle, so I knew full well that it worked. I wanted Joe to find a job. If only I could just get that intensity back like I'd had for Michael. I was so tired. No, I was exhausted. I wanted to get the feeling of total surrender back, and yet I hadn't been completely giving things up to God. I had been counting on Joe to find the perfect job posting, and on the recruiters to follow through with their promises. God had healed Michael, surely a job for Joe was a drop in the bucket. I made a conscious decision and a daily effort to offer up everything I did to God. All the mundane things in my day, the laundry, and the crumbs I swept up off the floor after the kids left for school. I tried to offer up the humiliation of being on food stamps. The big house was conducive to my new prayer ritual. With the glorious sun pouring in, and with absolutely every window framing a breathtaking nature scene—foliage, flowers, birds, and butterflies, I felt like I was in a heavenly treehouse. I began my morning devotions before the kids woke up, right after having coffee with Joe and sending him off to work.

Prayers continued to come to my lips easily, little conversations with God throughout my day. I got into a groove and soon had a pep in my step each day as I vacuumed and mopped, shined bathrooms, and changed bedding, while the little boys played at my feet in whatever room I was in. I decorated for the fall season with the decorations we had brought with us, pumpkins and garland, baskets and wreaths, making the Mazzucas' house our home with familiar and personal items. I baked and cooked our favorite comfort foods, while marveling at the awesomeness of the changing colors all around. I seemed to be worrying less and praying more. Life was calm, the kids were happy, and we were connected and hopeful that God would answer our prayers. The job would come, I could feel it. We prayed our family rosary without fail. It had become a sort of habit for us, one that I depended on. It was understood by everyone that the rosary was part of our day. It was our way of all being together, and it became more meaningful over time. We knew that we were being provided for by God and that we would always have each other. We prayed for each other and for Joe to find a job; we prayed for our friends and for those who were much worse off than us. We counted all our blessings and tried to draw our kids' attention to all the blessings that we had witnessed, reminding them that it was all due to God's provision. We wanted them to see the power of prayer.

TWENTY-SEVEN

The Investigation

Beaver Falls, Pennsylvania, October 2011

October 4, 2011, is a date that will forever remain burned in my memory. The kids had an early release day from school. Clare, who was in sixth grade, was the first to arrive home, shortly after noon. She found me upstairs in the boys' room where I was putting away laundry. I had spent the day freshening up the house. Not that it ever really had a chance to get dirty, but that day, I had done a deep cleaning, changing the linens and organizing cabinets, drawers, and closets. The whole place smelled fresh with the windows open and a fall breeze blowing in. Ryan and Michael were still napping. Clare sat down on the bed and said, "Um, I got called down to the office today."

I looked at her, questioning her with my eyes. Clare had always been a model student and had never been in trouble, so I knew there had to be logical explanation. I continued putting the clothes away, waiting for her to explain. She continued, "I had to go into a room with some lady who asked me a bunch of questions. Like, if Daddy beat me."

I spun around and looked at her with my mouth gaping open, waiting, searching for some twisted punchline, anything. Clare had a wide-eyed, open-mouthed look on her face and said, "I know, right?"

She then told me that the lady told her that someone had made a call to some Kids Helpline, and that was the reason she was being questioned. I had no words, and I am certain that my heart had stopped beating entirely. All I could gasp out was, "Whaaat! Who was this lady?"

Clare said she didn't know who she was. She said the lady told her that she would be coming to the house at four o'clock to talk to Joe and I. Oh, really? She was, was she? Well, good, because I had some questions I wanted to ask her. How dare she? We had lived in Beaver Falls for less than two months, and our daughter was being questioned, at school, about being beaten? I wanted to throw up. It was insanity. Where in the world had it come from? Clare was angry. She kept asking me over and over again who would have made such a call, and why would someone make something like that up? Clare told me that she had told the lady that whoever had reported that she had been beaten was a liar. She said that she was embarrassed about getting called to the office. She hadn't done anything wrong, but she felt like her friends would assume that she was in trouble. I grew angrier and angrier the more I thought about my daughter being put into such a position.

An hour or so later, the high school kids came through the door. I overheard Joseph, Christina, and Grace chattering away. Joseph had been called to the office at his school and was questioned in much the same way. Had he been beaten by his father? Christina and Grace, who attended the same school, had not been questioned, but they said that Patrick had. I heard the sound of the John Deer riding mower running in the yard. When I looked out the side door, I saw Patrick's backpack leaning against the side of the house, and Patrick mowing the lawn. He hadn't even come inside. Joseph handed me the business card that the caseworker from Beaver Country Child and Youth Services had given him. She had explained to him that a call had come into their Childline number the day before, about Patrick specifically. Someone had called to say that he was being beaten. She had been assigned to investigate the allegation. Again, all that I could utter was, "Whaaat!"

We didn't even know anyone in town. How could we have
enemies? We didn't have any enemies anywhere. Who in the world
would have ever made such a call? It made absolutely no sense to any
of us. Joseph gave me the same message as Clare, that the caseworker
would be coming to the house around four o'clock that afternoon.
I was shaking with anger. I called Patrick into the house. He parked
the mower, leaving it running, and came toward me slowly shaking
his head. He told me that yes, he had also been called down to the
office where some lady had questioned him about being beaten. He
said that the woman had also taken his picture for her records. I
was furious and demanded out loud, to no one in particular, who
would have made such a vicious claim. Why would someone make
such an accusation? Our children had never been beaten or abused.
Disciplined? Yes. Spanked? On occasion, when we felt the circumstances warranted it. Patrick said that he had told the woman that
no, he had never been beaten. He told her that when we lived in
Texas, he did get paddled with a wooden paddle, but that by his own
admission, he had deserved it. He explained that he had been doing
things he shouldn't have been, like repeatedly sneaking out of the
house to go to parties and hanging out with friends that we didn't
approve of, smoking, drinking, and doing drugs. He told her that he
wasn't doing any of those things anymore. Not since we had moved
to Pennsylvania. I was beyond flabbergasted. I couldn't believe that
what was happening could really be happening. I felt certain that I
must be in the most vivid nightmare I'd ever had. I could not for the
life of me come up with one person who ever would have made such
a call. Such a false claim. None of it made any sense.

I looked around at my children who were gathered together,
looking back at me. Waiting. They wanted to know what I was going
to do and what I planned to say to this person when she came to the
house. I told them that I would tell her the truth. Patrick said that
the lady seemed nice enough. She had explained to him that she had
to, by law, follow up on the claim and question him and the rest of
his brothers and sisters. Christina and Grace were very angry. Joseph
and Clare were angry and felt humiliated. Callum, Sarah, and Katie
came through the door next. They walked in on the rest of us deep

in discussion, wanting to know what was going on. They had obviously not been questioned. When the older kids filled them in, they had the same reaction, wide-eyed disbelief. They too questioned who would make up such a thing. They all grew angrier.

Joe wasn't home. He was on his afternoon bus run, picking his kids up in Zelienople, and he planned to pick Angela up from Geneva on his way home. I knew that he would not have his cell phone on, not that I would have called to tell him something so shocking while he was on the road anyway. He was already on blood pressure medication.

Patrick went back to mowing the lawn, and I sent the other kids off to start their homework while I waited for the caseworker to show up. None of us could concentrate on anything but the events that had taken place that day, and what would happen in the following hours. The low whispers of my children's conversations were all about the lady and her investigation. None of them could get their heads wrapped around it. They continued to ask me what I was going to say. Would I even let her into the house? I told them that of course I would let her in, we had nothing to hide. I would tell her the truth.

At four o'clock on the dot, a small blue car pulled around the circle driveway. I called for Christina to put the dogs, who had already let me know with their barking that she had arrived, outside on the deck. I opened the front door before she could ring the bell, inviting her into the foyer. I am sure that my eyes were wild and accusatory when she handed me her card. I wanted to know what the meaning of her investigation was, and I demanded an explanation. She didn't seem at all surprised or bothered by my cold reception. She said that she gathered I must have heard from the kids about her meeting with them and that she would be coming by. I told her that yes, indeed, I had heard that three of my children had been questioned by her at school. They had been pulled out of their classes, called down to the office, and interrogated about whether or not they had been beaten by their father. I was livid. I told her that I wanted to know just exactly what was going on. I told her that I did not at all appreciate the insinuation or accusation that any of my children were being abused. I remained controlled and confident, but I was angry. She remained calm, and actually sounded somewhat sympathetic when she explained to me that an anonymous call had come through on the Childline, claiming that Patrick, specifically, was being abused. I told her that the claim was an outrageous lie, that Patrick had been physically disciplined, and that yes, we absolutely used a wooden paddle. I explained to her that we had done so out of desperation, fear, and parental concern after multiple attempts to stop his dangerous behavior. I told her that we had done so at the encouragement of more than one police officer. Patrick had been sneaking out of the house, drinking in cars, smoking pot, using pills, and going to parties that we didn't approve of. We were responsible parents trying to protect our son and save his life. The police had told us that their hands were tied. Because he hadn't broken any laws and was a minor, they couldn't put him into a juvenile detention center or even detain him at the local police department. Had we refused to pick him up, we would have been charged with child abandonment. They told us that as his parents, we had the right to physically discipline him. Removing privileges and giving him extra chores hadn't worked.

I asked her what she would have done. I told her emphatically that we made no apologies for paddling him and that we would do it again in a heartbeat if we were in the same situation. What I told her was the God-honest truth, and I said it loud and clear. If she had been a caseworker on a power trip, she would have no doubt had me hauled off in handcuffs, but I was not afraid. I also shared with her that on that very day, ironically and very tragically, the funeral for one of Patrick's friends had been held in Texas. A friend of our family's son had ended his life, and drugs had been involved. I told the caseworker that that was why we would do everything in our power to keep Patrick safe. I told her to look around her. All my kids were standing around the foyer, a couple of them were sitting on the steps leading upstairs. Grace had Michael in her arms, and Christina was holding Ryan. None of them wanted to miss the exchange. They all dared her with their eyes to say something to their mother. I think she may have been tackled had she tried to pursue the claim. I asked her if my children looked like they were, or had ever been, abused. They seemed to have contempt in their eyes. I understood later on, after I had cooled down, that it had been misplaced. She was only doing her job, but we were all angry. I told her that our family was our very life. We loved our children, and we were raising them to be of good character. Our life centered around them, and we were proud of each one of them.

When I got through speaking my mind, she told me that she could tell that our kids were not abused. She said that the three that she had spoken with so far had been articulate, polite, and respectful. She told me that Patrick had been honest and forthcoming with her and that she understood our position completely. She explained that she was bound by the law to question each of the kids at their schools and had to physically see the two that were still at home. She said she would also have to speak with Joe. Angela was eighteen, so she wasn't required to answer any questions. I told her that Joe was working and wouldn't be home for another forty-five minutes, but that she was most welcome to wait. She said that she didn't feel that it was necessary, she had no concerns. There was obviously no problem from what she could see and that she would come back the next day. I'm pretty sure she didn't want to hear me rant anymore.

I told her as I walked her to the door that I wanted to know who had made the claim. She said that she didn't know because the call had been made anonymously. I didn't buy it. Surely if she didn't know, she could find out. There had to be a way of tracking numbers. How could they not have a way of verifying claims? She assured me that the call was anonymous and that there was no way of finding out. All she had were the details of the accusation. That angered me more. I told her that I thought it was ridiculous. What would stop people from making false claims just to cause trouble? She told me that sadly, that did happen, and that it happened more often than I might think. I was in shock. I could never ever, in a million years, ever consider doing such an ugly and horrible thing to anyone. Not even to my worst enemy, of which I had none. She left, promising to return the next morning.

Numb doesn't come close to describing our state of being. We mulled around in a fog, unable to fully digest it. I dreaded telling Joe, but at the same time, I was anxious for him to get home to share the load with me. The kids continued to hash and rehash the entire event, comparing their experiences with each other. The ones who thought that they'd escaped questioning had been made painfully aware that they would be getting called down to the office the next day. Grace and Christina asked me if they could refuse to be interviewed. I told them that there was no reason for them to refuse, they had nothing to hide. All they needed to do was tell the truth. They all continued to repeat the same questions.

"Who would do that to us?"

Then, almost as if it were a complete revelation realized by all of them simultaneously, they said, "I bet it was Grandma."

Shivers crawled over my skin. My stomach dropped, and my heart thundered in my chest as I listened to them discuss their conclusions. They all seemed to be in agreement. I felt nauseous as I contemplated their suspicions myself. Could it be possible? I didn't have any proof, but judging by my physical reaction to the idea of it, I knew that it wasn't entirely out of the realm of possibilities. Joseph said he knew that my mother didn't at all like it when I called her out on her rudeness toward Romaine. He felt that it could be her way of retaliating. Could my very own mother do such a thing? I hadn't spoken to her or even heard from her since the day they left after their visit, almost two months earlier. No e-mails, no phone calls. I knew that my mother tended to be passive-aggressive, but I didn't want to believe that she could stoop to that level of torture. I couldn't, however, completely dismiss the possibility either.

Joe walked through the doorway with Angela and hadn't even made it into the foyer before the little kids rushed to tell him about the whole episode. Angela stopped halfway up the stairs, a look of total disbelief on her face. News travels fast when you live with a house full of kids. He looked at me completely confused, searching for some sensible explanation to what he was being bombarded with. I stood facing him while the older kids told the little kids to shut up so that I could tell him what had happened. I gave him a quick synopsis of what had transpired that afternoon. I have never seen such a look of utter confusion and disbelief, followed by pain, on my husband's face. His mouth gaped open, his shoulder's dropped, and he shook his head incredulously. The first thing he uttered when he could finally speak was, "Who hates us that much?"

I just shook my head.

In unison, the kids said, "Grandma."

Joe looked at them wide-eyed before returning his troubled gaze to me, wondering if it could possibly be true. I didn't want to believe it, and I don't think Joe wanted to believe it either, but how could we know for sure? My mother's behavior had become increasingly hostile, in a passive-aggressive way. I told him that the caseworker would be returning to the house the next day to question him, and that she would be talking to Christina, Grace, Callum, Sarah, and Katie at their schools. He was crushed. The very thought of our kids being subjected to the humiliation of being interrogated at school about their father, whom they loved and respected, was sickening to us. We did the best we could to reassure them that it would be okay. They hadn't done anything wrong, and all they had to do was tell the truth. They had nothing to fear or hide. It made us both sad and physically ill, knowing that the experience would be etched into their memories forever. A part of their childhood had been tainted, their innocence robbed from them by a phone call. No, a lie.

We prayed our evening rosary, and at the end, after blessing each other, our relatives, friends, neighbors, favorite priests, the poor and homeless, all the Knitterbugs ladies, and sick babies in the hospital, we added one more prayer.

"Help us find out who made the call."

We kissed our kids goodnight, hugging them extra tight, and sent them to bed. Joe remained silent between the incredulous question he asked out loud, more to himself than to me, "Who would make up such a lie?"

I sobbed into my pillow that night, not so much about the false accusations, but because my kids thought that they had been made by my mother, and the possibility that they could be right.

My mind found no rest. I prayed over and over to the Holy Spirit that we would find out the truth, that we would discover who had made the call. I needed to know for my own peace of mind. I don't know how much I slept, but each time I woke up, the prayer was the same, "Holy Spirit, shed Your light on this darkness and reveal to us who did this." I didn't want revenge. I needed to know who to protect my family from. It was obvious to me that the perpetrator had to be a tragic and unfortunate soul with a tortured life. No rational person would mess with a family, my family, in such a twisted way. The next morning, we were met with worried looks from our two youngest girls, and a lot of brave talk from the older ones, threatening to tell the caseworker off. We told them that we expected them to be nothing but respectful, and simply answer her questions truthfully. It would all be over soon.

We sent the kids off to school and waited for the caseworker to show up. She was late. Joe had turned down an extra school run that McCarter's had called him for. Never one to turn down the extra work, he was frustrated, but I felt that it had been a blessing because he was still quite distraught. He had been hurt deeply, and I was worried about him. I questioned God, "Hasn't Joe suffered enough? How much more does he have to take?"

As much as Joe was hurt, I was mad as hell. The dogs began to bark, announcing the arrival of the caseworker. Joe opened the door while I held them both back. Michael was napping, and Ryan was building Legos on the floor in the family room. When I excused myself to put the dogs out onto the deck, she assured me that she didn't mind dogs, so I let go of Maverick and Scamp. They greeted her and happily let her pet them before settling down on the area rug near where Ryan was playing. She sat down and told us that she was basically going through the formalities required of her by law, but she reassured us that she had no concerns. She informed us that she had spoken with Christina, Grace, Sarah, and Katie that morning before coming to the house, the reason for her delay. She would be going to Callum's school after she finished up with us. She congratulated us on our family, saying that it was obvious to her that we were doing a wonderful job of raising our children. She commented on how polite, respectful, and articulate they were and how much she appreciated their honesty. She also said that she wished that there were more parents like us. We thanked her for the small consolation and asked her, "Then why is this happening to us? Who would do such a thing?"

She said she didn't really know what motivated people, but that it happened quite often.

I asked her what our options were. I wanted to know what we could do about the injustice. It was wrong, and I wanted to know who did it so that I could protect my family. She told me that she didn't know who had made the call because it had been made anonymously. She said that the success of the Childline depended on protecting the anonymity of the callers. Most callers didn't want to be identified for fear of retaliation. If people were afraid of their identities being discovered, they wouldn't make the calls at all, and kids would suffer. I thought that the rationale was cowardly. I know for a fact that if I was certain that a child was being abused, I wouldn't have a problem identifying myself to the authorities. I would report it, and I would welcome an open discussion about it. I wouldn't hide in the shadows. I asked her if there were any laws to protect those who are falsely accused. She wasn't entirely sure, but said that there may be some legal action that we could take. We would need to get a lawyer. She said that we could request a copy of the call record, detailing the actual call from Childline. That was something. Then she added that it was best to just forget about the whole thing. I laughed sarcastically and said, "Forget about it?"

I knew that would never be possible. I asked her what she would do if it was her or her husband who had been falsely accused. She looked at me, smiled gently, and said that she would do exactly what I was doing. I thanked her. At least I wasn't being unreasonable. Uncovering the truth would be my new mission.

As we walked her to the door, she informed us that when she got back to her office, she would send off two letters—the first letter would be one informing us that a claim had been made, the second one would be a letter explaining that the claim was unfounded. The claim would be expunged, and there would be no record of it. Before she left, Joe pulled out the certificate that he had received in the mail only days earlier. It was the background check that had been done in order for him to work at McCarter's. It dated back to 1975, and certified that he had no history of any type of child abuse. We all thought it was quite ironic. The caseworker said that sadly, most of the people that she dealt with would never be able to attain such a document.

As soon as we shut the door, I began to search the yellow pages for a legal aid lawyer. We didn't have money to pay a lawyer, but I remembered reading somewhere in the Beaver County paperwork that we could consult with a legal aid lawyer for a nominal fee. I found the number and set up a one-hour appointment that would only cost twenty-five dollars. It would at least give me the opportunity to ask questions. I felt like I was doing something. There was no way I could just sit still and do nothing. I wasn't about to let it go as if it had never happened. The two letters couldn't come fast enough. I continued to pray to the Holy Spirit, "Just show me who did this." I just wanted to know who. The why didn't matter to me anymore, I just needed to know who. I felt a little better, vindicated somewhat, after our meeting with the caseworker. She had assured us that we had nothing to worry about, and Joe and I knew that we had done nothing wrong. She could see that we were a normal loving family. She had complimented us and commended us on the job that we were doing.

I called Cathy and Nanette to tell them what happened. The two ladies had become my mentors, my sounding boards. All the ordinary and mundane goings-on in our life. I kept them updated on the kids and how they were going at school, the recruiter calls, interviews, new job possibilities, and the rejections. The experience in the Welfare office and life in general. It seemed like there was always something going on, new highs and new lows, hopes and disappointments, excitement and worries. I shared everything with them. I bared my soul to them, and it helped me in so many ways, almost like therapy. I needed to tell them what had happened in order to help it sink in. It all still seemed so unreal, a living nightmare. They were shocked to say the least, heartbroken was more like it. They prayed along with us and for us that we would get some answers, and they helped me to keep calm. Part of me wanted to retaliate. I wanted to confront whoever had assaulted my family, but I was still not certain who had actually done it. I had suspicions, but I didn't have proof. I continued to pray for answers and for the wisdom to know how to deal with them when they came.

On the evening of the caseworker's visit, I went to adoration and Mass at Christ the Divine Teacher. I brought Michael with me. No one else was in the church when I arrived, but I went into the nursery. As I sat in the quiet room holding my baby, adoring the Blessed Sacrament, I thanked God for the good outcome of the horrible event. I couldn't help but wonder how it might have ended up. God had protected our family through the ordeal. Life had thrown some really hard balls at us, and many of them came at us at the same time. It often felt like all we could do was bat them away to defend ourselves. We were in self-preservation mode. Bad things kept happening, but we continued to turn to God through it all, and He remained faithful to us. I felt a peace wash over me in the little room. Overcome with emotion and gratitude, quiet tears filled my eyes while I pondered just how blessed we were.

Fr. Joe Freedy, a priest I hadn't met before, said Mass that evening. During his homily, he very emotionally informed all who were gathered there that there had been false allegations made against our beloved bishop, Bishop Zubik. It was the first I had heard of it. The allegations had been made long before we had arrived in Pennsylvania. Fr. Freedy praised God that night because that very day in court, a judge had thrown the case out. There had not been one shred of evidence to support the false claim that had been made against him. I shuddered. I was instantly convinced that the Holy Spirit had prompted me to go to church that night just to hear that news. I felt less isolated and actually quite fortunate. How devastating it must have been for him. We had been falsely accused and humiliated, but it had been kept private for the most part. He, on the other hand, had been falsely accused and publicly humiliated with stories all over the media. I was grateful to hear that his name had been cleared, but I was heartbroken for him and our church.

Two days after the caseworker's visit, Angela, who was home early after a short day at Geneva, showed me a Facebook post that she had found. She had taken it upon herself to do some detective work of her own. The event was still obviously very much on her mind, and she hadn't even been part of the investigation. I did not have a Facebook account, so it hadn't occurred to me to search there. I looked at the page that had been posted by my mother. It read: "Sometimes silence is not golden, if children are suffering abuse in any form we need to speak out."

It had been posted on August 16, 2011, only days after her visit with us in Beaver Falls. My heart began to pound. I knew then that it had to have been my mother who made the call. A Facebook post was obviously not the sort of evidence that would convict her in a court of law, but it was enough for me, and it was enough for Joe. He shook his head and said, "Kick him when he's down."

When the rest of the kids got home from school, Angela showed them the post, and they were convinced as well. They said that they already knew it was Grandma. The Holy Spirit had answered my prayers. I prayed to know who, and He had revealed it. I felt numb. I did have a sense of relief, but I felt no emotion. I wasn't angry or sad, I wasn't even disappointed. I'm pretty sure I was in shock. The relief was that the horror was finally over, the threat was gone, and I could protect my family. None of us would ever be subject to my mother's torment again. I prayed a silent prayer of thanksgiving as I pondered what to do with the new information.

Joe went out to collect the mail. The weight had lifted off his shoulders. Any injustice I felt was for my husband and my children, none of it was for myself. He handed me an envelope. It was a card from our friends Tracy and Blair Korschun. The note in the card was handwritten:

> They sold property and possessions to give
> to anyone who had need. (Acts 2:45)
> Praising God and enjoying the favor of all
> the people and the Lord added to their number
> daily those who were being saved. (Acts 2:47)

Then Tracy wrote:

Hi Nicole and Joe,

We were told by the Holy Spirit to send you a gift. This is a gift and not to be repaid to us. In the future when you get on your feet I know you will pay it forward to someone else in need! Hope to hear good news soon!

Love you,
Tracy, Blair & family

I about collapsed when I read the card. *The Holy Spirit* had told them to send us a gift? Had I not just been talking with the Holy Spirit myself? Begging Him for an answer? Inside the card was a personal check for five thousand dollars. It was most definitely one of those "hit me over the head with a sledgehammer" God moments. God was telling me to not be afraid. He was with us. He had never left us. Not only had I received my answer, but just in case I had any doubts, the Holy Spirit was making sure that I knew that He had been the one to answer me.

The Korschuns didn't know anything about the investigation, but I called Tracy immediately to thank her and to tell her the whole story of the events that had taken place only days before. I wanted to let her know that God had used them to help reassure us. Tracy was shocked to hear the story, but she wasn't at all surprised to hear how God's hand was in it, turning the storm into a blessing. Being a Godly woman, she offered me wise words of advice. I told her how conflicted I was. I was numb, but the more it sunk in, the more different emotions whirled through my head and heart. Knowing the truth, I felt a need to do something about it, I just didn't know what. I wanted justice. I told her that I had an appointment with a lawyer to find out how we should handle it. She told me not to fall into the temptation of trying to get retribution. She also advised me to sever contact with my mother in order to protect my children. Keeping my children far away from my mother was a no-brainer for me. I had no interest or desire in having any kind of relationship with her as her daughter. What troubled me was whether or not my dad and siblings knew what she had done. What kind of lies had she been feeding them? I agonized over whether or not to tell them. I wanted them to know, and yet I didn't want to disrupt their lives with what she had done to us. I wanted to inform them so that they could protect themselves, but then I second-guessed myself. Would they even believe me? My mother was good at twisting the truth to serve her own agenda.

I wrote a long e-mail, detailing everything, a sort of warning to my brothers and sisters. If she could do such a despicable thing to me and my family, she could do it to them and theirs. I couldn't hit the Send button. I decided instead to say and do nothing. Silence became my weapon of choice, and prayer was my armor. I knew my mother. She would expect me to go into panic mode, calling everyone to tell them what had happened. I didn't want to give her the satisfaction. I kept silent. There was a war going on in my very soul. Angels and demons. Part of me wanted revenge, and the other part of me wanted to surrender. I told no one, other than my three friends.

In the following days and weeks, my kids continued to come to me with their stories. Things that they had remembered when my mother had come to watch them during Michael's birth and from her visit to Pennsylvania. I knew that they needed to vent to deal with their feelings. They were angry and disappointed and had been robbed of their innocence. It pained me to hear how they had been so deeply injured by someone that they should have been able to trust. I told them that I wanted them to each write out their own account of what they had dealt with, their thoughts and feelings and about being questioned by the caseworker. Each of them did so willingly. When I read each of their pages, some of them had written several; I felt tremendous guilt. How could I have allowed it to happen? I had allowed my mother to torment my children, making them feel badly, bringing them to tears, ridiculing and criticizing them, leaving them out, talking about them behind their siblings' backs, playing favorites, and making them feel uncomfortable by being rude to my friends and neighbors. We had invited her into our home, where my children should have been safe, and she hurt them. Their writing out their own personal stories and me reading them helped all of us. I apologized to them for not doing a better job of protecting them, and I promised them that I would never allow it to happen again. We began to heal. We still talked about things if one of them brought something up, but for the most part, we enjoyed the peace of the knowledge that we would never again be subjected to her behavior.

I received a call from my sister Thérèse. She called while on her way to my parents' house for Thanksgiving weekend. Her voice sounded upbeat as she shared her exciting news. Her boyfriend had proposed to her while on vacation in Greece. She apologized for not calling in such a long time; she had been working two jobs, and life was busy. I told her I understood completely. It seemed to me that she wasn't aware of what had happened, and I didn't want to ruin her Thanksgiving celebration by telling her. I was genuinely happy for her and her engagement. She and her boyfriend had been dating for several years. I had yet to meet him, but I knew that Thérèse was head over heels in love and wanted to get married more than anything. I was happy that she would finally realize her dream, but I was sad that I would not be able to share in her special day. My mother had ruined the possibility of that. We would never again be able to participate in family weddings or holidays. I wouldn't subject my family to her. I tried to sound genuinely happy, but it was clouded with sadness. I think Thérèse sensed it, though she didn't ask why. We corresponded several times after her call through e-mails, cards, and letters. She wanted Sarah and Katie to be her flower girls and Angela to sing at her wedding. We declined without giving her the real reason. I know that Thérèse must have been hurt, but I couldn't burden her by overshadowing her wedding with such a dark drama.

The two letters from the Beaver County Youth and Child Services office came in the mail on October 14. The first one informed us that a claim had been made of physical child abuse against Patrick; the second one stated that the claim of physical child abuse had been unfounded. On the back of the letter was a list of what our rights were, one of them being that we could request a copy of the Childline call report. I definitely wanted a copy and planned to type up a letter the next day requesting that one be mailed to us. I felt certain that it would contain clues that would help to put the pieces of the puzzle together. Not that I needed to be further convinced, but I wanted documentation.

The next morning, after the kids left for school, I quickly tidied up the kitchen from breakfast and threw in some laundry while the boys played. I checked my e-mail on my iPhone and was very surprised to see two e-mails from my mother, whom I hadn't heard a peep from in more than two months. I opened them up. Neither of them were personal e-mails, just forwards. I looked at who she had included on them and found it curious that she had only sent them to Nanette and I. Both forwards were about friendship. I called Nanette to tell her that I had received the e-mails, and we both commented on how strange it was. Nanette had been receiving forwards and e-mails regularly from my mother, up until our move to Pennsylvania, but since then they had ceased. Until that morning. I suspected that it was an attempt to worm her way back into my life. I told Nanette that we had just received the two letters that we had been expecting from Children and Youth Services, and that I planned to request a copy of the call report. She was glad that things seemed to be working out, but sad that it had happened at all. She said it was unfortunate that my relationship with my mother had been so deeply damaged. Nanette had been under the impression that my relationship with my mother had been strong prior to the investigation. I hadn't shared the long history of dramas with her. Sadly, I had been in denial about just how dysfunctional our relationship had always been. We hung up, and I got busy with my letter writing.

Early that afternoon while the boys were still napping, and the scanner copied the letters I had typed up requesting the Childline call record, the phone rang. The display showed private name, private number. I guessed it was probably a bill collector, and without thinking much of it, I picked up to answer.

"Hello?"

I had not been prepared to hear my mother's voice on the other end of the phone.

"Helllooo," she sang in her cheeriest voice.

My heart sank. All I could think was, *Really, do you think I'm falling for that?* But I didn't say it. "Hello," I answered flatly.

"How are yooouuu?" she continued to sing.

"I'm fine." Again, emotionless.

"How are the kiiids?" she was still singing.

Was she for real? "They're wonderful," I answered.

"Long time, no speak!" she cooed.

"Yup," was all I could muster.

"Well, we were just theeere … what haaappened?" More singing.

I found it incredibly curious that my mother chose the words "What happened?" Especially since she knew perfectly well what had happened. *She* was what had happened. Was she expecting me to dissolve into tears? Cry on her shoulder and tell her all about the child abuse investigation? What exactly was she trying to do? For all she knew, Joe could have been arrested, and all our kids could have been split up and put into foster homes. Was that what she had wanted? She was like an arsonist returning to the scene of the fire to see what kind of damage had been done. Did she somehow in her sick mind think that maybe she might be awarded custody of my eleven children? Like she could get some kind of do-over? Was that what she had wanted? There were so many things I wanted to spew out. I felt my face burn with anger. I wanted to tell her exactly what I thought of her, but I couldn't do it. I still couldn't stand up to my mother. Instead, in an exaggerated matter-of-fact tone, I asked her, "Why don't *you* tell *me* what happened?"

I turned it around on her, giving her an opportunity to come clean. I was giving her one chance. She responded with deafening silence. I decided to end the call.

"I'm really busy. I need to go."

Shaking, in utter disbelief over my mother's nerve, I hung up the phone. She was feeling me out. She had to know after her phone call that I knew what she had done.

Joe was just as surprised as I was to hear that my mother had called. I also told him about the e-mails that Nanette and I had received that morning. He shook his head and said what we both already knew; our silence was killing her. She was dying to know how we were dealing with the whole thing. She had to be wondering if we had been devastated by it, wondering why I hadn't run to her for support. I was seeing her through fresh eyes, through the eyes of my children. They had seen what I had been ignoring and denying, long before the investigation. I had enabled her, and I felt tremendous guilt. I couldn't help but wonder if the whole thing could have been avoided had I called her out on her behavior years earlier. Could I have saved others from being hurt by her? That is something that I will never know. The Childline call report couldn't come fast enough.

When Angela got home from college that afternoon, she told me that my mother had called her cell phone that morning. I asked her what she wanted, but Angela said she hadn't actually spoken to her. She was in class when the call came in, and my mother never left a message. I told Angela about my conversation with my mother that afternoon. Angela's response was simply, "Wow."

As if the two e-mails and two phone calls on the same day weren't enough to get our attention, that afternoon, the mailman delivered a stack of cards, all from my mother. What kind of planning had she done in order for us to be bombarded by her attention, all on the same day? Her cards were a reconfirmation of her passive-aggressive nature. She had sent two confirmation cards, one for Patrick and one for Christina. They had been confirmed in June. There was a birthday card for Grace, whose birthday was in May, containing ten dollars. A graduation card for Angela, who had graduated in May, with twenty dollars inside. A birthday card for Katie, whose birthday was in July, with no money in it. We suspected that she thought Katie had received enough from the big party in Texas that Nanette and Cathy had thrown for her. A birthday card for Patrick, whose birthday was in June, with a twenty-dollar bill. A birthday card for Christina, whose birthday was coming up on November 3, with no money in it. Christina was not at all surprised and felt that it was a result of her not hiding her distaste for my mother's behavior. Callum didn't receive a card or money. His birthday was August 18, roughly a week after my parents had visited. Callum had made the mistake of showing excitement over the fact that Cathy had told him that they would be shipping him a birthday package in the mail. He had also borne the brunt of my mother's meanness when Michael was in the hospital. I instantly regretted allowing the kids to open the cards and wished that I had simply returned them to her or tossed them into the trash. It was something that she had done before, so it was nothing new for them. She regularly remembered some kids and forgot about others on their birthdays, but we chalked it up to just that—forgetfulness. This time, however, was the big reveal for my kids, who all at once opened up cards, while those who didn't get one looked on. Each of them witnessed with their own eyes exactly how she operated. If I had thrown the cards away, they wouldn't have known. I never tried to influence or form an opinion of my mother for them. They had been forming their own opinions all along, according to what they saw and, most importantly, by how she made them feel by her actions. We were gathered together in the family room. As they opened their cards, the kids who received money took no pleasure in it. It really wasn't about the money, it was about the favoritism. It would have been less hurtful if she hadn't sent anything to any of them. It reconfirmed to all of us that having no contact with her was the healthiest option for our family.

It took a few weeks for the copy of the Childline report to arrive, sometime in November. After reading every word from the transcript of the call, none of us had any doubt whatsoever that my mother was behind it. I was not entirely certain whether or not she had put one of my sisters up to making the actual call. It read as though it had been reported by a third party. There was no question that she instigated it. The details in the report were impossible to ignore. No one would have known everything that had been typed into the report but her. One of the more obvious details pertained specifically to a letter. The letter that Patrick had written to my parents after they had visited us in Texas. In the letter, Patrick commiserated with them about being homeschooled. He wrote, "I agree with you that being homeschooled will ruin my education."

I had torn the letter up, resenting the fact that my parents, more specifically my mother, had undermined our decision to homeschool our kids. Worse, they had discussed it in a negative way with Patrick in our absence. I told Patrick—at the time that he had written the letter, which, by the way, he had handed to me unfolded, requesting that I mail it for him—that I would be happy to mail a letter when he wrote one that didn't undermine or discuss our parental decisions. When my mother came to help out for Michael's birth, Patrick told her that he had written her a letter but that I had ripped it up. That was the letter that was referenced in the report. That "the child had written a letter to the friend, which the mother had torn up." The second and probably most telling detail was the line stating that 'the incident occurred in August.' The only people who saw us in August were my parents any my youngest sister. We had moved from Texas to Pennsylvania on August 4th, and we knew no one in Pennsylvania. The rest of the report was filled with lies and embellished half-truths.

I did not at all doubt that Patrick had complained, and probably even lied, to my mother about our disciplining him. He was a rebellious teenager, spinning out of control. My mother knew perfectly well that neither Patrick nor any of our other children had ever been abused. We told her ourselves that Patrick had been sneaking out of the house and doing things he wasn't allowed to do. That we had talked to our priest, our friends who had been through similar things with their children, school counselors, and the police. We told her that after trying countless ways to deal with his behavior, we had run out of ideas. Feeling absolutely desperate by the fact that Patrick was repeatedly sneaking out, the police were the ones who encouraged Joe to "whip his ass." None of the other consequences had worked. The police were sympathetic when they told us that their hands were tied. They assured us that we were within our parental rights to use appropriate physical discipline, and a paddle was within that realm. My mother objected, and she saw to it that she would put a stop to it. What she didn't know was that after using the paddle on Patrick three or four times after catching him sneaking out, we realized that the paddle was not working either, so we gave it up. We took no pleasure in spanking our son. We hadn't even brought the paddle with us to Pennsylvania.

The report made me sick, and yet it confirmed what we already believed. Her name wasn't written on it, but she was definitely in all the details. I filed it away, along with the pages that my kids had written out, and the letters from the county and state. I was sad that our family would always have such an ugly stain on it. I wasn't certain if justice would ever prevail, but even if it did, the scar would always remain. Next came the letter that stated that although the claim had been unfounded, it would not be expunged until one hundred and twenty days, after one full year of the date that the claim had been filed. That made me angrier than the actual claim. It was completely unfair. The claim had been a lie. I felt that it should be expunged immediately, but that was how the law had been written, and we couldn't change it. The record would not be expunged until February 11, 2013.

TWENTY-EIGHT

Sold

Beaver Falls, Pennsylvania, October 2011

We finally got an offer on our house. The closing was set for the end of October, less than three weeks after the offer was made. It had been made by a real estate agent, and was insultingly low with several ridiculous conditions. We were in no position to haggle over price, but we put our foot down on many of the conditions. We accepted the offer, taking a huge loss, sixty thousand dollars less than what we had purchased it for. We tried not to think about the many thousands of dollars' worth of improvements that we had made over the five years that we lived in it. At closing, we got a check for five thousand dollars. We felt more than a little sick, but we were grateful that we had been saved from a foreclosure or bankruptcy. We complained that we could never get a break, but we caught ourselves and consciously tried to remind each other to look for the blessings. It was tough, but the more we worked on it, the easier it became. God was stripping things away from us, and it forced us to see what was truly important. With the weight of the house lifted off, we prayed for the ability to move forward.

We continued to pay the important bills with the money that Tracy and Blair had sent us, and the money from the sale of the house kept us afloat for a while. Joe continued to collect Texas unemployment, though it had been significantly reduced because of his job driving the school van. Bob and Nanette paid all the utilities for their house. We were able to breathe a little easier.

I had the house decorated inside with all our fall decorations, but outside was even more breathtaking. The trees were yellow, gold, orange, and red. The air was crisp and clean, and the little kids were excited about Halloween. Joe had scoped out the best trick-or-treating streets while driving his school route. The kids dug out their costumes from the bin that we had collected over the years. Even though Halloween has always been my least favorite holiday, I enjoyed watching their excitement. Patrick and Joseph asked if they could invite some friends over for a bonfire and food. Joe and I agreed, thinking it would be fun for them to have their friends over. We told Christina and Grace that they could invite some of their friends as well. Our rules had been clearly established, but we made sure that they were understood by all. No wild behavior of any kind and absolutely no alcohol or drugs. Joe and I and all the other kids would supervise. I baked cookies and cake pops, and we made pizza. We served pop, chips, and other snacks. Patrick built a fire in the pit and set chairs up on the deck. A lot of kids showed up, and everyone was polite and well-behaved. We laid the food out on the kitchen table, in front of the patio door that led to the deck where the fire pit was. The rest of us watched movies in the family room where we had a clear view of the party. Our boys were good hosts and very respectful of the fact that we were only borrowing the house. They did a great job of making sure that the crashers who'd heard about the party were turned away. We were happy that our kids had made friends and that they felt comfortable inviting them over. Football season would be ending in a couple of weeks, and we were relieved that Patrick seemed to be settled and in a much better place. He talked about doing track and field in the spring.

Joseph and Christina had auditioned and gotten significant parts in the high school musical *Hairspray*, and Angela was enjoying college life. She had tried out for and made the Genevans, Geneva's touring choir. It was an elite choir, and according to our neighbor Romaine, it was almost unheard-of for a freshman to be accepted, but she'd been given a spot. We were very proud of her. She had applied for a job at McDonald's and started to work part-time around her already busy college schedule. Joseph had also begun looking for a job. Callum stayed somewhat busy with Webelos, though his initial enthusiasm had worn off. He had also started altar serving at Christ the Divine Teacher. Life gradually became fuller as each of our kids made friends and discovered their interests.

Using food stamps was something that I didn't believe we would ever get used to. We wanted to get off of them as soon as we could, but we knew that it was a necessity for our family. It was a dark secret that I didn't want anyone to know about and tried to keep hidden. When I got a call from Callum's school nurse, informing us that they had a large donation of food for our family, which had been collected during their school's Thanksgiving food drive, I knew the secret was out. We were on a list. I humbly thanked the nurse, telling her how much we appreciated the gesture, but that we had more than adequate food. Surely, there had to be another family that needed it more than us. She insisted that it had been divided up among other families and that she really wanted us to have it. I didn't want to pick it up. I was so proud, and I knew that my pride was one of my biggest sins. I swallowed it and went to the school, driving around the back as I had been instructed by the nurse, to protect my identity and save me from embarrassment. When she opened up the back door and showed me the piles of bags filled with boxes and cans, my eyes filled with tears. I choked back a sob, not wanting to lose my composure. The nurse hugged me and told me not to feel bad. I again attempted to explain away our circumstances, wanting her to understand that we were not lazy deadbeats. She was anything but judgmental. She was kindhearted and compassionate, but in my own prideful mind, I felt the need to justify the situation. Pride is ugly.

I received a call from my sister Andréa. She told me that she was planning a trip to Pennsylvania to do some Black Friday shopping with her boyfriend, and she wanted to know if they could come to see us. Joe and I had discussed how we would handle such requests more than once. We still hadn't told any of my family about the investigation. We didn't know if any of them knew about it, or what they had heard from my mother. No one had called to ask or verify anything. We wondered if my mother had acted alone and kept it a secret from everyone else, or if she had told all my siblings some twisted version of the story. They all had to be wondering about our silence and lack of contact. We could only speculate about what they knew. We decided that if any of my siblings called to visit, we would welcome them, but that we wouldn't speak of the investigation unless they asked us specifically why we had been out of touch.

The evening that my sister arrived in town with her boyfriend, they texted for directions. Joe drove down the road to meet them on the hill near the apple orchard. The visit was polite and friendly but more than slightly awkward. There was definitely an elephant in the room, but no one brought up my mother, not even once. We had dinner and visited in the family room, and then went out onto the deck for a family bonfire. As the nights were getting colder, we were having regular weekend fires. We didn't have any money, but we spent plenty of time together doing simple things. Andréa had brought bags of clothes and shoes for the girls. Hand-me-downs from her closet that they were more than happy to sort through. They only stayed for a few hours, but their visit was pleasant for all of us. It was nice to see my sister, and we felt that it was good for her to see that we hadn't changed at all as a family. Despite the hard financial times, we were still just as connected as we had always been. If she had been sent on a mission to report back to my mother, which we believed was not only entirely possible, but very likely, she wouldn't have much to tell.

Joe and I spent a lot of time talking about how much we had been through and how very aware we were that God had been with us through all of it. We were also very aware that the devil was trying to do everything in his power to discourage us and make us lose hope. That knowledge made us stronger and more resolute in our faith. We prayed even harder. We were closer as a family, and we felt loved and cared for by our friends and community.

No sooner had things settled down, did they begin again to go awry. Joe had cashed the check from the closing of the house, and he put the money in our safe. We had purchased a small safe with a code, as well as a key. We set the code and put the keys on our keychains for safekeeping. Joe had counted the cash several times before putting it into a white envelope inside the safe. Patrick started behaving suspiciously. He was spending more time alone and stayed out of sight except to check on where Joe and I were. I noticed him going in and out of Joe's office quite a bit. He had no business in there. Joe kept a logbook for the jobs he'd applied for, as well as our legal documents and personal files. When I spotted Patrick sitting at the desk in the dark, I questioned him about being in there. He got defensive and said he wasn't doing anything. The house was more than six thousand square feet, not counting the huge basement, so there were plenty of other places for him to sit. I told him to get out. When I saw him in there again a few days later, I noticed a glow, like from some sort of electronic device. When he spotted me walking toward him, he hid whatever it was that he had.

Because we were living in a rural area, we couldn't get Internet service at the house, so Joe purchased a MiFi WiFi, from Verizon. We only turned it on when we needed the Internet, primarily for job searches, and sometimes the kids needed it for homework. When we were done, we shut it down because there was a usage charge for it. Joe kept it in the desk drawer. Joe couldn't find the MiFi in the drawer when he went to use it, but he just happened to notice it tucked inside the glass cabinet in the office. I hadn't put it there and neither had he. I suspected that Patrick had because he had been standing in that area of the office when I saw the suspicious glow. We didn't say anything to him about the WiFi being in a different spot, we just kept our eye on him. He was showing the all too familiar signs of his old ways. The way he had been in Texas, mulling around and checking where we all were. We figured out that he was checking to see if the WiFi was on. When it was, he stayed out of sight.

One of the little kids told us that Patrick had a phone or an iTouch. They had seen something glowing. We questioned him about it, but he denied having anything. Christina had an iTouch. She had bought it from Joseph when he got his phone, but it had mysteriously gone missing, and she was convinced that Patrick had stolen it. I went through his room while he was at school. I had learned how to search his room when we grew suspicious of him in Texas. I hadn't done a thorough search since moving into the Mazzucas' house. Since the move to Pennsylvania, I never felt a need to; there hadn't been any red flags. Patrick had always been good at hiding things. I went through all the clothes in his closet, patting them down, checking pockets, sleeves, pant legs, and hoods. I found a bottle of cough medicine that we had not purchased, some folded-up notes from a girl, a couple of cans of chewing tobacco, several lighters, and an empty cigarette pack. I took all the drawers out of the dresser, went through the clothes, turned the mattresses over, checked the bed frames, changed the sheets, and ran my hand along door and window frames. It was on the top of the window frame that I found a small key with a black plastic coating over it. It looked strangely familiar, but I couldn't recall what it was for.

After going through the boys' bathroom and drawers in much the same way, I carried down all the contraband to show Joe. He took the key and walked back to our room and into the closet where the safe was. Joe opened the safe, took out the envelope, and counted the money. Then he counted it again. He looked at me in disbelief and said, "There's five hundred dollars missing."

We were stunned. I couldn't believe it. I did not want to believe that one of our kids had stolen from us. I was sick because I knew which one of them had stolen it. His suspicious behavior had not been imagined. Joe and I both checked our key rings. The key to the safe had been removed from mine. When Patrick came home from school, we showed him what we had found in his room. He claimed that he had brought the lighters and cans of chewing tobacco with him from Texas. Because I had been the one to pack his room and had thoroughly searched it before moving, I didn't believe him. I told him so, even though I couldn't prove it. The items would have surfaced before then, especially since my mother had organized his closet during her visit. If he'd brought them from Texas, she would have seen them and would have definitely reported it to us. He denied it. When we told him about the missing money and that the key to the safe had been found in his room, he swore he knew nothing about it. He said he had no idea how it got into his room. Patrick's initial reaction had always been to deny everything, even if all clues pointed to him and he'd been caught red-handed. He wanted to know how we could prove that he had been the one to take the money. Joe told him that he knew it was him, and he wanted it back.

I was mad about the missing money, but I was sick over the breach in their relationship. We thought Patrick had made a fresh start, a new beginning in Beaver Falls. It had been refreshing to watch him and Joe working together in the yard, on the riding mower, grilling and building fires in the pit, just spending time together without the suspicions and second-guessing that had become the norm before our move. We had been through hell in Texas. Life had finally begun to feel somewhat normal. Normal until that day. We hadn't turned up any cash anywhere, so we were at a loss. Patrick wasn't forthcoming with any information. We didn't have any concrete proof that he had taken the money, so we dropped it, but we continued to watch him very closely.

When Callum came to us to tell us that he definitely saw Patrick with something like a phone again, I went on a rampage. He again denied it, but I knew he was lying. What had he been hiding? Why wouldn't he just come out and say what he had? The fact that he was lying and sneaking around with whatever it was caused me to believe that he was up to no good. Anytime he had possession of an iTouch in the past, he used it to plan his sneaking out. I got that all too familiar sinking feeling in the pit of my stomach. I did not want to go back down that road again. Immediately after Callum informed me about the glow he'd just seen, I stormed upstairs to the bedroom and questioned Patrick. Not surprisingly, he denied having anything; so after patting him down, I told him to get out and go downstairs. I turned his room upside down—closet, drawers, clothes, and pockets. I then did the same in his bathroom. When I pulled out the middle drawer, I saw it inside the drawer box, resting on the track. I proudly carried the iTouch downstairs and showed him that I had found it. He smiled smugly and said, "Congratulations."

And so it began. I asked Patrick what he had been up to and what he was hiding. He got angry and said that he wasn't doing anything wrong. I asked him where he got the iTouch and why he was hiding it. He told me he bought it. I asked him how he could buy it, since he didn't have any money. He claimed that he had saved the money from Texas. I didn't believe it. With football season over, he had changed. Joseph and Christina said that they had seen him hanging around with different kids at school. Kids that they were pretty sure used drugs. I told him that I wouldn't object to him having an iTouch if he was honest about it, but the fact that he had been lying and sneaking around with one raised my suspicions. I reminded him that previously, anytime he'd had one, he'd used it to communicate for the purposes of sneaking out of the house, drinking, and doing drugs. I told him that I would definitely discuss it with his father, who had left with Callum to go to a Webelos meeting, and we would decide what to do with the iTouch. Joe and I told Patrick that we would be keeping it. Patrick didn't seem at all bothered about losing his device, which also raised suspicions. We locked it into our new safe. A bigger, heavier one with a combination lock.

We watched Patrick like a hawk. Around the beginning of December, Christina happened to stumble across his Facebook page, and our world crashed again. Much of the conversations on his wall was drug related. They talked of where and when the parties were taking place. There were also pictures. One of the most recent pictures caught my attention. It was a photo of him and another kid who I didn't recognize, holding up a handful of cash with a post, "Got into the parents' safe." I was sick. He had stolen five hundred dollars from all that was left of our life savings from our safe. Worse than that, much much worse, he was using drugs again. There were messages to kids who we didn't know, in which he discussed buying Adderall, an ADHD prescription drug. The kid who was selling it joked about how his dad had questioned why he was running out of his prescription so quickly. The kid had lied to him, telling him that his pills had spilled out in his backpack and been crushed. In reality, he had been selling them for five to ten dollars a piece. There were messages about where to meet to do a deal—in the brown cafeteria, at the bus stop before or after school. There were even messages about his intent to sell and inquiries about purchasing a scale from someone. We confronted him again about stealing the money and the drug talk, and he flat-out denied it. He swore that he didn't steal the money, that he was not using drugs. Even when we presented him with the Facebook evidence, he claimed that it was just talk. They were just being stupid; they weren't doing drugs. We didn't believe him.

I bought a home drug test kit and hid it in my closet. I wanted to have it handy. Some of the Facebook posts and pictures had been taken in the middle of the night, and not from our house. A sure sign that he had been sneaking out. His bedroom was upstairs, but the house was so huge, with many windows and doors on the three levels that he could easily slip out after we had all gone to sleep. Joe and I left our bedroom door open and the lights turned on in the stairwell, giving us a clear view should anyone get up or come down the stairs. I did bed checks in the middle of the night. We had relaxed too much and become complacent after moving to Pennsylvania, believing that life could be normal. We had finally been able to sleep soundly again, after more than a year of keeping one eye open and our ears finely tuned. I was still nursing Michael a couple of times through the night, so I checked the whole house after putting him back in his bed. Joe stayed up later than usual every night, and we put a locking door handle with a key lock on the basement door, cutting off access to the basement. We found evidence that he had been stashing his clothes and shoes downstairs earlier in the day so that he could sneak out at night. There were two sets of patio doors in the walkout basement, and lots of windows to escape from. We never caught him in the act of sneaking out, but after we found unlocked doors and a screen out of a basement window, we decided we had to do something different.

He became very creative. He kept clothes hidden in the garage, in the van, and stashed in the yard in different places. He would sneak out in his pajamas and then wait around for a while to make sure that he hadn't been detected. He'd change into his clothes, and then knowing that our dogs would bark at the slightest sound, would have his friends meet him down the road. After a night of drinking, smoking, using pot, and other popular drugs, he would somehow find his way home and sneak back in. If I happened to discover him missing during a bed check, I searched for the compromised door or window and locked them, leaving him no way of getting back inside.

Joe and I were unable to sleep, knowing he was out there somewhere. I stayed awake, praying rosaries all night for his safety. That he wasn't driving around with someone who was drunk or high, and that he wasn't getting beat up or passed out somewhere. I listened for the slightest sound and ran to the windows, watching and waiting for him when I heard anything.

Once we knew that he had made it home, usually around four or five in the morning, I could relax. I prayed more rosaries in thanksgiving, but we didn't let him in the house. We heard him trying the doors, but made him stay out in the cold until everyone else woke up around seven or eight o'clock. His escapades almost always occurred on a weekend or during a school break. He'd been able to get away with his escapes for several weeks before we had caught on. If one of the younger kids let him in in the morning, he tried to lie his way out of it, claiming that he had woken up early and decided to go for a walk, or had let the dogs outside and got locked out. We knew it was time to act.

On a Monday morning after a weekend of partying, I pulled the drug test out of my closet. I read the instructions in the dim light of the bathroom and tiptoed up to his room. I shook him awake and ordered him to get up and go into his bathroom. I didn't let him close the door. I stood in the doorway while he peed in the little cup. He smiled smugly as he handed it to me and asked me if I knew how to read the drug test. I ignored him and went back to my bathroom to do the test. Just as I had suspected, he tested positive for THC. That morning, after everyone had gone to school, I started making phone calls. I called a drug rehab and told the lady who answered that my son was using drugs, primarily pot, but possibly others as well. I told her that he was not in any immediate danger, he was in fact at school, but that we needed to do something to stop his behavior. She was very sympathetic and told me that we could set up a consultation with a drug counselor. We made the appointment for that same week and didn't tell Patrick until the morning of the appointment.

He was not at all happy when we told him why he wasn't going to school that day, but he resisted showing any emotion. He tried to act aloof, but he was very obviously ticked off. Joe and I drove him to the rehab center in Aliquippa, where we spoke with a drug counselor and told her our concerns. The counselor then talked to Patrick separately. She tested him and told us that she would call us with the results and her recommendations. Patrick was silent in the car on the way back to school. When the counselor called us later that afternoon, she said that he had tested positive for THC and that Patrick had been forthcoming about his pot use. She felt that the best treatment plan for him was to place him in a partial hospitalization program, where he would attend sessions three days a week. Each session was three hours long, with one of them being a family session that Joe and I could attend with him. The treatment center was in Ambridge, not a short drive. Gas was expensive, and we had been very careful about unnecessary driving, trying to make as few trips as possible. Instead of making four trips to drop off and pick up, Joe drove to Ambridge and stayed in town, using the WiFi at McDonald's to work on his job search or to study for his Farmers Insurance course.

Patrick hated rehab. He hated the loss of his freedom and sitting for three hours, listening and sharing with other addicts. He swore that he was not an addict and that he used pot because he enjoyed it, not because he was addicted. He said he could quit whenever he wanted. We didn't know whether he was an addict or not, and it didn't matter to us one way or another. As far as we were concerned, he was drinking and using illicit drugs, he was a minor, and he was our child. We wouldn't allow him to continue the behavior, and we would do whatever was in our power to prevent him from destroying his life. We'd had many conversations with him before that point. He wanted us to relax and let him have fun. He wanted to know why we couldn't be cool like his friends' parents. He claimed that some of them used drugs and even partied with their kids. We had no idea when he had become so delusional. We had always talked openly about drugs and how damaging they were. We frowned upon the Hollywood glamorization of partying and drug and alcohol abuse. He hadn't been serious when he asked us to loosen up, but he tried to lead us to believe that we were in the minority, that partying and using drugs was a normal part of growing up. He tried to convince us that it wasn't a big deal and that most kids were doing it. We told him not to believe the lie, which he may have thought that was the case because he had surrounded himself with kids who used drugs, but the majority of kids were not of that mind-set. We felt hopeful that the rehab would help him to see the light. That he would be exposed to people who had been devastated by drug use and want something better for himself. We hoped that hearing the truth and facts about the harmful effects of drug use from people other than us would make a difference.

Patrick was required to attend regular Narcotics Anonymous meetings and was randomly drug tested at the rehab center. He grew increasingly angry with us and maintained a bad attitude about absolutely everything. Any and every attempt I made to talk with him about even the most mundane thing was met with hostility. When I offered to make him a dinner of his choice or surprised him with his favorite snack, he held only contempt for me. My heart ached for the son that I knew before he had taken the first step down the wrong path. I am certain that his bad attitude was due to withdrawals, mixed with the frustration of being under constant surveillance and scrutiny by his family and the rehab. He was never left alone. We had no choice but to watch him. We had been through too much—the lying, the stealing, the hiding, and sneaking. We scoured the yard and found cigarettes, lighters, tobacco chew, beer cans, and alcohol bottles—none of which had been purchased by us. They were stashed in the garage, shed, and hidden in the yard. Each time something turned up, he claimed that it must have been left by the previous owners. He brought home and hid more iTouches, no doubt purchased with the money he had stolen from us. One of the iTouches was found by Joseph, quite by accident, hidden on a book-shelf between some of my knitting books. Joe and I decided to give it to Christina since Patrick had finally admitted to taking hers from her. We still had the one we had confiscated from him in November locked up in the safe. We told Christina that she was allowed to have it but that she had to turn it in to us every night. We told her that she needed to guard it vigilantly because we felt certain that Patrick would take it at his first opportunity. Our kids were held hostage once again, unable to keep money in their rooms. They had to hide or lock up anything of value.

Within two days of giving Christina the iTouch, it disappeared. It was a Saturday morning, and we had just called everyone down to get their new chore lists. Christina left the iTouch in her room, charging under her pillow, when she came down for her list. When she went back upstairs less than three minutes later, it was gone. Patrick had come in from the garage right about the same time that Christina discovered that it was missing. Patrick stood in the kitchen, wide-eyed and feigning innocence when he heard of the disappearance. We knew better. It was the weekend, and that meant that there were parties to get to. We tore the house apart. We pulled sheets and bedding out of closets, and books, toys, and games off of shelves. We emptied drawers and looked high and low. We turned over mattresses and pulled out beds and dressers. Joe kept Patrick in our bedroom with him while the other kids helped me search, but we found nothing. Patrick refused to tell us where it was. We knew he had it, and he knew we knew he had it, but he refused to come clean. He had nothing to lose. He had already been deprived of everything because of his behavior. Joe sat in the chair in our bedroom holding Michael on his lap, while Patrick sat on the love seat. Joe lit a candle and said a prayer to St. Anthony that it would turn up. While I searched the house in a mad frenzy, Joe prayed. Five minutes after he lit the candle, I walked into the garage and pulled up the sheet that we used to cover the van seat. We had removed it before the move to make room for our pets on the road trip, and we still hadn't put it back in the van. There, lying on the seat, was the shiny silver iTouch. I picked it up and walked through the house with it. By the time I reached our bedroom, I had a following of little kids who were amazed that it had been found. I held it up for Joe and Patrick to see. Joe's jaw dropped, but Patrick looked at me smugly and again said, "Congratulations."

Somehow we had begun a sad and tragic competition. Joe and I did our best to stay a step ahead of Patrick, and Patrick always seemed to be two steps ahead of us. We felt like wardens. Christina reached for the iTouch, expecting me to hand it over to her, but I told her she couldn't have it. I sent Joseph for the sledgehammer. The kids begged me not to destroy it. They all wanted to keep it, promising to take turns with it and only use it in our presence. I refused. I took the iTouch out to the front driveway. With all my kids crowded around, and Patrick watching from our bedroom window, still under Joe's supervision, I bashed it to smithereens. I wouldn't have it in my home.

The next day was Sunday. Fr. Melee, a visiting priest, said Mass at Christ the Divine Teacher. In his homily, he talked about keeping a truly Catholic home. He said that there were certain things that have no business in Catholic homes, and he challenged us to get rid of them. My lips formed into a smile as I glanced down the pew at Joe and the kids. They too were wide-eyed at what we knew was not a coincidence. More and more, we had been making a conscious effort to keep a Catholic home. Joe looked back at me with the same knowing smile. The Holy Spirit always seemed to deliver the message that I most needed every Sunday.

The iTouches continued to be smuggled in, and somehow we always managed to discover them. We wouldn't have had an issue with them except for the fact that Patrick insisted on using them for his demise. We simply wouldn't allow it. Joe bought a metal detector wand like the ones they use in the airports. At the rate that the iTouches were being brought into the house, he felt it was a necessary tool. Patrick would never admit to how he acquired them, but Joe believed that he was buying them with the money he had stolen from the safe. The iTouches had all been used, older versions. At one point, we had five of them locked up. One afternoon, one of our older kids told us that Patrick had yet another iTouch. One of the blessings of a large family is that during a crisis, you have a team of snitches that rally together. We all wanted Patrick to stop his craziness. None of his brothers and sisters wanted to see him go down the wrong path. They had all witnessed how his behavior and attitude had changed and was growing uglier. They saw who he was hanging around with at school, and it worried them. We had no control over who he chose as friends or associated with at school. Several of his teachers and counselors had warned him and had also talked to Joseph about the choice of kids he was hanging out with. They were concerned. Joe took Patrick to his treatment session without mentioning the fact that he had been seen with another iTouch. Joe texted to tell me that he planned to search him when he got home. We had decided that whenever possible, our strategy would be the element of surprise, catching him off guard. I searched the house while they were gone, hoping to find the device, but Joe was convinced that he had it on him somewhere. We got into the habit of searching his backpack each day after school. After finding cigarettes and chew, he quit hiding stuff in his bag and, instead, started stashing things on the property, under bushes, or in the woodpile. When Joe got home with Patrick, he took out his wand and made him strip down to his shorts in the garage. He found the iTouch wedged between his cheeks. Not the ones on his face.

The game that we were playing was not fun. We wanted it to stop. Patrick showed no sign of giving up, and we had no intention of quitting. He was miserable to live with. He had become belligerent, and at times violent with his brothers and sisters. I made every effort to keep the peace, avoiding arguments and conflict, keeping the younger kids away from him. He egged them on and went out of his way to upset everyone over the slightest thing. He continuously defied us and purposely did exactly what we told him not to do. We didn't allow him to leave the property. If he wanted to go for a walk in the forest or do anything outside, he had to have one or more of his siblings with him. He was never left alone or unsupervised. We told him that once his attitude and behavior changed, we would let up on him. Our control over him made him madder. He cooked food without asking at random times of the day. He wouldn't just eat the fruit or other snacks that we made available, he used up items that I had bought to prepare meals for the family. He refused to eat at dinnertime with the rest of us, claiming that he wasn't hungry. He would return to the kitchen a few hours later and start cooking things, leaving his mess behind. We made him sit with us at dinnertime; whether or not he chose to eat was up to him, but we wouldn't allow him to make a meal later on. It worked to a certain extent. He just waited until late at night after we all went to sleep to eat something. He pushed every button he could, hoping to wear us down to the point of giving up. We refused to give him an inch. When we prayed our evening rosary together, he sat stone faced on the couch and refused to participate, but we insisted that he be in the room with us. We prayed openly for him after our rosary, asking God to help him and heal him of his addiction. I wasn't seeing any results or feeling that my prayers were being answered, but I continued to pray nevertheless. I received the strength I needed to get through each day, and each new challenge that I was faced with. New challenges continued to come every day.

I called Patrick's drug counselor and told her that he wasn't showing any signs of progress. He was angry, disrespectful, and was still sneaking out of the house. She tested him at his next session and found him positive for marijuana. I called the high school and spoke at length with his coach, Coach Hamilton, as well as the vice principal, Mr. Marsilio. Both gentlemen were incredibly supportive. I told them that we needed help but had no idea where else to turn. I wanted Patrick away from the kids he was hanging around with. I shared with them all the Facebook postings, and even made copies for them. I hoped that the information would help them to deal with the kids who were selling drugs. I told them that they had a problem at the school and that something needed to be done about it. I had contacts, names and phone numbers that I had taken from his iTouch, as well as his Facebook page.

Mr. Marsilio told me that there was an alternative school, based out of the high school, that we might try. It operated in the evening, and Patrick would not have contact with anyone other than his teachers. We both agreed that it may be a solution, but I worried that he wouldn't be able to continue his drug counseling because of the evening hours. I tried to discern which was more important. After discussing the alternative school with his drug counselor, she suggested we try to find a rehab who could assign a counselor to come to the house, and she gave me some numbers to call. Before the end of the school day, everything had been arranged. Patrick would attend the alternative school and would also begin in home drug counseling after the Christmas break. We didn't tell him.

TWENTY-NINE

A Medical Whirlwind

Beaver Falls, Pennsylvania, 2012

*O*ur kids all had their well-child checkups prior to leaving Texas. Once I received our Medicaid cards in the mail, I made an appointment for Michael's six-month well-baby check. After going over his medical history, I told the new pediatrician, Dr. Whistler, that Michael had seen Dr. Beauchamp, a pediatric ophthalmologist, in Texas. Dr. Beauchamp had recommended that we follow up after our move to Pennsylvania. Dr. Beauchamp had been Sarah's ophthalmologist, and he had taken a look at Michael's eyes at her last appointment. Michael had been a newborn at the time, and I explained that the prenatal MRI doctor suspected that he may have septo-optic dysplasia. Dr. Beauchamp, out of his kindness and without a separate appointment, checked Michael out. He told me upon his examination that Michael's optic nerves looked smaller than normal, but that he was confident that he had good vision. He recommended he be rechecked in six months. Dr. Whistler noted that Michael continued to follow his own growth curve, still in the tenth percentile for height and weight, but his head circumference was in the ninetieth percentile. He seemed pleased with his ability to track and follow with his eyes, but was a little concerned that his head was still lagging, and he wasn't yet sitting up on his own. He referred him to Dr. Cheng, a pediatric ophthalmologist in Wexford. I also made an appointment with Dr. Canon, the urologist that we had been referred to by Michael's urology office in Dallas.

We drove to UPMC, University of Pittsburgh Medical Centre, Children's Hospital in Pittsburgh, for the urology appointment. It was a long wait, but Dr. Cannon was very nice and extremely thorough. He had gone to school with Michael's previous urologist in Texas. It was a relief to get the referral, and I couldn't help but believe that God had put all the right people in our paths when we needed them. Dr. Cannon said that Michael definitely needed surgery to descend his testicles. They were up in his abdomen, and just as his previous urologist had explained, Dr. Cannon said that he may need more than one surgery to correct it. If the vas deferens were very short, they would have to be clamped until they grew long enough to be descended. A second surgery would need to be done to descend them. The best-case scenario would be to simply descend them, but he wouldn't know for sure until surgery. Michael had already had an ultrasound, in which they couldn't detect testicles at all. There was a possibility that they were completely absent or that they had atrophied, in which case they would need to be removed. Dr. Canon scheduled surgery for March 28. I had hoped that they would descend on their own, but it wouldn't be so. I hated the thought of Michael having to go through surgery, but I knew that it was for the best.

Dr. Cheng, the new pediatric ophthalmologist, was also very nice. He was, however, very concerned by how puffy Michael's soft spot was. He was very pleased with Michael's ability to track and follow with his eyes. He noted that he had some nystagmus, a kind of shaking of his eyes, but said that it was not severe. On a scale of one to ten, it was a three. He noted that his eyes were straight and even, and he felt he had good vision, even though his optic nerves were smaller than normal. He asked me to request a copy of the MRI that had been done at birth, and told me that he wanted to refer us to a neurosurgeon. That threw me. Neurosurgeon? When I asked him why, he told me that he was concerned that there was fluid building up on Michael's brain. Even though it wasn't affecting him then, he was afraid that it could eventually put pressure on his optic nerve, which could potentially cause him to lose his eyesight. How could that be? I had taken him to all his doctor's appointments. He had been well monitored. I was the one who had rushed him to the pediatrician's office in Southlake the morning that his head mysteriously puffed up, but his doctor had not been concerned. Now all a sudden, this doctor was telling me that I needed to take him to a neurosurgeon, and quickly. Feeling panicked, I drove directly home. Joe was concerned when I told him, but he told me not to get stressed out. If something was wrong, we wanted to know. It was better to check it out and err on the side of caution. Dr. Cheng's office made the referral, and the neurosurgeon office called me that same afternoon. After answering a series of questions, the neurosurgeon's secretary told me that she felt Michael should be seen by a neurologist, not a neurosurgeon. That made more sense to me. I was relieved. I called the neurologist office and made the appointment.

It was December, and we were all excited for Christmas. We knew it would be a slim year, gift-wise, but we planned to go all out with decorating and baking. Food was our only indulgence and source of pleasure. Collected over many years, we had accumulated loads of Christmas decorations with which to make a festive, family holiday.

Michael's neurology appointment with Dr. Cleves-Bayon had been booked for late December, just a few days before Christmas. She was serious and exceedingly thorough. She did a series of tests with him, noting that the only delays he demonstrated involved gross motor skills due to his low muscle tone. At eight months old, he was not yet sitting up on his own, nor was he bearing any weight on his feet. She gave me a list of specialists that she wanted him to see, and further tests she wanted performed. Instantly, I didn't like her. I did not want to believe that anything was wrong with my baby. Certainly, I knew that he hadn't met some of his milestones, but we had all seen progress. He could roll over both ways and was able to creep all over the floor. He was a happy, smiling, social, and active baby who spent his days in the open family room. He was surrounded by his siblings, toys, pets, and music. He played, rolled, crept, and explored his surroundings. He was beginning to babble and hum along to familiar songs. He had a good appetite and had begun eating a full range of baby foods, cereal, fruits, vegetables, meats, as well as a few tastes of table food, and continued to nurse a few times a day. He slept through the nights and never got so much as a cold. After Dr. Cleves-Bayon listed off the specialists, she said that she expected me to schedule appointments with them at Children's Hospital of Pittsburgh as soon as possible.

One of the specialists that she referred us to was a neurosurgeon. I couldn't get my head wrapped around the sudden bombardment of medical intervention when I hadn't noticed anything even remotely concerning. Also on the list were a geneticist, endocrinologist, and physical therapist. She ordered a series of blood work and an MRI. She wanted all the tests done immediately. I left her office feeling like someone had played a dirty trick on me. Couldn't this woman see with her own eyes that my little baby was perfect? I had been with him around the clock every day since his birth. I would have known if something was wrong. I refused to believe it, but I dutifully made all the appointments. Because it was so close to the Christmas holidays, all the tests and appointments were made for after the new year. It was both a blessing and a curse. As much as I tried to enjoy the holidays, it loomed over my head and weighed heavy on my heart. There is much truth to the saying, "Ignorance is bliss." I wasn't completely ignorant anymore, but I didn't want to borrow trouble. Michael was happy and healthy, and I would continue to enjoy him. We all would.

We dove into our holiday baking. Having bought giant bags of sugar and flour at Costco, the girls poured over the butter-stained recipe cards and the old standby, *Better Homes and Gardens* cookbook, that Joe and I got as a wedding gift. They picked out their favorite recipes, writing out lists of the ingredients that we still needed. The food stamps were very helpful over the holidays, giving us the ability to cook and bake nice things and enabling us to celebrate and indulge. It was a gift. The kitchen was a hub of activity over the Christmas break for the whole family. Everyone got involved, carrying out big bags of flour and sugar, organizing, measuring, and mixing ingredients. We baked for days, turning out dozens of several varieties of cookies, pies, squares, and breads. Everyone pitched in, wiping down counters, sweeping floors, washing pots, pans, and utensils. We wrapped tins and containers that would last us more than a few months. It was how we had always prepared for Christmas and one of our favorite ways to bond. I was grateful for the ability to maintain that tradition, even through our hardship.

With our decorations set up throughout the house, the Christmas tree glistening with its clear lights and familiar baubles in the family room, the illuminated village houses in a row along the bar, scented pinecones in baskets in every room, and the Nativity on the table in the foyer, it felt like home. The sparkle, the smell of fresh baking, and the warm fire burning in the fireplace. All of us together watching Christmas movies and listening to carols while the little kids played on the floor or out in the snow reminded us to count our many blessings. We knew things could be much worse.

Cathy, Al, Bob, and Nanette mailed us a very generous check so that we could buy Christmas presents for the kids. We had not planned on Christmas shopping, other than possibly buying a few new clothes on my Old Navy card. They wanted to make sure that our kids had something under the tree. Tracy and Blair also very generously adopted our family and shopped online, ordering several Christmas gifts for each of the kids, and had them delivered to the house. It was overwhelming that all our friends were so incredibly and consistently generous to our family. We were absolutely humbled. We had always been able to provide a nice Christmas. We realized that Christmas isn't about gifts; but as parents, we enjoyed giving our kids a few of the items that they had on their lists, and seeing their smiles on Christmas morning. Especially the little ones. Understanding our situation, none of our kids had asked us for anything. They knew we simply did not have the money to spend. Our friends knew that too, and they stepped in. I shopped carefully with the money that our friends sent; and every day, for nearly two weeks, the dogs barked announcing another online delivery made by the Korschuns. It took hours to wrap everything. I covered the ever growing pile on the sofa in our bedroom with a sleeping bag, to hide it from peeking eyes.

Christmas morning arrived with a dusting of snow. The kids' surprised squeals at the sight of the gifts piled up under the tree woke us up. Joe and I breathed a sigh of relief and whispered a prayer of thanks, for sparing our kids from disappointment. We took pictures of everyone with their loot and texted them to our friends, wanting them to share in the fun they had provided. They received more than Joe and I would have bought, even if he hadn't been out of work.

Patrick assembled Ryan's riding toy and Michael's new bouncy seat. He seemed to be in a better mood, was less combative, and more engaged. Being home for two weeks on Christmas break away from his friends seemed to be the reason. The kids spent the day playing with their new games and toys. We all watched movies and snacked while I got the turkey stuffed and into the oven. It was a quiet, peaceful, and restful day perfect in every way and a wonderful Christmas break altogether. We enjoyed the unscheduled days, playing outside, playing inside, and simply being together. I did some knitting, we all ate too much, and none of us looked forward to school starting back.

When Patrick came down to the foyer with the rest of the high school kids to head out for the bus, we informed him that he wouldn't be going back to school that day. We told him that we had arranged for him to attend Blackhawk's alternative school. His school day would start in the evening. The information caught him very much off guard, and he was not at all happy about it. He told us that he thought it was a stupid idea and that it wouldn't solve anything. We told him that he may be right, but he had left us no other option. It was either alternative school or a live-in drug rehab. That got his attention. He slowly began to realize that we were not going to give up. We hadn't told any of the other kids about our plan either, so the first morning back to school was filled with more excitement than usual. Patrick grumbled around the house most of the day, and we kept a close eye on him.

The alternative school was held in the high school building. It ran four nights a week from 3:00 p.m. till 8:00 p.m., with Fridays off. It was not a well-publicized arrangement, and there were very few students enrolled. It had been set up for special circumstances, and we were grateful that Patrick had been accepted. Once a week, a drug counselor came to our house to meet with and test him. I finally felt like we had begun to gain some ground. We believed we had found a solution that the new arrangement would fix him. Patrick wouldn't have access to his druggy friends; he would continue his education, and still get drug counseling. He would have around-the-clock supervision. Would I ever learn? Before the end of the first week, Patrick snuck out of the school. He told his teacher that he needed to use the bathroom and never went back to class. Joe and I were shocked when the teacher called to tell us that she didn't know where Patrick was. When I returned to the school that evening to pick him up, he got in the car acting like everything was just fine, pretending that he had been there the whole time. He thought he had gotten away with it. I looked directly at him and told him that he had better quit being an idiot, he was only hurting himself. He told me to put him back into regular school and he would stop. I told him that he needed to prove to me that he was improving before I did that. It was a battle of the wills. The next day, I walked him into the school and delivered him to the vice principal, who walked him to his class. I told Mr. Marsilio that I was prepared to stay for the four hours while Patrick was there, to ensure that he stayed where he was supposed to. He assured me that that wasn't necessary. He was certain Patrick wouldn't pull another stunt like the night before. He was wrong. Patrick did it again. Twice. Each time with a different teacher. The third time we received the call that Patrick had left and never came back, I drove my van to the church parking lot across from the high school. I parked facing the school and watched for him. The longer I sat there, the angrier I grew over, yet again, being duped. What in the world were we doing? Would it ever end?

I decided to call the police. Patrick was truant, and I was going to report him. I was tired of dealing with him, and obviously the school wasn't able to handle him either. They only had one kid to watch, and he had duped them as well. I told the dispatcher what was going on and where I was parked. She told me she would send an officer right over. I was surprised to see not only one, but three cruisers pull into the lot. Four police officers and the chief got out. I stepped out of the van and explained the whole story, giving them the background, leading up to the decision to place Patrick in alternative school. They shook their heads sympathetically and assured me that

I wasn't alone. They had seen it all before, but they were impressed by the lengths at which we were going to keep our son from a life of destruction. I asked them what else we could do. I asked them if there was a scared straight program. There wasn't. I begged them to take him somewhere, on a jail tour to teach him a lesson. I was afraid that he would end up dead. They told me that they wished that there was something that they could do, but they were between a rock and a hard place. Unless he broke the law, there was nothing they could do besides talk to him. One of the officers said it sounded like he needed his butt beat. I laughed and said, "Yeah, we've been told that before, by more than one cop in Texas. We tried it, and it ended badly."

He then asked, "How so?"

I told him that we'd had a claim filed against us with Children and Youth Services shortly after moving to Pennsylvania. He asked me what came of it. I told him that the claim had been investigated, deemed unfounded, and would be expunged. He told me that we were within our parental rights to use physical discipline with our children, especially in a situation such as the one we were currently dealing with. He said he highly recommended it. That if it were his son, that's what he would do. I told him all of what we had tried—the constant supervision, no friends, no electronics, alternative school, and drug counseling. The other officers listened in. They told me that they wished that more parents were as relentless as we were. I told them that it all seemed fruitless and we were exhausted. Patrick was still rebelling, and he was still using drugs. They said that even though it may not seem like it, what we were doing was making a difference. We were showing him that we were not going to make things easy for him. We were also setting a precedent for our other kids, who were watching it all very closely. They told me not to give up and to tell Joe to dust off his paddle.

With a description of what Patrick was wearing, the chief and two of the officers left with the photo I gave them. One of the remaining officers asked me what time I usually returned to pick Patrick up. I told him around eight o'clock. He instructed me to go home and come back at eight, that he would meet me there to talk to him.

He assured me that if he was spotted before then, they would call me. I went home and told Joe the whole story. Once again, we felt like we were at least doing something. Being validated by the police officers was something worth celebrating. We hated that we were going through such a nightmare, that Patrick was being reckless and destructive. We loved him and felt powerless over the addiction that had gripped his life. We were fighting him every step of his way to destroying his future. We were beyond exhausted, but the assurance from the officers that we were doing the right thing was the boost we needed to keep at it. If they hadn't encouraged me that night, I'm not entirely sure, but I may have given up. I do know that God always seemed to send the right people exactly when I needed them.

It was cold when I went back to pick Patrick up at the school that night. I pulled the van up along the curb and waited. He walked along the sidewalk in front of the school as if he had been there all along, with his head bent down and his hood pulled up against the cold. I popped the locks, and he got into the van. I very calmly asked, "Where were you?"

He answered, "At the school."

Disappointed but not surprised, I looked directly into his eyes. He was so used to lying. I didn't respond. In my rearview mirror, I caught a glimpse of the police cruiser pulling up behind me. Patrick glanced over his shoulder when I rolled his window down, meeting the officer who was standing next to it, face-to-face. He told Patrick that he needed to quit being stupid and that he should appreciate the fact that he had parents willing to go to great lengths to help him stay on track. Parents who were making sacrifices for him despite all the other things that they were dealing with. Going out of their way to bring him to the alternative school so that he could continue his drug counseling. He told Patrick that he seemed like a smart kid and that he shouldn't waste his time mixed up with the wrong crowd. He also told him that if he heard from us again or got caught skipping school, he would see to it that he was placed in the alternative school in Zelienople or Pittsburgh. He assured him that they were not the kind of places that he wanted to be in. Those were the schools that

Joe drove to. They were the end of the road. That was the last time Patrick skipped alternative school.

Michael's endocrinology appointment and MRI were scheduled on the same day. The endocrinologist used the opportunity to request a picture of his pituitary gland on the MRI, as well as order a series of blood work. I was annoyed that he needed more blood work done since he'd already had a ton taken for genetics, only a week earlier. The endocrinologist was very sweet to Michael and said that he looked great. He promised to call me with the test results as soon as they came in.

Michael was sedated for the MRI. I was allowed stay with him for the few seconds it took him to go to sleep, before heading to the family waiting area. When he was done, I was called back to the recovery room where I held him until he woke up again. He came out of the sedation quickly while I sang to him and rocked him in the chair. I was grateful to have the MRI over with and very anxious to take him home. The nurses commented on how sweet he was and said that he had done remarkably well during the scan. While they checked his vitals and monitored him, I shared his story with them. I never passed up an opportunity to tell people about what a miracle Michael was. Not only did it reconfirm that very fact for me each time I repeated it, but it amazed everyone who heard it. I especially loved sharing Michael's story with medical professionals. I prayed that it would inspire them to give hope to other patients who were faced with difficult health concerns. I made sure I told everyone that prayer was what had given us hope and brought our miracle to us.

Michael had an appointment with Dr. Green, the neurosurgeon, the very next day, so I would be driving him right back to Children's Hospital in Pittsburgh early in the morning. The recovery nurses called to see if he could be released. It so happened that Dr. Cleves-Bayon, Michael's neurologist and the doctor who had ordered all the tests, was on call. She and the radiologist both looked at the MRI. It was the radiologist who came to speak with me in the recovery room. He said that there was indeed fluid on Michael's brain, but that because his head was so large, no pressure was being put on it. He called it a compensated hydrocephalus. He felt that he would need a shunt, but didn't feel that it was urgent. Dr. Cleves-Bayon came into the room next. She wanted us to stay for an emergency shunt operation. I was confused by the conflicting reports. I told her that the radiologist had just spoken with me and what he had said. I also told her that we had an appointment scheduled with Dr. Green the next morning, and that I wanted to discuss surgery with her first. Dr. Cleves-Bayon let us go home. It had been a long day. It was nine o'clock at night before we were released. With our big bag slung over one shoulder, I carried Michael, bundled in a blanket, down to the parking garage and buckled him into his car seat.

I was emotionally exhausted. If it hadn't been for the GPS, I never would have found my way home. I hate driving at night anyway and driving in the unfamiliar big city of Pittsburgh, combined with the anxiety that was building up—was a bad combination. I didn't want Michael to have surgery. I had prayed that he wouldn't need a shunt, but I wanted what was best for him. Driving home with my sleeping angel boy and a million emotions battling through my head and heart, I gave it up to God. If a shunt was something that he needed, God would protect him through it. I told God out loud that I expected Him to take care of my boy.

When we got home to the sleeping house, I nursed Michael, changed his diaper, and put him to bed. I repacked our same bag for the next morning's appointment before changing into my pajamas and laying my head down on my own pillow. I was desperate for what little sleep I knew I would get.

The drive to Children's Hospital had become all too familiar. It was still dark when we left the next morning, and despite my prayers, the knot that had begun on our drive home from the hospital had grown overnight. I talked and sang to Michael along the way, slowing and stopping through the many construction zones, in an attempt to reassure him and comfort myself. Michael was a good little travel companion. He played with his toys and sucked noisily on his pacifier, cooing and babbling in response to my questions and silly songs before falling asleep. I got three rosaries said along the way. I was not exactly certain how or what to pray for, other than Michael's well-being. I tried my best to leave it all in God's hands. His will be done.

Dr. Green was very nice, and I especially liked the resident neurosurgeon who came in with her, Dr. Karandahkar. Dr. Green went over the findings of the MRI with me and said that it was very good news. Although there was indeed fluid, no damage had been done to Michael's brain. His head was large, and the fluid was not enough to create pressure. Her concern was that it was likely that the fluid would continue to accumulate, which would be dangerous, potentially fatal. Although she didn't feel that it was an emergency, she did want the shunt placement done soon. She said she had an opening the following Friday. That was faster than I would have thought for not being an emergency. I thanked both doctors. I wasn't happy that Michael would have to go through the surgery, but I accepted it. I called Joe on the way home to tell him, and then I called Cathy, Nanette, and Tracy. They were all an incredible source of support and encouragement and assured me that Michael was in good hands.

I tried to prepare myself mentally for Michael's surgery. I prayed constantly and did my very best not to worry. I found it amazing that God had protected him. Yes, it appeared that he needed the shunt, but the fact that he hadn't suffered any brain damage was a miracle. God had ensured that his skull was large enough to give the fluid plenty of room and not put pressure on his brain. His skull was large enough because the fluid had been there during his prenatal development. A lot of fluid. It had forced his skull to form largely. The fluid had miraculously disappeared completely, before it could create problems. For some reason, it had begun to fill up again, making a shunt placement necessary. The doctors couldn't explain why it had happened. They said that it was very fortunate that Michael hadn't shown any symptoms of brain pressure, excessive sleepiness, vomiting, or seizures. I guess some things we won't ever know. I know God planned it that way to teach me things. Lessons in trust and patience among others, and to keep me on my knees. I had become comfortable, slacking off in my prayer life, and I think God wanted me to keep talking to Him. He knew that he could get my attention with my kids.

Nanette and Bob told me that they would be in town when Michael had his surgery. We knew that they were planning to come to town before the surgery had been scheduled, and we had planned to have them over for dinner. We hadn't seen them since we had moved in. The week before the surgery, a stomach bug tore through the house. It was a violent ugly bug, and none of the kids, or Joe, were spared. Each of them got it, two at a time, within a day of each other. At one point, there were six down at once. Thankfully, I had been spared. I kept Michael away from everyone, quarantining him in our bedroom. I didn't want him getting sick before his surgery.

I packed a bag for Michael and a few things for myself for our overnight stay in the hospital. Because he couldn't eat for several hours before the surgery, I woke him up at 4:00 a.m. to nurse him and fed him his cereal and fruit before his fast began. Joe put the bag in the van, and I pulled out of the driveway, again in the dark, en route to Pittsburgh at 6:00 a.m. Michael looked so small and fragile in his stroller, where he sat playing happily in the waiting room with the rattle that Nanette had bought him. My heart swelled with love as I looked at his beautiful innocent face. He had no idea what he would be enduring that day, which was a blessing. I had prayed all the way to the hospital. My dread and anxiety had been replaced with resignation, and I begged God to guide the medical team who would be caring for Michael from start to finish and that the surgery would be a success with no complications.

I was permitted to carry Michael to the operating room and hold him while he was sedated. The anesthesiologist told me to kiss his little cheek, before I was escorted out by one of the nurses to the family waiting room. I sat in a chair, surrounded by several other families, and watched the monitor that displayed Michael's ID number. It showed what stage he was at in surgery. I had taken along my knitting and worked on a pair of wool socks I had started for Bob. They were supposed to be part of his Christmas gift, but I hadn't had the time to finish them. Knitting kept my hands busy and my mind from worrying. I tried to pray along with the rhythm of the movements, stitch after stitch. When the surgery was over, Dr. Green came into the waiting room to find me. We went into a tiny consultation room where she told me that everything had gone very well. She said that I would be able to see him soon in the recovery room. She told me what to watch for and how to care for him once I brought him home. She wanted to see him back in four weeks.

I couldn't get to him fast enough. I was taken to the recovery room where Michael lay in a crib. I stifled a gasp when I saw his poor little head. His incision looked awful and was a lot bigger than I had expected. A large semicircle of stitches on the right side of his head, with a bump under the skin where the valve had been placed. It looked painful. The nurse assured me that once it was cleaned, it would look a lot better, and she assured me that it would heal just fine. A tube had been connected to the valve and placed under the skin, going down his neck and into his abdominal cavity, where the fluid would drain. All I wanted was to hold my little boy. The nurse busily checked his vitals and entered things into the computer. I stood next to the crib and rubbed his back until he began to stir. I picked him up, still connected to an IV and monitors, careful not to disconnect anything. Rocking him in the chair, Michael guzzled a bottle of Pedialite. As I rocked and talked to him, the nurses chatted with me and commented on how sweet and beautiful he was and how he obviously loved his mommy very much. Yes, he did. Not wanting to spare the opportunity, I told them about his journey and just how special he truly was. Just like all the others, they were amazed to hear how far he had come and how blessed we had been. Then I told them about Bob and Nanette and our journey to Beaver Falls. Sharing the stories of our struggles and how God had carried us through had become second nature and helped to remind myself of my blessings. The reaction was always the same. People seemed to be inspired, and more than once I was told, "Wow. You should write a book."

The nurses were wonderful. When we were brought up to a room on the pediatric floor, I held him in the chair, grateful for the successful surgery. Seeing my exhaustion, the nurse told me to stretch out on the sofa at the end of the crib. I was too afraid that Michael would roll over and pull out his IV or get tangled in the leads and wires, so I leaned back in the chair with him nuzzled under my chin and closed my eyes.

When Nanette walked through the door to the dimly lit room that evening, I felt much less isolated. It was comforting to have Joe home with the rest of the kids, holding down the fort. God had seen to it that the timing of Michael's surgery and Bob and Nanette's visit coincided. She and Bob had just finished dinner with their friends, and he had dropped her off at the hospital. Her company gave me blessed relief. We chatted in the quiet of the room while we took turns rocking Michael. We had never really been able to enjoy a visit on our own without the business of little kids running around. Though the circumstances weren't the greatest, it was a sweet time, visiting with a very kind lady who had touched our lives in profound ways.

Nanette stayed the whole night and held Michael for much of it, insisting that I sleep. She had given up the comfort of a hotel bed and time with her husband during their vacation to sit and keep me company in the hospital. The night nurse came in to check on Michael and saw Nanette holding him in the chair, and me lying on the sofa, trying to sleep with one eye open. I overheard her comment on how nice it was to have Grandma there to help. Nanette and I exchanged a knowing look and started to giggle. I was grateful to be able to lay my head down and shut my eyes, but I slept with my ears pricked for any sounds that Michael needed me. Nobody sleeps well in a hospital with nurses dashing in and out at every hour, turning on flashlights and checking vitals, but I'd gotten just enough rest to keep alert. I was anxious for Michael to be discharged so that I could take him home.

Nanette bought us coffee and Danishes in the morning. Our mood was light as we chatted and marveled at Michael, who seemed to be doing really well. The doctor came in and checked him out, giving him the all clear, and said we could go home. Michael had begun to eat some of his baby cereal and fruit, and I had nursed him. Nanette left, saying that she would call the next day to see how things were going. She hoped that she and Bob could come by the house to see everyone before they headed back to Texas. I was glad that we would get the opportunity to have them over after all. The nurse took out Michael's IV, gave him some liquid Tylenol, and he immediately threw up. A lot. We weren't certain if he'd had a reaction to the medication or if it was something else, but the nurse didn't feel comfortable letting us leave. I certainly didn't want to take him home until I knew for sure that he was okay. Several hours passed, and he continued to throw up. He was taken down for an x-ray to make sure that there wasn't some sort of shunt malfunction. Everything appeared to be working fine. He didn't have a fever, so they ruled out an infection. Any time I tried to feed or nurse him, he refused. I urged him to drink the Pedialite, but he continued to vomit. There was no explanation. I called Joe to tell him that we wouldn't be coming home as we'd expected. Joe was worried but assured me that it was fortunate that we were still in the hospital.

I called Cathy, who was cat-sitting for Nanette, to give her an update. Cathy always made me smile. Just hearing her sweet voice made me feel better. I told her that the nurses would be returning to put in another IV. It broke my heart that after all he had already suffered through, Michael would have to endure more pokes. Cathy told me that she would pray that the IV would go in quickly, easily, and not be too painful. I thanked her and hung up the phone when two nurses came into the room. They looked at both of Michael's little arms and determined that the lighting was very poor in his room, so they decided to take him to a treatment room down the hall. I asked if I could go with him, and they told me that I absolutely could. I was very grateful for the parent-friendly environment. I am sure that children must benefit greatly by having moms and dads close by during such scary ordeals.

The two nurses chatted away with each other while they studied Michael's hands and feet. Bending his wrists and ankles, turning them this way and that, trying to find a good vein. They seemed concerned and, after some debate, decided on his foot. They turned on a special light. One nurse got the elastic around his leg and poked in the needle, carefully moving it around a little, trying to get a result. Nothing. Just as she was about to pull the needle out, the little tube started to fill up. She looked surprised. Both nurses remarked at how unlikely it had been, but seemed very pleased that it only took one poke. I told them that my friend Cathy was at home praying for them both. They smiled and told me to thank her for them.

Bob called me that evening from the steakhouse, where they were having dinner, and asked me how I liked my steak. He told me that Nanette planned to come back to the hospital that night and that she would be bringing me dinner. It was the best steak I'd ever eaten, and it came with a loaded baked potato. I felt bad that poor little Michael couldn't eat, but I was starving; and I knew that if I didn't keep my strength up, I wouldn't be able to nurse him. Nanette held Michael while I devoured my meal. She had brought along a big bag of things that she and Cathy had bought for the kids, goodies and little gifts. She also brought loads of Eat 'n' Park smile cookies for the nurses on Michael's floor. She was always thinking of ways to make people feel appreciated, and the nurses were thrilled with the treats. Michael had a much better night. He hadn't thrown up for most of the afternoon and all the night. Whatever it had been, it seemed to be over. I suspected it was the stomach bug that everyone else had at home, and when I mentioned it to the nurses and the doctor, they all agreed that it was entirely possible. Nanette slept on two chairs pushed together in the waiting room, while Michael slept soundly in his crib, and I—very lightly on the sofa.

The next morning, we were all smiles, Michael included. He had found the soft Sophie Giraffe teether that Cathy had sent for him. He chewed away on it, drooling and smiling with each squeak it made. We were discharged and sent home with our instructions before nine o'clock. We couldn't get out of there fast enough. I drove Nanette back to her hotel, deciding that we'd try to visit again in March when they returned to see the high school musical. With Joseph and Christina both having parts, she and Bob planned to come and see the performance. Michael's surgery had been the scariest and most worrisome time in my life, but having Nanette there for support had been a huge comfort. She continued to live out the gospel, blessing us all once again.

Michael recovered remarkably fast. In no time, he had regained his strength and was back to his happy sweet self eating, babbling, rolling around, and creeping along the floor. Once he had completely recovered, and had his follow-up appointment with his neurosurgeon, who gave him the all clear, he started physical therapy. At first,

I took him to Wexford once a week to a UPMC facility, but we soon arranged for a physical therapist to come to the house through Beaver County. Dana was wonderful, always upbeat, energetic, and happy. She came to work with him once a week for an hour, and Michael quickly took to her. He wasn't always happy with the new equipment and challenges, but he worked really hard and continued to make steady progress.

Having what I thought was the worst behind us, all the specialist appointments and surgery, things calmed down a lot. There was more time to just enjoy the kids and the simplicity of our days. We were ever so grateful for the successful surgery, and we celebrated each new thing Michael learned to do. We discovered that he really enjoyed music. Whenever Angela played piano, he squealed and kicked his feet, reacting to the music. I sat at the electronic keyboard with him on my lap and let him bang excitedly on the keys. We played the recorded songs that had been saved on the keyboard while he played on the floor with his toys. I sang to him all day long, silly kid songs, ABCs, and rhymes that I remembered my aunt Mary singing to me when I was little. He began humming along, remembering them all, and kept the tune perfectly. He loved the music at church. When he got restless and fidgety while we waited for Mass to begin, he instantly became attentive when the music started. Watching our little miracle thrive and grow, he revealed his bright personality and displayed his interests, and we were filled with awe and wonder. We knew that he would continue to shine. We celebrated each new day and were excited for what the future had in store for him.

CHAPTER-THIRTY

Trials and Blessings

Beaver Falls, Pennsylvania, 2012

J oe had reached out and introduced himself to the dean of Geneva, shortly after Angela started college. Never missing an opportunity to network, it was not in vain. The dean introduced him to Keith Wing, a local business owner who worked in the energy field. In the span of a few months, he and Joe met several times over coffee and lunch, and Joe hoped to start some consulting work for him once their government contract was renewed. Joe had been burning the candle at both ends, between driving the school van and studying for the Farmers Insurance test. He finally came to the conclusion that he simply could not continue the Farmers Insurance thing. It just didn't feel right. The day before he was scheduled to take his test, he called and cancelled, telling them that he had decided not to pursue it. That very same day, Keith Wing called him with a consulting job. It wasn't a huge contract, but it was enough to pay some bills and was a better fit for Joe's skills. He also decided to quit driving the school van. He wasn't making enough money to make it worth his while, and there were no benefits. He had reported the income to Texas unemployment, and they in turn made big deductions from his unemployment check. The hours that he put in driving the van were hours missed searching for a better-suited job. It was exhausting, and we both grew frustrated. We had begun to see the problem with the system, and we wanted to get out of it.

We gathered up our tax information, receipts, and all the things that Tax Masters had asked us to send them. We were working with them to resolve our tax problems, and had paid them $4,500 on our credit card to get the process started. They told us that they would put our profile together and file it with the IRS on our behalf. From their calculations, they estimated that we would have to pay back twenty-five hundred dollars of what had grown to a sixty-thousand-dollar debt. A tremendous relief for us if it was true. The Tax Masters person that we dealt with was astonished at our ability to survive under the circumstances. He calculated all our bills and expenses, comparing them to what little income we had and the number of our dependents. After a long pause, he flatly asked Joe how we were managing it. It was just too unbelievable to him. Joe told him that we were living rent free in our friends' house and that they were also paying all the utilities. The guy was amazed that we had such generous friends. Joe told him that God had provided for us and that He had used our friends. We told the story to practically everyone that we came into contact with. We wanted to make sure that we shared our faith because it had become clear to us, judging by the common reaction, that it was an inspiring story.

The Tax Masters representative said that someone would call to let us know the status once everything was filed. A month went by, and we still hadn't heard anything. When we mentioned it to Bob, who had informed us that he knew the CEO of Tax Masters, Patrick Cox, he made a phone call. A representative called us with an update within an hour. Our case hadn't been filed yet, but they promised that it would be done before the end of the day. A couple of weeks later, as we were going about our morning routine, Joe working on his project for Keith, and me taking care of the boys and the house, we listened to Fox News in the background. One of the breaking news stories caught our attention, causing Joe and I both to stop what we were doing and focus on the television. As we read the banner, TAX MASTERS FILES FOR BANKRUPTCY, Joe and I looked at each other, mouths open, in total disbelief. Would we ever catch a break?

It just seemed like any time we got a step ahead, we were knocked down again. We had no idea what to do next. We had already paid them, and we were pretty sure we wouldn't be getting our money back. Joe tried to call our contact person, but not surprisingly, he didn't get an answer. We were screwed. We called Bob to tell him what we had just heard, and he was just as surprised as we were. We decided that our only option was to call the IRS ourselves and tell them our situation. Joe called them, they gave him a number and said that someone would get back to him.

Angela wanted to move on campus for her second semester at Geneva. There was absolutely no way we could afford it. She may have been able to qualify for a loan, but we knew that our credit was sinking, due to our financial situation, so we couldn't cosign. Without our knowledge, she sent an e-mail to Bob, asking if he would cosign a loan for her. He told her that he wouldn't cosign but would instead give her a personal loan. He told her that he wanted to invest in her and that he would rather loan her the money than have her deal with a bank. We were not at all happy about what she did, but Bob wouldn't take no for an answer. He knew that Angela was thoroughly enjoying college, and he wanted her to have the ability to stay in school. We felt terrible that we couldn't help her ourselves, but there was absolutely no way. We had exhausted everything, savings and investments, just to survive and provide for our family. Angela was just as surprised by Bob's loan and was happy to be on campus for her second semester, giving her the full college experience.

Joseph and Christina rehearsed for hours every day for months for the high school musical *Hairspray*. We were proud of them and terribly excited to watch them perform. The practices were almost every night and most weekends, from October until March. They were at the school more than they were home. The cast really bonded, and they loved being part of their musical family. They hung out together even when they weren't rehearsing. It was a joy for us to watch them be part of something so fun and exciting, with such a great group of kids. Bob and Nanette planned to come to town, specifically to see the musical, and they invited a bunch of their friends and family to come to show their support. We invited all of them to the house for dinner before the show, laying out a Mexican feast of chicken and beef fajitas, guacamole, rice, salsa and chips, and of course, loads of desserts. It got our evening off to a festive start. There were twenty-five of us that went to the show, babies included, and it was a fantastic performance enjoyed by all. We were incredibly proud of our kids. Watching them up on stage singing, dancing, and performing with all their friends was amazing.

The day after the show was my birthday. Bob and Nanette met us at Christ the Divine Teacher for Mass in the morning. I introduced them to Fr. Schreck. I had told him shortly after we'd met about how they had given us their house for almost a year, rent free. Fr. Schreck thanked Bob and Nanette for not only hearing God's call, but for acting on it. He then pulled me aside and asked me if we would consider sending our kids to Divine Mercy Academy. I laughed out loud and told him that we would love to but that there was no way we could afford it. Joe needed a job, and we needed to get back on our feet before we could even consider it. Even then, we probably couldn't afford it. Fr. Schreck laughed next and said that there were scholarships available and that there was always a way if we were interested. I didn't believe it was even a remote possibility for us. We couldn't afford to pay anything extra. We had nothing extra. To us, Catholic school was a luxury. Once I got into the car, I told Joe about what Fr. Schreck said. Joe laughed and said, "Is he crazy?"

Bob and Nanette followed us to Ohio, where we had discovered a Tim Hortons. They treated us all to donuts and coffee after church. When we got home, Bob and Nanette said that they needed to pick up a few things, but that they wanted to treat us all to dinner later that evening for my birthday. They took Callum and Patrick along with them, and when they returned, we told them that we would love to just order pizza and visit with them at home. Nanette got the kids to come outside to help her unload her car. I was completely surprised when they carried in two birthday cakes, balloons, hats, and decorations. All the fixings for an impromptu birthday party. Overwhelmed that they had gone out of their way to throw me a birthday party, on top of everything else that they had already done. The coffee and donuts was more than I would have hoped for, but dinner and a birthday party was way over the top. They brought gifts and placed a birthday crown and feather boa on me. It was a fun and special time that I will never forget. My friends made sure that we felt loved and cared for. They knew we were going through a very rough patch, and their kindness kept us afloat. My kids were just as thrilled and amazed as Joe and I were by Bob and Nanette's thoughtfulness. Bob and Nanette were amazing role models for all of us, showing us care and concern over and over again, inspiring us all and planting seeds of desire to give back. Just like they helped us, we began to pray that we too could one day be there for someone in need.

After Bob and Nanette left, we found empty beer cans hidden in the linen closet. Patrick admitted to us, after much interrogation and denial, that he had taken them. Bob had bought the beer for the dinner party and put them in the beer fridge in the family room. We told his drug counselor about it, and she was not impressed. While his attitude had improved slightly, making him less difficult to get along with, we still didn't trust him. I wished I could trust him. I longed for a normal parental relationship with him, but he lied constantly, which made it very difficult, if not impossible. We weren't feeling that the counselor was making much of a difference. Nothing seemed to be changing. Patrick hated that he had to talk to her, so we took that as a sign that we should continue. The only real benefit for us was that he was randomly drug tested, an incentive for him to stay clean. His counselor made it clear that if he came up dirty, she would see to it that he was put into a live in rehab or a juvenile center. That was more than enough to keep him straight. She was tough, and Patrick was never 100 percent sure whether she was bluffing or not.

Life for us stayed in a constant state of living on the edge of a cliff. All our energy was spent trying to keep everything balanced, a juggling act of sorts. With each new ball tossed our way, we adapted while remaining on guard, with a constant eye watching for the next one to be tossed in, praying that they wouldn't all come crashing down at once. We lived with locks on doors and windows and checked them multiple times, day and night. We got up two or three times a night to check beds, always making sure that Patrick was visible. We unplugged all but two phones, monitored where they were at all times, and hid them at night because he used them to make plans to sneak out with his friends. One night, we heard him in the basement, directly below our bedroom, talking to one of his friends on the phone. I picked up another extension and listened to their whole conversation. Patrick had told the friend to wait for him to call him back because he was waiting for his parents to go to sleep. Joe and I stayed awake, not saying a word about what we had discovered, foiling his big escape plans. It sometimes seemed like we were playing a tragic game, trying to outwit one another. We felt a sense of accomplishment when we intercepted a plan, but we knew that each time his plans were spoiled, Patrick stepped up his game and got sneakier and more deceptive. We worked that much harder, but there was never a winner. We were all losing the game. I prayed constantly that he would stop fighting us and that he would get off the path to destruction. We altered our routines and kept all exits, and Patrick, in sight until much much later in the evening than usual. We lost incredible amounts of sleep, but we learned to function on what little we did get. On top of everything, our big concern was for Joe to find a job. He had worked on a couple of projects for Keith Wing, but he needed something permanent and full-time. Our nerves were shot.

Joe and I shared the task of driving kids around to their activities, school functions, giving Angela rides to work at McDonald's, and Joseph to his server job at Franciscan Manor, an assisted living center. The regular daily chores and activities would have been a piece of cake if it hadn't been for all the emotional stress caused by the unemployment, and much more, Patrick's craziness. Another worry loomed. Michael's urology surgery. Not something that we looked forward to. The surgery had been scheduled for March 29, the day before Ryan's third birthday. It was a day surgery, so he would be home the same evening, in time to celebrate his big brother's birthday the next day. I was less worried about the urology surgery than I had been about the neurosurgery, I suppose because I had known that he needed it since his birth. His neurosurgery had been successful, and other than the stomach bug he came down with the following day, he had recovered quickly and without complication, so I expected the same outcome.

When the day of surgery arrived, we loaded Michael into the van with the bag I had packed for us the night before. The trip to Pittsburgh seemed to have gotten shorter. I easily maneuvered the van into the parking garage, pulled out a ticket, and found a spot close to the elevator. I flipped out the double stroller, buckled Michael in with a toy, and popped the bag into the empty seat before locking the doors. I had learned my way around the hospital. I confidently pushed the elevator button to our floor and pulled out the Medicaid card before stepping out. Michael was calm and smiled happily at the clerk while I checked in. She told him how adorable he was, and he ate it up. I beamed with delight at my beautiful son, wishing he didn't have to suffer, but grateful for the access to the medical treatment. Michael was called back quickly and prepped in the examination room where we waited for Dr. Cannon. When he came in, he explained that there were several possible scenarios that I should to be aware of, and that I was required to sign consents for. The first being the most desirable scenario, finding and descending both testicles; second, in the case they weren't able to find them at all; third, if they had atrophied and needed to be removed; and fourth, if the vas deferens were too short and needed to be clamped and then descended in a secondary surgery. I signed all four consents with less certainty than I had arrived with. Dr. Cannon hoped that he could take care of everything in one fairly simple surgery, but he wouldn't know—until he got inside—what the case might be. I prayed that it would be a good outcome. The nurse allowed me to walk Michael back to the operating room where I kissed his little head just before he went to sleep. I thanked the anesthesiologist and nurses that were in the room and told them that I would be praying for all of them.

I waited in the same little family waiting room. Again, I had brought along my knitting to keep my mind from worry, praying along with each stitch. I glanced around at the families that were there, wondering about the loved ones that each of them were waiting for. I wondered what kinds of surgery they were going through and said a prayer for them as well, that their surgeries would be successful. When Dr. Cannon came to find me to tell me that he was done, I followed him into the consultation room. He was all smiles.

He said that he was very happy to report that he had been able to find both testicles and descend them. Michael wouldn't need a second surgery.

"Thank God!"

Was all I could exclaim. It was an incredible relief. He was done. I could hardly wait to see him and hold him. When I got to the recovery room several minutes later, he was still pretty out of it. He managed to drink a little of his Pedialite, and I nursed him some, but he wasn't very interested. He just seemed really sleepy. Basking in the knowledge that he was finished with surgeries, and that all he needed to do from that point on was get strong and be a kid, I rocked him in my arms. I excitedly told the nurses about his journey and how thrilled I was that we wouldn't be back to the hospital for anything other than follow-ups. It could have been a lot more complicated, but Dr. Cannon had done it all in one shot. The anesthesiologist who had taken care of Michael was standing at the nurse's station in the recovery room, writing out a report and talking to one of the nurses. When he saw me, he smiled and waved. I thanked him and told him that we were so thrilled to be done, that only one surgery had been needed. We wouldn't have to come back. His response stopped me cold.

"That kid has a VP shunt. He'll be back."

He said it so matter-of-fact, like, "Don't be so naive." I had no words as I held my baby a little bit tighter. He was still really groggy, more than he had been coming out of his sedation the last two times.

It was almost eight o'clock at night. He'd had a very long day, and I figured he had to be exhausted from the ordeal, besides the fact that it was past his usual bedtime. I stayed in the recovery room with him for more than a couple of hours. The nurse felt that he seemed alert enough but had low energy. He hadn't eaten since early that morning. She agreed that he'd had a long day. The surgery had been delayed two hours, and he was worn out. She told me that I could stay the night if I wanted to, but I declined. I told her that I wanted to take him home. We'd both sleep better in our own beds. It was Ryan's birthday the next day, and I wanted to be there for him. I bundled Michael up and wheeled him down to the parking garage, loaded him into the van, and drove home in the dark. We didn't get home till after ten o'clock. He ate all the baby cereal and fruit that I fed him, but nursed very little before I put him to bed in his crib in our room. Exhausted, I crawled into bed and had a fairly decent sleep.

I woke up around five o'clock to the sound of Michael's not quite crying, but soft moaning. Picking him up, he snuggled into my neck and didn't seem at all like himself. I walked him out to the family room and sat with him on the big sectional couch where I tried to nurse him. He refused. I took a bottle of Pedialite out of the fridge, and he drank a little bit of it. Looking at him in the glow of the dim lights, his soft spot appeared to be puffed up more than usual. So were his hands and feet. I assumed it was due to all the IV fluids that he had been given. He seemed really uncomfortable. When Katie came down the stairs, she asked why Michael's head looked so big again. Since he'd had his shunt placement, his head had gotten quite a bit smaller and his soft spot had sunken in. He started to throw up. I called the hospital to explain what was going on. The urologist on call called me back right away. After telling him about my concerns, he told me that according to Michael's report, he didn't have any worries about his surgery, but that I could bring him in to get checked out for my own peace of mind. I threw some things into the bag that I had yet to unpack and drove back to Pittsburgh.

The hour drive had become more familiar than I cared for it to be. I rushed Michael into the emergency department where he was seen by a triage nurse. I told them that he'd had surgery the day before, but that I was worried about him being so lethargic, and now vomiting. They took him to a room right away. A nurse came in, followed by the emergency room doctor. They suspected a possible shunt malfunction. I called Dr. Green, Michael's neurosurgeon, whose office was on another floor in the hospital, to let her know that we were there. We waited in the little room for hours, but no one seemed to know what was going on with him. Dr. Green was in surgery, but her nurse told me that she would let her know that we were there. The neurologist on call ordered a shunt series, a CT scan, and an X-ray. They tapped his shunt, a test where they checked the pressure by inserting a long needle into the valve on his head. It was difficult to watch, but I refused to leave my baby boy and helped hold him down while the doctor performed the procedure.

The CT scan showed that the shunt was still intact, but the test showed that the valve wasn't working. It was decided that Michael needed a shunt revision. I was not at all prepared for such news, but I didn't have time to think or worry. I simply prayed and was thankful that we were in the right place. I called Joe to tell him and sent out a prayer request to our friends. We would miss Ryan's birthday. Angela and her boyfriend, David, decided to take him to the college for the day. They played at the park, took him for lunch in the dining hall, and David rode him around campus on his long board. Ryan had way more fun with them than he would have had at home, with Michael recovering from his urology surgery.

Since it hadn't been a scheduled surgery, we had to wait for an opening. It was a long day and reminded me a lot of our wait with Callum before his heart surgery. Every couple of hours, someone came to tell me that it wouldn't be much longer, only to return a couple of hours later to say there was another delay. They started an IV and took us to a room around five o'clock. Finally, at nine thirty that night, fifteen hours after our arrival, they came to tell us that they were ready for him.

Dr. Green was long gone. We never did see her, but Dr. Karandahkar, the intern who had assisted with Michael's first shunt surgery, said that he would be doing the revision. The surgery was a lot shorter than the original shunt placement. Much like our experience with Callum's long delay, I was far too exhausted to even pray, all I could do was surrender everything over to God.

Seeing Dr. Karandahkar walk through the doorway was a huge relief. He explained the reason for the shunt malfunction, a blockage in the valve, but couldn't answer what had caused it. He cleaned it out and said it seemed to be functioning properly. He repeated what Dr. Green had told me after Michael's first operation, that shunts can fail at any time for unknown reasons, and that we needed to always be aware of the signs. He confirmed that bringing him into the ER as quickly as I had was the right thing to do. He said Michael did very well during the surgery, and he expected him to recover quickly.

We waited in a long line for another CT scan, to make certain that everything was working as it should be before returning to his room after midnight. Michael slept soundly in his hospital crib. Overcome with sheer exhaustion, I curled up on the vinyl sofa, succumbing to sleep. I awoke to the sounds of cooing and singing, "Da-da-da-da-da-da."

Music to my ears. I felt as though I would burst with joy. My baby boy was back. The nurse beamed when she saw him voraciously eating up all of his food, not at all like the sick little boy from the day before. He still wasn't interested in nursing, but drank up all of the bottled formula that the nurse brought in, which left me feeling somewhat troubled. It was four days from his first birthday. He had always been a fantastic eater, so I knew he was receiving plenty of nourishment, but I loved nursing him. I was a little sad that he seemed to be weening himself when I wasn't quite ready to give it up.

After seeing Dr. Karandahkar that morning, we were discharged. He told me that it was great to see how in tune I was with Michael, that I was able to observe the signs. He reminded me how critical it was to get him checked out if things didn't seem quite right, and said it was best to err on the side of caution. I asked him if there could be a connection between the urology surgery he'd had the day before and the malfunction. He said he didn't believe so but agreed that it was quite a coincidence. Once Dr. Karandahkar gave us the okay, Michael's nurse wasted no time taking out his IV. I signed all the paperwork and headed to the elevators. Pulling out of the parking garage into the bright sunshine, I hoped to make it home before lunch, but not before making a quick detour to the pharmacy for a pregnancy test.

Having us both home again was a great relief for Joe and the rest of the family. We celebrated Ryan's birthday in our bedroom, where he excitedly opened up the packages that Bob and Nanette and Cathy and Al had sent him in the mail. With Michael kicking his feet happily in his pack and play, cooing at the mobile that danced over his head, we all breathed a sigh of relief. Angela saved the day by baking cupcakes. Being three, Ryan didn't expect much and was thrilled with the special attention, packages in the mail, and treats. He kissed his baby brother's head carefully and expressed great concern over the incision. He asked me if Michael would have to go back to the hospital again. I told him that I hoped he wouldn't.

Michael recovered remarkably fast. His first birthday was four days after his surgery, and we had plenty to celebrate. He had been through a lot in his one short year. The back-to-back surgeries had stalled his physical therapy, since he wasn't allowed to strain or do anything that could tear his stitches. Never missing a birthday for any of our kids, another big package arrived in the mail for Michael from Bob and Nanette and Cathy and Al.

The morning of Michael's birthday, I did the pregnancy test, and just as I had suspected, it was positive. I had been feeling a little off, fatigued, and a bit queasy, but I had attributed it to the stress and worry over Michael. When my period was also late, I just knew. The timing wasn't great. Actually, I thought it was the worst time. We were broke and barely keeping it together. Michael had gone through a huge ordeal, and Patrick was a constant concern. Now there would be a new baby added to the mix. Joe had enough stress to deal with. Another mouth to feed would be more for him to worry about. I decided to keep the pregnancy to myself. I questioned what in the world God was doing. I had been working on a deeper prayer life. Getting up early in the morning before anyone else, in order to spend my first couple of hours with God, praying my favorite novenas and prayers from my pieta book. It seemed to help lessen my anxiety. Even though there was always a new drama or concern, I felt like God was helping me to handle it all more calmly. I had begun to take each thing in stride without panicking.

My new prayer routine was something that I protected and refused to give up. I had experienced the feeling before, several times in my life. I had gone in and out of it and knew that it worked. When I became immersed in prayer mode, life was easier and trials were bearable. When I was out of it, I was frustrated and agitated and any little thing would set me off. I don't know why I ever fell out of it, knowing that everything worked better when I prayed. I was determined to keep at it. I wondered if God was testing me. I wasn't disappointed about being pregnant. The instant I saw that little pink plus sign, I was overcome with emotion over the new precious life within me. I just wished that the circumstances had been better. Joe needed a job. I also worried about what people would think. My pride was always just below the surface. Surely people would judge us, thinking we were irresponsible. I was forty-two years old, and my last pregnancy had been anything but easy. I worried about how the pregnancy would go, if it too would have complications. I prayed that I would have the strength to progress through nine months, and for the grace to accept whatever God gave me.

I baked Michael a birthday cake and spent the day reading books to him and Ryan. We put together Ryan's giant fire truck floor puzzle and played with the musical train that Cathy had sent them, and with the building blocks from Nanette. It was a peaceful and beautiful day. The sun shone, and I smiled to myself. I knew I couldn't keep my new little baby to myself for long. My belly would be growing bigger quickly, but I planned to enjoy the little secret for as long as I could. Our little miracle Michael was a year old. When we sang Happy Birthday to him that night after dinner, I was flooded with emotion. Hormones no doubt played a role in the sudden surge, but it was undeniable that our life had been abundantly blessed. Despite all the struggles and hardships, Joe's unemployment, the loss of all our savings and investments, our home and our comfortable life. Despite the betrayal of my mother, the humiliation, having to swallow our pride and depend on food stamps and medical assistance, and all the worry over Patrick, we were incredibly blessed. We had our beautiful family, all of us together, under one roof. Our little boy who wasn't supposed to survive the pregnancy was now a whole year old, sitting up in his high chair, picking fruit puffs off his little cake, one by one, and licking the icing from his fingers. His big bright eyes were so innocent and beautiful. He had no concept of the struggles or worries; all he knew was that he was loved very much by all of us.

THIRTY-ONE

Tested Again

Beaver Falls, Pennsylvania, May 2012

The economy began to show signs of progress. Joe seemed to be receiving more recruiter calls than usual. Since giving up on the Insurance sales course and quitting with McCarters, he had more time to focus entirely on his job search. He drove to New Jersey and Kentucky for two separate interviews, all within two weeks of each other, and had completed online assessments for a third potential job in Pittsburgh, a chief operating officer position for a law practice. All the positions were in line with his skills and experience. Things were looking up, and we felt hopeful. Nanette would be moving into the house in June, and we prayed that Joe would have a job offer before then; otherwise, we'd be homeless. With three serious job prospects on the go at the same time in three different states, we didn't bother searching for housing. We had no idea where we would end up— Pittsburgh, Kentucky, or New Jersey. We were not in any position to plan, so we decided to sit tight and wait to see what God's plan was for us. Joe received his final Texas unemployment check. They told him that it had run out and that he could not reapply for it. I felt like a job was within reach, but not surprisingly, another stumbling block had been thrown into our path.

I went to confession at Divine Mercy Church and talked to Fr. Farnan. Distraught, I must have sounded like a basket case. I told him how hard I had been trying to remain hopeful, but I was beginning to lose it. Joe still hadn't found a job, we were broke, our friends would be moving back into their house, we had no idea where we would end up, and now his unemployment was running out. To top it all off, I was pregnant. Fr. Farnan told me not to despair, that God would provide, and that our new little baby would be a light in the world. He blessed me and told me to call the church, the St. Vincent de Paul would help. I told Joe what Fr. Farnan said about the St. Vincent de Paul, but I didn't tell him about the baby. Within days, the St. Vincent de Paul paid most of our bills, the main ones, like the insurance for the van and our phone bill. On Easter Sunday, Fr. Schreck handed us a fat envelope from some anonymous donors. When we opened it up after Mass, there were hundreds of dollars in cash and gift cards. While we were still sitting in the parking lot with our jaws dropped, speechless at the huge gift, Deacon DeNome tapped on our window and handed us a giant ham. From that point on, our parish rallied around us. Before then, no one knew how dire our situation was. I had been too proud to tell anyone. When I finally opened up about it, our parish community rushed to help, and it was overwhelming.

Joe continued to move forward with the job prospects and was invited to second and third interviews. The New Jersey job fizzled, but the Kentucky and Pittsburgh ones had yet to be decided. We remained open to either one. I would have gladly stayed in the Pittsburgh area, but I also welcomed a new place. We just wanted a job. A good one. One that would provide for our family and be a good fit for Joe. We tried to prepare ourselves for the possibility that neither job would be offered, but we remained hopeful. We searched the Internet for housing and rental properties in Kentucky and Pittsburgh, in order to get an idea of prices and availability. We even looked into finding some house-sitting jobs. I begged God for this one last favor.

Patrick had done well in alternative school, passing all his classes. He asked us if he could return to regular school. We told him that we were interested in more than just good grades, we wanted a total transformation. He appeared to be working at it. His report card was the best we had ever seen from him, and his attitude was much better. He seemed less angry and definitely less disrespectful, choosing to walk away rather than engage in an argument. We were even beginning to enjoy pleasant conversations with him. It melted my heart to watch him interact with Michael. He never held back when he picked him up off the floor, kissing and smooching his little face. Michael lit up every time Patrick walked into the room. They had a bond. At the end of the six-week grading period, we agreed to let him return to the regular school setting. We knew that once he went back, we wouldn't be able to switch him into the alternative school again. It was a one-shot deal and a gamble. His vice principal and drug counselor advised us against it, but we had made a deal with him, and he had kept up his end of the bargain. We couldn't go back on our word. He went back to his old ways almost immediately. He displayed no behavioral issues at school, but his grades slid again. School was his social outlet and drug source. His bad attitude returned, and when the mouthing off started up again, we knew we had been played. We were so tired. The arguments wore us out, the tension was unbearable, and I didn't need the stress in my condition.

Grace's confirmation was in May, and she had asked Nanette to be her sponsor. Nanette flew in from Texas, and I picked her up in the pouring rain from her hotel near the airport. She treated us all to pizza at Mario's in Beaver before the confirmation. Bishop Zubik celebrated the evening Mass in the packed church. I stood at the back with Michael, who had become restless. As I gently swayed him back and forth, praying for him to stay quiet, I noticed a lady had been watching me, glancing back and forth in my direction. Each time I caught her looking, I smiled before she looked away. After the Mass was over, as I was walking out the door, making my way to the hall for the reception, I heard someone whisper in my ear, "Are you expecting?"

My heart stopped. Speechless, I turned to see the lady who had been looking at me during Mass. I had no clue who she was, and I hadn't told anyone that I was pregnant. Was it that obvious? I lied, "No."

And quickly walked away from her before she could ask any more questions. I knew I wouldn't be able to keep my secret much longer, not if random people continued to approach me at church. Nanette flew back home the following day. It had meant a lot to us that she would make the trip to be there for Grace's confirmation. Her visit had been short and sweet, and it was the last that we would see her before her move. It was obvious that she was getting very excited about moving into their house. I was a nervous wreck, worrying about the possibility of being homeless.

A few days after the confirmation, I told Joe I was pregnant. His reaction was not one that you'd expect from a first-time father. It was not the sort of news that he had been expecting to hear from me. Mostly due to crazy hormones, I judged his reaction to be one of disappointment rather than—what was in reality—complete surprise. I left the bedroom in a flood of tears. I'd had the advantage of time for the news to sink in, but I was upset when Joe didn't jump for joy. I was unfair. He followed me into the living room where I sat on the couch, trying to read my prayer book through tears. He pulled me up into his arms and told me that he was sorry for his stunned reaction. He had been caught completely off guard by the news. He reassured me that of course he was happy and that everything would be okay. He reminded me that God was with us and that He hadn't let us down yet. There was so much going on, so much to worry about, and so much drama in our lives already. I wondered how we would ever get through it all. I slumped into his arms, sobbing while he held me up, bearing all of my weight, and I knew instantly that we could get through everything together.

We didn't tell the kids. I wasn't ready to tell anyone yet. I saw the lady who had asked me about being pregnant at Mass. Joe told me that she was Deacon DeNome's wife and a member of the Saint Vincent de Paul. I had no idea. I had never met her before. I told Joe about the night of the confirmation and how she had asked me if I was pregnant. The next time that Joe spoke to her, he told her that I had lied to her the night she had asked me if I was expecting, only because I hadn't told him the news yet. She laughed and said that she understood. She said she knew I had to be pregnant, because she recognized the glow. Our kids found out that there was a new baby on the way on Mother's Day, and not because we had made the announcement. It didn't happen at all the way we would have planned it.

After returning from Mass, we planned to enjoy a relaxing day at home. We relished our family time together on the weekends after the long and hectic school week. The kids enjoyed playing outside in the beautiful weather. Patrick was outside as well, which was not unusual. We didn't think much of it since they were all together, until one by one, most of them came inside, and our neighbor knocked on the front door. He wanted to let us know that Patrick had come by to ask him for a ride to his friend's house. We were stunned. That was a new one. The neighbor said that he thought it had been a strange request, and that, in hindsight, he probably should have asked us first. In any case, he wanted to let us know. Joe told him that he wished he had talked to us before taking him anywhere. The neighbor apologized and told Joe where he had dropped Patrick off, the white house next to the church on Blackhawk Road, across from the high school. We knew the house. Joe and I immediately got into the van and drove there. We pulled into the driveway and banged on the door. No one came out. The back of the house faced the front of the high school. There was a large storage shed on the property. Joe looked in the windows and called out, "Hello, hello."

But no one seemed to be home. Then, a little girl about the age of seven, came around from behind the shed. We asked her if she had seen Patrick. She said she hadn't. We asked her if her parents were home. She said her mom was in the back, and she went to get her. The mom and another woman came around to the driveway where we were standing, followed by a kid who looked to be about the same age as Patrick. We told the mom that we were Patrick's parents and that our neighbor had just informed us that he'd dropped Patrick off at her house. We asked her where Patrick was. She and the other woman said they had no idea. They had been in the backyard, building a gazebo all day, and they weren't having much luck with it. They laughed about it being harder than it looked, but it hadn't dampened their Mother's Day celebration. They joked about the bottle of wine that they'd just finished, possibly being the reason for the trouble they were having with the project.

The kid stood silently next to the shed looking at us. I turned to him and asked him where Patrick was. He stared back at me stone faced and said he hadn't seen him. I told him he was a liar, and I demanded to know where he was. I had heard that the kid was a druggie and had been in trouble with the police, and I told him so. Still, he wouldn't tell us where Patrick was. I pulled out my cell phone and called the Chippewa Police, who were on my contact list. I told them who and where I was and that my son was missing. Within minutes, two cruisers pulled into the driveway. One of the officers was the same one who had come out the night that Patrick had skipped school. It was like old home week when they arrived. The mom was on a first-name basis with the officers. I didn't want to know why. We explained the situation and how our neighbor had come by to tell us that he'd dropped Patrick off at the house, but mysteriously, Patrick was nowhere to be found. They took down a description and said that they would be on the lookout. They instructed us to go home and wait, just in case he returned home. Just as we were getting into our vehicles, one of the officers pointed down toward the road in front of the high school and asked, "Is that him?"

Sure enough, it was Patrick, casually walking along the road in his familiar blue sweatshirt. Two officers drove toward the school in opposite directions while we followed. Joe and I didn't see Patrick get into the car that was driving down the road, but one of the police officers did. We saw the cruiser lights flash and the car pull over. The two frightened teenaged girls who sat in the front seat nervously rolled down the window while Patrick, who had ducked into the backseat, knew he had been caught. I was amazed at how quickly it had all happened, marveling at the cop's sharp eye. The girls were both crying. They hadn't done anything wrong that they were aware of; they had simply given Patrick a ride. Patrick was the one who was in trouble.

After sending the girls on their way, the police officer gave Patrick a talking to, but we knew it wouldn't make any difference. More talking and no real consequences, we had been down the same road before too many times. We would drive Patrick home; he would shower, eat, and sleep. No big deal. Patrick got into the van while Joe talked to the officer on the side of the road. He told him that we were close to the breaking point. He wanted to know what our options were and if he had any ideas. He told the officer that I was pregnant and that he didn't want me being stressed out with Patrick's nonsense. The officer told him the same old story: unless Patrick broke the law, his hands were tied. Patrick overheard their conversation but remained smug. He knew he could continue being a delinquent as long as he didn't break the law, or at least as long as he didn't get caught. We thanked him and apologized for the trouble.

We drove home in silence, and the moment we arrived, Patrick told the other kids that I was having another baby. I knew something was up when they each came into our room and sized me up, looking at me strangely with an occasional giggle, but without coming right out with the question. When one of them finally asked, while the rest of them hung around outside the bedroom door waiting to hear the answer, we couldn't deny it. They were very excited with the news. A new baby in the house was something to look forward to. It meant joy and hope. They immediately began talking about whether it would be a boy or a girl and started tossing out baby names. I prayed for the energy and strength I needed to get through the next seven months. I had calculated my due date to be December 8, the Feast of the Immaculate Conception. We were relieved that we didn't have to keep the new baby a secret anymore, even if Patrick had been the one to blab the news.

Patrick snuck out again. The temptation was greater with the arrival of the warmer weather. Always the opportunist, watching and waiting, he managed to slip out while we were distracted. When we discovered that he was gone, Christina said that she'd heard around the school that there was a party, but she didn't know where it was. Joe called the police. He told the dispatcher that our son had snuck out and that it wasn't the first time. We were concerned about him drinking and using drugs or, worse, driving around with kids who were under the influence. The dispatcher told Joe that there was nothing they could do unless he was caught breaking the law. We were beyond frustrated. Wasn't sneaking out of the house while still a minor, breaking a law? I drove around town with Joseph and Christina to a house where we thought the party might be. They even got out and knocked on a door to ask if Patrick was there, but it was the wrong place. We went back home and locked up the house. I was scared for him, dreading the worst, praying rosaries over and over that he would make it home safely. I stayed awake all night. I didn't get mad until he got home. We didn't let him in the house until everyone was awake, and then we didn't let him go to bed. We made him stay up all day, putting him to work. It was much more exhausting for us to stay on his case all day, shoving him awake when he'd fall asleep on the couch, forcing him up, and making him do whatever jobs we could find.

The fact that Patrick seemed to have absolutely no regard for the enormous amount of stress that we were already under, instead, choosing to add to it with his behavior, was disheartening. His behavior was more worrisome for us than all our other struggles combined, but all he cared about was having fun. We wanted him to enjoy wholesome activities like the rest of his brothers and sisters, but that never seemed to satisfy him. We allowed him and the older kids to go to the mall or a movie, and they often had fun together, but Patrick always turned around and snuck out again, sometimes the very same night. It had become almost a normal part of our life, and we had no idea how to stop it. Joe wanted to kick him out. He was sick and tired of the turmoil. He was sick of not having any control. There was nothing he could do to stop him, and yet we couldn't just kick him out. He was a minor, so anything he did, we would be held accountable and financially responsible for. I wasn't willing to relinquish my parental responsibilities. Things got really ugly, to the point where Joe and Patrick didn't speak to each other at all. After the five hundred dollars disappeared, Joe essentially wrote him off. Patrick continued to deny taking it, despite the pictures he'd posted on Facebook and the post he'd made about getting into the safe. I couldn't hold on to the anger. I prayed constantly for their relationship to be repaired. I hated to see them so angry. The younger kids were afraid of Patrick. He lashed out at them verbally and even physically. If any of them snitched him out to us, he retaliated. I talked to Fr. Schreck. He told me not to give into his behavior and to continue doing what we were doing. I continued to pray.

Nanette's move-in date, June 15, was fast approaching. She, Bob, and Al planned to drive from Texas along with Nanette's friend Linda, who lived in Beaver. They would drive straight through with their eight cats and Buddy, their dog. I started packing things up around the beginning of May. We had kept most of the boxes from our move from Texas, and one by one, I filled them. I had the older kids pack up their winter clothes and things from their rooms. We had eliminated a ton of stuff before leaving Texas, but surprisingly, we bagged up a ton more while packing for our next move. I made multiple trips to the donation bin where I stuffed bags of clothes, shoes, toys, and household items. We knew we would be hearing about the two job prospects any day, and we wanted to be prepared. I began to hope that the Kentucky job would be the one, partly because I didn't think I'd have the energy for another self move. I also wanted a fresh start in a new place, for Patrick's sake. Even though I was certain that a job offer in Kentucky would include a full relocation package with professional movers, I still felt that I should continue packing up what I could while we waited.

After Wednesday night Mass and adoration, I asked Fr. Schreck to pray that one of the jobs would come through. He said that he would, and assured me that God would provide. On Friday, Joe heard from the law firm in Pittsburgh. He didn't get the job. Not entirely surprised, he'd begun having strange vibes after his face-to-face interview, when they began sending him multiple assessments. With each one that he completed, they sent another, giving him the impression that they were looking for a reason not to hire him. They had also switched the original posted title of chief operating officer to a director position and significantly reduced the salary. In the end, they informed him that they had decided not to fill the position at all. It was somewhat disappointing, but no doubt a blessing in disguise since Joe felt that it was a little sketchy. We held out hope for the Kentucky job, but grew nervous when we hadn't heard back from the recruiter in the timeframe that she had given.

Joe called the recruiter on the same day that he got the rejection from the Pittsburgh job. She told him that she hadn't heard back from the hiring manager either, but said she would call to check on the status. She promised to let Joe know by the end of the day. I prayed my head off. It was our last hope. We had no idea what we would do if he didn't get the offer. Thirty minutes later, the recruiter called back and told Joe that the company had decided to hire someone internally. The recruiter seemed annoyed that they had not chosen one of her recruits. Joe was defeated. I was at a complete loss and felt that God had let me down. What in the world would we do? What would become of us? I cringed at the thought of us living in Welfare housing somewhere in downtown Beaver Falls.

I sent an e-mail to Bob and Nanette, Cathy and Al, and Tracy and Blair to let them know. They had all been praying for us and for Joe to find a job since the beginning, but most especially for what seemed to be two very promising prospects. I told them about both rejections and how we'd received them on the same day. I asked them to pray that we would find housing before we had to move out of the house. I called our next-door neighbor Romaine to ask her if she knew of any rental properties. Being a professor at Geneva, I figured she might have an idea about where we should start looking. She e-mailed me a housing list that the college gives to new students. On my way out of Mass on Friday morning, I did my best not to crack. The floodgates opened when I told Fr. Schreck that Joe hadn't been offered either job and that I had no idea what we were going to do. He told me not to worry. God would provide.

Joe went to work, calling numbers on the housing list, starting from the top, while I called from the bottom. We didn't have much luck. Most of the numbers were no longer in service, and many of them were wrong numbers altogether. A few told us they didn't have any rental properties available, and we left several messages on machines. Joe dialed the last number. A lady answered, and he repeated the same pitch that he'd practically memorized after multiple calls. He'd gotten the number from a Geneva housing list, and our family was in need of a rental house. The lady told him that the list must have been an old one because all their properties had been rented by the same tenants for years. Joe thanked her and was about to hang up before she said, "Hold on, I'll let you talk to my husband."

The husband confirmed that the housing list was definitely an old one, but that he had, that very same week, made an offer on another property that had been accepted. The closing day was June 15. If you are thinking to yourself, "Wow, what a coincidence," think again. Joe told him that the timing was perfect, since that was the exact date we needed to move out of the house we were currently living in. He said that if we were interested, we could come by to see it that Sunday.

On Saturday, Tracy called me to tell me that she was sorry to hear about the job rejections. She and Blair had moved from Southlake to Denver, where after a brief layoff, Blair had accepted a job, but their Southlake house still hadn't sold. Tracy told me that she and Blair had discussed it, and they wanted us to consider moving back to Texas, to house-sit for them. They offered to pay our moving expenses and told us that we could live there, rent free, until it sold. I was speechless. Their house was a showplace. Listed on the market for well over a million dollars, it was a dream home. The fact that they were willing to entrust it to us was unbelievable. She told us that their goal was to sell the house and that if they did get an offer before Joe found a job, they would help us find and pay for a rental property, for as long as we needed. They wouldn't allow us to be homeless. I thanked her immensely and told her that I would discuss it with Joe and let her know. Joe was just as astounded as I was. How and why had we been so incredibly blessed with such generous and compassionate friends? It was more than enough to keep us both from crumbling in despair and worry over the possibility of having to move next to a crack house. A completely surreal proposition had been offered to us once again, and it was next to impossible to get our heads around it in order to even begin to discuss it.

Our kids overheard us talking about Tracy and Blair's offer, and they unanimously favored the idea. We had been to their home, so they dreamed about how amazing it would be to live there, even if only temporarily. The thought of another long-distance move was daunting, and the uncertainty of how long we would live there was a little concerning. Their house might sell within weeks, or it could take several months. None of us had a clue. The biggest concern for us was bringing Patrick back to the very place where his craziness had begun. Sure he had been acting crazy in Beaver Falls, but we worried that it would escalate if he was brought back to even more familiar territory. Still, it was comforting to have an option.

That night, at around eleven o'clock, I jumped out of bed at the sound of the dogs barking. Peering through the window, I saw a car in the driveway. I immediately assumed that Patrick had snuck out of the house. Rushing to the door, prepared to chew someone out, I saw a familiar face but couldn't place who it was. I hadn't seen David, Joe's brother, in nearly fifteen years. Once I realized who it was, I threw the door open wide and welcomed him and his family in. They had been traveling home to North Carolina from Ohio, after two family funerals. Having heard the commotion, most of the kids came downstairs, squeezing into the living room to join in the surprise reunion. David and I had stayed connected through e-mails and letters over the years. He knew that we would be moving soon and didn't want to pass up an opportunity to visit us while they were so close. David is a solid Christian, with an enormous faith, and we had always shared that connection. We told him about what was going on, the job rejections, and the offer of our friends' home. He celebrated God's goodness with us and told us how encouraged he was to hear and see how hugely God continued to bless us through our struggles. He promised us that God had big plans for us. We knew deep down that he was right. God must have big plans. But what were they? And when in the world would He ever reveal them to us? David and Bettie's visit was very short but oh so sweet. The love that we shared, all squished in that living room, filled us to the brim. After hugs all around and long goodbyes, we all went back to bed. Joe and I giggled about David just showing up out of the blue. The timing couldn't have been better. It felt good to be loved. We fell asleep with smiles on our faces, counting all the blessings of the day. Right on the brink, God had shown us that He was still there.

On our way into Sunday Mass the next morning, I saw Fr. Schreck in the parking lot, standing next to his car. With a pep in my step and a smile on my face, I told him about Tracy and Blair's offer. God had scooped us up again. He kept showing us, in undeniably huge ways, that He was with us. Before Mass began, I saw Fr. Schreck writing something on a notecard at the lectern. He was fascinating to watch before Mass, as he checked to make sure that everything was in perfect order. I was always humbled when I observed him sitting on the floor, hidden behind the altar facing the tabernacle. Sometimes he would be on bended knee, head down in prayer, alone with God, preparing himself for Mass as the church filled up. It was a beautiful sight to see such humility and reverence as he showed his love for God. As usual, after Mass, we stood in line waiting our turn to greet Fr. Schreck on our way out. We loved that he always stuck around outside to say hello to his parishioners. Shaking hands and cracking jokes, talking to the seniors and little kids, encouraging young parents, always making eye contact, giving each person a smile and attention. Joe told him what I had already shared with him about Tracy and Blair's offer. Fr. Schreck looked at him seriously and asked him if that was what he really wanted to do. Joe stopped and thought for a second before answering, "No, not really." The rest of us just looked at him. Then he continued, "But what other choice do we have?"

Fr. Schreck said that we should pray over it. He told us to give God a week to let us know what we should do.

I laughed and asked him, "Oh, is that how it works? I've been doing it all wrong all this time. I didn't know I could give God a time frame."

He said, "Sure. God has a way of coming through at the eleventh hour."

We told him we would pray about it and that we would give God a week. Joe mentioned to him that we had an appointment to look at a rental property that afternoon. We would most certainly have to apply for Welfare housing in order to pay rent. Fr. Schreck said that it was too bad that we couldn't move in to St. Philomena's rectory, which, in his words, was *ginormous*. It had something like seven bedrooms. That definitely would have been sweet, but it was against diocesan rules. He handed us a little notecard, the one I had seen him writing on before Mass. It read:

> Allen Family
> Pancake Breakfast
> Paid in Full, Fr. Schreck

He told us to go have breakfast on him at St. Rose of Lima, where he was heading to say the next Mass. We thanked him and drove to the church. When we got down to the hall, Fr. Schreck called Joe over. He told him that he had discussed our situation with Fr. Farnan, the pastor of Divine Mercy and St. Philomena Churches, and that they had come up with a figure. Our rent would be covered, up to $650 a month, by someone in the community. An anonymous benefactor. We were speechless and almost collapsed after hearing the news. Incredibly humbled once again, we couldn't sort any of it out. What we really wanted was to support ourselves. For Joe to find a decent job so that we could just take care of ourselves without having to rely on charity, but God was showing us that we needed to rely on Him. That He was providing for us. We drove home after breakfast, settled the babies down for their naps, and left the older kids in charge before going to meet the landlord.

The rental house was in Chippewa, on Blackhawk Road, one of the busiest streets in town. It was a two-story house, between a law office and a pizza place, and directly across the road from McCarter's Bus Barn. From the outside, the house looked decent. It was very small but seemed to be in pretty good shape from what we could tell. The yard wasn't fenced, but there was a small deck on the front with a gate. We parked in the Dad's Pizza parking lot and waited for the landlord to show up. When a car pulled into the driveway, Joe got out to see if it was Tom, the landlord. He waved me in when he discovered it was. Still dressed in my church clothes, a black maternity dress and heels, I carefully walked across the grass and over the thinly graveled driveway. Tom unlocked the side door and showed us in. We followed him up the crooked stairs and into a tiny kitchen. My heart sank. The house was nothing like any place we had ever lived before.

A little over one thousand square feet, it was old and very dated, with cracks in the ceiling and up the walls. The kitchen was dark, and the cabinets were shabby, the carpets were stained and tattered, and the wallpaper was curling. Tom walked us through the tiny dining room and into the small family room. We made our way up the narrow stairs and peeked into the only bathroom, which was tiny and basic. There were two fair-sized bedrooms upstairs and another room that had most likely been intended as a dressing room. Not nearly deep or wide enough to fit a bed, it had a large closet. As the three of us stood in one of the upstairs bedrooms, Tom told us that he would be willing to replace all the carpets, paint, and get the kitchen and bathroom functioning. The home had belonged to an elderly lady who had passed away. Tom told us that the funeral home had taken possession of the house when the family couldn't pay her funeral expenses. Joe and I looked at each other, wondering if it would work. It would certainly be tight. Tom said Joe looked familiar. Joe told him that we belonged to Christ the Divine Teacher parish. Tom then asked, "Do you have, like a lot of kids?"

Panic set in. That was a deal breaker. Surely he would never rent us the house, knowing we were expecting our twelfth child. We had not planned to disclose how many kids we had unless we were asked directly. Joe told him we had eleven kids and were expecting our twelfth in December. He told Tom he was looking for work and that we had been house-sitting for the Mazzucas for nearly a year. They would be moving into their house on the fifteenth of June. He also explained to Tom that Fr. Schreck and Fr. Farnan had seen to it that our rent would be covered up to $650 a month. Tom said that he had seen us at Mass and told us that he was on the parish council. He told us we could have the house for up to a year and a half. After that, his plan was to convert it into a commercial property. He said he would do his best to get it fixed up in time for us to move in on the fifteenth. We thanked him and left with our heads swirling.

It was way too incredible to absorb. God continued to wow us at every turn. In less than twenty-four hours, we had been given two incredible housing options, and we wouldn't have to pay for either one of them, nor would we require government assistance. We drove to Long John Silvers for lunch to discuss our options and to share our amazement at God's hand in our lives. We sat across the table from each other, holding hands with silly grins on our faces, sharing a fish dinner. We both agreed that the best option for us was to rent the house on Blackhawk Road. There was no question that it was God's providence. We decided to call Tracy and Blair to thank them for their incredibly generous offer and tell them that we decided to stay in Beaver Falls. Joe called Tom on the way home to tell him that we wanted to rent the house, and he sent Fr. Schreck an e-mail to tell him all about what had just happened. Fr. Schreck knew Tom well and told us that he was a good man. He had told us many times that God would provide, and boy had He ever.

Just as I was about to call Tracy, I received an e-mail from her. I read it from my phone while we drove back home. Incredibly, she and Blair had been discussing their offer and were having reservations because of our two large dogs. Their priority was to sell their house as quickly as possible; they worried that the dogs may be a detracting factor. Joe and I laughed. God was really something else. He had planted the idea in Tracy and Blair's hearts, just long enough to give us the hope we needed to get us through the weekend. Tracy said that she and Blair still wanted to help us out with finding a house. Helping with rent and whatever else we needed. I replied to Tracy's e-mail, telling her not to worry about anything and told her I would call her when we got home. We told the kids that we would be moving into the little house on Blackhawk Road. They were not exactly excited, after dreaming about living in the Korschuns' house and its spacious grandeur. The gourmet kitchen, endless pool, theater room, patio fireplace, and all the luxuries that went with it. No doubt we all would have enjoyed it, but we knew it wasn't the right option. I called Tracy and Blair to tell them what had transpired over the previous twenty-four hours. Tracy was relieved, fearing that they had gotten our hopes up, only to let us down. She was amazed to hear how things had worked out so perfectly, but being a woman of God, she was not at all surprised. She felt blessed to witness such a miracle with us. I called Nanette to tell her and asked her to fill Cathy in. Everyone was relieved. The last thing Joe and I wanted was for Bob and Nanette to be stressed out, worrying about us. We wanted them to fully enjoy their move into their retirement home.

I continued packing, eliminating much of our possessions for donation, packing away seasonal things and items I knew we wouldn't need. The rental house was tiny, so we decided to only bring what was absolutely necessary—clothes, beds, kitchen table and chairs, our washer and dryer, pots, pans, dishes, and a few toys. We packed up all our decorations, large living room and family room furniture, artwork, home decor items, piano and keyboard, most of my yarn and knitting supplies, and set it aside to be kept in a storage unit. We felt certain that once Joe secured a good job, we would move into a larger house where we could once again enjoy our possessions. We doubted we'd be able to afford to replace them, so storage made the most sense.

Having secured a rental house gave us peace of mind, but the worry about a job and no income was always there. It was all we could manage, to walk in the direction that God pointed us in. There were varying degrees of worry. We were grateful for the roof over our heads and incredibly humbled by the knowledge that people we had never met were paying our rent. We felt blessed to be welcomed into a parish family that rallied around us in our time of need. A parish that we had only been part of for nine months.

At the end of May, right after school let out for the summer, Joseph left for Minnesota. He had applied for—and was hired to work at Northern Tier Boy Scout Camp. He would be gone all summer and wasn't at all disappointed about missing the whole move. We were happy for the exciting opportunity and experience that he had been given, with a wonderful recommendation from Bob Mazzuca.

The time passed quickly as our move date approached. It was getting down to the wire for the work to be completed at the rental house. We drove by each day, noticing that they had cleaned up the yard, trimming back the big tree and shrubs. There seemed to always be work trucks parked out front, a good sign that work was being done. At Bob and Nanette's house, we kept busy right up until moving day, packing and cleaning.

After receiving the notice from Texas unemployment that his benefits were exhausted, Joe and I went to the county office to find out what our options were. The caseworker said that Joe was definitely employable. She was very sympathetic to our situation and said that she felt that the economy was slowly turning around. She offered us a one-time bridge allowance. It was something that they only offered to families that they felt were in a temporary hardship situation, not lifetime Welfare recipients. The timing of receiving the help was perfect for our move. We got a deposit on our Access card for four thousand dollars. Joe rented a U-Haul truck and bought extra boxes. Patrick disassembled all the bunk beds and the whole family pitched in, helping to haul boxes and furniture out of the bedrooms. I wanted all the big jobs done as early as possible. I cleaned every window and washed all the walls. We planned to leave the house in better shape than when we moved in. I called the Salvation Army to pick up all our donation items, and they filled a good portion of the truck. Dressers, bed frames, toys, electronics, clothing and household items, some garden supplies, and tools were just some of the things we got rid of. It boggled my mind how much stuff we had eliminated once again. It hadn't been that long since we'd purged an incredible amount of stuff before leaving Texas, and there we were with more still. It was like a cleansing. The stripping away of layers, like peeling an onion.

We got a call from Bob Javens, the kids' old bus driver. He had called to check in on us and to tell us that Peggy had been diagnosed with multiple myeloma, cancer of the blood. She was receiving treatment and seemed to be responding well. I was very saddened by the news and started working on a prayer shawl for her. I had just finished making one for the wife of our dear pediatrician, Dr. Hadad's wife, who was also battling cancer. I questioned why such beautiful people continued to be ravaged by such a horrible disease. Bob asked Joe about his job prospects. Joe filled him in on the current leads and status of his interviews. He also told him that we were preparing for a move into a rental house, right across from McCarter's. Bob was happy to hear that we would be staying in the area and told Joe to call a guy named Matt Nance, from Tiger Pause. He said he was a great fellow who could help us with our move. Joe thanked Bob and said he would call. I'm fairly certain that Bob called Matt himself right away to tell him about us because Matt didn't seem surprised when Joe called. He told him that we had rented a U-Haul and let him know our moving date. Matt told Joe that he would provide some guys to come and help us.

We had everything staged before moving day, separating the items that would be going to the storage unit from the stuff we would be taking to the house. Matt's guys showed up ready to work, along with a few of Joseph's friends. They loaded the truck and delivered everything to the storage unit, packing it wall to wall and floor to rafters, in record time. The following day, Joe, Patrick, and Joseph's friends packed up a smaller truck twice, and delivered everything to the house where the work was still being completed. They packed boxes in the basement, in the makeshift garage with the tarp curtain at the end of the driveway, and on the front deck. Miraculously, the workers finished in time for us to sleep in the house that night. While Joe and the guys took care of the loading and unloading, I continued cleaning our way out of the Mazzucas' house, making sure that everything was perfect.

Bob and Nanette had driven straight through from Texas, stopping only for gas and food. Al Morin had ridden along with Bob and their eight caged cats in a large utility van, while Nanette drove with her friend Linda, and Buddy the dog. They promptly unloaded all the kitties upon their arrival and set them up inside one of the bedrooms with food, water, and litter boxes, before heading to their hotel to sleep. I'm certain it was an exhausting trip for them, but we knew they were very excited about beginning the new chapter in their lives. Turning over the house keys, we hugged them all and said goodbye. Joe and I packed the last few items into the van before pulling out of the driveway, leaving the big house behind, heading to the little house on Blackhawk Road to begin our new adventure.

The rental house cleaned up pretty well. It was small and dated, but the carpets were new, and even though the paint job wasn't even close to perfect (they painted over most of the wallpaper), it looked clean. They had installed a new sink and toilet in the bathroom, and the shabby floors had been replaced with a tile-look, stick-on, roll-out floor. It was cute in a college apartment sort of way. I decided that I would make the best of it. The house was a Godsend and a haven for our family. Tiny as it was, we would all be together. I told the kids to pretend that we were on an extended camping trip. At least we had an indoor bathroom and shower, laundry facilities, and a kitchen. They were good sports about it. They had grown accustomed to a comfortable life, so it was quite a change for them. We all knew that it could have been worse. I shuddered each time I thought about where we might have ended up.

We were experiencing a heatwave, with temperatures in the high nineties, climbing into the hundreds. The house did not have central air. The landlord brought us a third window air-conditioner unit, for which we were extremely grateful. I scrubbed the mini blinds that I found in the basement and hung them on all the windows. They helped to shade the baking sun that poured in. Patrick and the older girls worked together assembling bunk beds, an exceedingly challenging chore, due to the minimal amount of space in the bedrooms. They set three up in the girls' room and two in the boys'. Maneuvering the long rails in such tight spaces took skill, but they managed to get the job done. We were on a mission. We all wanted the same thing, to get the house set up quickly so that we could relax. All of us were exhausted, both mentally and physically. Moving is labor intensive under the best conditions, but with the added worries of our situation, it was much more stressful, not to mention the combination of oppressive heat and being five months pregnant. I could have easily dropped and fallen fast asleep at any given moment, but I knew I couldn't stop. I needed to make the space feel as much like home as possible for my family. Nesting was my specialty.

The morning after our move was Sunday, and we got up for nine o'clock Mass as usual. Sitting in our regular pew, I was overcome with emotion as I pondered all the events that had led us to that moment. Tears welled up in my eyes. I couldn't keep them from flowing, something that seemed to be happening more often than usual, and I don't think it was purely hormonal. I felt truly blessed in every way. Each time it seemed like we were hitting the bottom,

God lifted us up. As we drove home, we commented how close the house was to the church, only a three-minute drive with no winding mountains to navigate. I was excited about how easy it would be to get to morning Mass.

After church, we got straight to work, unpacking the rest of the boxes and setting up the rooms. Even though we had put three quarters of our stuff in storage, the house was still packed. I worked on the main floor, scrubbing out the six cabinets and three drawers in the tiny kitchen, a far cry from the gourmet kitchens we'd had in our last four houses. Our fridge was too tall to fit into the spot where it was supposed to go, so we put it on another wall where it stuck out. We put one of the tall storage cabinets that we had used in our garage, in the kitchen, to use as a food pantry. The cabinets were not big enough, and I had seen evidence of mice on the shelves, which totally grossed me out. There was no way I'd be putting food in them. I bleached everything and put down shelf liner on every surface. The counters, sink, and dishwasher were new, but the overhead fan didn't work. The stove was used, but looked like it was in fairly decent shape and appeared clean on the outside. It was an older-style range with the four round elements. When I lifted up the top of the stove to wipe it out, I discovered a mouse nest, complete with bits of insulation, straw, tissues, and loads of mouse poop. I gagged and stifled a cry at the realization that we had sunk to an all-time low. We had caught the odd mouse while living in Bob and Nanette's house, but they had run in to get out of the cold, they hadn't set up housekeeping. We'd had mice in our shed when we lived in our first house in Niagara Falls, but they never came into the house. We didn't see any live mouse activity, and we never found any dead mice, but it was obvious that they had been there at some point, and their leavings were still around. I cleaned and scrubbed with a vengeance. I was not about to expose my family to any potential diseases. It felt great to get everything disinfected and sanitized.

I spent the entire day in the tiny kitchen and was quite pleased with the results. It not only looked and smelled clean, it was clean. Just as I finished washing the floor, before moving on to the dining room, the ceiling light fixture flickered. It was brand-new. In fact, the entire kitchen ceiling had been replaced because of water damage. When it flickered again, I called out to Joe. The two of us looked up, and all of a sudden, water began to first drip, then run, and then pour, out of the light fixture. I grabbed the bucket I had been using, dumped the contents into the sink, and placed it under the flow. Joe ran up the stairs to the bathroom, directly above the kitchen, where he found Patrick plunging the toilet. Toilet water was pouring into my freshly scoured kitchen. I was beyond tears. We could not get the toilet unclogged. We had noticed that the water seemed to drain very slowly in the bathroom sink the day we moved in. Joe called Tom and told him what was going on. Tom asked Bill, his partner, to come over and check it out. Bill told us that they too had noticed that the water drained slowly, and they had put some Drano down the pipes, figuring it would do the job. Because it was Sunday evening, a plumber wouldn't be out until the next day. With only one bathroom and no ability to flush, we knew we had a big problem. When Joe discovered that the basement drain was backed up as well, it was more than we could bear. The basement was unfinished, and thankfully, we hadn't put anything where the water was pooling, so no damage had been done, but the thought of what was floating around down there was a nightmare.

Our new neighbor, Gary Snyder, the owner of Dad's Pizza, showed up at our door with two giant pizzas. It was the kindest thing that anyone could have done for us at that precise moment, and it pulled me out of my self-pity. He welcomed us to the neighborhood and told us that if we needed anything to call him. The pizza was delicious, and we were delighted to have met a good neighbor.

When the plumber arrived the following day, he snaked the drain and told us that he had been to the house in the past for the very same problem. He said that because the house had been empty for so long, whatever was clogged in the pipes had hardened. All of the water we'd been running since we'd moved in, showering, cleaning, flushing, and laundry, had not been able to pass the clog, causing it to back up. The plumber left, confident that the problem had been fixed. I resanitized the kitchen and bathroom, and Joe bought industrial-strength biohazard chemicals to defunk the basement. Exactly one week later, it was déjà vu. The lights flickered, water poured down through the kitchen ceiling, and the basement backed up. I thought I would lose it. The plumber returned and said that he may not have snaked the drain far enough. The second time around, he snaked it out to the main drain on the street; and after that, we were clog free.

That was probably the lowest point for me. I felt like I was being tested over and over again. I was trying incredibly hard to keep it together and make the best of our situation. I felt like it was my job to stay brave for my children and strong for my husband; but the more I tried, the more difficult everything became. I felt like I was under attack. Nothing was easy, everything was a struggle, and for each step forward, there were three steps back. Despite it all, I clung to hope, believing that God was still there. He kept revealing Himself in subtle ways. I continued to remind myself that God was with me, even though bad things were happening, and things literally got pretty crappy at times, but He made sure that we saw how He was carrying us along.

After sanitizing the entire kitchen for a third time, things settled down. To say that we lived in close quarters would be a huge understatement, but it was organized and clean, and we had everything we needed. Our biggest challenge was making room for all the girls' clothes. With six of them sharing one room, in three sets of bunk beds, and just enough space between them for one person to squeeze through, it was almost claustrophobic. They had a decent-sized closet for their hanging clothes; but for their other things, we improvised, using the cubby part of the wall unit we had bought in New York for a clothes organizer. We set it up in Michael's room on the wall opposite his crib, leaving less than two feet of space in between. He had the tiny shoebox room to himself. The four older boys slept in the third bedroom in two bunk beds, and Joe and I set up our bed in the family room on the main floor. There was enough room for our dresser, a small pull-out sofa, and Joe's big leather chair and ottoman.

We used the side kitchen door as our main entrance and kept the front door locked. It was challenging keeping the doors secured. The screen didn't close tightly unless it was pulled shut. Scamp, our rescue dog, soon figured that he could push the door open with his nose and escape, which he did more than once. The older kids had to chase him, which was dangerous being that we were on one of the busiest streets in Chippewa. The scariest thing that happened was when Ryan, who was three, followed our older kids out as they were heading to the store across the street. The kids hadn't noticed him following them, but a passerby did and brought him up to the door. Joe and I were panicked. We were grateful for Ryan's guardian angel watching over him, but we knew we needed to do something different. We decided that we needed to not only keep the side door locked, we also put an alarm on it. We added a chain lock, up high on the door, and put a baby gate between the screen and wooden doors. We were constantly watching and checking doors, making sure we knew where Ryan was at all times, and always reminding the kids to keep them locked. Each time we heard the alarm, we ran to count heads. It was more than stressful.

We were grateful for summer break. The reprieve before the kids returned to school. The time to decompress from our move was much needed. It was convenient being right around the corner from Walmart, where I did most of the grocery shopping, and I loved being so much closer to the church. We were closer to everything. Joe took all the kids who wanted to go on walks every day, usually early in the morning before it got too hot. They would either drive to the Blackhawk High School track down the road or to Brady's Run walking trail. It became a routine for them, and they very much looked forward to it. As soon they got home, I headed to morning Mass. It was my new routine. The more I went, the more I craved it. I loved the hour of adoration and the opportunity to go to confession before Mass, which I began to do at least once a month. My relationship with God deepened, my faith was strengthened, and I became very protective of my devotional time. Life felt calmer. I thanked God for providing so much for us—food, a humble roof over our heads, the support of our friends, our parish community, and our health. I focused my prayers on Joe finding a job and us getting back on our feet. I knew that God was listening to my prayers and felt confident that in His time, the job would come.

THIRTY-TWO

Old Habits

Beaver Falls, Pennsylvania, July 2012

$\mathcal{A}$ lady from our church, Winnie, had some work to do around
her house, cleaning up her gardens and landscape, power washing,
staining trim, and some other odd jobs. She asked us after Mass
if our boys would be interested in a job. She'd pay ten dollars an
hour, cash. Joseph was still away, working at the Boy Scout camp in
Minnesota, but Patrick wanted a job. He was strong and hardworking, and he jumped at the opportunity. We drove him to Winnie's
house, where she showed him all of what she needed done. Patrick
started right away and worked from seven in the morning till one
o'clock in the afternoon. He worked hard, and Winnie paid him
right on time. Patrick was also offered a job by Gary, at Dad's Pizza,
and soon he was working two jobs. When he finished at Winnie's for
the day, he took a shower and headed next door to work at the piz-
zeria, sometimes until midnight. Patrick seemed to be much happier,
less moody, and a lot easier to get along with. He enjoyed having
money to buy new things. He bought an iTouch, which we approved
of since he had worked for and earned it. We were proud of him and
how he seemed to be handling his new responsibilities. His counselor
continued to see him at the house once a week on Saturdays. He had
been testing clean for several months, and she too was pleased to see
his growth and progress. After a few weeks of working long hours, he

informed us that he didn't want to work at Winnie's house anymore. We were disappointed. He had completed nearly all the work she wanted done. He could have finished the rest in a little more than a week. We knew he was tired from the early mornings and late nights. Joe told Winnie that if she wanted, he would finish the work. Winnie agreed, and Joe took Clare and Callum with him to finish up the next several days of work.

We started finding cans of chewing tobacco around the house—some empty, some full—and several empty water bottles used for spitting in. Patrick was buying chew again. When we asked him about it, he said that he had bought them before the move. We didn't believe him. Now that he was earning money, he had the means to purchase it, and we discovered that the people at the store across the street were selling it to him. Joe went into the store to talk to the owner and his wife. He told them that Patrick was underage and that he knew they were selling him tobacco. Joe told them that he wasn't looking to start anything, but if they continued to sell tobacco to Patrick, there would be trouble. The owners promised that they would not sell it to him anymore, and we told Patrick not to bring any tobacco into the house.

Shortly after moving into the house, we got a call from the IRS. The lady Joe had spoken with months earlier had finally gotten back to him about the status of our tax bill. She said that she needed a few other copies of certain documents, but from what she had calculated, we would only be required to pay $1,250. Half of what Tax Masters had calculated. Another stipulation was that we would have to surrender to the IRS any tax returns for the following year. It was a huge relief. Our original bill was forty thousand dollars, and it had grown to more than sixty thousand, due to interest penalties, a crushing debt. Joe and I were completely aware that God's hand had been in the resolution.

Patrick started sneaking out of the house again. Living in the heart of Chippewa with money in his hands was the perfect setup for him. We aren't sure how many times he had snuck out before we caught on, but we'd been in the house for less than a month when we found out. One night around eleven o'clock, after everyone had gone to bed, Joe and I heard a thud. We got up and checked all the windows and doors. I went upstairs and discovered that the boys' bedroom door was locked. There was an old-fashioned slide lock on the door inside the room. It was strange for the door to be locked in the middle of the night. Being pregnant, I regularly made multiple trips up the stairs to the bathroom throughout the night, and the door had never even been shut before. All the bedroom doors were left open so that the air-conditioning unit at the top of the stairs could reach the rooms. I banged on the door, over and over and over, until Callum, who had been sound asleep, got up and unlocked it. By that point, some of the girls had woken up too. I shuddered when I wondered what would have happened if the house had caught fire. We wouldn't have been able to get in to save Callum and Ryan. Patrick's bed was empty, and the screen was out of the window. He had climbed out onto the roof. The thud had been him landing, either on the ground right outside our window or onto the front deck. Joe walked around outside and didn't see him anywhere. When he came back in, we locked all the doors and his bedroom window. He wouldn't be getting back in the same way he had gotten out. We laid awake for the rest of the night with our hearts sinking. The nightmare had begun again. We had given Patrick the opportunity to prove himself, and we had hoped that he would choose the right path. We wanted him to succeed, but it had been too tempting for him.

I got up several times to scan the yard through the windows. We heard movement on the deck and up on the overhang, just under the boys' bedroom window. Patrick was attempting to sneak back into his window, no doubt surprised to find it locked. Joe and I sighed with relief that he was home, and we waited to see what he would do next. He never came to the door, knowing he had been discovered. When I went upstairs to use the bathroom again, I looked through the window at the top of the stairs. It faced the backside of the house next door. I saw him walking away from the big fridge behind Dad's Pizza with something in his hand. When I told Joe, he got up to look out the kitchen window. Patrick had pulled out a lawn chair from the shed, sat down under the spotlight, and proceeded to open up a can of beer. He had taken a beer out of Gary's fridge. I was shocked. Not so much that he was drinking beer, I knew that was nothing new for him, but I was shocked that he would just blatantly help himself to Gary's beer. As far as I was concerned, he was stealing. We left him outside. After everyone had woken up and it was time to put the dogs outside, he sauntered through the door. When we began the inquisition, he told us that he never left the property, that he had been sitting out front with his friends the whole time. We knew he was lying because Joe had gone out to look in the yard and walked around the whole house after we'd heard the thud. I called his counselor and told her what had happened. It was Saturday, his regular counseling day. She was not at all happy when she got to the house. She told him that she was not only very disappointed, she was angry. She believed that he had made progress and was showing signs of responsibility. She told him that she was tired of dealing with him, and if he didn't want to work on improving himself, she didn't want the hassle. She said she was ready to play hardball. If he wanted to continue that sort of behavior, she encouraged us to involve the police. We were beginning to think the same thing. We had already tried everything else, and we didn't have the energy to go through it all over again. I was tired of playing games. We told Patrick that he would have to tell Gary what he had done. I was so ashamed that he would steal from him. Gary was not only a kindhearted neighbor, he had given Patrick a job. Joe went to the pizza place and asked Gary to come over for a minute. He came in and sat down at our kitchen table, and Patrick proceeded to tell him what he had done. Gary wasn't mad. He was disappointed that Patrick was drinking beer underage. He said that he had no problem with Patrick going into the fridge to take a pop or water, but didn't approve of him drinking beer. We told Gary that we would understand completely if he fired him. Gary said he didn't want to do that. He felt certain that Patrick wouldn't do it again and that he surely had learned his lesson. We thanked him for being so generous, but we didn't let Patrick off the hook. We put him on lockdown. Other than work, he wasn't allowed to go anywhere unless he was supervised.

When we found more tobacco and spit bottles in the house, Joe brought a wallet-sized picture of Patrick back to the store and told the owners to post it. He told them to make sure that everyone who worked there saw it and warned them not to sell tobacco to our son, or we would go to the police. I was heartsick. I continued going to morning adoration and Mass Tuesday and Thursdays at St. Rose of Lima, and Wednesday evenings and Friday mornings at Christ the Divine Teacher. The peace and comfort it brought me helped me to deal with all of the anxiety. I got comfort from all of the regular morning Mass goers. I knew they were praying for us. I longed to sit in adoration of the Blessed Sacrament. I looked forward to it each morning, thinking about and anticipating the next opportunity each night before I went to sleep. When I missed a daily Mass, I craved it. I wished that I had discovered how powerful adoration and daily Mass were years earlier. How many Masses had I missed out on? How many opportunities to go to adoration had I not taken? It became my sustenance.

Patrick continued to work but was angry, not only because he had been caught, but because of his once again restricted life. He continued to sneak out of the house. He snuck out of Michael's window the next time we discovered he was missing, making us extremely uneasy. The fact that he would go into his baby brother's room and sneak out through his window while he was asleep made my skin crawl. Joe and I had said that the worst part of Patrick's escapades was that he left the house unsecured and his family vulnerable to potential predators, or other criminals. If he was sneaking out and his friends knew about it, people could just as easily sneak in. We put a wooden stick in the window because the lock was not working, and waited for him to come home. Because it was summer, he didn't care about being left outside overnight. When he returned home early in the morning, he was obviously hung over. We made him quit his job and confiscated his iTouch. It was clear to us that he was using it to plan his escapes. He was spending all his money on cigarettes and beer. He hadn't been using drugs as far as we knew, because his counselor continued to test him, and he was always clean. Still, we wouldn't allow him to continue his behavior. As much as we liked that he was working, he was not doing the right thing. He was not at all happy that his cash supply would be ending. He became very angry with us. We felt supported by our pastor, our friends, and the drug counselor. We needed to set an example for the rest of our kids. We did not want his behavior to be repeated by any of them.

We moved Patrick down to the basement. We didn't want him sneaking out of the windows anymore, and the basement was inescapable. There were block glass windows down there, and we put a padlock on both the walkup basement and the side kitchen doors. We started using the front door because we could more easily monitor all the coming and going from the family room. Patrick didn't seem too bothered by being banished to the basement. He brought down his hand weights and a radio and organized all his clothes in the dressers that were stored down there. We soon felt a slight sense of security.

Within a few days of us forcing Patrick to quit his job, we got a call from Gary. Someone had broken into his fridge and stolen all the booze that he kept in there. All of it—beer, wine, liquor. It was his personal stuff and that of his adult employees. Patrick had been the only minor working there. We were devastated. We knew it couldn't have been Patrick since there was no way he could have gotten out of the house. We had taken all the measures we could think of to prevent it. Our house was like Fort Knox. He said that whoever had stolen it had to have had a vehicle to get it all out, because there was no way someone could have carried it all and moved it on foot. We asked Patrick what he knew. His reaction was one of complete surprise, but of course, how did we really know? He had lied to us so many times before, and very convincingly. We knew that he couldn't have done it himself, if indeed he had been involved, but we knew it was very possible that he knew who did it. He swore he didn't know. He said that he had talked about how much booze was available while he was with friends, bragging about how he was able to get beer whenever he wanted it. He said that he might have mentioned to his friends that the fridge was never locked. We were sick.

Joe went over to talk to Gary. He told him what Patrick said, that he swore he didn't know anything about it, but that he had told his friends that he'd been able to sneak beer. Joe told Gary he should probably get a video camera and lock up the fridge. Gary said that he had been in business for ten years and never had anything like that happen. It was really embarrassing. I told Patrick that he had better start talking to his friends because I planned to talk to the police. I would not sit back and allow something like that to happen and do nothing about it. Gary had been more than good to our family. Patrick called his friends while I listened on the other end of the phone. He told them that he needed to find out who had stolen the booze and that his mother would be going to the police if he didn't get any names. I could hear the nervousness in one of his friends' voices. He swore that he wasn't involved in the theft, but he said he didn't need the cops showing up at his house because he had "stuff" all over the place. I wasn't exactly sure what kind of "stuff" the kid was talking about, but I was pretty sure it wasn't legal. He also threatened to go crazy on me if the cops did show up.

After a few more calls and no real leads, and after discussing it with Patrick's counselor, I went to the Chippewa Police Department. I just showed up and rang the buzzer, and they let me in. I talked to Officer Herndon, the same officer who had come out on Mother's Day, when Patrick had disappeared and ducked into the car. He remembered us, and I updated him on the events that had taken place since that day—about our move, Patrick's job at Dad's Pizza, and about the robbery. Gary hadn't called the police and wasn't planning on filing any charges. I gave Officer Herndon names and phone numbers of kids I knew Patrick hung out with, and contacts from his iTouch. The police officer agreed that it was more than likely a case of Patrick talking big and bragging about the easy access, which gave some of his buddies the idea of stealing the booze. Officer Herndon said that he would go by to talk to Gary and would let me know what he found out. I told him about Patrick's consistent sneaking out and the measures we had taken to prevent it. It seemed like every time we thought we had come up with a new solution, he managed to find another way around it. Officer Herndon told me the next time he snuck out to call them. I told him that the last time we had done that, back when we were still living in Bob and Nanette's house, they told us that unless he broke the law, they couldn't do anything about it. Officer Herndon looked irritated and asked, "Who told you that?"

I told him that the dispatcher who had answered the call told us. He seemed very annoyed and told me that the dispatcher had no authority to tell us such a thing. Because Patrick was a minor, we could call the police anytime he left the property without permission, day or night. That was news to me and something we could use. Patrick had been confident that nothing would happen to him, and he was growing more and more arrogant about it. We felt like our hands were tied. None of the consequences we gave him seemed to bother him. Sure, we kept him on lockdown all day, but once we were able to finally fall asleep, he could sneak out whenever he wanted and have his fun. Officer Herndon said that he wouldn't even bother locking the doors. He told me to just let him sneak out and then call the police when he did. Once there were enough calls, he would be considered a habitual runaway, and they could involve the courts.

When I went home and told Joe about my conversation with Officer Herndon, he seemed pleased that we had a little power. We didn't say anything to Patrick. His counselor tried to convince us to emancipate him, but we refused. She believed that he would continue to rebel and get himself into trouble, possibly with the law, and we would be held accountable when he did. We wanted to protect him. He was a minor, and he was our child. We kept the locks on the doors. We still had a little more than a year to help him straighten up, and we were not about to relinquish our parental responsibilities.

The oppressive heat continued all summer. We kept the window air conditioners running around the clock, two on the main floor, and two upstairs. We also kept the ceiling fan running in the family room, which doubled as our bedroom, along with a big box fan in the dining room entry. The whirring sounds of all the machines created a white noise, day and night in our little house. At night, the added whooshing sound from Joe's CPAP machine drowned out the traffic from the street and any other sounds in the house. Late one night, we awoke to our dog Maverick's low growl. I shot up out of bed, onto my feet, and Joe, startled more by my sudden movement than the growling dog, got up as well. I went directly to the basement, turning the light on, on my way down. Patrick was gone. I walked back up the stairs to the kitchen, checking the two basement doors on my way. They were both locked. When I got back to the kitchen, I saw Joe standing at the sink, holding Patrick's hat in his hand. It was one of his party hats. He always seemed to have a ball cap when he snuck out that he never wore any other time. Joe said that he had found the hat in the sink. The kitchen window was partially open, and there was a ladder leaning against the house. We were willing to wager that one of his friends had put the ladder there to help him escape. Joe locked the window and put a wooden spindle that he had found in the basement inside the frame so that it couldn't be opened. The kitchen was literally eight steps away from our bed. He was definitely getting bolder, taking advantage of the noise being generated from all the fans and air conditioners. We were about to call the police when Patrick knocked on the front door. He had obviously only just gotten out of the window minutes before. I'm sure he saw the lights being turned on in the house and knew he was caught. He told us that he was just going to walk to the store to get a drink. It was after eleven o'clock at night. We knew that he had other plans, and we told him so. He went back to bed, and we waited for his next escape attempt. We knew it was only a matter of time. It was difficult to enjoy any sort of summer fun with the weight of Patrick's behavior always hanging in the air. We couldn't leave him unsupervised, but he was unpleasant to be around, always in a bad mood, disrespectful, and argumentative. We felt like prisoners in our own home, constantly having to be on watch and refereeing arguments.

One night in late August, Joe saw a light flash across the window, like a flashlight or car headlights, directly in front of the house. It was about ten thirty, and the lights were all turned off inside the house. The kids were asleep, and Joe and I had just turned off the TV. Joe got up to look out the window, and I went downstairs to check Patrick's bed. I turned on the light and saw a form in his bed, but when I went closer to check, I noticed that he had stuffed his blanket to make it look like he was sleeping. A trick he had used before when we lived in Texas. I called up the stairs to Joe to tell him that Patrick was gone. I checked the basement doors and kitchen window, but they were all locked. I couldn't figure out how he had managed to get past us while we were watching TV. I knew he hadn't come upstairs. Or had he? I wondered if I had missed something. We checked upstairs. Every window in the house was secure and all the doors were locked. How in the world had he escaped? I felt like I was losing my mind. I looked through the basement again. Wondering if he was hiding out down there. The only windows in the basement were block glass ones that didn't open. There were tiny vented windows that not even the smallest of our kids could fit through. I was beyond baffled. Joe went outside to walk around the perimeter of the house with a flashlight. When he came back in the house, he told me that the block windows on the back of the house had been chiseled out and replaced, to make it look like they hadn't been touched. I asked him how he had figured it out. He told me that the old electronics and computer stuff that he had stacked on the table in the basement, just beneath the chiseled-out window, had been rearranged. Patrick had climbed on top of the table, moved out the blocks, slipped out the window, and restacked the blocks from the outside before sneaking off. I called the police. I explained to the dispatcher that our son had again snuck out of the house and that I wanted an officer to come over. We were less than a mile away from the Chippewa police station, so it took no time for an officer to get there.

The cruiser pulled up, lights flashing, and we invited the officer into the house. We explained Patrick's history up to that point. I showed him a picture, and he told us he would be on the lookout for him. He asked who he might be with, and I gave him some names and phone numbers. He said he was familiar with some of the names. The officer left, and within twenty minutes, Patrick was standing on the front deck knocking on the door, trying to get in. He gave us the same story: he had walked to the gas station to get a drink. Joe and I were convinced that he had seen the police lights flashing and was afraid of the consequences. I called the dispatcher again, and when the officer returned my call, I explained that Patrick had returned. He asked me if I wanted him to come back to the house to talk to him. I told him that it wasn't necessary. The main thing was that the incident would be on record. We told Patrick very calmly, in a matter-of-fact way, that every time he snuck out, we would be calling the police; and eventually he would be classified as a habitual runaway. At that point, they would have no choice but to place him into a juvenile facility. We were tired. We were not going to continue living that way. It was his future and his choice.

We moved Patrick back upstairs to his old room and made him reseal all the basement windows he had chiseled out. Joe went to Home Depot and bought several two-by-four boards; and while the kids were at school, he measured, cut, and fit them into the window frames. He not only screwed them in, but glued them with wood glue first. Patrick wouldn't have an easy time of removing them, though he did try, always getting caught before the time-consuming task of getting the screws out was complete. Joe eventually stripped the screws, making it next to impossible to get the boards out. We told Patrick that he would be constantly supervised, something that was way harder on us than it was on him. We didn't let him hang out in his room either. He had to sit wherever the rest of us were. If he went outside, someone had to be with him. If Joe went walking with the younger kids and I wanted to go to Mass, I made him get up and come with me. I wouldn't risk leaving him home with the other kids. He regularly got into the girls' rooms, in search of money or anything else that he could use. We locked up all valuables in our safe and kept it by the front door.

Patrick wasn't happy about having to get up early to go to Mass with me, but he got used to the routine. I used the time to tell him that I wasn't enjoying keeping him under my thumb, but he had left me little choice. He said he just wanted to have fun. His idea of fun and our idea of fun were in completely different realms. Our other kids enjoyed hanging out with their friends, working on projects, going to the movies and out for lunch, being involved in basketball and track and field, school musicals, and other extracurricular activities. Patrick wanted us to give him permission to hang out late at night with the bad boys and girls, smoking cigarettes, using pot, drinking beer, and driving around high. We told him that we would never give him permission to do any of those things, so he snuck out at every opportunity. He believed that what he was doing was normal teenaged behavior. He claimed that all his friends were doing it and some of their parents even partied with them. He told me how cool his friends' parents were and asked why we couldn't be cool like them. He used a lot of different angles to try to wear us down, but we stayed consistent and prayed our heads off that he would come to his senses before something tragic happened.

Fr. Schreck stopped Patrick one day after daily Mass and asked him if he wanted to earn some money. They planned to renovate some of the classrooms in the church building to transform them into a Perpetual Adoration Chapel. They needed help with pulling up old carpets, replacing the ceilings, and knocking out walls. Patrick said he'd like the opportunity, and he started that same day. God had given him another chance. It was his third job offer in as many months. A couple of weeks later, when Fr. Farnan saw Patrick working in the church, he asked him if he'd be interested in helping out at Divine Mercy School. Their regular custodian was recovering from a foot injury, and they needed someone to fill in for him. Pretty soon he was working regular hours at Divine Mercy Church and School doing all sorts of jobs. Joe and I thought that working in two churches and the Catholic school was the best place for him to be. We were grateful that he had been given the opportunity. Joe joked about Patrick having nine lives. I just kept praying that they wouldn't run out.

School started for the youngest kids two weeks earlier than it did for the high school kids. It was an unbelievable privilege and gift to be able to send them to Divine Mercy Academy. We never would have been able to afford the tuition, even if Joe had been working, but Fr. Schreck insisted that there was always a way. Between the Angel Fund, scholarships, and some very generous private and anonymous donations, tuition for five of our kids had been paid in full for the entire year, with money left over. We asked that the leftover funds be donated to another needy family. We loved that the class sizes at Divine Mercy were small and that the teachers were solidly Catholic. The school building was beautiful. It really hit me as I walked through the hallways, realizing where my children would be spending their days, how truly blessed we were. Surrounded by life-sized statues of the Blessed Mother and several saints, where sunshine poured in every window of the historic and authentically Catholic school, my heart soared. Our kids were immersed in their Catholic faith every day, and I felt a tremendous amount of comfort sending them to school. They attended and participated in school Masses on Fridays, they were nourished spiritually while receiving a solid well-rounded education. They were loved and cared for by everyone from the principal to each of their teachers, teachers from other classrooms, the lunch ladies, and the parents of their friends. It was a holy place.

Joe got a notice that his Texas unemployment was being continued. We were happy, but also worried about the one-time benefit we'd received from the Beaver County Assistance Office. We still had some of the funds left, but we'd used some of it for our move and wondered if we would have to pay it back. We called the caseworker to explain what had happened. She assured us that we had nothing to worry about and that we weren't required to pay it back. She said that she was certain that we could use it and that the unemployment wouldn't last forever. She wished Joe luck on his interviews.

Once high school started, Patrick continued working at his custodian job after school, and Angela got a job at Franciscan Manor, the same place that Joseph worked. Angela mostly worked the day shift, and Joseph worked after school. Angela didn't return to Geneva for her second year of college. We just didn't have the funds to send her, and she didn't want to take out any more loans. Joseph had gained a lot of experience with cooking during the summer, working for the Boy Scout High Adventure Camp. When he let his manager at Franciscan Manor know, she allowed him to cook on occasions when they needed someone. It gave him more experience and a little better pay.

Joe had two job leads that were moving forward and seemed to be getting more serious. One of them was in Denver, Colorado, for a financial institution, and the other was in California, in the San Francisco Bay area, for a health network. We prayed for the one in Denver, Colorado. Our friends Tracy and Blair Korschun had just settled there, and we loved the idea of living close to them. We researched housing and the cost of living in both areas. We knew that

California was a very expensive place to live, but we had no idea that it would be more than double the cost of living in Colorado. I was also somewhat afraid of California. From everything that I had heard about it, mostly from the news, I imagined it to be extremely liberal. I worried about education, knowing we could never afford private school there, and I didn't want to send my kids to public school, especially not after being so blessed with a school like Divine Mercy Academy. I begged God to please let Joe get the Colorado job.

A third opportunity was presented when another call came from a recruiter about a job in the Pittsburgh area, for a school board position. It would have paid a lot less than the other two jobs, but we both agreed that staying in the Beaver Falls area would be wonderful. The salary would have been enough for us to live off because the cost of living in Beaver County was so low. It wouldn't take long for us to save up for a down payment on a house. Best of all, our kids could continue going to Catholic school. We decided that we would pray for either Colorado or Pittsburgh. Joe had several interviews for each of the three jobs. Most of them were phone interviews. He went to the school board to meet with the members twice, and in early October, he flew out to California for two days of interviews.

Ryan started preschool twice a week, and with the new routine established, it was a treat to have a couple of hours of quiet and calm with just Michael. I was able to get to morning Mass most days, as well as visit the Perpetual Adoration Chapel at Divine Mercy Church. The church itself was no longer open, due to the near collapse of the roof. The cost to repair and restore the church was in the millions, and the decision to close it permanently and merge the four area parishes into one had been made. We knew that we would be losing one of our pastors, either Fr. Schreck or Fr. Farnan, but no one knew which one would be getting moved. There was a lot of emotion surrounding all the changes. Divine Mercy Church was a landmark, and generations of families for more than a hundred years had been part of it, celebrating weddings, baptisms, and all the other sacraments and funerals in between. We were newbies to the area, but we felt the sadness, excitement, and anxiety of our fellow parishioners. There were also feelings of anger among some of the community, and our priests worked and prayed hard to help them through the transition. It would be a monumental undertaking.

Even though there were serious interviews taking place for all three prospective opportunities, Joe never stopped applying for others. We had been on that ride more times than we could count, and we knew that there were no promises or guarantees. He got notice that unemployment would be running out again. Joe had received the very same notice before, causing us to panic, and then within a few weeks, he was sent a letter telling him that he could reapply. It was nerve-wracking. He heard that a security company, Centurion Security, was hiring in the Pittsburgh area. He went to the job fair location that they'd advertised on the Internet and was one of fifteen people who got hired. He started right away. He had a drug screen test and a background check the same day as his interview. His job was to work as a guard for the Chevron gas drill site, close to Pittsburgh. His shifts were eight at night till eight in the morning. The graveyard shift was a pretty huge culture shock for all of us. He bought some steel-toed boots and was issued a pair of coveralls, a hard hat, and vest. The pay was only thirteen dollars an hour, and there were no benefits, but at least he got plenty of hours. The biggest challenge for him was getting enough sleep. He would get home around nine o'clock in the morning, after all the kids had left for school. I tried my best to keep Ryan, on the days he wasn't at preschool, and Michael, quiet. I took them to the park or on errands with me until their nap time. Of course the dogs barked randomly, and Joe wasn't used to sleeping during the day, so it was difficult to get used to the new schedule. He managed to sleep about four or five hours before the rest of the kids got home from school. When he was at work, he had a really hard time staying awake past midnight. He said he spent a lot of time walking around outside. The weather was getting colder, so the night air helped to keep him awake. He and his partner radioed each other and talked to pass the time.

We were just skimming by. Food was never lacking, thanks to the food stamps, nobody ever went hungry, but everyone's clothes were wearing thin, and although no one asked for anything, I knew they would have liked a few new things. I used my Old Navy card to buy the little kids their back-to-school uniforms and some of the essentials for the other kids. None of us were in desperate need of anything, but it was more than a little depressing, not being able to shop for some new things. I consciously tried to force myself not to reminisce about the old days when money was no real consequence, and we could just go buy the things we wanted or needed.

Bills were still tight. We were paying our own utilities in the little house, and of course the car insurance, the van payment, and gas. Our cell phone bills and other credit cards were being partially paid, and the payments were usually late. We just didn't have the money. We called a meeting with Angela, Joseph, and Patrick. We told them that we needed them to help out with the bills. They were all earning money, and we asked them to contribute most of their paychecks so that we could pay the bills. It was probably the lowest point for us to have to ask our kids to help us pay our bills. That's when they really understood the situation, that things were getting desperate. We told them that we would be keeping track of what they contributed, and that when Joe finally did get a job, we would pay them back every penny. Angela and Joseph turned over their paychecks willingly. Patrick cashed his and told us he hadn't gotten paid yet.

We noticed that one of the bikes was missing from the shed. It was a bike that had been left by the previous owners. Callum rode it often on the street behind our house. When we questioned Patrick about it, he told us that he had used it and left it at a friend's house after one of his nighttime escapades. He said the kid lived somewhere near the high school. I told him that I expected him to pick it up and ride it home from school. He came home three days in a row without the bike. On the fourth day, weary of all of his lame excuses, I waited for him to get home. When he got off the bus, obviously without the bike, I told him to get into the van. I informed him that we were going to pick it up. He grumbled and told me that I was wasting my time because there was nobody at his friend's house. I wasn't swayed. I drove toward the high school and made him show me where his friend lived. Patrick was annoyed, mostly because he didn't want me to know where his friend lived. When he pointed to the house, I noticed several cars in the driveway and that the garage door was wide open. I looked over at Patrick and, with a hint of sarcasm in my voice, remarked, "Well, it looks like they are having a party here. I thought you said nobody was home?"

He didn't respond. I pulled into the driveway and waited while he walked to the garage. I saw him wheel the bike out, so I backed out of the driveway onto the street. He gave me a puzzled look and told me to wait so that he could put the bike in the van. I rolled down my window and told him to ride it home. He hadn't been expecting that. He told me he wasn't riding it home. I told him that he'd had no trouble riding the bike to his friend's house, so he shouldn't have any trouble riding it home. He tried to haggle with me, "Just let me put it in the van."

I told him no, that he could ride it home. Then he announced that he would just ask his friend to put it in the back of his truck and drive him home. I told him that he didn't have permission to do that either. We caught the attention of a neighbor who was putting his trash cans out on the street. I told Patrick that I didn't really care about making a scene; if he didn't get on the bike and ride it home, I would call the Chippewa Police and ask them for an escort. He was not happy, and he knew I wasn't bluffing. It was a small parental win, in a sad and tragic sort of way. He had been making our life a living hell for far too long with his manipulations, lies, and defiance. I was not about to pass up an opportunity to take some of the arrogant wind out of his sails. He got on the bike and proceeded to ride painfully slow, while I followed at a snail's pace behind him. He did so until he got to the corner of Blackhawk Road. My window was still down. He stopped alongside the van to tell me that I would be responsible for his fine if he got stopped for riding with no helmet on a busy street. I asked him if he had worn a helmet when he snuck out in the middle of the night, while visibility was zero, on that very same road that had no streetlights. He glared at me and proceeded to ride at warp speed, across a bunch of front lawns. I drove along the road, pulling over onto the shoulder until he caught up. He continued to ride fast and then slow, just to mess with me, but I wasn't flustered. I continued to keep him in sight. At one point, he stopped and pulled something out of his pocket. It was a chewing tobacco pouch, and he made a big display of putting it under his lip. He gave me a big grin before he started riding again. I shook my head and prayed that he would stop the nonsense.

When he finally got home, I told him to get into the van because he was going to work. He told me he wasn't going. I insisted that he was. I would not allow him to just not show up for work. I delivered him to the door of the church and watched him go in. I sat out front and watched for a while, making sure he didn't leave. Several days later, the regular custodian returned from his sick leave and Patrick wasn't needed anymore. He had drifted right back into his old ways, moody, defiant, and hard to get along with. The high school kids noticed that he was hanging around with the wrong crowd again. We received a letter from the school, informing us that Patrick had missed some classes. I watched him get onto the bus every day, and there were no reasons for him to miss classes. He hadn't been sick, and I hadn't taken him out for any appointments. He had obviously been skipping out. When we questioned him, he told us that he left school during an assembly and one other day after lunch claiming he hadn't missed anything important; he blew the assembly off as a waste of time and went to his friend's house. I told him that if he skipped school again, I would call the police and report him as being truant. He laughed it off.

THIRTY-THREE

Adoration Miracles

Beaver Falls, Pennsylvania, October 2012

The kids caught the school bus right in front of the house every day, and I drove Ryan to preschool on Tuesdays and Thursdays. Divine Mercy Academy was in downtown Beaver Falls, about a ten-minute drive from the house. One Tuesday morning, I noticed that my gas tank was almost empty. Joe's van had just enough gas to get him to work and back. He had to drive to Pittsburgh, so I didn't dare drive his van and risk him running out on his way home. I had two options: I could either keep Ryan home from school that day, or I could take him and spend the two hours in the Perpetual Adoration Chapel until he was done. Joe told me to go ahead and take him. After delivering Ryan to his classroom, with my prayer books in hand, I walked around the corner to the chapel, looking forward to my two-hour retreat. There was only one other lady inside when I settled into the short pew. It was a delight for me to have two uninterrupted hours with Jesus. I prayed my regular prayers from my pieta book, and all the ones from the prayer scrapbook that I had made, a simple notebook that I had glued my favorite prayers into. I had also written out my own personal prayers on some of the pages and put pictures and names of all the people that I wanted to remember to pray for.

After finishing the prayers from my books, I sat in silence, pondering the state of our life. How had we arrived at that point? I had

447

no idea why it was all happening. It felt like we had been under attack for months. It was depressing, and yet at the same time, it had all been an incredible blessing. We had lost everything, and we had gained more than we had ever had. Financially we were a wreck, but spiritually we had grown tremendously, though I knew we still had a long way to go. It was hard to wrap my head around it all. Joe was spending more and more time in prayer, and he too was seeing the signs. He knew that it was God who was providing for our family, but we were both growing so weary of scraping by, not being able to find a job. The thought of him being a security guard, working the graveyard shift for the rest of his days was not at all comforting. As I thought about the empty gas tanks, I wondered how Joe would make it till payday, still three days away, with probably not enough gas for both of his shifts. The tears started to well up in my eyes. I didn't want to feel sorry for myself, but it was getting to be more than I could take. Everything was just so hard. When would we ever get a break? Joe finally had a job, not a great one, but it was a job, and he wouldn't even be able to get to it. I was just thinking about all those things, not necessarily telling them to God, just mulling them over in my head. I was sitting in the presence of Jesus, so I figured that my thoughts had to be known to Him, an unspoken petition. I didn't have to speak, and I was truly tired of asking. He already knew what I needed. I felt somewhat numb. I let it go and thought to myself, hoping Jesus was hearing my despair, "Just fix it."

The lady who had been praying when I arrived, left, and another lady came in. I had seen her at the various morning Masses many times before at the different churches. I didn't know her name, but we smiled at each other when she sat down in the chair. A few minutes before I was about to leave, she looked up and asked me my name. I introduced myself, and she told me that her name was Pat. She asked if I had children at Divine Mercy Academy. I told her that I did, and that in fact, Ryan was at preschool at the moment. I told her what a treat it had been to spend two hours in the chapel while he was at school. We chatted a bit, and I asked her to please pray that my husband would find a job. I told her it had been three years since his layoff and that things were getting really grim. I mentioned that we had a few leads that seemed promising, but of course, we had no idea for sure if any of them would be offered. She said that the breaks usually happen when things look the most bleak. I told her that that would be about now. She flipped through the book she was reading about St. Gertrude the Great and found a prayer. She said that she had a great devotion to her and believed that she would intercede. I listened while she prayed the prayer out loud, and she promised that she would continue to pray for us. I hugged her and thanked her as we walked out together, feeling a real sense of peace and comfort. The feeling of desperation that I had come into the adoration chapel with was gone. My gas tank was still empty, but I believed that everything would be okay.

I picked Ryan up from his class, and we drove straight home. I fixed lunch for both him and Michael and put them down for their naps. Joe went to sleep upstairs in the girls' room where it was a little quieter. After tidying up the lunch dishes and making a cup of tea, I flipped through the stack of mail that I had collected from the box on my way into the house with Ryan. I opened up what looked like a card. There was no return address on it, but it was stamped with a United States Post Office Stamp from Pittsburgh. I opened it up. There was no writing on the card, but inside were two fifty-dollar gift cards for Giant Eagle. My jaw dropped. Giant Eagle is a grocery store with an affiliated gas station. Joe and I could each put fifty dollars' worth of gas in our vans. He would be able to get to work for the rest of the week, and I'd have gas in my van for us to take the older kids to work, and Ryan to school on Thursday. It was a miracle. God had heard my thoughts and my tears. St. Gertrude the Great had no doubt whispered into God's ear for me, pleading for some relief. I couldn't wait for Joe to wake up so that I could show him the cards. All I could do was thank God over and over. He was so amazing, and no one would ever be able to convince me otherwise. When Joe came down the stairs from his nap, I told him about my experience in the adoration chapel, how I had been feeling like we were pretty close to rock bottom. He agreed. I told him about Pat, the lady who had prayed with me, and how she said that something good would be happening soon, not to worry. Joe said he hoped so, but he didn't look convinced. Then I showed him the two gift cards that had just arrived in the mail. They had been delivered as I was pulling into the driveway after driving Ryan home from school; I had seen the mail truck drive away myself. His jaw dropped. He was speechless. I gave him one of the cards, and he went straight to the gas station to fuel up his van.

That afternoon, he got a call from the recruiter for the California job. They wanted to set up another call with him. They scheduled it for Thursday at four o'clock Pacific time, which was seven o'clock Eastern time. He would be working at the Chevron site, but he said that he would just get one of the other guys to keep a watch for him while he took the call. The recruiter said that the call should only last about twenty minutes. We weren't sure if he would be getting a job offer or a rejection. Since the beginning of May, he'd had a total of nine interviews with the same company. It had been five months' worth of talking and waiting. Strangely, I was not thrilled about the possibility of the job. I was still praying that he would get one of the other two. Joe had decided that he would take the first offer he got. That made sense to me, and I vowed to support him with whatever his decision was, but I continued to pray that the Colorado job would call to make their offer first. I didn't want to move to California.

Patrick grew increasingly defiant about anything and everything that we said and did. He wasn't getting along with anyone. He was mean to the little kids, hostile with Joe and me, and we were suspicious of everything he did. The only time we saw his soft side was when he interacted with Michael. I could see the love in his eyes and how Michael lit up when he was around. I knew he had goodness in him, and I knew he had a soft heart. I prayed that he would let go of the anger he had bottled up, and that the demons who were tempting him and trying to wage war on our family would leave us all alone. He said that he didn't want to meet with his drug counselor anymore. He told us it was pointless and a waste of time. We told him that he needed to continue services with her. The random drug testing kept him honest. He informed us that we couldn't force him to stay in treatment or counseling if he didn't want to. After asking questions and checking it out, we discovered that he was right, so we cancelled the services. I knew that I could easily buy a drug kit myself and test him if I saw a need.

Joseph and Christina had auditioned for the high school musical for the second year in a row, and both of them got parts in *Beauty and the Beast*. Joseph was chosen for the role of Lumière, and Christina got two roles—a villager and as a knife in the "Be Our Guest" scene. We were happy that they would be participating in the musical once again and that they were still very much enjoying their high school experiences. Grace had made a lot more friends than she had in her first year in Beaver Falls. She was a freshman, excelled academically, and although she was not interested in being involved in any extra-curricular school activities, she was social, and we liked her friends. Clare decided to run cross-country for the first time, and both she and Callum planned to try out for basketball. They were both doing very well at school and were making nice friends. Patrick was not doing well academically, but he enjoyed school because it was his only social outlet, other than Teen Fusion, the church youth group. It was the only time we weren't around supervising him. He was well-liked by his teachers, though his coaches had caught onto his game and had warned him about the kids he was hanging with. They knew we didn't approve. He was handsome and charming and enjoyed being the bad boy. We weren't happy with the kids he was hanging out with. We were sick at the thought that he was one of those kids, but we had no control over who he interacted with at school.

Other than feeling emotionally drained, I felt pretty great. I had plenty of energy to do what I needed to do every day. At forty-two years old, and seven months pregnant with my twelfth baby, it was my easiest pregnancy health-wise that I had ever had. I had not once felt nauseous, though I had gained quite a lot of weight, probably because food was one of our only comforts. My blood pressure was perfect, and there were absolutely no concerns about the baby what-soever. A huge relief. God had spared me the kind of worry I had endured with Michael.

I started seeing a new ob-gyn, Dr. Dumpe. His office was much closer to us, in downtown Beaver Falls, in the same building where our dentist was. The first practice that I had gone to early on during my pregnancy was in Aliquippa. I had chosen it because while doing an online search, I discovered that one of the doctors in the practice was listed as being pro-life. Unfortunately, I had to see whoever happened to be on rotation for my appointments and would have to wait until it was her turn to come to that particular office. I was seen in a sort of satellite office, not the main practice, because I was a Medicaid patient. The main office was reserved for people who had private insurance. That rubbed me the wrong way. We'd always had private insurance, and I had been blessed with pro-life doctors of my choosing for all my other pregnancies. I was seen by a nurse practitioner for my first two appointments, not a doctor.

The waiting room and office made me feel very uncomfortable. It did not look or feel like any OB-GYN office I had ever been to before. It actually felt more like a birth-control dispensary. Every picture and bulletin board on the walls listed policies and requirements for specific contraception methods. For example, some of the shots had to be purchased by the patient from their pharmacy and then brought to the clinic to be injected by the nurse. It was almost impossible not to overhear the receptionist speaking to patients over the phone, even behind the closed glass, telling them that they needed to make an appointment before they could have their birth-control prescription refilled. There were advertisements for every pill, injection, sponge, ring, and device I never wanted to know existed, displayed on the walls of the exam room. I wondered to myself what kind of place it was. I didn't get a warm and fuzzy feeling from the doctor that I finally did meet either. When I was called back to the examination room, it was the nurse practitioner who did all the measuring, and used the fetal monitor to check the baby's heartbeat. Don't get me wrong, she was very nice and actually quite pleasant to talk to. I got the sense that I wasn't their typical patient. When the doctor came in, he introduced himself from across the room, barely looking up from my chart, and asked me when I wanted to schedule my C-section. He didn't examine me and made no attempt at small talk. I made the decision that day to search for another doctor. Surely there had to be a legitimate office somewhere. When I did more research that evening on the Internet, I discovered, to my horror, that the practice I had been going to was actually a Planned Parenthood satellite office. I wanted to vomit. I couldn't believe I had actually been in an office where they had dispensed so-called emergency contraception. Chemical abortions.

I did a search for pro-life obstetricians and found Dr. Dumpe. There was only one other doctor in his practice, as well as a nurse practitioner, and all three of them were pro-life. I immediately developed a rapport with Dr. Dumpe and his staff. The office was welcoming, everyone was friendly, and they all seemed to celebrate the new life with me. I found myself looking forward to my appointments as the anticipation mounted for the birth of our newest addition. I found out that I was having a boy. The kids were all so anxious to know if they'd be getting another brother or a sister, and I wanted to know for the sake of what baby clothes to hang onto and which ones to donate. The biggest conversation in our house was picking a name for our new little guy. Joe insisted that he would be choosing the name this time around, and I let him think that he would have the final say. I would be the one filling out the birth registration in the hospital, so ultimately, I had the last word. All the kids offered up names to be either approved of or tossed out, but Joe wouldn't tell them one way or another which one he had decided on. He enjoyed getting them all riled up.

Joe worked the "eight in the morning till eight at night" shift on the day of his call with the California recruiter. It was a typically busy day for all of us. We had anticipated hundreds of recruiter calls over the course of three years that hadn't been fruitful, so I didn't spend an unusual amount of time thinking about it. I said my morning prayers and got to Mass. The days were long for me when Joe was at work because of all the shuttling to and from work, and picking up from basketball. I was the only driver, and I also had to bring Patrick with me every time I left the house. He hated it, and I didn't particularly enjoy it either. It was a huge hassle. The few times that I did leave him at home, there was always trouble with one of the other kids. A fight of some kind would break out, or he would go out to smoke cigarettes in the backyard. He always seemed to have cigarettes or chewing tobacco since school was back in. Bringing him with me everywhere was frustrating for everyone. He would take forever to get into the car, purposely taking his time, needing to get a cup of water or a snack before going out the door. He took forever to put his shoes on, not caring that Angela and Joseph would be late for work or that Clare and Callum were at their school waiting to get picked up from basketball practice. He made sure he let me know that it was my fault if anyone was late, because it was dumb that I was making him come with me. I began allowing for an extra ten or fifteen minutes, calling him to the car earlier to avoid the delays. Driving around with him in the car was just as irritating. I made a habit of reciting the Divine Mercy Chaplet because it always seemed like I was driving around at three o'clock, the hour of mercy. The more I tried to pray, the stronger the attacks came. I became convinced that it was a spiritual warfare, and I refused to let the evil one win. Patrick used the time to disparage me and criticize our parenting, always trying to get me to react, but I learned how not to. I had learned through a lot of prayer to remain calm and unfazed by his shock tactics. When he asked me if I would consider allowing him to move to Canada with my mother, I screamed inside. That was the most shocking thing that he had come up with yet. Without blinking an eye or so much as a stutter, I calmly told him, "Absolutely not."

He continued to rationalize his request, trying to convince me that it would make my life so much easier if he wasn't around. He said he could finish school in Canada. I told him that under no circumstances would we relinquish our parental responsibilities. I especially would not agree to hand him over to my mother. The woman who had falsely accused his father of abuse and tried unsuccessfully to destroy our family. I asked him if he had forgotten the drama that had unfolded the year before. He told me that he didn't really care and that he had been in communication with her by e-mail. I knew that he was using my mother and that she was using him. I shuddered to think how alike they were. I asked him how the whole plan had come about. He said that he had discussed it with my mother and one of my sisters. He planned to move on his eighteenth birthday, but he could go earlier if I was nice enough to give him permission to do so. My response was a flat, "Never."

I was more than anxious for Joe to get home from work. After helping the little kids with their homework, and dinner was finished, the older girls gave Ryan and Michael their baths. Our bathroom was so tiny, and my belly was so big that I couldn't fit between the sink and toilet in order to lean over the bathtub. We all sat down in the family room to watch a DVD. We didn't have cable or satellite TV, but we had a lot of movies, and they saved our sanity. I settled on top of our bed with my knitting. I had been working on blanket squares since the beginning of summer. Red, white, and blue, each color was a different pattern, and I had planned to assemble them into a blanket for the new baby. Just after seven o'clock, the phone rang. Even though I had been expecting his call, my heart thundered in my chest. With no idea what the verdict would be, I held my breath before answering, "Hello?"

Joe whispered into the phone, "It's over. I got the job."

He sounded as if he didn't believe it himself. I could hear his smile and feel his relief, sensing how weak he must have been in his knees. I pictured his eyes twinkling. It felt like a dream. Then he said again, "It's finally over."

There was still close to an hour left on his shift. I couldn't wait for him to get home. I told all the kids, who had been listening to my end of the conversation, waiting to hear the news. There were huge sighs of relief all around. It didn't exactly sink in right away. We had waited so long for this news, and it seemed like it would never happen. We all sat around with big eyes, mouths open, just looking at each other. When Joe got home, he stopped in the doorway and looked at all of us with a giant grin on his face. We all stared back smiling. Then the kids bombarded him with questions.

"When are we moving?"

"Where are we going to live?"

"What about school?"

Joe was expected to start on November 5, less than two weeks away. He would be getting a signing bonus, a decent relocation package, and a fair salary. It was not as big as his salary with KPMG, but it was nothing to thumb his nose at. It was a good role, Director of Human Resources for the Human Resources Service Center, for

Kaiser Permanente, one of the largest private health care networks on the West Coast. He had held a similar role with KPMG when we had first moved to Texas. He knew he was more than qualified to do the job. He would have to wait a couple of days to get the offer in writing. The recruiter let him know that they would be calling all his references and conducting a background check, so it wasn't completely sown up, but he didn't have any concerns.

Over the next few days, while the finalizing was being done and the logistics were being figured out for the relocation, Joe and I sat staring at each other, rarely breaking the silence. We each knew what the other was thinking. It had been one hell of a ride. It was finally over, but it was also a little scary. We had adapted to our situation and had grown accustomed to surviving, clinging onto each other for dear life. Joe had essentially been home for three years. His consulting business start-up, Empowered Voyage, his work with Mir Group, the projects for Keith Wing, studying for the Farmers Insurance course, and driving the school van hadn't kept him away from home much. He'd only been working at the security guard job for a month or so. Despite the struggles of the unemployment, the blessing was that we had all bonded tightly as a family. We were more than a little nervous about the drastic changes that would be taking place.

Joe and I discussed, to the point of exhaustion, all our options. We knew that we couldn't all move right away. It simply would not be possible to manage a move across the country with a family of our size, in two weeks. It would be challenging enough for Joe to find a place for himself in that amount of time. He would be getting the relocation money up front, and we would be managing our own move, choosing our own moving company and scheduling everything ourselves. We could move on our own time table. The kids were only two months into the school year, which didn't seem like a long time, but they had already become actively involved, and we didn't want to just pull them out. Not to mention the fact that our five younger kids had received full scholarships to Divine Mercy Academy. And then there was the small fact I was seven months pregnant, not exactly in any shape for a cross-country move. I loved my new doctor and didn't want to have to go through the hassle of finding a new one in another state. Even though Joe's new job would be with a private health network, his probation period on the job included only basic insurance coverage. The full package wouldn't come into effect for ninety days. We decided that Joe would go to California on his own, and the rest of us would join him in June, as soon as Joseph graduated and school was out. Joe had quite a few frequent-flyer miles saved up from all the travel he'd done while working for KPMG, so he planned to come home for monthly visits. He would of course come home for the birth of our new baby, and then probably once a month after that.

Joe booked his flight for November 3, Christina's sixteenth birthday. The day after he received his signing bonus, the two of us went out for a day of clothes shopping. He desperately needed new clothes and shoes for work. He wasn't required to wear a suit, but needed business casual clothes. He was getting excited, but I know he was nervous too. I loved watching Joe try on new clothes. The saleslady and I chatted while he came in and out of the dressing room. I told her all about his new job after such a long time of unemployment, and about the support of our friends and community. The more I shared with her, the more questions she asked and the more amazed she was by our story. She told me how we had inspired her, and she wished us all the best. We both needed tissues by the time Joe was done with his shopping. He bought a lot of stuff, mainly because he needed it, but also because there is no sales tax in Pennsylvania, and everything would cost a lot more in California.

After our shopping trip, we went out for lunch. Bob, Nanette, Cathy, and Al had given Joe a gift card for Sal's restaurant in Chippewa for his birthday in August. Joe said he didn't want to use it until we had something to celebrate. We decided that the new job was the best reason we had at the moment, even though it still didn't seem real to us. He would be leaving so soon. It had been three years of searching and waiting, hopes and disappointments. We'd had so much time, but we still weren't prepared. I just couldn't make sense of my emotions. I had encouraged him to call off on his next shifts at the gas site, telling him that he needed to rest and prepare for his trip and spend the last few days with the kids. We both agreed that it would be a life-altering ordeal. When he went into the office to return his coveralls and hard hat, everyone congratulated him. He had shared some of his story with his coworkers, and they were genuinely happy for him. They told him that they had figured he would end up finding something that he was better suited for. His supervisor told him that they had been planning to offer him a training supervisor position the very same day he got the California offer. It would have paid better than his security guard job, but still not nearly enough to support our family.

Joe and I talked about all of what we had been through and how far we had come. We had remained faithful and hopeful despite the desperate and difficult times. God had carried us, using good people all along our journey to help. It hadn't been our plan. It had always been God's plan. We tried our best to accept it without resisting it, knowing that we would eventually see glimpses of how it all fit together as we continued on the path. Of all the places and jobs that Joe had applied for, that was where God wanted us to be. I never wanted to move to California, and neither did Joe. He purposely avoided looking for any jobs there. He had never even heard of Kaiser Permanente, but after two and a half years of searching, he opened up to it and applied for the job. Like Joe has said more than once, "God is a strange person."

We learned from experience that the changes that we had been the most resistant to, always ended up being the best, so California had to be good.

Joe's biggest worry about going ahead of us was leaving me on my own with Patrick. There was no question in his mind that Patrick would take full advantage of his absence. I told him that he couldn't worry about that, he needed to focus on his new job. We would be fine. I wouldn't put up with any of Patrick's nonsense, I would simply call the police. Only a couple of weeks earlier, we had called them when Patrick had disappeared during the day. It was a Saturday, and he had slipped off somewhere. When he finally returned, he offered a vague story about going to the basketball courts with his friends. When we called the police to tell them that he had finally come home, they came to the house to have a word with him. They were getting the hint that we were sick and tired of his complete disregard for our authority. I am pretty sure they were getting tired of him too. They told him that he really needed to quit being stupid. They knew the kids that he was hanging out with, and they were bad news. They told Patrick that he obviously had parents who cared about him and that we would give him more freedom when he earned it. They reminded him how we had allowed him to work at Dad's Pizza and about the fact that we hadn't taken his freedom away, he had given it up by making the wrong choices. They told him to stop blaming his parents and to start accepting responsibility for his own actions and make the necessary changes to improve his situation. It was encouraging to have the backup and support from the officers. They reiterated and reinforced everything that we had already told Patrick. All the same things that he had been told by his teachers, our friends, his coaches, the vice principal, his counselor, and more than one priest. It had always been the same message, there were no contradictions. We weren't being unreasonable, we were being responsible. They told him that they wished more parents were like us because their job would be a lot easier. I pondered what they said. If more parents had been like us, our job may have been easier too. They told Patrick that if they continued to get calls about him leaving the house without permission or sneaking out at night, they would take him to a juvenile facility. They didn't want to do that. They knew he was smarter than that. He would be eighteen in eight months. He could move out and be his own man at that point, but for the time being, he needed to live by our rules.

Joe picked Joseph up from his shift at Franciscan Manor one night, just days before he was scheduled to leave for California. Seconds after Joseph got up to his room, he called down to us that Patrick had a phone. We had suspected that he had one a couple of days earlier. Callum had seen a flash of something shiny, but Patrick denied having anything. We knew he had something, but we didn't press him, figuring that in time it would resurface. That time had come more quickly than we had anticipated. Joe ran up the stairs, demanding to know where it was. A phone meant that he was scheming. Joe looked around while Patrick stood smugly, denying having anything and daring Joe to search the room. I waddled up the stairs and helped him look. I knew it had to be in there somewhere. We searched every inch of the room with a fine-tooth comb and could not find the thing. We were completely baffled. We made Patrick come downstairs to sit on the couch and wouldn't let him out of our sight. Several minutes later, Christina called down the stairs to say that she had found it. Patrick had made a slit in the bottom of his backpack and slipped it between the lining and the outer shell. He was a genius. It amazed us how his mind worked. If only he would put all his creative genius and energy into something good and productive, instead of criminal. He was brilliant, and yet he continued to use his smarts for all the wrong things. He told us that he wasn't doing anything wrong, he was only talking to his friends. What was the big deal? I told him that if he didn't have anything to hide, he wouldn't have a problem giving me the password for the phone. He told me it was none of my business. I asked him why he wouldn't tell me. If he wasn't doing anything shady, what was the big secret? That's when the next big bombshell fell. As he walked up the stairs, free to go back to his room now that the contraband phone was securely in our possession, he looked over the railing and said, "I'm not the one with a secret."

Joe and I looked at each other and knew instinctively what Patrick was alluding to. It could only be one thing. He had been in communication with my mother, and I knew that she would have so enjoyed being the one to tell him.

With all our other children's eyes on us, questioning what it was, we knew that we had no choice but to lay it all out. We had been putting it off long enough. We told the kids that Joe had been married before and that he had a son, Christopher, whom he had only recently reconnected with six months earlier. They were extremely surprised to hear such information, but when the initial shock wore off, they were also quite excited to learn that they had another brother. Joe told them that he had received a text from his son on Father's Day. Christopher had been in the military, was married, and pursuing an acting career in LA. Joseph was especially excited to hear that part, since he had always been very interested in acting and hoped to become involved in performing arts and comedy. We answered all their questions. It was a surprisingly calm, matter-of-fact conversation. There was no drama, no meltdown, and no anxiety. Although we had been carrying the secret for more than twenty years, it wasn't something that we dwelled on daily. Still, it had always been there at the back of our minds, and we were relieved to finally have it out in the open. We were happy that our kids finally knew about their brother, and we were also excited about the fact that he lived in Los Angeles. We would soon be moving to California. Surely we would get to see Christopher and meet his wife. God's plan for our family was unfolding, and we hoped that Christopher would be part of it.

Patrick stayed upstairs while we laughed and talked about how incredible it was that we would be moving to the same state as their newly discovered brother. We knew better than to believe it was a coincidence. I doubt that our reaction was the one that Patrick—and most especially, my mother—had expected us to have. Patrick had revealed that he had been talking to my mother regularly, via his e-mail account at school. He told her that we suspected that she had been the one to make the Child Helpline call or that she had put one of my sisters up to it, but he said she denied it. He mentioned something about one of my sisters being friends with someone who worked for customs at the Canadian/US border. It all sounded very fishy to us. He said that my mother and sister had discussed a plan to drive to Pennsylvania over the Thanksgiving break. My sister would do some shopping first, pick Patrick up at a neutral place, and then drive him to Canada where he would live with my parents. Joe and I laughed at the plan. There was no way we would ever allow it. Patrick thought that we would go along with it, simply out of frustration over his behavior. We were beyond frustrated. We were more than exhausted with his craziness and acting out, but we would never relinquish him to my parents. We would not shirk our responsibility. We were his parents, and until he turned eighteen, he would live under our roof. He told us that my sister had already planned to pick him up and that all he needed was his passport and a letter giving her permission to take him across the border. They had done their homework. I explained to him that his passport had expired and all of our immigration paperwork was locked in our safe. We told him that we would not give anyone permission to take him across the border and that if any of them had any plans to sneak him out of the country, we would have them charged with kidnapping. The border police would be notified immediately the minute he went missing. Patrick felt that the plan would be his ticket to freedom, but I knew better. I knew that my mother would have enjoyed playing the role of rescuer and all the drama that went along with it. A couple of days after Patrick had revealed his plan to us, we were all watching television together. I had dozed off, but was startled awake by the sound of the phone ringing next to me on the night table. When I answered it, I heard a click. The caller had hung up. I looked at the caller ID and recognized my mother's home phone number. The kids all urged me to call back, but I refused. I told them that if she wanted to talk to me, she would call back. She never did.

Joe was even more worried than ever about leaving me to deal with Patrick. I was one month away from delivering our baby and had eleven other kids to care for. I had plenty on my plate to manage, even if Patrick had been an angel. I told him to focus on his new job, I would be fine. He couldn't afford to be stressed out about what was out of his control. With his bags packed with all his new clothes, I drove him to the airport early in the morning. His brothers, who lived in Oakland, had found an apartment for him in Alameda. They set it up for him with a bed and the basic essentials for survival until he got settled in properly. I was glad that he would have family around him to make his transition relatively smooth. Joe had spent some of his summers in Oakland as a kid. His parents had divorced when he was very young, and his dad had remarried and settled in Oakland, California, so it was not completely foreign to him. I cried all the way home from the airport. Joe and I had been married for twenty years, and our twenty-first wedding anniversary was only a few weeks away. We would be celebrating on separate coasts. Still, we were grateful. No matter how tough we knew it may get, we knew that it was temporary. There would be a paycheck coming in. We wouldn't starve, we could pay our own bills, and finally relax a little bit.

THIRTY-FOUR

Taking Charge

Beaver Falls, Pennsylvania, November 2012

I was scheduled to have a C-section on December 5. The first thing I did on the Monday after Joe left town was call the Beaver County Welfare office. I told them that Joe had gotten a job and that we no longer needed food stamps. We did, however, need to remain on medical assistance until his insurance kicked in on March first. I needed to be reassured that my delivery would be covered, as well as our kids in the event of an emergency, especially with Michael. Our caseworker told me that she would make all the necessary changes. She said that because Joe was not living in the home, I would still be eligible for food stamps. I thanked her and told her that we did not want or need them. I told her that Joe had moved ahead of us to start his job and that I stayed back because we didn't want to take our kids out of school, but that we would have an income. I was never so happy to turn down help. I had been grateful to have had it while we needed it, but I was even more grateful that we didn't need it anymore.

Life continued on. I missed Joe like crazy, but the days were so busy that I didn't have a lot of time to dwell on it. I had all my kids around me, so I definitely wasn't lonely. Joe, on the other hand, being all alone in his apartment, missed us terribly, especially when he got home from work. Every time he called or texted me, I told him to enjoy the peace and quiet because it wouldn't last forever. I secretly wished that I could live on my own for six months. The kids were all good sports and pitched in a lot. They all had their chores to do, they helped with the meals and with their little brothers. Because I was the only driver, I spent a lot of time in the van, shuttling kids around to and from work, preschool, musical rehearsals, track and field, basketball, playdates, and parties. I will be forever grateful to our friends the O'Learys, who were so good to Clare and Callum. They did almost all the basketball pickups and drop-offs, and had them over to play practically every weekend. I relished and was so grateful for every daily Mass and adoration I could get to. Angela was a tremendous help. She had moved out to live with her college friends and quit her part-time job at Franciscan Manor to work full-time as a child care provider for a family. After only a couple of months, the family moved, and she found herself out of work and unable to pay her rent. I told her that I would pay her if she wanted to move back home to help. She was a lifesaver for me. With my own doctor appointments, Michael's appointments, school functions, and the grocery shopping, it was a relief to have her there to take care of little ones.

Patrick was still acting crazy. I had no real way of knowing what he was doing at school because I wasn't there, but the other kids told me that he was still hanging around with druggies at lunch. I had no control over who he hung around. I had some sense of security at home, especially at night, because the windows were virtually inescapable. There were padlocks on all the doors except the front one, and I slept directly across from the front door with both dogs lying next to the bed; so if he tried to open it, I would hear him. I carried my keys with me everywhere. I switched the regular padlocks out to tumbler locks when I discovered that he had been trying to pick them. He was still blatantly leaving spit bottles from his chewing tobacco around the house, and I found lighters in his room, which made me crazy. My worst fears were that one of the little kids would set the house on fire, or that Ryan, who was three, would drink from his tobacco chew spit bottle. I had grown accustomed to the argumentative banter. I hated it, but it had become almost normal. He was repeatedly caught searching through the other kids' stuff, looking for money.

On the weekends, the older girls would take the little kids to the school playground across the street from us. Sometimes Patrick would go with them. One weekend, he and Callum, who was eleven, asked me if they could go shoot some hoops at the school. It was a nice day, so I let them go, warning Patrick not to do anything he shouldn't. When they came back home sooner than I would have expected, and Callum had a bag of chips, candy, and a slushy, I asked them why they weren't playing ball. Callum said that they had played for a little while, but Patrick wanted to go to the store. After Patrick went up to his room, Callum told me that he had bought a can of chewing tobacco. He said that the lady at the store asked Patrick if she was going to get into trouble for selling it to him. Patrick told her that she wouldn't because his dad had just moved to California and that his mother didn't care if he had chew or not. Patrick had bought Callum a bunch of hush treats, hoping to get away with it. I called the police. An officer came to the house, the same officer who had come to talk to Patrick at the school the night he skipped out from his class. He was very familiar with the history. I told him about the store and how Joe had not only asked them twice not to sell his son tobacco, but that he had also given them a picture to post. I told him what had happened that day. He told me that the store was known for selling tobacco to underage kids and that he would go talk to the salesclerk. When he returned a few minutes later, he told me that the woman who had been working on the counter had admitted to selling Patrick the tobacco. She explained to the officer that Patrick told her that his mother didn't care if he had it. I laughed at the ridiculousness of it all. I absolutely did care, but that was beside the point; she had sold tobacco to a minor. The officer agreed and asked me if I wanted to press charges. I told him I did. I told him that they had been warned multiple times. He informed me that if he fined the store, Patrick would also get a fine for purchasing tobacco underage. I asked the officer if Patrick's fine could be converted into community service hours, since he didn't have a job, and I wouldn't be paying his fine. I wanted him to have some consequences. The officer said that when we spoke to the judge, I could ask him that question.

Patrick was extremely annoyed that I had called the police. The officer told him that he needed to follow the rules. He told him that he really should be more sensitive to our family's situation, that he should be trying to help out, stepping up and being a man, instead of causing more trouble and adding to the stress. I told Joe about what had happened when he called that night. He was not at all happy about it, but he was glad that I had called the police. The citation came in the mail a few days later, and I called to set up a time to talk to the judge. Surprisingly, when I did call, I got to speak to the judge himself. I told him about what had happened, gave him a little background about our situation, and the fact that we had been dealing with Patrick and his rebel ways for far too long. I let him know that we were expecting our baby in a few weeks, so we needed to have the situation resolved before December 5. The judge scheduled the hearing for December 3, the day after Joe was scheduled to arrive for the baby's delivery.

Thanksgiving has always been a huge feast and celebration for our family, but we decided that since Joe wouldn't be home, it would be just another day. Or so I thought. I got a call from Weaver's Market in Darlington. Someone had donated a Thanksgiving meal to our family; all I had to do was come by and pick it up. I didn't know what to say. We weren't planning to have a traditional Thanksgiving meal. I told the lady on the phone that we really didn't need a meal this year, but thanked her anyway. She insisted, saying that an elderly gentleman had come in and requested several meals and that one of them was set aside for our family. She wouldn't tell me who it was. The man preferred to remain anonymous. Not wanting to insult the donor, I agreed to pick it up. I drove to the market and gave the person at the counter my name. An employee came out with a rolling cart filled with large trays of turkey, stuffing, mashed potatoes, vegetables, cranberry sauce, gravy, rolls, and two pies. It was a feast. Tears filled my eyes as the girl wheeled the cart out to my van. I waddled, very pregnant, behind her, thanking her over and over again. She wished us a Happy Thanksgiving. I drove slowly and carefully down

Constitution Boulevard, wondering to myself who I knew that could use a Thanksgiving meal. We were the poorest people I knew, but we were doing okay. We had food. Only a few days earlier, I had bought all the groceries we needed; and the fridge, freezer, and pantry were full. I didn't have room to even store the food. I asked God to find me a person who could use it.

I needed to buy a new broom and an ironing board, so I pulled into the Walmart on my way home. As I turned into the parking lot, I saw a lady standing on the grass, holding up a cardboard sign. The sign asked for help with food and diapers. My head spun as I parked the van. I muttered something to God about how fast He had worked a miracle. I kept telling Him how amazing He was. I hurried through the store to get the broom and the ironing board, before walking down the diaper aisle. I realized that I had no idea what size I should buy. I paid for the items, hitting the Cash Back button on the PIN pad, requesting twenty dollars. I went back out to the parking lot, scanning the spot where I had seen the lady, praying that she was still there. She was. I drove up alongside the lane, pulled over, and turned on my hazard lights. I got out of the van and asked her what she needed and if she had a home. She told me that she wasn't homeless but that her husband was in jail for unpaid parking tickets. They didn't have any money, and she had no income. She had tears in her eyes when she told me that she couldn't believe she was standing on the side of the road with a sign, but she was desperate. I asked her how old her baby was. She told me that he was two. I told her that I knew what she was going through. My husband had, only just a couple of weeks earlier, started a new job after a very long unemployment. I told her that I would pray for her and her family and that things would get better. I gave her the twenty-dollar bill so that she could buy diapers, and I told her that if she wanted it, I had a fresh Thanksgiving meal in my van that I had just picked up from the market. The tears were rolling down both of our faces by that point. She pointed to a van that was parked across the lane. I drove around, and she walked across to meet me. I pulled up alongside her van, and she helped me unload all the food. She thanked me over and over again. I told her that I had asked God to show me someone who needed it, and there she was. She was amazed. I am pretty sure that was the most meaningful Thanksgiving I had ever had. I drove home on a cloud, and I called Joe to tell him what had just happened. He was just as amazed as I was. Only one year earlier, we had been showered with a huge donation of food from the school's canned-food drive. It was nice to be back on the other side again.

Our new baby would be arriving in a couple of weeks, and I couldn't wait for Joe to come home. I had asked my sister Bridget, and her husband, Stéphane, to be godparents. We had scheduled the baptism for the week after the birth so that Joe could be there. My sister and her little boy Maxime, who was eighteen months old, planned to fly into Pittsburgh the day after the delivery. Stéphane would leave a day earlier by car. He planned to drive from New Brunswick, and they would all drive back together, visiting friends and family on their way home. I was more than excited. I hadn't seen my sister in more than ten years. We had only reconnected the previous January, less than a year earlier, after a very long time. We had been separated by distance, in both miles and communication, mainly because of old loyalties to my mother. Bridget had severed ties with her years earlier, and I never reached out to her to find out why. Reconnecting with her had been a tremendous blessing for both of us, and I was so excited to see her.

I picked Joe up from the airport. I hadn't realized that I had been holding my breath the whole time he was gone, until I saw him walk toward the van and exhaled. The kids waited up late to see him. They had all missed him. Little ones and big ones alike piled onto his lap when he sat down on the couch.

The next morning, I took Patrick to the courthouse, which was right next to the Chippewa police department. The judge was very understanding. He told Patrick that he felt he was smarter than the way he was behaving. He could see that he had good parents who were responsible and truly cared about his well-being. He told him that he would be referring him to the Beaver County Court to determine his community service hours. He agreed that he should have consequences and that us paying a fine for him wouldn't teach him anything. He told Patrick to be more considerate of what his parents were trying to do for him and the family. From what he could see, we were being very generous by not pulling him and his siblings out of their schools to move to California right away. We had considered their feelings and well-being in our plans. We had made sacrifices, and he should, at the very least, show some respect. The judge told me after Patrick left the courtroom to stand firm and keep up the good parenting. He told me that he could see Patrick had been raised well and that we had done a good job. He seemed to think that Patrick was going through a rough patch but was confident that in time, he would smarten up. I told him I was praying that it wouldn't get any worse. He said we had a lot of responsibilities with twelve kids and a big move ahead of us. He congratulated me and wished us the best.

I dropped Patrick off at school, before driving to the hospital to register for my delivery and get pre-op lab work done. I mentally prepared for the few days I would be away from home. We had been through it all before. I was grateful that we were living in a tiny house, where life was simple and low maintenance. I'd gotten the house cleaned and organized from top to bottom, including the basement, before Joe came home, and my bag had been packed for weeks. I had bought two new nightgowns and a new bathrobe, all Christmas themed. It would be my first Christmas baby. I had knitted a baby cocoon, a little sac, out of red-and-white cotton yarn, striped like a candy cane, with a matching red hat to bring the baby home in. I bought a few new onesies, receiving blankets, and a pack and play, and set it up in the corner of the family room. I was glad that we kept the little musical swing that had been Michael's, and I set that up as well. All the baby things had been washed, folded, and put into the dresser. Since Joe had moved all his clothes with him to California, half of the dresser was empty, perfect for storing the baby clothes and diapers.

On the morning of the delivery, we left Angela in charge. She would see the little kids off on the school bus. I had all their clothes and backpacks laid out the night before, to make it as easy as possible. Grace and Christina skipped school and stayed home, without our knowledge or consent, but we didn't get mad at them. We knew they were excited. Joe and I left the house at five o'clock in the morning, all smiles and with absolutely no worries whatsoever. We had been through it so many times before, but I had never felt so calm. I had complete confidence that everything would go smoothly and easily. Joe dropped me off at the door of the Beaver County Hospital, and I waited in the lobby for him to park the car. We walked to the labor and delivery floor together. I was brought into a room, given a gown, and within minutes, was on a bed hooked up to a monitor, getting an IV, and chatting away excitedly with the nurses. I absolutely love labor and delivery nurses. They are a special breed—kind, compassionate, and upbeat. I have no doubt that there must be plenty of stressful situations that they have to deal with, and I am certain that there are times that are sad, difficult, and frustrating. In our experience, our nurses have always been wonderful, easygoing, and happy; and we have been told that we have been that way for them too, with every birth. It has always been a wonderful and joyful time.

One of my nurses, the one who was there for all the prep and the delivery, Judy Manna, was an absolute doll. Joe sat on the chair while she asked questions, checked vitals, made notations, and bustled around me. We chatted away about this and that, and of course it was no big secret that we were having our twelfth baby. She gushed about how blessed we were, saying that she had always wanted to have a big family, but was so grateful for the one daughter that she was able to have after many years of trying. She too was a Catholic and had lived in the Beaver Falls area all her life. She had come from a big family, and her cousin, who also worked at the hospital, just so happened to be my anesthesiologist that day. If I said it once, I said it a thousand times: Beaver Falls was indeed a small town. We shared stories about our faith journey, and she told us how grateful she was that God had connected us that day. She didn't believe it was a coincidence. I felt the exact same way. Dr. Dumpe came in to say hello before the C-section. I introduced him to Joe since they hadn't met before that day. They chatted back and forth, joking about our huge family and how it seemed like we really knew what we were doing. We told him that we were learning on the job but that we were working hard at it.

I was wheeled into the operating room while Joe was left to suit up in his coveralls. Everything started moving really fast. Having a C-section isn't exactly fun. It's a pretty major surgery, and it's a really strange feeling to be wide-awake but completely numb. With my rosary in my hand, I tried to pray; but with all the excitement and chatter back and forth between Dr. Dumpe and Dr. Lauer, joking with Joe and me, and Judy Mana, bragging about Joe and I to her cousin, it was difficult to concentrate. It felt kind of like a party. Noah Joachim James Stewart Scott Allen was born kicking and screaming. A healthy baby boy, another mini-me for Joe. It was such a relief to be delivered of my little one. Joe went with the nurses to the nursery while I got put back together. The entire pregnancy had been unbelievably easy. Other than catching a nasty cold shortly after Joe left town, I had been completely healthy. There had been no complications whatsoever. God was so good to us. We had gone through entirely enough. I spent only two days in the hospital. I was anxious to get home so that I could spend as much time with Joe as possible before he had to return to California. Dr. Dumpe discharged me, only after I promised him that I would take it easy. No lifting or driving. I promised I would behave myself. One of the pediatricians from Tri State Pediatrics, Dr. Deacon, checked out little Noah from head to toe and announced that he was absolutely perfect. Music to my ears. I dressed Noah in his little sleeper and packed up my bag. Joe held him while I showered and dressed, and we left as soon as the discharge papers were signed. The discharge nurse informed us of the available services and benefits that we were entitled to, WIC and other programs, but we declined. We didn't need the assistance.

We arrived home to a clean, quiet house, where the little boys were napping and the older kids were still at school. It was so good to be home. I was tired, but it was a good tired. There is absolutely nothing like coming home with a brand-new baby. It's such a high and relief to have that tiny little person, who seems enormous before birth, on the outside. We'd had twelve babies in twenty-one years. They had all been born in a lot of different places, small houses and large ones. We had built and grown our family as Joe built and grew his career. We had brought Michael home to our beautifully decorated and remodeled home in Texas, by far the biggest and most beautiful place that we had ever owned. Noah came home to our tiny little outdated and cramped rental house, definitely the most humble place we had ever lived, but the experience was just as beautiful. Baby Jesus had been born into a stable, and He was the Savior of the world. Our humble home didn't matter. Our beautiful, precious, perfect baby boy was with us, safe and sound.

Joe was only able to stay with us for a week. He had informed his boss at the time that he was hired that we were expecting and would need to take time off. A week was all he took because he planned to come home for Christmas. We cherished every minute we had together, and we all anxiously awaited my sister Bridget's arrival with little Maxime. We had scheduled Noah's baptism for December 9, the first Sunday after his birth. I was thrilled that Bridget and Stéphane had agreed to be godparents, and overjoyed that they were making the long trip. I could hardly wait to see her and meet her new husband and little boy after such a long separation. It was a joyous time.

We had put all our Christmas decorations into storage before moving into the rental house, and they were buried deep, out of reach. I wanted to make sure that our kids had a Christmas tree. I bought a small prelit one at Walmart, and we decorated it before Noah's birth, knowing I would not be in any shape to do much of anything after he was born. I bought some Christmas plaid tablecloths and made a tree skirt and matching stockings out of them and hung them from the white-painted wooden railing. I also cut out and hand-stitched twenty-five mini felt stockings and hung them on the garland over the dining room doorframe, as an Advent countdown. Just a little bit of garland and some lights made a big difference. Our little house was cozy and festive. I don't think I had ever felt lighter on my feet or more joy in my heart. We had much to celebrate and be grateful for—Joe's new job and a brand-new beautiful baby. A fresh start. Bridget and Stéphane's arrival with Maxime was icing on the cake. It was like there had never been ten years of absence. Seeing my sister again and hugging each other erased the gap of time. Her new husband instantly became my brother, and her little boy melted my heart. It was a joy to see what incredible, loving, and dedicated parents Bridget and Stéphane were to their bright-eyed, curious, and gentle-natured little boy.

Noah's baptism was beautiful. We named him Noah because he was the rainbow that God had sent us after a great flood. There had been times we really felt like we were drowning. *Joachim*, after our beloved Fr. Kim and the Blessed Mother's father. *James* after our other beloved priest, Jim Farnan; and *Scott*, after Fr. Scott Seethaler, the Franciscan priest who had come to do our parish mission for Easter, a real inspiration the week that Noah was conceived; and *Stewart* after Joe's youngest brother. My actual due date had been December 8, the feast of the Immaculate Conception. Grace had asked me to schedule my C-section on December 12, the feast of Our Lady of Guadalupe, Patroness of the Unborn, because he was the twelfth baby. She thought it would be very cool if he was born on the twelfth day of the twelfth month of the year 2012. I agreed that it would have been very cool, but when I asked, my doctor wouldn't hear of it. He was concerned that I may go into labor before that date and need an emergency C-section, a risk that he didn't want to take. Noah was born on the day God wanted him to be.

Stéphane drove Joe to the airport two days after the baptism. It was hard to say goodbye after such a beautiful celebration. Bridget and Stéphane picked up where Joe left off, stepping up to help me out in every way possible—cooking dinner, lifting Michael out of his crib from his naps, changing diapers, running to the grocery store, shuttling kids around to and from rehearsals and basketball practice, and taking Ryan on outings during the day.

On that same Tuesday that Joe flew back to California, Michael had his regularly scheduled physical therapy session with Dana. Bridget and Stéphane decided to take Ryan to Bradys Run Park to play, while Michael did his physical therapy. Right after Dana left, I got a call from Patrick, who was at school. He told me he needed to stay after school to finish working on something for science, so he wouldn't be taking the bus home. Not being a very conscientious student, it was not at all typical of him, so I questioned it. He insisted that he was working on a project with another student and they needed to finish it up. I told him that was fine and asked him what time he would be finished. He hesitated and then asked me if Joseph and Christina had rehearsal for their musical that night. When I told them that they did, he said I could just pick him up when I picked them up after their rehearsal. That wouldn't be until at least eight thirty at night. I told him that was much too long and that I would be at the school to pick him up at three thirty sharp. He said he would be ready at three thirty. Mommy radar is a powerful thing, and something didn't seem quite right to me. I had learned not to ignore that sixth sense. I felt a lot more in tune with those uneasy feelings and warning signs, especially since my prayer life had grown so much. I was convinced that the Holy Spirit was the one giving me the sense that there was something amiss.

When the rest of the high school kids got off the bus, I left Christina and Grace in charge of watching Michael and Noah while I took Joseph with me to the high school. I wasn't supposed to be driving yet, but something told me to go. I told Joseph about Patrick's call that afternoon, and he shook his head. He too figured something had to be up. It was not quite three o'clock when we left, and I knew full well that I would arrive much earlier than I had said I would. Being early would enable me to see where Patrick came from, whether he was truly at the school or not. I didn't park in front of the school in the bus lane where he would have expected me to. Instead, I parked in the church parking lot across from the school, where I had a better vantage point.

Joseph and I weren't there more than three minutes when we saw three pairs of legs walking behind some tall pine trees, coming from the house next to the church. The house where Joe and I had gone to find Patrick on Mother's Day, when the police saw him duck into a car. I caught a glimpse of his jacket as he and his two buddies did their best to hide behind the trees. Joseph and I laughed at the ridiculousness of it all. All their legs were exposed behind the tree trunks. I laid on the horn, drawing more attention than any of them wanted, forcing Patrick out from behind the trees, while his friends remained partially hidden. He got into the car, smelling strongly of cologne. I asked him what he had been doing. He told me that he had just smoked a cigarette. I told him he didn't smell like cigarettes. I asked him why he had not been in the school working on his science project. He told me that they had finished early. I asked him again what he had really been doing at his friend's house. He grinned at me and said that he just had a cigarette. I told him I didn't believe him. He told me I didn't have to believe him. I asked him if he could pass a drug test. He laughed and said, "Sure."

I replied, "Okay."

I proceeded to drive directly to Walgreens to purchase a drug kit. Buying a drug kit was embarrassing and humiliating, but I felt it was a necessary indignity to endure for the sake of my son. I paid for the kit, went back to the van, and made him pee in the cup right there in the parking lot. I read the results before I left. It was positive for marijuana and amphetamines. With the evidence that he had smoked more than a cigarette, I asked him again what he had been up to. He told me that he had smoked a joint with his buddies and also taken an Adderall, an ADD prescription. I had the evidence. My suspicions had been confirmed, but I had no idea what to do with it. Joe hadn't even landed yet in California. His flight had been delayed more than five hours, and he was still stuck in Dallas. Patrick hadn't even met with the Youth Services Worker about his community service hours for his tobacco charges yet, and he was already smoking pot. I was sick. I drove home. The rest of the kids had arrived home from school, and Bridget and Stéphane had returned with Ryan from their outing at the park. Bridget was busily cooking dinner and was surprised that I had been out driving, much sooner than I should have been. I told her what had just happened, and she too was heartsick. Patrick thought it was funny. No doubt still under the effects of the pot, he smirked and laughed as he walked through the kitchen. My head was spinning as I wondered how in the world I would get through the next six months.

The next morning, I called the judge that I had talked to about the tobacco charge a week and a half earlier, hoping he could help, like order a live-in rehab or something. I didn't want his behavior to continue. I shared with him what had happened. He told me how sorry he was to hear it and was very sympathetic, but unfortunately there was nothing that he could do about it. He told me to continue doing what I was doing and not give up. I was tired of hearing it. Everyone we talked to told us that we were doing the right thing, that we were good parents, and that we shouldn't give up, but nothing was changing. What would it take? Joe wasn't at all surprised when I told him what had happened. He knew that Patrick was just waiting for him to leave town so he could start his fun again. He told me to call the police if he did anything else. I told him that I had called the judge already and that he said there wasn't anything he could do. We both felt powerless.

Bridget and Stéphane stayed a week longer than they had planned. They didn't want to leave yet, and I wasn't ready for them to go. We knew that it would be a very long time before we would be together again once we moved to California. We would be on opposite sides of the continent. Stéphane took Ryan and Callum to the Beaver County airport museum and taught Callum how to geocache. Stéphane is a soldier in the Canadian Armed Forces, the sort of man that anyone would admire and respect. He is kind, considerate, quiet, and unassuming, but strong and confident. He has the strength of character that citizens expect from the military, and I felt so proud to call him my brother. We all went to the Christmas concert at Divine Mercy Academy and drove the long way home in the dark to look at the Christmas lights. Bridget and I enjoyed quiet afternoons while the boys napped and the other kids were at school, having marathon chats, trying to catch up on as much as we could while drinking a lot of tea. Watching our little boys play together, eating snacks, and getting to know each other gave us much joy, but it made saying goodbye that much harder. It had been such a perfect reunion for all of us, and we knew we would cherish it forever.

Our little friend Bob Javens, the bus driver, came by every few weeks with bags of canned items and other treats for us. Once, he brought us a big bag of oranges. He said he loved oranges, but the bag was so big he couldn't possibly eat them all, so he took a few out and gave us the rest. He'd sometimes bring the kids cookies and ice cream, little treats that he knew would make them smile. It was always a pleasure to see his little frame at my door. He always wore a Steelers ball cap, and I never saw him when he wasn't smiling. He never stayed more than a few minutes, just long enough to check in and say hello to the kids, and then he was gone again. He told us that his wife, Peggy, was home, and he was hoping that they could come by to visit us soon so that Peggy could meet the kids and see Noah. Bob came by with a beautiful big fruit basket one afternoon before Christmas. He seemed to always be thinking of our family. He shared, with a twinkle in his eye, that when he told the lady who took his order for the basket at Giant Eagle what a wonderful family we were and that we had twelve children, she put in extra candy and cookies, at no extra charge. I had no doubt that she did so because Bob was such a sweetheart. The basket was both beautiful and delicious, and it gave me the idea of buying a smaller version for our friends Bob and Nanette. I went to Giant Eagle and put in my order. They said they didn't deliver. I would have to pick it up later and drop it off myself.

Although it wasn't all that cold, it was a very snowy night, and it was accumulating quickly. I had to drop Angela off to a babysitting job, so decided I would pick up the fruit basket and deliver it to the Mazzucas'—all in one trip. I left the older kids home with the younger kids and made Patrick come along. Patrick wasn't thrilled about coming with me. Tensions were still high after I had drug tested him, but I was resolved to remain tough. It hurt my heart to have to constantly be so rigid, but he took any kindness or gentleness for weakness. After we dropped Angela off, I pulled into the Giant Eagle parking lot. Patrick announced that he wasn't coming into the store. I told him that he didn't have the luxury of making that decision and that he would definitely be coming in. I was not about to leave him in the van alone. I had done that once when we went to pick Michael's glasses up at the mall. While I was inside, Patrick stood outside smoking a cigar right next to the van. It had left a sickening smell that both Michael and I, still pregnant, had to breathe in all the way home. I told him that he was coming into the store. He refused. I got out of the van and walked around to the side door, opened it, and told him to get out. He refused and then proceeded to utter abusive language at me. He was not at all happy that I was treating him like an insolent child. I stood my ground and told him that if he did not get out, I would call the police. He told me to go ahead. I really didn't want to call them, but I fumbled for my phone, hoping that he would get out of the van. As he shifted in his seat, making it look like he was about to get out, he made a big display of popping a tobacco pouch into his mouth. I don't know why I did it, and looking back on it now, I wish I hadn't reacted the way I did. I should have not reacted at all. I stepped up onto the running board, grabbed his face, and pulled the tobacco pouch out of his mouth. Then I pulled him out of the van. Still recovering from the C-section of a couple of weeks earlier, it was a stupid thing to do. I didn't want him in the van alone, and the fact that he wanted to stay in it so badly meant that he had some kind of plan. I didn't want him believing that he was in control. He thought he could bully me when Joe wasn't around. He did try, but I resisted. He finally got out of the van, and I informed him that he would be walking home. He glared at me and said he definitely wouldn't walk home. I told him that I was not about to drive him home after he had been so verbally abusive to me. He followed me unnecessarily closely throughout the store. I picked up my fruit basket order and a few other items that we needed, checked out, and walked back to the van with Patrick still at my heels. I put the groceries into the back of the van, while Patrick walked to the passenger side. I hit the button to lock the doors, replaced my shopping cart in the bay, and unlocked my door with my key. I climbed in, started the van, and drove off, leaving Patrick standing in the parking lot. It about killed me to see him standing in the lot in his hoodie with the snow falling down. He had been so incredibly rude, and I wanted him to know that I would not tolerate it.

I drove around the store and out to the traffic light, watching my son standing in the middle of the parking lot through my rear-view mirror. I had planned to deliver the basket to the Mazzucas' that night, but after the episode with Patrick, I didn't want to be away longer than necessary, so I went directly home. Giant Eagle was only a few blocks away from our house. Patrick walked miles farther than that, regularly, in all kinds of weather, when he snuck out. He didn't come home that night. I had left him in the lot at seven fifteen, and when he didn't return by eleven o'clock, I called the police. When Officer Herndon showed up at the door, I explained what had happened. He told me that he would call me if they found him and asked me to call him if Patrick returned home. I promised I would. Officer Herndon told me that my reason for leaving him in the parking lot was perfectly reasonable. He said that some kids are just tougher than others. My older kids sat all lined up on the couch, listening attentively. Officer Herndon said it was obvious that Patrick was testing us. He didn't believe that he was that bad, he had seen much worse, but he was still testing us. I told him that Joe and I both believed that Patrick would have been much worse had we given up the battle and given in to his behavior. Officer Herndon agreed.

It wasn't until seven o'clock the following night that Patrick called. He had gone to his friend's house. I told him that the police were looking for him. I told him that he should have simply walked home from Giant Eagle, not go to his friend's house. He said that he had waited at the store until a friend of his who worked there got off her shift. She had given him a ride to his friend's house, which was more than five miles away. They had driven right past our house to get there. It would have only taken him ten minutes to walk home. When I asked him why he did that, he told me it was because I had left him in the freezing cold and snow. It was obvious to me by the tone in his voice and the dramatic effect he was aiming for that he had an audience. I asked him why he didn't have his friend drop him off at home instead. He had no answer. I told him he needed to get home immediately. I then called his friend's mother, who was well aware of what had happened the night before. I told her that I didn't appreciate her allowing Patrick to stay at her house without calling me first. I informed her that she was harboring a runaway. That caught her attention. I was grateful that Patrick was safe, but I wanted her to realize that it was not cool to not inform us where he was. She was familiar with the troubles we had been having with Patrick. We'd had several lengthy conversations about it, and I thought she was sympathetic. Sadly, I later learned that she had been enabling her son to use drugs and alcohol and that Patrick had spent more time at their house than I knew about because of the freedom his friend had. She told me that she would bring Patrick home right away. I let her know that I had to inform the police that Patrick had been found and that they would likely be at our house when she arrived, which they were.

Patrick came in just in time to greet Officer Herndon and his partner, who were standing in the doorway. It had to be embarrassing for Patrick to keep running into those guys like that. They did their usual back-and-forth talk. Patrick told them that he knew he was being stupid. They told him he was smarter than that, to knock it off and think before acting. They told him to think about what our family had already been through, what I had to cope with on my own, while Joe was trying to establish himself in a new job in California. They pleaded with him to think about his family just a little bit and stop the nonsense. I told them about the incident only a week or so earlier, when I had bought the drug kit and tested him in the Walgreens parking lot. Officer Herndon told me that if I had only brought the test to them at the police station, they could have tested him there and done something about it. It seemed as though the helpful information always came a day late and a dollar short. I had no doubt that Patrick, having heard the information, would find a way around it. I continued to pray that he would just give it up altogether. Officer Herndon went out to the Dad's Pizza parking lot to tell Patrick's friend and his mother to go home and not get involved anymore. Poor Gary. His pizza customers must have wondered what kind of neighbors lived next door, with the cops always parked out front, lights flashing. I doubt that there had ever been that much excitement in the neighborhood before we moved in. The police left and told Patrick to behave himself. They didn't want any more calls about him. I was always relieved to have Patrick home. No matter what kind of trouble he caused or grief he gave me, I loved him and wanted him home and safe. All the chaos that followed him everywhere he went was worth the peace of mind I had, knowing that he was safe at home. I just wished that there was some way to reach him. I kept praying that we would find a way.

Patrick came with me to pick Joe up from the airport the night he flew in for his Christmas visit. It was a very quiet ride home. Joe had been in constant communication with the other kids and me through texts, e-mails, and phone calls, so he was well aware of everything that went on at home. Neither Joe nor Patrick had much to say to each other. Christmas was quiet, sweet, and simple for us. We didn't overspend or overeat. We had received several anonymous gifts in the mail, cash and gift cards from "Santa." Even after finally getting a job and being able to provide for our family, people continued to be generous and supportive of us. Whenever I protested gifts and assured Fr. Schreck that we were okay, that they could help out another family, he told me that the community realized that it would take us some time to get back on our feet. He smiled and told me to just accept their generosity. It was humbling, but I knew that it gave people joy to help. Joe and I remained determined to someday give back in whatever ways we could.

The day Joe was scheduled to fly back to California, I got a call from Bob the Bus Driver. He wondered if he could stop by the house for a few minutes with a tie that needed altering. He was part of a choral group, and they had all received new ties, but his was much too long. I told him that I was heading out to the airport with Joe, but that I would be happy to stop by his place to take a look at it on my way home. I told him I would even bring Noah along. I wasn't able to fix the tie. I'm just not that good of a seamstress, and I didn't want to mess it up. I was thrilled to finally meet sweet Peggy, Bob's dear wife, though. I had heard so much about her and felt like I had known her forever. She was small and frail as she sat in her chair. Cancer had taken a tremendous toll on her body, but she had such love in her eyes. Bob showed me around their cozy little house, Peggy's piano, and all the family pictures, and the prayer shawl that I had made for her draped over the back of their living room sofa. He held Noah and had me stand next to Peggy for a picture. She thanked me for making meals for them back when we lived in Bob and Nanette's house. It seemed like such a small thing for me, but to them, it was really a big deal. Peggy had been quite a servant in her day. Very active in their church, playing the organ from the time she was a teenager, doing meals-on-wheels, and helping children and the poor, she was a godly woman. She told me in a thank-you note that she had written after I'd sent some meals home with Bob that she had always been the helper and that it was difficult being on the other end, being helped by me. I remember reading it and knowing exactly what she meant. That was how I had felt when we were at such a low point. I didn't much like being helped either, but I knew how good it made me feel to help others. I realized that sometimes we have to let other people be the helpers so that they can feel that joy. I told Bob that I was sorry I couldn't help him with his tie. He walked me out to the van and thanked me for coming by. He looked very tired and worried about his wife, but he was grateful to have her home with him. I told him I felt so blessed to have met Peggy the Great. A few weeks later, Bob called and left a message on the answering machine telling me that Peggy was back in the hospital. My heart sank. I dropped off small meals to him a few times a week, leaving them in the back breezeway of his house on the little bench. I had learned not to bring too much food because he didn't eat all that much, just a small portion in a little container. I knew he had a sweet tooth, so I included a small dessert every day. He called me a few times from the hospital to give me updates on Peggy. Our whole family prayed for all of his. One night he called to thank me for all the food and told me that there were several people from his church who were also bringing meals. He said I could take a break for a while, but he asked me if I would shorten a pair of pajama pants that Peggy had bought him for Christmas. I was delighted to and felt honored that he would ask. I lovingly hemmed and pressed Bob's pajamas.

The kids' Christmas break lasted until after New Year's. We all wished that Joe could have been home for the entire holiday, but because he was still very new in the role and had already taken a week off for Noah's birth, it wasn't possible. He left two days after Christmas. One of the biggest challenges for me to manage on my own was Sunday Mass. It wasn't a problem getting the kids up, dressed, and arriving there on time, but making sure that Ryan, who was three and a half, behaved properly was a real chore. Joe and I have always been like bookends in the church pew. With Joe on one end, keeping Ryan next to him, and me on the other with Michael. Now that Noah was with us, the older girls took turns holding him so that I could hold Michael. No one was able to keep a rein on

Ryan. He fidgeted and flopped in the seat, slid down onto the floor, messed with the books, complained loudly, and cried when I told him to stop, which got Michael agitated. I must admit that I had Michael spoiled for me. I had been the one to hold him every Sunday from birth, and he was used to it. So used to it, that he would cry if I passed him to anyone else. I am sure that he would have gotten over it in time, but I didn't feel like it was worth upsetting him over, so I continued to be the one to hold him. With Joe gone, I had to be the strong arm with Ryan, while keeping Michael calm. Every Sunday, we sat close to an exit. I almost always ended up walking to the back entrance of the church with both boys to keep from distracting other people. I often left feeling like I could commit murder on the way home, but we never missed Mass. Christmas break was a much needed reprieve from the school routine, even though the kids continued their regular activities. They saw their friends; there were still musical rehearsals, basketball practices; and Joseph still had work. Despite the fact that they were all busy, we enjoyed the more relaxed schedule. We stayed up a little later watching movies together and eating snacks, and we slept in a little longer. I got to morning Mass every day that I could and brought Noah with me.

Two days before New Year's, there was another kerfuffle. It was early evening when Angela came downstairs to tell me that twenty dollars of her babysitting money was missing. She had been upstairs in her room. Patrick had been in his room, directly across the hall from hers. They were the only two upstairs. Angela came downstairs to get a drink. I noticed that when she went back up the stairs, Patrick came down a few seconds later, heading to the basement. Angela said that when she returned to her room, her wallet was open and hanging out of her purse. Not the way she had left it. She had been downstairs for less than five minutes. It was not the first time that money had gone missing. Angela was adamant that the money had just been there. I confronted Patrick, who had been in his room for most of the day, up until that point. He denied the accusation flatly as he walked back upstairs. I asked him why he had gone down to the basement. He told me he hadn't been doing anything. The basement was dark, dank, and unfinished, with a thousand places to hide things. I went down to look around but couldn't find anything. I went upstairs to his bedroom and demanded that he hand over the money. He continued to deny taking it, and I continued to press him. I was all up in his face, telling him I knew he had it and to just give it back. It wasn't his, and he needed to give it back. I stayed in his face. All my anger and frustrations had built up from the years of his rebellious behavior. I am sure I sounded like a yappy dog. I hated losing my composure with him, but I was at the end of my rope. I'm five foot one and a half. Patrick is a solid five foot nine. I pushed him with both hands on his chest, insisting he tell me where the money was. He shoved his way past me, pushing me aside with his body. Joseph, who had followed me up the stairs, had had enough. He wanted to get into it with Patrick, but I told him not to touch him. Joseph told me that if I didn't call the police, he would, because I had just been assaulted.

We were all tired of being held hostage. Having to constantly watch Patrick's every move and second-guess everything he did, locking up valuables, and hiding keys. It was exhausting. It was an extremely intense and highly emotional moment. I called the police. I explained to the dispatcher what had happened, and she assured me that an officer would be there shortly. Two female officers arrived at the door moments later. We had almost always dealt with male officers. There may have been one occasion when a female officer had accompanied a male one. I invited them in. The other kids were all still awake, watching television. Our Christmas tree and lights were still up and turned on, the house was tidy, and everything would have seemed normal, except for the constant underlying negative energy that we all felt. I told the officers what had happened. Angela had been upstairs in her room, and her purse had been next to her bed. Everyone else had been downstairs watching TV except for Patrick, who had been in his room. Angela came down for a drink of water and went back upstairs, just a few minutes later to find her wallet open and sticking out of her purse. Patrick had come downstairs, seconds after Angela had gone back up and went down to the basement. I had gone down to the basement to try to find the money, but there was no telling where he could have stashed it. I told the officers that I had gotten up in his face when I confronted him, and after arguing back and forth about it, he shoved past me. Not outright hitting me, but nonetheless, moving me roughly with his body to get away. The officer told me that she was familiar with the address and with Patrick's name. She said she understood that he had been causing problems for quite a while and asked me if I wanted to press charges. I asked her what that meant. She said that they would take him to a holding cell for the night until a judge heard the charges. I thought quickly. It may be the only opportunity I got to teach him a lesson. All my kids were watching me, waiting for an answer. I looked at Patrick, who still had a smug look on his face, and told her yes, I did want to press charges. She asked Patrick if he had ever been arrested before. He told her no. She said, "Well, you are getting arrested tonight."

She told him to put his shoes on and then ushered him out onto the front deck where the other officer patted him down and put handcuffs on him. My stomach was in knots, and my heart pounded. It was the hardest thing I ever had to watch, but I felt like it was our last hope of waking Patrick up. The little kids went to bed asking when Patrick would get out of jail. I told them that I wasn't sure, but they needed to pray that he would learn a lesson and turn his life around. I wanted him to see, before it was too late, what his life could be like if he didn't change his ways before he became an adult. I prayed he would live to become one.

That night, there were several calls from the police department and from the Family and Youth caseworker who had been assigned his case. It was no small ordeal I would quickly learn. They wanted to know if there was any place that I would allow Patrick to go until he saw the judge. Where there any friends I would approve of him staying with. He had told them that he had friends that would let him stay, but I had to give my consent. Knowing his choice of friends, I refused to give him permission to stay with any of them, and I didn't want to burden any of my friends. Staying with friends would have been like a vacation for him. I wanted him to get a taste of what really losing his freedom would be like. The arresting officer said that they would be taking him to a place called Keystone, a juvenile facility.

He would stay there until he had a court hearing. Because it was the holidays, that would likely not be until after New Year's. My heart hurt, but I knew I needed to stay strong. The officer told me over the phone that she could tell Patrick was not a hardened criminal. She said she knew the kids that he ran with and that they were trouble. She said she thought that cooling off at Keystone was exactly what Patrick needed. She told me not to worry, that he would be fine, and she wished that more parents were like us. That didn't make it any easier, but I hoped she was right. I called Joe to tell him what had happened. He told me later that he'd had the best sleep he'd had in years that night. He had been so stressed and worried about me dealing with Patrick alone. I, on the other hand, didn't sleep much at all. By morning, I felt like I had a hangover, and I am not even a drinker. I did feel somewhat less stressed when morning came, knowing that Patrick would be under twenty-four hour supervision. We could all finally let our guard down at home.

A worker from Children and Youth Services came to the house the next day. She took pictures of all the kids, got their names and ages, and asked me to tell her what had happened. We told her the story, and I filled her in on the background as well. She said that it sounded like we were a caring and loving family and that the incident might just be what Patrick needed to smarten up. I put a bag together with some of his clothes and toiletries, as well as his coat, for her to bring to him. She said she would be in touch with me when she got a court date. She informed me that I would have to go to court to talk to the judge. It was all more than a little confusing, and I wasn't exactly sure what the whole process was, how long he would need to stay in the facility, or what would happen once he got out. I hoped he would be there just long enough to learn that it wasn't the kind of life he wanted.

THIRTY-FIVE

Calling in the Troops

Christmas Break 2012

I called Patrick on New Year's Day, from the parking lot in front of the Chinese food restaurant where I was picking up our New Year's meal. The caseworker had given me the phone number for Keystone when she came to the house and encouraged me to maintain contact. I told him I loved him and that I wished he could be home with us for New Year's dinner. I told him I wished we could just have a normal happy family life. I asked him again if he had taken Angela's money. He admitted that he had. I asked him where it was, and he told me that it was gone, that he had given it to his friend. I had no idea when he would have had the opportunity to give it to his friend, since there was no time between the time the money went missing and when the police showed up. He hadn't gone outside, he'd only gone to the basement. The only thing that I could think of was that he had slipped it out of one of the tiny porthole windows in the basement. I wondered if that was how he had been buying his tobacco products. I never found out for certain, but I had my suspicions. I asked him if he had gotten the clothes that I had sent. He said he hadn't and asked me when we would have to go to court. I told him I didn't know. I could hear in his voice that he wasn't happy about his restricted situation and new living quarters. He was very somber. We had tried so many things for so long to reach him, but nothing had worked. He just grew more defiant, learning new ways around us and the law. It was the first time he seemed to be at a loss, out of tricks. He was on lockdown, under constant supervision, with no way to sneak out. He couldn't just go to the kitchen for food, shower when he wanted to, or watch television. He was getting a taste of what jail might be like. I prayed that his stay at Keystone would be a turning point for him.

After a few days, I received a notice in the mail to appear in court. Angela stayed home with Ryan, Michael, and Noah. I met with the caseworker from Youth Services. She let me know that I had the right to have an attorney, or I could be appointed one by the court. I waived my right. I didn't feel like I needed one. Call me a fool, but I knew in my gut that the truth was all I needed. Patrick had been appointed a lawyer through the court. I told the caseworker about Patrick's history, his most recent antics, and his blatant disregard for authority. I shared with her my fear for his life, well-being, and the safety of my other kids. She seemed sympathetic. I told her that I had drug tested him only a couple of weeks earlier, and he had been positive for pot. After telling the caseworker about the drug testing, Patrick's lawyer excused himself and disappeared into a conference room. I really had no idea who I should be talking to or what I should or should not be disclosing; I found myself suddenly rethinking my decision to waive my right to an attorney. I was completely transparent and truthful. My one and only concern was for Patrick. We were all called into the conference room to talk with the judge. Patrick wasn't there; he was still at Keystone, but he could see and hear us on a video screen. After we had all greeted and introduced ourselves for the record, it was Patrick's attorney's chance to speak. He told the judge that Patrick had been a model resident at Keystone since he had arrived and that he was trying to arrange a foster home for him to go to. I had been told by the Youth and Children's Services caseworker that finding a home for a seventeen-year-old rebellious male would not be an easy task. I didn't want him to go to a foster home. Knowing what we had been through and how vigilant we had been, a foster home would make it easy for him to go downhill at full throttle.

The Youth Services caseworker spoke up next. She told the judge that a long history of sneaking out, using pot as recently as a few weeks earlier, and alcohol, not following the family's rules, causing problems at home involving the police—these were the reasons Patrick was taken to Keystone. Patrick's lawyer chimed in saying that he had spoken with Patrick that morning. (The reason for his quick exit into the conference room.) The lawyer said that Patrick had assured him that he hadn't used pot in several months. He said that Keystone had tested him just prior to the hearing, and he was clean. I shook my head.

When the judge asked me if I had anything to add, I told him that I had tested Patrick myself a couple of weeks earlier, and he had been positive for marijuana. The lawyer spoke up again, saying that *if* I had in fact tested Patrick, stressing *if*, as if he had some doubt, the test hadn't been performed under controlled conditions. I stared at the lawyer, who was clearly trying to make me look like an idiot. I was foolishly under the impression that he had my son's best interests at heart. Obviously his goal was to free Patrick from Keystone and put him into a foster home. I suddenly felt ill. The lawyer was crooked. The judge asked Patrick if I had indeed tested him a couple of weeks earlier. Patrick said yes. He admitted that he had smoked pot and that the test had been positive. That was a first. Patrick had actually told the truth. I am not sure why he did it. He could have easily lied, since the test he had just taken had been negative, but he told the truth. It may very well have been his vulnerable situation, but I would like to believe that he too had sensed how smug his lawyer had been, and he wanted to validate what I had told the judge. I looked directly at the lawyer, not needing to say a word.

The judge asked me if I thought that Patrick would change his ways. I told him I wasn't so sure. I had my doubts because we had been down the same road so many times before. He asked me if I was ready to take him home. I told him no. He said that he would set another date to determine whether I wanted to give up parental rights, making Patrick a ward of the court, which meant that he would either stay at Keystone or go to a foster home. I had ten days to decide whether or not to allow him to come home. My heart wanted to bring him home, but I didn't think that three days was enough time to learn a lesson. It was definitely more peaceful at home. We could all let our guard down, and there were no arguments. We also felt the emptiness. Despite all the negativity, we all loved and missed Patrick.

When I returned to the courthouse the following week, Patrick was there. I had no idea if he would be present or on a video screen from Keystone again. I was glad to see him sitting on the bench when I arrived, and I hugged him tightly. He seemed sober and uncertain, out of his element and clearly vulnerable. I had decided to bring Noah with me, after being told by the caseworker that there were almost always delays in family court. Because Noah was only one month old, and because I was breastfeeding, I couldn't leave him home. Patrick was very happy to see Noah. He took the infant car seat from me, placed it in his lap, and rocked and kissed his baby brother, a little piece of home. Bringing Noah had worked to our advantage. When the court officials saw us waiting with a newborn, they called us in first. I told Patrick and his caseworker that I would agree to bring him home as long as he promised to follow the rules. I told Patrick that I would be setting up an appointment with the PA Cyber School intake people to register him in cyber school. I didn't want him returning to his high school or anywhere near his old friends. He would have to play by my rules if he wanted to come home. Patrick said he would behave and thought that cyber school was a good plan. The judge agreed to release Patrick back into my custody, but not without additional conditions. Patrick would continue to be monitored by Children and Youth Services, and we would be provided with support resources from Presley Ridge. We were finally getting what we had been asking for all along. Presley Ridge was a kind of mediation service that we could call on if things got out of hand. The judge also reserved the right to have Patrick returned to Keystone if he failed to follow the rules, and he fully supported the cyber school plan. I hoped that the conditions would be enough of a deterrent to keep Patrick on track.

We drove directly to the PA Cyber School center from the courthouse. We consulted with an intake counselor, brought home all the paperwork, and were decided on signing him up. I did have some concerns about the length of time it would take to process all the paperwork. They would need to obtain all his course information from Blackhawk and personalize his curriculum, which would take some two to three weeks. While everything was being processed, he was required to attend school at Blackhawk, which meant that he would be around the friends we wanted him away from. Another issue was the distance between the cyber school center and our house. It was a good forty-five-minute drive, even without traffic. Should there be any glitches with computer equipment, or if Patrick needed assistance with any of the courses, we would have to drive to the site, which would be a huge inconvenience. They also could not guarantee that Patrick would graduate by the end of the current school year, something we really wanted him to be able to do. Our family would be moving to California in June, immediately after graduation. Patrick had made it clear that he would not be moving with us. He planned to move out on his eighteenth birthday. I did not want to leave town with him not graduated from high school. I knew that the odds of him dropping out were very high. I weighed all my concerns with the alternative, him being back in his element at Blackhawk, and decided that cyber school was the best option.

I called Blackhawk High School and talked to the vice principal, Mr. Hedrick. We had been in communication all year, so he was up to speed on our struggles and concerns. He was both sympathetic and supportive. When I informed him of our decision to remove Patrick from Blackhawk and enroll him in PA Cyber School, he discouraged it. He understood my reasons but told me that he wanted me to first speak with the Blackhawk cyber school teacher. I had no idea that Blackhawk even had a cyber school program. I was reluctant to talk to her, wanting Patrick's ties to be completely cut at the school, but I decided I should at least hear her out. Patrick returned to his school the day after he got home from Keystone and informed all his friends and teachers that he was going to enroll in PA Cyber School. When the Blackhawk cyber teacher called him down to her room to have him look at their program, and essentially sell him on it, he told her he wasn't interested. I told him that the decision was ultimately his, and if he didn't want to do it through Blackhawk, we would go ahead with PA Cyber. The next morning, I collected all the required documents to get the process started for registering him in PA Cyber School. I was about to head out the door to fax all the paperwork off when I got a call from the Blackhawk High School principal's office. He informed me that he had Patrick with him in his office. He had been caught with one of his buddies smoking a cigarette before school. My heart sank. He put Patrick on the phone. Patrick told me that he had indeed done what the principal claimed. My exact words were, "What the hell is wrong with you? Why are you doing this?"

All he could answer me was, "I don't know."

Mr. Nelson, the principal, came back on the line. He told me he thought Patrick seemed like a good kid. He hadn't met him before, which he said was a good thing, but that he would be keeping his eye on him, now that he had. He said he would be giving him a three-day suspension. I informed him of our plan to move Patrick out of the district, and our reasons for it. He had only been back to school for one day, and was already getting into trouble. Mr. Nelson then asked me to consider Blackhawk cyber school. I told him that I wanted Patrick out of the school completely because his friends and temptations were obviously more than he could resist. My only concern with PA Cyber was that until all the processing was done, he had to attend Blackhawk. Mr. Nelson told me that if I came to pick Patrick up that morning, he would count it as the first day of his three-day suspension, which would carry us over into the weekend. The Blackhawk cyber school paperwork and process would only take a day or two, and there wouldn't be any reason for him to come back into the building at all. I decided to call Mrs. Boggs, the Blackhawk cyber teacher, to tell her that I was taking the power back to make the decision that I had let Patrick make. As far as I was concerned, he had forfeited the privilege when he broke the rules. Patrick was livid when he found out that I made the change. I told him he could blame himself. Because of his very hostile and negative reaction, I decided to call in the troops. We had been given access to the support of Presley Ridge, so I figured I may as well use it. I called Teresa and

Brian, the counselors who had been assigned to us; and after explaining what had transpired, they told me that the decision I had reached made perfect sense to them. They appreciated how I had handled it all—first giving Patrick a choice, and then taking control after he had broken the rules. It was a reasonable consequence for his behavior. Brian also spoke with Patrick, in an effort to help him understand the reasoning. It definitely helped to buffer things.

When we met with Mrs. Boggs to go through all the paperwork, I told her that my number one goal was for Patrick to graduate by the end of the school year. He had failed several courses, and his grades were terrible. Because he would still be considered a Blackhawk student, she could get all his missed work from his teachers. Rather than have him retake entire courses, he could simply complete the unfinished work for a final grade. Patrick could work at his own pace. Mrs. Boggs told him that it was entirely possible for him to graduate, but it would depend on him. If he put in the time and work, he could do it. Patrick was enrolled into the program, and within two days was issued all his equipment—laptop, printer, paper, and workbooks. The high school was on the same road as our house, less than a two-minute drive. Mrs. Boggs told him that if he ran into any glitches, all he had to do was call her. If he needed help with anything, he could go to the cyber room for twenty minutes or a whole day.

Patrick worked from his room or from the kitchen and seemed very motivated to get his assignments completed. He wanted to graduate. He had been talking to my brother who was a crane operator in Ottawa. He told Patrick that once he graduated, he would love to have him come and work for him. He would help him get into an apprenticeship program, teach him everything he needed to know, and assured him that he would be able to "write his own ticket." Patrick had a goal. He was already dreaming of the dollar signs, being certified to work on a crane, and maybe one day owning his own business. It was refreshing to watch to him working toward something positive. He very quickly worked through his classes and proudly showed me the progress he had made. Each course had a graph that showed the amount of work he had completed and how much he had left to finish. Color-coded, red, meaning he was behind; blue, on track; and green, working ahead. Patrick's classes were fairly consistently in the green.

There were only a handful of times when I had to call Teresa and Brian to mediate or intervene. They came by the house once a week to check in, as ordered by the court. If things got heated, they were only a phone call away. The stress level was high in our household. The rest of us managed to cope remarkably well under the circumstances, but Patrick had a low threshold for the stress and was easily frustrated. With thirteen people living in extremely close quarters, multiple personalities, and Joe out of town, keeping things ordered and peaceful was a big challenge. As the only parent in the house, I was "on" twenty-four hours a day, seven days a week. Sometimes a phone call to Brian and Teresa was enough to calm things down, and other times they had to come to the house. They were good listeners and a great support. They told Patrick that he had such a short amount of time left, they knew he really didn't want to blow it. They knew what his goal was, and they wanted him to reach it. He was counting down months, not years. We had to go to court twice more to give the judge updates on Patrick's progress, before his case was closed and he was officially placed back into my custody. The whole process had been extremely inconvenient for me, but I felt that it was worth it, simply for the support of Presley Ridge, and because Patrick had to hold himself accountable for his actions. He had a healthy fear of the consequences. There was always the possibility of going back to Keystone if he did anything crazy. Even after the case was closed, we still had the support from Presley Ridge and his Youth Services caseworker, Ian.

Patrick was under the impression that he was home free from the threat of going back to Keystone after his case was closed. Some of his old buddies showed up while I was taxiing kids around, having opted not to bring him along. He smoked a joint on the street behind our house, in clear view of the older kids who were at home. I about lost it. I called Brian immediately and told him what was going on. The next morning, Brian, Teresa, and Ian came to the house. They were not only shocked and disappointed, they were pissed off.

They had been really decent to him all along. They had treated him with respect and honestly believed that Patrick had turned a new leaf. After his relapse, they got tough. Ian—Patrick's usually easygoing, calm, and mild-mannered caseworker—told him in no uncertain terms not to mistake his good nature for weakness. He promised Patrick that he wouldn't think twice about marching him right back in front of the judge. Yes, he could do that, and yes, he would do it. Any worries I had about the case being closed and Patrick going back to his old habits died that day. I wished that we'd had that sort of support years earlier. It may have saved us all from the years of heartache, worry, stress, and sleepless nights. I was so grateful for them. Patrick treaded carefully after that, but I never fell asleep on the job. I watched him like a prison guard, monitoring his every move, still not trusting him. I could see the goodness in him. Despite his sneakiness and rebelliousness, he had a softness, especially around his baby brothers. He was easily frustrated and had a very short temper, but he had a sensitive, caring, and loving side as well. As exhausting as it was to live with him, I was glad to have him under my roof.

In the final months of our time in Beaver Falls, our days remained full. Life was busy, and it was stressful in a different kind of way. Joe was working and earning a paycheck, so we weren't worried about paying the bills or buying what the kids needed, like clothes and shoes. Being a pseudo single parent, albeit temporarily, was challenging in and of itself. I also had the daunting task of planning and managing a cross-country move looming over my head. Joe's third and final visit was at Easter. I had already begun packing and sorting through items to donate before he got home. We had decided to hire Tiger Pause to move us to California. They were the organization that had helped us move our things into storage from Bob and Nanette's house. When Matt Nance called us at Thanksgiving time to tell us they would be keeping our family in their prayers over the holidays, I shared our good news with him. He was happy to hear that Joe had found a job, and he told me that if there was anything we needed or that they could do for us, to give him a call. I told him we would be moving in June, but that it would be a cross-country move to California. I jokingly said, "Too bad you guys won't be able to help us move this time."

He said, "We are on our way to Seattle, Washington, right now, doing another move. If you want us to move you, we will beat any price quote you get from any mover. We'd love to move your family."

I was floored. I thanked him and told him we would be in touch. I immediately called Joe. He had already done some research, and the cheapest quote was fifteen thousand dollars. Of course we wanted to stretch our relocation funds as much as possible. When Joe got home, he called Matt. Matt quoted us five thousand dollars for the move. On top of it all, he agreed to take our two dogs at no extra charge, if we could guarantee that they were friendly. To fly the dogs by Air Animals, or even on a domestic flight, would have cost more than a thousand dollars each. We assured Matt that Maverick and Scamp were the sweetest dogs he'd ever met. Joe and I planned to drive our fifteen-passenger van with eleven of the kids and our baggage for the three-day trip. We wouldn't have room for the two dogs. With Tiger Pause taking care of our move at such a low price, and their willingness to take our dogs on top of it all, was unquestionably God's providence. We told Matt that we would be leaving town on Father's Day, the Sunday after graduation, right after Mass. He told us that he would be in touch with us as the date approached. He would need to assess how much stuff we had, what size truck he would need, and how to pack it. We told him that most of our things were still in the storage unit and that we would be donating a major portion of it to his organization, as well as a lot of the stuff we had in the house. Tiger Pause owns and operates a thrift store, and their organization helps at-risk youth and needy families.

I had not been excited about moving to California at all in the beginning, and I still wasn't totally thrilled about the idea, mainly because the cost of living is incredibly high there. When Joe told me that his office was in the Oakland area, all I could think of was drugs, crime, and bad schools. I didn't want to live in a house with bars on the windows like a prisoner. We had always owned our own home—six of them—before Joe got laid off. Moving to California would kill any chance we would have of saving up to buy a house.

Rent alone would keep us broke. I didn't want to live in an old run-down house, and I knew it would be very expensive to live in a newer one. I worried about finding a place that would allow us to keep our dogs. Unlike the kids, I was not excited at all. I had a lot of anxiety and fear. After spending a lot of hours worrying and obsessing, I remembered to put it all into God's hands. He had not let us down yet, so what did I have to worry about? When would I ever learn? When Joe e-mailed me pictures of the houses he was planning to look at, I was positive that they were too good to be true. They were all newer homes. One was brand-new, recently built, and never lived in. They were all just under four thousand square feet and had fenced yards. Rent was very high, three thousand, eight hundred dollars a month, almost as high as the mortgage payments on our last house in Texas. The yards were tiny, but the square footage inside made up for it. When we both decided on the brand-new house, and he had gone through the approval process, I finally relaxed and dove full steam ahead into packing and moving mode.

Patrick was in regular communication with my brother about his plans. He updated him on his progress in school and told him he was on target to graduate. I was grateful for the opportunity that he had offered Patrick. It was the incentive he needed to stay focused on graduating. I told my brother that if he was interested in any furniture, we would be traveling as light as possible to California. Because the plan was for my brother to pick Patrick up before we left town, he could have first pick of whatever he wanted. He said he had a big truck and that he could even bring a trailer; he was interested in whatever we wanted to get rid of. As the weeks went by, and the time for him to come and pick Patrick drew closer, he was harder to contact. When we did catch him, we couldn't get him to commit to a date. Patrick, suddenly less certain about his plan, grew frustrated and restless. I tried to keep him encouraged and told him to pray. I took him to get his passport and a replacement social security card because he had lost his original one. I collected all his other paperwork for him, his birth certificate, and naturalization papers. Everything was in place, except for his pickup date.

I went through every room, packing boxes to move and filling up bags for donation. I delivered bags to the donation bin daily— clothes, toys, winter coats, boots, mittens, and scarves, certain that we wouldn't need them in California. I packed up whatever I could, leaving out only the items we used every day and the necessary clothes. Joe had used up all his frequent-flyer miles. We didn't want to spend any extra money, so he didn't come home again after his Easter visit. He booked his final flight for the move, just a day before Joseph's graduation. He missed us more than we missed him. When he got home from work, he was alone, wishing we were with him. None of us were ever alone, and when I went to bed, I went to sleep instantly out of sheer exhaustion. I had baby Noah as a bed buddy, so I wasn't lonely. Still, I couldn't wait to have my family all together under one roof and to have Joe to share the load with me.

THIRTY-SIX

So Many Goodbyes

Beaver Falls, Pennsylvania, May 2013

On May 7, 2013, Bob Javens called to tell me that his beloved wife, Peggy, had passed away. She had lost her long battle with cancer. I could feel Bob's heartache over the phone. He told me that when their pastor asked her if she knew what her situation was, she said she knew that she had a terminal disease, but she was ready to go home to her Lord and Savior. I brought Clare with me to the funeral home for the visitation. I had only met Peggy once, the day I went with Noah to see if I could help with Bob's tie. She was a sweet soul, frail and weak, ravaged by the disease that had claimed her life. Her eyes were kind, and her smile was genuine. I could see that she had inner strength. It was at the visitation, though, that I caught a glimpse of what her life had been like. Collages of photos of her and her family filled up the funeral home room. Peggy had been a true beauty, inside and out. I learned that she was only fourteen years old when she and Bob had met. He was four years older than her, and they promised to remain true to each other when he left for the service. They married when he returned and had four children. Bob once shared with me a story about how Peggy nearly died after an operation. It was a story of their solid faith and belief in prayer. After round-the-clock prayers and vigil in her hospital room, her health was restored. Theirs was a love based on God and service. I couldn't miss noticing the love in her eyes in each and every picture I saw of her. In almost every photo, she was holding a baby. Her babies, her grandchildren, and great-grandchildren. When I went to the funeral a couple of days later with Noah, I listened to tribute after tribute to Peggy. How she had touched so many lives and how she had given of herself. I felt like I knew her. She was the sort of woman that I aspired to be. I knew that the loss was enormous for Bob and their children and everyone who knew her. I felt so sad that Peggy had died before we moved, yet at the same time, I felt blessed to be part of her beautiful service and to be able to give my condolences to Bob. He came by the house before our move to bring me a CD of Peggy's funeral service and a copy of her obituary. He broke down as he told us how he missed her and how he was just coping. A part of him was missing. It was so sad to see Bob hurting, yet encouraging to witness his hope in the Lord that Peggy was in His loving arms. That was his only comfort.

Fusion, the parish youth group, had been a wholesome outlet for our teenaged kids. It's always tough to be the new kid. It's even tougher when you are a teenager, but the members of the youth group welcomed our kids warmly. It was the only place we allowed Patrick to go to each week. When we didn't have the funds, they offered our kids scholarships go to Northbay Camp. When Noah was born, they collected hundreds of diapers and wipes for him. Five of our kids had parts in *The Passion* play, which was performed at Easter. Joseph acted as the crucified Jesus, and baby Noah played baby Jesus. Fr. Schreck remarked that it was the first year that baby Jesus and the man Jesus looked alike. Fusion hosted a farewell picnic for our entire family, close to our departure date. When the youth group leader asked Joseph to emcee a coffeehouse talent night fundraiser, he couldn't refuse. Joseph had gained a reputation as an emcee, entertainer, comedian, and actor in the two years we lived in Beaver Falls, so it was an exciting pursuit for him. All of us, everyone who knew him in the community, anxiously anticipated watching him in action. The kids had invited their friends from school, and Nanette came out in support as well.

Patrick finished all his courses four weeks before the end of the school year. It was a veritable miracle. I was not only proud, but utterly relieved that he would receive a high school diploma. Patrick was glad to have high school behind him, but he had no desire for any fanfare. We celebrated with Dad's Pizza and Wings. There was still no word from my brother about when he would pick Patrick up, so we began to discuss other options, like taking a Greyhound bus. It would be a long ride, but it was a cheap way to travel. When I finally did get ahold of my brother, he assured me that he would definitely be making the trip to get Patrick, but remained vague about exactly when. My biggest concern was leaving town without having a housing arrangement for Patrick. I couldn't just leave him wandering around Beaver Falls, flopping with friends, or worse, homeless. I needed to know he was in a safe place. When I told my brother about my concerns, he told me not to worry. Work was busy, but as soon as he had the time, he would be there. He said that he would be traveling to Niagara Falls to see his kids in the next couple of weeks. Beaver Falls was only a four-hour drive from Niagara Falls, so he said he'd plan to pick him up then. I had my doubts.

Angela's boyfriend, David, had finished his second year at Geneva College and was getting ready to return home to New York for the summer. When he came to the house to say goodbye, Patrick asked him if he could go back with him, thinking that he could take him to Niagara Falls on the way. I had relatives who could pick him up that he could possibly stay with until my brother came to get him. I called my aunt Kathy and left her a message, but David had to leave before she returned my call. When she did call me back on the night of the coffeehouse fund-raiser, I explained the plan that we had come up with. She was absolutely thrilled to have Patrick stay with them for as long as he needed to. I thanked her, but told her that David had already left. It had just been a spur-of-the-moment thought, but the window of opportunity had been missed. Then it dawned on me. I could drive him myself. I hadn't seen my aunt Kathy in years, not since before we had moved to Texas, but we had recently reconnected on Facebook. We couldn't cross the border into Canada because our passports had expired, and Patrick was the only one who had a valid one. If Aunt Kathy and her family were willing to meet us at the border on the US side, we could have dinner together and visit with all our kids before they took Patrick home with them. We decided to make the trip the very next day. I was giddy with excitement. I couldn't wait to see my aunt Kathy, and I was reassured in the knowledge that Patrick would be safe and in good hands. He would soon be on his way to his dream of apprenticing and crane operating. I would have preferred to have him come with us to California, but he wanted no part of it. He was ready to be on his own, and this was the next best thing.

Patrick had left early with Joseph to help get the hall set up for the fund-raising event, so I couldn't tell him about the new plan. All his stuff had been packed up for a couple of weeks, with the expectation that my brother would come to get him like he had promised. It was two days before his eighteenth birthday, and I was sure he would be thrilled that things were falling into place for him.

There was a great turnout at the coffeehouse night, and I was so proud to watch Joseph—confident and in his element—as he hosted the event. Christina performed a song with her friend. It was bittersweet to watch my two kids perform one last time onstage together. They had both blossomed in Beaver Falls. Nanette was very happy to hear that Patrick had completed his classes and was excited about his new venture. When I told Patrick about the plan to drive to Niagara Falls the next day, he was stunned. He grinned, seeming excited at first, then hesitated and said that it was too soon. I wondered if he was having second thoughts. He asked me if we could leave the day after his birthday. Suddenly, I understood his hesitation. He had hoped to have a big birthday bash with his buddies. Eighteen had been the magic number for Patrick for years. He felt that once he turned eighteen, he would be free from all parental restrictions. I told him that our schedules wouldn't allow it. It had to be the next day. It had all worked out more perfectly than I could have ever planned, God saw to that. He reluctantly agreed, knowing he really didn't have any another option.

The coffeehouse night was a lot of fun and a big success. We would be moving in just a couple of weeks. Our kids and all their friends wanted to squeeze as much time together as they could. Joseph and Patrick asked if they could invite some of their friends over for a bonfire in the backyard after they cleaned up the hall, as a sort of impromptu birthday celebration and goodbye party for Patrick. They promised that only approved friends would be there, so I allowed it. They stayed up late, talking around the fire pit, reminiscing, and promising to keep in touch. I smiled as I checked out the kitchen window, drifting back to my own memories of football games, talent shows, musicals, Mr. Cougar contests, Mr. Beaver County homecoming, dances, and fund-raising events. They had only spent two short years in Beaver Falls, but they made a lifetime of wonderful memories.

The next morning, after the kids had gone to school, Patrick and I went to Mass and then to Walmart to shop for some supplies for him. Stocking up on toiletries and snacks, I bought him his own clipper set so that he could cut his hair, something he did regularly. He repacked his things into our biggest suitcase. I gave him two hundred dollars to add to the hundred that Bob and Nanette had given him for his graduation. I wanted to make sure he had enough funds to last until my brother came and he started working. My aunt Kathy's husband, Chris, had been working on a house renovation job. He told Patrick that he'd love to have his help. Patrick was grateful for the offer and happy he would be working and earning money while he waited. Patrick had gotten his learner's permit a week earlier. I let him drive us back to the church office so that he could say goodbye to Fr. Schreck and Mary Ann, the youth minister. They had been a huge part of his life over the last year. They wished him well, and Fr. Schreck told him to remember that the prodigal son could always come home. We had been through a lot, and Fr. Schreck understood. I truly hoped and prayed that Patrick would come home, but I knew I had to let him go before that could happen.

It was an early release day. When the kids got home from school, we filled the van up with gas at Giant Eagle and hit the road to Niagara Falls. The plan was for us to meet at Chili's Restaurant in Niagara Falls, New York. It was a quick and easy trip. We made it in four hours flat. I wished I'd thought of making the trip before. We were the first to arrive and waited for Aunt Kathy, her husband, Chris, and their two boys, Ethan and Aaron. I hadn't seen my aunt

Kathy in more than twelve years and had never met her husband. Our reunion was tear-filled and joyous. Hugging her melted the huge gap of time that we had missed. All I felt was love from her forgiving heart. I still felt horribly guilty for simply walking away so many years earlier, when I had replaced everyone else with my mother after she reentered my life. I wished I had handled things differently, but I had come to understand that God always seems to make everything good in His time.

It was wonderful to meet my new uncle and cousins. Aunt Kathy hadn't changed a bit, if anything, her loving heart had grown even bigger. I had no worries at all about leaving my son in her care. Chris treated us all to dinner. We took a group photo, and I got one last picture with just Patrick and me before we went our separate ways. Letting him go was one of the hardest things I had ever done, but I knew it was what he wanted. He had been difficult, to say the least. He had been downright torturous to live with at times, but as his mother, I loved him fiercely, and I knew I would miss him. We said our goodbyes, stopped for gas, and went to Walmart for a few snacks. We wanted to hang around close by, until we heard from Aunt Kathy that they had crossed the border without any hassles. After they called to let us know that they had made it to the Canadian side with no problems, we headed back to Pennsylvania. The drive home was just as easy as the trip there, until the last forty-five minutes when Michael started to throw up. He had a sensitive stomach, and the eight hours in the van had been more than he could handle. The cross-country road trip to California was something I suddenly began to dread. After a warm bath and fresh pajamas, we settled him and the rest of the kids into their beds.

Patrick texted me regularly to update me on how he was doing. Chris and Kathy took him to all the tourist attractions in Niagara Falls; they showed him the sights and treated him like one of their own. Chris took him along on his renovation job and said that Patrick was a good worker, and he was happy to have him. He paid him well, and Patrick was glad to be there. My brother still had not committed to a date or even a time frame to pick Patrick up. Even when he had driven to Niagara Falls to visit his kids, he left without picking

Patrick up. I was beginning to think that we had all been duped. When Patrick finally spoke with him, my brother told him that he was still working on things, that he had to make sure that his boss approved of the plan. We had been under the impression that it had already been approved, but apparently it hadn't been. All of us were frustrated. My brother had been the one to offer the opportunity to Patrick out of the blue; it wasn't something that we had sought. We couldn't understand why he was dragging his feet. Patrick told him that if he wasn't serious about the apprenticeship offer, or if he had changed his mind, he needed to let him know so that he could pursue something else. My brother told Patrick to be patient, that he would let him know when things were ready for him. I wanted Patrick to realize his goal. To learn the trade and make a career in the crane business, but I had a knot in my stomach and some serious doubts. I prayed for whatever God's will was for Patrick and put it into His hands. I couldn't do anything about any of it, but I had confidence that God had it all under control.

One of the sacristans at Christ the Divine Teacher, Paul Chiappetta, was being installed in the Secular Franciscan Order at the Wednesday evening Mass. It was a week before our move. Gramma Hubbard had been a Third Order Franciscan nun, and though she never wore it in her daily life, she had been buried in a brown Franciscan habit. Wednesday evening Mass was not easy for me to get to regularly, but I really wanted to be there for the ceremony. St. Francis had always been one of my favorite saints, and I had recently begun considering the possibility of one day becoming a Secular Franciscan myself. I arrived at the church early so that I could spend some time in front of the Blessed Sacrament. It was such a blessing to have so many opportunities for adoration before Mass. When I arrived, there weren't many people in the church. Pulling out my rosary, I knelt down and started to pray. As I knelt, focusing on the Blessed Sacrament, I suddenly felt a presence very close to me, and it wasn't just Jesus present in the monstrance. I glanced to my right, without turning my head, and saw Gramma Hubbard. Her presence was so real and so close that I became frozen, afraid to blink or move a muscle even the slightest bit, for fear that I would lose sight of her. I wasn't looking at her straight on. I saw her more in my peripheral vision, but she was only inches away, close enough that I could feel the hairs on my skin standing straight up. I could make out her gray hair, freshly set, just as I always picture her when I think of her. I saw her clear watery eyes behind her glasses, not looking at me, but at the Blessed Sacrament. Her lips were moving, as if she were also praying a rosary with me. I didn't see her in color, not like a person would see another person; she was more of a haze, but it was unmistakably Gramma Hubbard. I had thought about her every single day for years. I had missed her and wished that I could ask her so many things about her life. From her childhood to her motherhood, and beyond, her struggles and her joys. With each life-changing event that I experienced, the good and the bad, and all the mundane daily chores I tended to in between, I had thought of her and felt a connectedness. Surely, she had walked along many of the same paths, years before I had stumbled across them. We had lived in different generations. The world was a much different place for each of us, but I believe our hearts and souls had experienced many of the same joys and sufferings. I had always sensed that she watches over me and my family, but I had never had a vision of her like I did that night. I was so overwhelmed by it that I needed to share it with someone, but I didn't want to sound like a crazy person.

The following Friday after morning Mass, I asked Fr. Schreck if I could talk to him for a few minutes. He told me to wait for him at the office, that he would meet me there after tending to a couple of things. He invited me to sit down while he quickly made a note. His office door was open, and I noticed Fr. Farnan walk in, all smiles as he greeted the office staff. We would be leaving town in two days, on Father's Day, and I hadn't expected to see him before we left. I was happy for the chance to say goodbye. It had only been announced a week or so earlier that Fr. Farnan would be moving to another parish, and that Fr. Schreck would be staying on as pastor of the four parishes. Divine Mercy, St. Rose of Lima, St. Philomena, and Christ the Divine Teacher would be merging together as St. Monica's, and he would be overseeing it all. It was a bittersweet time for all the parishioners. I was sad that we would be already gone before the merge, but excited for the new journey and opportunities that St. Monica would bring to the community of Beaver Falls.

I was glad that Fr. Farnan was present to hear about my experience, along with Fr. Schreck. I told them both about what had happened, having no idea whether they would think I was a kook or not. The vision had been so real, and I wanted to know what I should think or do about it. I told them that my gramma had also been a Third Order Franciscan and that I had been thinking of looking into possibly preparing for the order myself. After doing a very minimal amount of research, I realized that it was quite an in-depth process. At the stage I was at in my life, I wasn't certain that the timing was right. I quickly shared with the pastors what a great example of faith Gramma Hubbard had been for me and how I felt like her influence on my life seemed so much clearer the older I got and the more our family went through.

They didn't think I was crazy. In fact, Fr. Farnan said that the vision I had of my gramma had been a gift. He said I should pray for discernment, to see if the Secular Franciscan Order was a calling for me or not. I told them I would. I took the opportunity to thank them both again for all that they had done to help our family on so many levels. I had already written a thank-you letter to the parish to be included in the bulletin, but I wanted to personally thank each of them. They had blessed our family in so many ways, surrounding us in prayer, educated our kids, and had provided for our family's needs, housing and help with paying bills. God had brought us to Beaver Falls, a place we had never heard of, because He knew we would be loved and cared for by the parish community. They embraced us before they even got to know us. We had lived in other cities for longer periods of time where we knew more people, but we had never felt so cared for as we did in Beaver Falls. They had rallied around us. How the fathers responded to my thanks and gratitude startled me. Fr. Schreck spoke, "No, Nicole, we need to thank you. Before your family arrived, our parish had not been involved in outreach at all, and you gave us that opportunity by allowing us to help you. Your family has helped our parish more than you will ever know."

He also added that there had been a lot of stereotypes and misconceptions in the community that we managed to help overcome without even being aware of it. Joe was a well-educated, African American man. A solid father who had always been involved and had provided exceptionally well for his family, up until his layoff and the twists of life. Beaver Falls was a very small town, and we were highly visible in the community. We attended Mass regularly as a family—clean, neatly dressed, and well-behaved. He said that we had set an example for other parishioners. Fr. Schreck said that Beaver Falls had been a fairly racist town at one time and that there were still some lingering sentiments. The population of downtown Beaver Falls was predominantly low-income and African American. The crime rate was higher, and there were more drugs. Because a lot of the middle-class whites didn't want their kids associating with them, Blackhawk School District was formed. Fr. Schreck said that the witness of our family had done much to break down the stereotypes and prejudices. All I could think about the entire time we had lived in Beaver Falls was how much we had been blessed by the community. Never once had I considered that we were also blessing them.

The last few days were packed full with our kids trying to fit in as much time and fun as they could with their friends. There were end-of-the-year parties and, of course, graduation. I was sad that I couldn't watch Patrick walk with his brother, the rest of his classmates, and fellow graduates. He had finally, at the eleventh hour, resolved to focus and finish school and worked hard to graduate. He had spent so many years messing around and not caring about his studies. It was refreshing to see his determination, and it would have been an incredibly proud moment for us to watch both our boys graduate. He had made it clear that he wasn't interested in the ceremony. All he wanted was his diploma. He didn't need the pomp and circumstance.

By the time Joe arrived, the day before graduation, all the packing was done. Having kept out only the essentials, we lived in camping mode for a week or so. All our clothes and items we needed for our road trip had been organized and lined up along the wall in the family room. We tried to eat up whatever food we had left in the pantry, fridge, and freezer; and we ordered pizza and wings more than once in the last few days. We all knew that we would definitely miss Dad's Pizza once we left town, so we got our fill. All the prior moves we had made over the years had prepared us for that one. They taught us a lot, and I was quite proud of how organized I had become, though I was definitely getting tired of picking up my whole life and family. I wondered if we would ever settle and stay in one place.

Joseph's graduation was a proud moment for all of us. Although he had only been a student at Blackhawk for two years, it felt like four, because he had become so involved and had made a lot of great friends easily. Bob and Nanette came to the graduation. It was fitting to have them there as we ended our time in Beaver Falls. We had taken an incredible leap of faith to pick up and move to the little town and into their big house. We had no clue what we were heading into, but it had changed our lives and blessed us beyond measure.

Matt Nance and his crew from Tiger Pause met us at the storage unit on Saturday, the day before the move. When Joe opened up the big doors of our compartment, I was shocked to see how crammed it was and wondered how we had accumulated so much stuff. We had donated and sold a ton of stuff before we had moved from Texas. Only a year earlier, we donated another huge amount before moving out of Bob and Nanette's house. Weeks earlier, I had given away bags and boxes of things in preparation for the move, but there was still so much more. It was sickening to me that we had so many possessions. All the things that I had been so reluctant to part with a year earlier, I suddenly no longer felt attached to. We had lived without all of it for a whole year and, for the most part, hadn't missed any of it. We would bring the leather sectional couch that we had bought in Texas, the one we had ordered extra sections for in order to fit our whole family. We would keep our formal living room furniture, piano, electronic keyboard, the antique bookcase, and keepsakes from both of our deceased relatives. Then there was the old Peg Perego pram that had been given to me from the little old man at church before Angela was born. All my babies had ridden in it, all except for Noah. A lump formed in my throat when I saw it, but I realized someone else would get enjoyment out of it. Matt and his crew had brought two trucks, one for items that we would be moving with us, and the other for the things that we would donate to Tiger Pause. We systematically went through the items as they came out of the unit, glancing at the labels on the boxes, and without pondering for more than a second, we told them which truck to load it onto. The donation truck received the bulk of the items—bedroom furniture, appliances, garden tools, toys, books, home décor, artwork, dishes, and clothes. I vowed to continue to simplify our life, beginning with our possessions. I knew we still had plenty of stuff to get rid of, still peeling away the layers of the onion that had become our life, a little bit at a time.

Matt and his crew drove both trucks directly to the house from the storage unit, and we did the same thing there, separating the donations from what we planned to keep. There were items at the house that we would have brought with us, but because we wanted to avoid renting a second moving truck, we parted with them. We kept pictures and sentimental items, but left behind tents and office supplies, some of the newer toys, and outdoor furniture. We told Gary that he could take anything he wanted from the items we stacked inside the shed. We had already given him several shelving units. It was our way of showing our appreciation for so many things—his kindness and for putting up with us as neighbors. We had decorated the front of Dad's Pizza for Memorial Day. The kids and I planted red, white, and blue flowers in our old wire-hanging baskets and hung them up on the front-porch posts early in the morning before he got to the shop. We stuck American flags in each basket and all along the front of the flower beds. Patrick carried over our two white wicker chairs and table and put them on the front porch, and he touched up the paint on the railing. It was a spontaneous project that we worked on as a family.

When the Tiger Pause truck left the house, I collected the last of the cleaning supplies and the baskets of food items that we had left in our fridge and freezer. I loaded them up into our van to take them to our friends who also had a large family. I also loaded up bags of yarn and Michael's little riding toy. They were items that just wouldn't fit in the truck. A few of the kids came with me for the ride to drop the things off. When our friends didn't answer their door, I worried that I would have to throw the food away. It was hot outside, and I couldn't leave perishable items out in the sun, so I just left the cleaning supplies on their front step. A little voice told me to drive to downtown Beaver Falls with the food. I had no idea who I would give it to, but I had learned not to ignore the voice. I drove around looking for someone. The kids asked me where we were going. I told Clare to keep her eyes open for someone to give the food to. She asked me if I was seriously going to just give our food to a random person. I told her that was exactly what I planned to do.

We didn't have to drive far before I saw two little girls standing on the sidewalk with a man who I assumed was their father. He was talking on a cell phone. Judging by the look of their house and how the little girls were dressed, I got the impression that they could use the food. I pulled up along the curb, got out of the van, and walked toward the man on the phone. As I passed by the little girls, I smiled and said hello. They smiled back, following me curiously as I waited for their dad to finish his call. I explained to the man that our family was moving out of state and that I had just cleaned out my fridge and freezer. Not wanting him to think that I was just dumping my garbage on him, I told him that I had planned to bring it to our friends but that they weren't home, and I really hated to throw away good food. The man thanked me and said that they would take it. He followed me to the van with the two little girls following closely behind him and helped me carry out the baskets of food. There were cold cuts and cheese, bread, buns, eggs, jelly, condiments, and vegetables. Enough to fill some little bellies, I hoped. Next, I drove to another friend's house who had a little boy, Michael's age, who I knew could use the little musical riding toy. After dropping that off, I headed to Mary Ann Tarpin's house, the lady who led the prayer shawl ministry at church. I asked her if she had room for the yarn because we just couldn't fit it into the truck. She was happy to take it. I had intended to start up a Knitterbugs group in Beaver Falls, but it never worked out. I had donated yarn and blanket squares to the prayer shawl ministry shortly after we had arrived in Beaver Falls. I went to a couple of the meetings, but with our life being so hectic, I didn't get there as often as I would have liked to. It felt good to do those last little random acts of kindness. It seemed small in comparison to all the blessings that we had received, but I wanted to leave a little bit of us behind before we left.

About a month before our move, I received a card in the mail from Beaver County. The same type of Access card that had been issued to us when we were first signed up for food stamps. After informing our caseworker at Beaver County that Joe got a job, I cut up our original card. I thought it was strange that a new card had been mailed to us. I immediately called the number on the back of the card, keyed in my password, and was shocked to hear that there was a large balance on it. I called the county assistance office and left a message for our caseworker to call me back. I had no intention of using the card. We didn't need it, and I was certain that they had made a mistake. When our caseworker called the next day, I told her that I had received a new Access card in the mail, most certainly by mistake. I reminded her that I had called her more than six months earlier to inform her that we no longer needed assistance because Joe had started working. I waited while she looked up our case to verify what I had told her. She came back on the line and informed me that the balance on the card was ours because it had been processed before I had called to discontinue the assistance. I told her that she could just go ahead and put the balance back into the system. I asked her if I should mail the card back to her or destroy it. She told me that the system didn't work that way. I asked her if I could return the card for her to give it out to someone else. She said that wasn't possible either since it had been issued in our name. She said, "The money is yours. I'm sure you can use it."

I just didn't feel right about using government assistance when we didn't need it. I called Joe, and we came up with an idea. We decided that we would donate it to the food pantry at our church before leaving town.

Most of our kids had grumbled about moving to Beaver Falls when we had first mentioned it to them. The road trip had been long, and they were apprehensive about making new friends. They complained about starting at a new school, though they didn't want to be homeschooled. They criticized the little town and everything in it. How depressed it all looked, nothing like the polished and clean city of Southlake. They doubted that they would have any fun, and felt like their lives were over. In less than two short years, our kids had made incredible friends and had more fun than they had ever had anywhere else we had ever lived. We were the poorest we had ever been. We were living in the oldest, tiniest, crappiest house that we had ever lived in, but life had been better than ever in so many ways. It was hard for all of us to say goodbye. It was hardest for the kids who had complained the loudest about moving there in the first place. Once it got down to the wire, we had all their friends in our house around the clock, coming and going, day and night, having fires in the pit, and sleepovers. Cramped as it was, we let them have their time.

When we arrived for the nine o'clock Mass on Father's Day, Joe and I spotted Fr. Schreck in the parking lot. We told him about our food stamp card and that we wanted to donate it to the St. Vincent de Paul's food pantry. We worried about giving him the actual card, fearing he may get into trouble for fraudulent use of it. Fr. Schreck laughed, telling us he wasn't afraid of getting into trouble, but that if we wanted to, we could simply purchase the food items and leave them in the church. Because our kids told all their friends that we would be leaving shortly after Mass, many of them came to church that day. A bunch of them showed up, whether they were Catholic or not. Nanette, who usually went to Our Lady of Fatima, came to Christ the Divine Teacher and sat with our family so that she too could say goodbye. There were a lot of tears shed throughout the Mass, mostly by me, and afterward by our kids and their friends. Our parish had become a part of us, and I loved it. I was sad about leaving it behind, and I worried that we would never find a parish that would come anywhere even close to it. It had become our lifeblood, a little piece of heaven on earth. Fr. Schreck called our family out during the homily, mentioning the fact that we would be leaving town that afternoon. He wished us well, and after Mass, we had our picture taken with him on the altar.

As we walked out of the church, and the kids said their final goodbyes and hugged their friends before loading up into the van, Nanette handed each of them a baggie with spending money for the road trip. I spotted Joseph in the parking lot, huddled up with his friends Brandon and Frantzi in a group hug. It touched my heart to see those big boys hugging tearfully, not afraid to show their emotion. They had become such good friends. Nanette walked over to them and told Brandon and Frantzi that whenever they wanted to come and visit, she would pay for their plane ticket. That blew them and all of us away. Nanette, the forever sensitive and generous soul.

We drove home so the kids could get a snack and change clothes. While they were preparing for the long drive and saying more goodbyes to the friends who showed up at the door, I drove to Walmart to buy the food pantry items. I filled up two carts with nonperishables, peanut butter, jelly, tuna, jars of baby food, canned beans, vegetables, pasta, sauce, canned fruit, crackers, cereal, cake mixes, and frosting. I bought multiple boxes, jars, and packages of each item, and anything else that I could fit into the cart, using up the full balance on the card. Once they were loaded in the van, I drove back to the house, picked up Joseph and his friend Brandon, and went back to the church to unload it all into one of the rooms at the church. It was the one last contribution that we were able to make before leaving town, and it felt very good. We wished that we could have done so much more, but there wasn't time. Joe and I had many conversations about adopting a family, funding the St. Vincent de Paul, setting up scholarship funds for Divine Mercy Academy. Dreams that we prayed one day we could live out when we had the means.

We had arranged with Matt for Joseph to ride with him and his crew to help with the dogs. Our plan was to leave town by noon, but Matt wouldn't be leaving until that night. They would be driving straight through, alternating drivers, and would be arriving at the new house before the rest of us. Brandon and Frantzi stayed with Joseph at the little house until Matt came to pick him up. They were grateful for the extra time to hang out together. We said our goodbyes, hugged the boys, and told Joseph to make sure everything was clean and locked up before leaving. We were relieved that he would be helping to take care of the dogs. It would be a three-thousand-mile trip, and I prayed that we would all arrive safely.

Joe and I buckled the kids into the van and backed out onto Blackhawk Road for the last time. Unlike our trips to South Dakota and Pennsylvania, we didn't book any hotel reservations. We hadn't even planned out our trip. We decided to drive west until we got tired before checking into the nearest hotel. Of all the lessons we had learned along the way on our journey thus far, the most valuable one was trust. Trust in the Lord. He has the plan, and He always provides, usually through angels in human form.

The End

EPILOGUE

𝓕or now, California is home. I have no idea how long we will be here. We continue to be open to God's plan for us, but just between you and me, I hope we stay a while. Not surprisingly, it's better than I could have ever imagined. The people here are wonderful, we love our parish community, our kids are doing well and making friends. Life is still a roller-coaster ride, but I have learned to resist the urge to control it and strive to let God lead the way. I thank Him daily for the incredible gifts He has blessed us with, as well as the challenges He sends my way, no matter how painful they might be. I've learned that they are lessons that I will need for the next dip in the ride.

If there is one clear message that I have learned through this journey that I wish to share with you, dear reader, it is that the power of prayer is real. Life can be hard in the best of times. Raising a family in the world today is a huge challenge. It is essential to pray and pray often, individually and as a family. Cutting out time for daily prayer is a must for a peaceful life and the preservation of the family. You've read the story. The common thread throughout our journey has been how prayer sustained us and caused miracles to happen, both big and small. Prayer works.

As Catholics, we have a treasure trove of tools and an arsenal of weapons. In today's culture, the family is under attack, and the best weapon we can use to defend ourselves is prayer. The family rosary is powerful. It only takes about fifteen minutes to pray it, and fifteen minutes is something even the busiest of us can find. Our family gathers together at the end of the day, before the littlest kids go to bed, to pray the rosary. It's a perfect way for them to go off to sleep. Sometimes it's a challenge. The devil loves to cause a commotion at rosary time, creating distractions and moaning complaints about homework and more playtime, but we persevere. Our kids have witnessed the miracles firsthand, so it only takes a quick reminder to get them focused. We need to teach our children to pray and draw their attention to how their prayers are being answered, and they will get answered in God's way and time.

The one thing that we have always been consistent with during our entire married life has been attending Sunday Mass as a family. Unless one or more of the kids is sick, and that happens now and then, we attend all together. If we can't all make it together, we go to separate Masses, but we never miss Mass on Sunday. I believe that Sunday Mass attendance as a family is the glue that has kept us intact. It is a part of who we are as a Catholic family. The graces received from the Mass are treasures that will be stored up for us in heaven, and the benefits of being part of a parish community are invaluable for our earthly journey toward our eternal home. It is never too early. If you have babies and young children, pray with them. Bring them to Mass. Don't worry about them fussing or squirming around. Persevere, especially when you don't feel like it. If you bring them consistently, they will learn how to not only behave appropriately, but to participate actively from a very young age. It is never too late! If you have drifted away, come home. You will be welcomed with open arms. Return to the sacraments. Reconciliation is a gift, and it's free. We all sin, and we all need forgiveness. Reconciliation is a great way to keep our lives on track, to clear out those things that are holding us back from growing closer to Jesus, and freeing us to love ourselves and our families more fully.

We are all on a journey, and our destination is the same. Our whole purpose on this earth is to learn how to know, love, and serve God so that we might share in His everlasting happiness in heaven. Jesus is our guide, and the gospels are the roadmap to all the lessons. None of us is perfect, but we can all strive to live more perfect lives, taking care of our families, being kind to everyone, helping the poor, visiting the sick, easing the burdens of others with a smile, a word of encouragement, or by simply listening. Showing mercy, forgiving others, and praying constantly. God has given us all unique gifts and talents that He expects us to use in order to grow the kingdom of heaven. We are called to share our gifts with others to draw them to Christ. I would like to leave you with a quote that inspires me every day: "Let your light shine before men in such a way that they may see your works and glorify your Father who is in heaven" (Matthew 5:16).

ABOUT THE AUTHOR

 Nicole Allen was born in Niagara Falls, Ontario, Canada. She is happily married to Joe, and over the course of their twenty-six year marriage, they have had twelve children, ranging in age from twenty-five to five.

Career moves have taken them from Canada to several cities across the United States. Besides being a stay-at-home mom and homemaker, Nicole homeschools her youngest five children and is a member of the Catholic Daughters of the Americas. She is an avid knitter, with a project or two on the go at any given time. She gives away most of her projects, and she formed Knitterbugs, a charity knitting group, while she lived in Texas. When she isn't knitting, she can be found in her secret garden, an escape from the daily routine—planting, pruning, and doing her best praying.

Nicole currently lives in Northern California, with Joe and most of their children; their dog, Scamp; two cats, Koda and Franky and their German Shepherd Service pup-in-training, Apollo.

CPSIA information can be obtained
at www.ICGtesting.com
Printed in the USA
LVHW040514141118
596828LV00009B/314